STRIKE TERROR NO MORE

Theology, Ethics, and the New War

STRIKE TERROR NO

Theology, Ethics, and the New War

MORE

Jon L. Berquist, Editor

CHALICE
PRESS

ST. LOUIS, MISSOURI

Proceeds from the sale of this book will benefit
The Interfaith Center of New York.

Cover photo: © Comstock, Klips #00903234
Cover design: Michael Domínguez
Interior design: Elizabeth Wright
Art direction: Michael Domínguez

This book is printed on acid-free, recycled paper.

Visit Chalice Press on the World Wide Web at
www.chalicepress.com

10 9 8 7 6 5 4 3 2 1   02 03

Library of Congress Cataloging–in–Publication Data

Strike terror no more : theology, ethics, and the new war / Jon L. Berquist, ed.
    p.   cm.
  Includes bibliographical references and index.
  ISBN 0-8272-3454-6 (alk. paper)
  1. September 11 Terrorist Attacks, 2001.   2. War–Religious aspects–Christianity.
3. Terrorism–Religious aspects–Christianity.   I. Berquist, Jon L.
  BT736.15 .S77   2002
  261.8'73–dc21   2001008583

Printed in the United States of America

Table of Contents

List of Contributors   ix

Preface   Jon L. Berquist   xi

PART 1: Observations of Terror and War

1. A War against Terrorism   John B. Cobb, Jr.   2

2. Subversion, Body-Politic, Scripture: A Question on the Limits of Power   Creston C. Davis   10

3. "I Have Been through This Before"   Ariel Dorfman   18

4. Business as Un-usual: Reconstructing Divine Economy   Marion Grau   21

5. Civil War, Civil Rights, World Trade Center   Cheryl A. Kirk-Duggan   30

6. "For This the Earth Shall Mourn" (Jer. 4:28)   Fumitaka Matsuoka   47

7. Roots of the Taliban   Judith Mayotte   56

8. Sovereignty, Empire, Capital, and Terror   John Milbank   65

9. September 11 and the Ethics of Violence   Jorge Secada   76

10. "Dealing in Straight Power Concepts": Justice and the Use of Force   Kenneth Surin   86

11. Errant Concepts in an Age of Terror   Edith Wyschogrod   98

PART 2: Visions

12. Fragments of a Vision in a September 11 World   Teresa Berger   110

13. The Armageddon of 9/11: A Counter-Apocalyptic Meditation   Catherine Keller   116

PART 3: Responses of Theology

14. "Make Them as Tumbleweed"   *David R. Blumenthal*   130

15. Truth-telling Comfort   *Walter Brueggemann*   138

16. The Theologian in the Twilight of American Culture   *M. Shawn Copeland*   142

17. Faith, Ethics, and Evil   *Robin W. Lovin*   154

18. When Listening Is Not Enough: Pastoral Theology and Care in Turbulent Times   *Joretta L. Marshall*   164

19. Four Ways of Worship in a Time of National Trauma   *Martin E. Marty*   172

20. Hope in a Time of Arrogance and Terror   *Jürgen Moltmann*   177

21. In the Face of Evil: Understanding Evil in the Aftermath of Terror   *Luis G. Pedraja*   187

22. Theologies of War: Comparative Perspectives   *Max L. Stackhouse*   200

23. The Last Word?   *Marjorie H. Suchocki*   212

PART 4: Just War and Just Peace

24. The Danger of Violence and the Call to Peace   *Lisa Sowle Cahill*   222

25. How to Fight a Just War   *Jean Bethke Elshtain*   231

26. The Just War Doctrine and Postmodern Warfare   *Peter J. Haas*   236

27. Christian Nonviolence   *Stanley Hauerwas*   245

28. Organizing Nonviolence   *Jim Lewis*   248

29. What Can We Hope for Now?   *M. Douglas Meeks*   253

30. New Wars, Old Wineskins   *Susan Brooks Thistlethwaite*   264

PART 5: Life and Faith after September 11

31. Dust and Spirit   *Karen Baker-Fletcher*   280

32. What Is the War on Terrorism Doing to Us?   *Tony Campolo*   287

33. A Dispatch from Security   *Amy Laura Hall*   292

34. In a Time Such as This   *Ada María Isasi-Díaz*   296

35. Christian Intellectuals and Escapism after 9/11   *Charles T. Mathewes*   306

36. Wounds of Hurt, Words of Faith   *Mary Elizabeth Mullino Moore*   316

37. How Should Christians Respond?   *Ronald J. Sider*   326

38. We Must Find a Better Way   *Walter Wink*   329

Notes   337

List of Contributors

Karen Baker-Fletcher is associate professor of systematic theology, Perkins School of Theology, Southern Methodist University, Dallas, Texas.

Teresa Berger is associate professor of ecumenical theology, Duke University Divinity School, Durham, North Carolina.

Jon L. Berquist is senior academic editor, Chalice Press, St. Louis, Missouri.

David R. Blumenthal is Jay and Leslie Cohen Professor of Judaic Studies, Emory University, Atlanta, Georgia.

Walter Brueggemann is William Marcellus McPheeters Professor of Old Testament, Columbia Theological Seminary, Decatur, Georgia.

Lisa Sowle Cahill is J. Donald Monan Professor of Ethics, Boston College, Boston, Massachusetts.

Tony Campolo is professor, emeritus, of sociology, Eastern University, St. Davids, Pennsylvania, and founder, Evangelical Association for the Promotion of Education.

John B. Cobb, Jr., is Ingraham Professor of Theology, emeritus, Claremont School of Theology, and Founding Co-Director, Center for Process Studies, Claremont, California.

M. Shawn Copeland is associate professor of theology, Marquette University, Milwaukee, Wisconsin.

Creston C. Davis teaches philosophy and theology at James Madison University, Harrisonburg, Virginia.

Ariel Dorfman is Walter Hines Page Research Professor of Literature and Latin American Studies, Duke University, Durham, North Carolina.

Jean Bethke Elshtain is Laura Spelman Rockefeller Professor of Social and Political Ethics, University of Chicago, Chicago, Illinois.

Marion Grau is assistant professor of theology, Church Divinity School of the Pacific, Berkeley, California.

Peter J. Haas is Abba Hillel Silver Professor of Jewish Studies and director of the Samuel Rosenthal Center for Judaic Studies, Case Western Reserve University, Cleveland, Ohio.

Amy Laura Hall is assistant professor of theological ethics, Duke University Divinity School, Durham, North Carolina.

Stanley Hauerwas is Gilbert T. Rowe Professor of Theological Ethics, Duke University Divinity School, Durham, North Carolina.

Ada María Isasi-Díaz is associate professor of theology and ethics, Theological School, Drew University, Madison, New Jersey.

Catherine Keller is professor of constructive theology, Theological School, Drew University, Madison, New Jersey.

Cheryl A. Kirk-Duggan is executive director of the Center for Women and Religion, and assistant professor of theology and womanist studies, Graduate Theological Union, Berkeley, California.

Jim Lewis is an Episcopal priest who lives in Charleston, West Virginia.

Robin W. Lovin is Cary Maguire University Professor of Ethics, Southern
Methodist University, Dallas, Texas.

Joretta L. Marshall is academic dean and professor of pastoral theology and
care, Eden Theological Seminary, St. Louis, Missouri.

Martin E. Marty is Fairfax M. Cone Distinguished Service Professor, emeritus,
University of Chicago Divinity School, Chicago, Illinois.

Charles T. Mathewes is assistant professor of religious studies, University of
Virginia, Charlottesville, Virginia.

Fumitaka Matsuoka is professor of theology, Pacific School of Religion, and
executive director, PANA Institute, Berkeley, California.

Judith Mayotte is professor and women's chair in humanistic studies,
Marquette University, Milwaukee, Wisconsin.

M. Douglas Meeks is Cal Turner Chancellor Professor of Theology and
Wesleyan Studies, Vanderbilt Divinity School, Nashville, Tennessee.

John Milbank is Francis Ball Professor of Philosophical Theology, University
of Virginia, Charlottesville, Virginia.

Jürgen Moltmann is professor of systematic theology at the University of
Tübingen, Tübingen, Germany.

Mary Elizabeth Mullino Moore is director of the Program for Women in
Theology and Ministry, and professor of religion and education,
Candler School of Theology, Emory University, Atlanta, Georgia.

Luis G. Pedraja is academic dean and professor of theology, Memphis
Theological Seminary, Memphis, Tennessee.

Jorge Secada is associate professor of philosophy and chair of the Corcoran
Department of Philosophy, University of Virginia, Charlottesville,
Virginia.

Ronald J. Sider is president of Evangelicals for Social Action, and professor
of theology and culture, Eastern Baptist Theological Seminary,
Wynnewood, Pennsylvania.

Max L. Stackhouse is Stephen Colwell Professor of Christian Ethics, Princeton
Theological Seminary, Princeton, New Jersey.

Marjorie H. Suchocki is Ingraham Professor of Theology, Claremont School
of Theology, and co-director, Center for Process Studies, Claremont,
California.

Kenneth Surin is professor of literature and professor of religion and critical
theory, Duke University, Durham, North Carolina.

Susan Brooks Thistlethwaite is president, Chicago Theological Seminary,
Chicago, Illinois.

Walter Wink is professor of biblical interpretation at Auburn Theological
Seminary, New York, New York.

Edith Wyschogrod is J. Newton Rayzor Professor of Philosophy and Religious
Thought, Rice University, Houston, Texas.

Preface

Why, O LORD, do you stand far off?
Why do you hide yourself in times of trouble? (Psalm 10:1)

In the days following September 11, 2001, questions and laments such as these filled the minds of faithful persons. Although we knew of God's presence, such knowledge connected to the events of those days only with great difficulty. When terror struck in the form of airplanes crashed into New York's World Trade Center towers and Washington's Pentagon, matters of faith and theological knowledge seemed so elusive and yet so much deeper in their import. How is God present in a time of terror? What can we affirm about God? How do our religious convictions compel us to act? The theological and ethical questions intertwine with the diverse and particular realities of the world around us, a world we did not see in the same way after September 11.

In the midst of trouble and confusion, Jews, Christians, and Muslims alike frequently turn to the Psalms of the Hebrew Bible for comfort and reflection. In such laments, people of faith express their frustration at God's seeming inattention to the tragedies of this world. We long for God's presence to be more visible. We desire God to be active in the world and to bring forth the changes we wish to see, instead of the pain that surrounds us. In times of trouble, we wish that God would end the fear and terror of this world. Thus, psalms of lament move toward conclusion in the faithful assertion of God's inevitable goodness and right action on behalf of the victims.

O LORD, you will hear the desire of the meek;
you will strengthen their heart,
you will incline your ear
to do justice for the orphan and the oppressed,
so that those from earth
may strike terror no more. (Psalm 10:17–18)

This vision of ultimate justice is familiar to those who read the psalms. God's presence will inevitably reside with those who are most needy in order to strengthen them from within. God will pay attention to the needs of the disadvantaged and the terrorized. God will perform justice for the unfortunate, the abandoned, and all victims. God will even remove the possibility of further terror from the world. Visions like this occur frequently throughout the Hebrew Bible, and they empower the quest for justice and the celebrations of God's eventual victory throughout the Abrahamic faiths.

Many of the essays in this book echo this psalm's movement toward the assurance of God's saving activity in the world, which will remove terror and the ability to terrorize. But even after this sure answer of faith, two questions remain: who are the meek, and how will God protect them from terror? Such questions propel this book and the reflections of the theologians and ethicists in these pages.

The fact that the psalm's original audience consists of the meek, who will enjoy God's justice, may not be of much comfort to readers today. Should we identify ourselves as the victims in the contemporary situations of terror, or are we the arrogant ones who disregard God's will? The psalm paints a portrait of stark contrasts, but we see things today with more ambiguity. We can recognize ourselves (or people like us) as victims, while at the same time finding other persons like us to be those who perpetrate evil (whether this evil or some other, separated from us only by time or geography). When we can see the world in clear-cut terms, with one set of innocent poor victims and another group of arrogant greedy oppressors, then it is easy to discern God's preference. But honesty requires us to admit that the world is not so simple. The complexities of the modern world have created many victims and left very few people truly innocent. In the U.S., people often see themselves as innocent and yet recognize the poverty of others around the world. If God is on the side of the innocent poor, then where is God, if there are poor people on every side?

The vision of a world that knows no fear and where no one will strike terror ever again attracts us all. Such is the world where we want to live, but we know that our own world is far from it. In the political rhetoric that followed September 11, 2001, we heard differing perspectives about how to attain a just world. Yet the psalm itself contains the same differences. In verse 18, part of the solution that creates a world without terror is the performance of justice for the orphans and the oppressed. Divine righteous activity that brings justice to the victims will bring about a world without terror. This logic reaches into the contemporary world, where many argue that feeding the hungry and providing liberty to the oppressed will lead to a world without violence. Only then will no one ever again need to resort to terror or uprising in order to gain for themselves and their loved ones basic human needs and rights.

Even though the psalm ends in this vision of liberty and justice for the oppressed, other parts of the psalm stand in possible tension with this nonviolent, pro-justice reading. In verse 15, the psalmist cries to God to "break the arm of the wicked and evildoers," expressing a desire for violence against the violent that resonates in the contemporary world as well. We have heard the rhetoric that labels people and groups as evil, thus justifying their destruction in order to remove the threats of violence and the realities of terror. This too is part of the biblical heritage at the heart of Judaism, Christianity, and Islam.

Psalm 10 is hardly the only place where this ambiguity exists. Justice and violence live in tension within many biblical concepts. One of the greatest testimonies to peace in the Bible and in our own contemporary world is Isaiah's magnificent speech in which nations "shall beat their swords into plowshares, and their spears into pruning hooks; nation shall not lift up sword against nation, neither shall they learn war any more" (Isaiah 2:4). This remarkable call reverberates from Isaiah 2 to Micah 4:3 to the foundations of the United Nations. Yet the careful exegete cannot overlook another prophetic passage:

> Proclaim this among the nations:
> Prepare war,
> > stir up the warriors.
> Let all the soldiers draw near,
> > let them come up.
> Beat your plowshares into swords,
> > and your pruning hooks into spears;
> > let the weakling say,
> > > "I am a warrior." (Joel 3:9–10)

Swords and plowshares are two valuable uses of metal. Each can mutate into the other, allowing people to tend the ground or to kill the neighbor. The prophetic texts never leave one certain about which is the right "biblical" response. Interpretation is a matter of discernment in which ethics are at stake, but the answer will not be reached easily.

The psalm rightly raises these questions about the identity of the meek and the process of God's justice, and these questions wind their way through many of the chapters in this book. As theologians and ethicists, we see terror in the world today and ask about what has transpired previously among all of the people involved—those who perpetrate the violence, those who are its victims, and the many who are its witnesses. Examining the complex relationships between all of these people is vital work for our time. Likewise, we discuss how God will respond, and how those of us who try to do God's will should respond. How do we work for a just world? How do we remove the terror from our midst, and indeed from our world as a whole?

Strike Terror No More: Theology, Ethics, and the New War offers responses from thirty-eight theologians concerning the events of Tuesday, September 11, 2001, and the U.S. reaction to these events, especially the war against Afghanistan. This war has been called "the new war" and "a war against terrorism," and this volume addresses the roots, prospects, and ethics of such a war.

The chapters of this book represent a remarkable array of theological stances. The book's goal has been to bring together important voices and compelling arguments from diverse people, not to develop a systematic reflection or to encapsulate one certain position. Each contributor was invited to write about her or his own perceptions of the central issues regarding terror and the war against terror. As will be clear, intelligent persons do not agree on the right answers—or even upon the identification of the right questions. But together, these essays combine into a vital investigation of the many issues at work in American culture, global relations, and the new war.

It is nearly impossible to write about terror; disaster transcends words and breaks down the boundaries of language. These authors have found words to share about the tragedies of airplanes crashing into buildings on the eastern coast of the U.S. and subsequent U.S. military attacks half a world away. But these are slippery words, uttered about an ever-changing matter that rips through the lives of persons in many parts of the world. We do not know where those ripples will stop, or what issues in this volume will seem antiquated to the reader and which topics will seem of most immediate interest. Hindsight will soon render these impatient words as bravery or foolishness—or much more likely, some strange and still-changing combination.

This book's essays proceed in five parts. The first part, "Observations of Terror and War," contains eleven chapters offering different insights into the root causes of the terrorist acts of September 11, 2001. In these pages, scholars address historical, social, political, cultural, and economic forces that have brought society to this point, and begin to show us how these factors are still with us now. These forces of history and realities of economics will continue to shape the effects and responses that result from September 11. Observation and insight provide analysis of the situation, but the religious traditions of the Abrahamic faiths have developed alternate ways of seeing. In the second part, "Visions," the reader will discover two apocalyptic readings. Apocalyptic literature does not see the world through the same lenses as other sorts of vision, but its deeply religious and impressionistic view mirrors the perceptions of biblical writers and much of the populace today.

The third part, "Responses of Theology," details ten modes of mapping future paths for theological reflection and development. These responses cover a wide range. All of them engage the richness of theological traditions in order to discern how religious communities should respond and how theological discourse should shape itself in the aftermath of the new war against terrorism. In the book's fourth part, "Just War and Just Peace," seven scholars suggest ways that the tradition of "just war theory," including its critiques and replacements, may assist us in evaluating the new war.

Finally, the fifth part deals with "Life and Faith after September 11." What is different in this new world? How should faithful life be different than what it was before? What differences will this make in personal life? The eight chapters in this part comment on ways that our individual lives and our communal life together should and must change in the time ahead of us.

Although the book is arranged into these five parts, the reader will readily recognize that any division of these chapters is somewhat arbitrary. The many themes of war and peace, cause and effect, justice and violence, oppression and victimization, theology and ethics, tradition and reflection, faith and action, vision and insight, hope and apocalyptic, and change and changelessness flow throughout these chapters in a variety of ways. I would challenge the reader to search for the many connections while watching these superb theologians practice their craft, for there is much to learn here about theological method as well as meaning, ultimate concern, the assumptions of thought, the ends of religion, and practical ethics. This is not merely a book about a specific day in history, nor about the war in the months that followed. Indeed, this book engages the multifaceted tradition of the Abrahamic faiths with the realities of a complex contemporary event. The multiple intersections of faith and world result in a panoply of entries into the whole subject of religion as it is lived and practiced in the world at large.

In these recent weeks, I have been immersed in the privilege of having the contributors to this book share their own best thoughts. They have struggled to find their own insights and to make their own meaning of the events of these months. They have examined terror and the American response, and they have assembled words that speak to the meaning that they are finding in the rubble and the loss of September 11 as well as in the war that followed. I owe deep gratitude to these contributors. Each of them worked to meet short deadlines; they wrote swiftly and with skill in order to make this book possible, and in every case, these writers remained pleasant even in the face of the inevitable editorial annoyances that were only enhanced by the project's speed. I am grateful for every one. Had time allowed another week or another month, other voices would have joined these chapters.

This book embodies the expertise and resilience of Chalice Press's capable staff. No book occurs without the work of a very long list of persons, including every employee of the press and many others. Some of the people whose support contributed greatly to the volume include Cyrus N. White, David P. Polk, Ulrike R. M. Guthrie, Laura Christian, Pamela B. Brown, Susan J. Burgess, Kristin Westphal, Lynne Letchworth, Ann Dauer, Carol Dunn, Kaitlyn Rose, Gail Stobaugh, Michael Domínguez, and Elizabeth Wright. Work among colleagues such as these is joy and privilege, and rarely more so than with this volume.

I also wish to acknowledge several people who offered advice about contributors to invite or who helped in making connections. Shawn Copeland, Creston Davis, Stanley Hauerwas, Catherine Keller, Mary McClintock Fulkerson, Douglas Meeks, John Milbank, Bill Nottingham, and Max Stackhouse each assisted in irreplaceable ways throughout this project.

Many friends and family members offer me the encouragement of their daily support, and this nourishment enables and enriches my life, including this book. I would name in particular Ronald J. Allen, Lori G. Beaman, Richard and Mary Beth Berquist, Jana Childers, Roy Herndon SteinhoffSmith, and Larry A. Thomas. Finally, my thanks go to my family, in whose midst I have lived the daily events of terror, war, and writing, which they somehow infuse with love and grace: Sally Greene Willis-Watkins, Rebecca Blake Willis-Watkins, Spencer David Willis-Watkins, and Margaret Mbagara.

Jon L. Berquist

PART 1

Observations of Terror and War

1

A War against Terrorism

John B. Cobb, Jr.

Will a War against Terrorism Reduce Terror?

Terror is a terrible condition. Terrorism, as the intentional effort to generate and extend terror, is a horrible evil. The evil is not only the death and destruction that is caused but also the widespread effect on the whole fabric of society. When people feel insecure, the patterns of life to which they are accustomed have to be changed. They are willing to sacrifice personal freedom. They look at neighbors with suspicion. National resources that should go toward meeting human needs are soaked up into defense expenditures. Business is disrupted.

It is possible that the United States can lead the world into a significant reduction of terrorism. If so, we may snatch real gain from the ashes of destruction in New York and Washington. But this depends on an honest appraisal of the role of terrorism in our own global actions and an appraisal of its complex causes.

Unfortunately, the greater likelihood is that we will extend and increase the role of terror in the world. Currently, we are undertaking to increase terror in Afghanistan. It is true that our target is in one sense limited to those responsible for attacking us. But the assemblage of huge military forces is accompanied by threats that create terror in the civilian population of Afghanistan. And this is clearly not unintended. Furthermore, their terror is not unrealistic. There is some danger that what remains of Afghan civilization will be wiped out by American bombs. There is danger that terror will be extended to such other countries as Iraq or even Syria.

If the United States really wishes to reduce terrorism, it can make profound changes in its foreign and military policies. For the sake of pursuing its global policies, the United States has made extensive use of terrorism. Much of the war we supported in Afghanistan against the Soviet-supported government involved terrorism. Indeed, we supported and trained Osama bin Laden in terrorist tactics.

In Latin America terror has been a major implement of military and conservative regimes in suppressing the opposition of peasants and indigenous peoples. We have called this "low intensity warfare," and we have instructed thousands of Latin American soldiers in these methods at our training camp in Columbus, Georgia. The disappearances and death squads that have been, and still are, so large a part of life in Latin America for decades have expressed our support of terrorism there.

Some define terrorist acts as those directed against governments. This means that the actions of police and soldiers against people who resist the government are not identified as terrorist even though their systematic intention is to instill terror. We might then say that low intensity warfare, as a means of keeping a government in power, is not terrorism. We might then suppose that the United States has usually not employed or supported terrorism.

But even when we limit terrorism to acts against governments, we cannot claim that we have held back. In 1973 we engineered the overthrow of a democratically elected government in Chile. This involved terrorist actions and initiated a reign of terror against the supporters of the legitimate government. From 1981 to 1990 we supported the terrorist tactics of the Contras against the Sandinista government of Nicaragua. Earlier, in 1953, we overthrew Mosadegh in Iran.

The truth is that moral horror about acts of terrorism depends very much on whom the acts are directed against. If they are directed against those who threaten our global policies, they are regarded as acceptable means in the maintenance of world order. If they are directed against us, they are simply vicious and wholly inexcusable. They even justify our intensification of the use of terror in retaliation and in defense of our interests.

Consider the situation in 1985. Ronald Reagan met with a group of leaders of the Afghan mujahedeen, with whom Osama bin Laden worked closely. Reagan called these men the moral equivalent of our founding fathers. At that time, Nelson Mandela, a prisoner in Robben Island, was listed as a terrorist on the official watch list of the Pentagon.

Now it would be an overstatement to say that the only reason that the attacks on the World Trade Center buildings and the Pentagon were so shocking was that, in this case, we were the victims rather than the actors. They were shocking also because of their scale, their visibility, and their extraordinary success. Also, they were directed at the most visible symbols of global power rather than at the relatively powerless. They showed that no one was safe.

Wealth, geography, and military dominance protect no one. Hundreds of millions of powerless people have grown accustomed to terrorism, learning how to survive in spite of it. Now other hundreds of millions, citizens of rich and powerful nations, have discovered that they, too, can be the objects of terrorist attack.

It would be a great exaggeration to suggest that we now understand the experience of the victims of low intensity warfare in Latin America or of those who were tortured in Chile because of their support of the legitimate Allende regime. It would be an equal exaggeration to suggest that we now understand the experience of the people of Afghanistan, who suffered through the years of warfare, fomented by us, that replaced a Marxist government with the Taliban. Our suffering cannot be compared with theirs. Nevertheless, there is the possibility that we will learn through this event some compassion for the sufferers from all forms of terrorism, including those that we inflict. It is possible that we may psychologically identify with the victims of terrorism and refuse to support its perpetration on others. Such a change in public opinion could redirect the course of history.

I have concentrated on examples of how the policy of the United States has fomented terrorism. Let me hasten to say that we are not alone. Most governments, when they believe their vital interests to be at stake, employ terrorist tactics if they believe they need to do so. What is historically unusual, in fact, is the extent to which such countries as the Western democracies and Japan have avoided the use of terror internally. Although people in other countries have suffered terror at their hands, those living within their borders have been largely immune.

Even here we must not overstate the case with regard to our own nation. For decades local governments in this country allowed the Ku Klux Klan to use terror systematically as a means of holding in check the aspirations for justice of the black community. Some ghetto dwellers to this day experience the police more as an occupying force that rules by terror than as a servant of society dedicated to justice for all. Terror was systematically employed against Native Americans for centuries in order to drive them off their lands. Even recently their efforts to find justice have sometimes been met by terror. Euro-Americans as well sometimes experience the police as terrorists when their protests seem to threaten the interests of the rich and powerful. In some of our prisons, order is maintained by terror.

However, if we compare all this with the use of terror in the Soviet Union against its own citizens, or that of the Taliban, we will be impressed by the fact that many, many citizens of the United States have never been victims of terrorism. Terror against our own people has not been a part of standard American policy. The Ku Klux Klan was finally disempowered, and other would-be terrorist groups have been marginalized. Blacks and Native Americans have had some success in getting public support against terror. Hundreds of millions of people in other parts of the world feel only envy for the extent to which our lives are free of terror. Reduction of the amount of terror in all other countries to the level that it still functions in the United States would constitute an enormous advance in international affairs.

A move in this direction is not easy. It would be comparatively easy for the United States to end its instruction in low intensity warfare. What little justification it ever had ended with the Cold War. We could stop using the Drug War as an occasion for supporting terrorism in Colombia and other Andean countries. We could resolve to allow democratically elected governments in Latin America to develop their own policies. We could cease fomenting rebellions in other parts of the world, especially those that we know will use terror as a major means of gaining and preserving power.

But there are uses of terror that are far more difficult to end. Consider the situation on both sides of the conflict between Israel and the Palestinians. The state of Israel came into being through the use of terror against the British rulers. The British had vacillated between opening Palestine to Jewish settlement and protecting the rights of the Palestinians. The Jews forced the departure of the British through terrorist acts. The heroes of Israel were once terrorists.

Are they to be condemned? They were passionately concerned that in a world that refused to welcome Jews, even when their lives depended on finding a new home, there be some place to which they could come. Killing a few innocent people seemed a small price to pay to achieve this goal. They succeeded, and they established the State of Israel. To do so they needed to reduce the Arab population of the region. To this end they employed terror against them, so that many fled. Was that use of terror justified?

Since the exercise of terror in relation to the Palestinians and their subsequent subjugation aroused deep resentment and anger among the victims, these also have resorted to terrorism. They attack civilians more often than police and soldiers. Their weapons are far inferior to those of Israel, and their voice of moral protest falls on deaf ears. From the point of view of many of them, the only way to get any attention at all to their oppression and suffering is to employ terrorist methods. Are they justified?

The response of Israel is like that of any government. It is committed to doing whatever it must to keep its people safe. Overall the effort is to terrorize the Palestinian people into submission to their fate. The methods include destruction of homes and orchards, assassinations of suspected leaders, bombardment of villages and neighborhoods, and torture of prisoners. Is this justified?

What will a war on terrorism mean in the context of Israel and the Palestinians? Many Israelis believe it should mean that we will support the ending of all restraint on their part in the suppression of Palestinian terrorism. Palestinians fear that this will lead to genocide. Many Palestinians believe that a war on terrorism should mean the end of terrorist acts against them and that they should be allowed to establish their own state according to the resolutions of the United Nations. Many Israelis fear that this means the abandonment of their numerous settlements in Gaza and the West Bank and a nation without defensible borders surrounded by enemies only too eager to destroy it.

It is encouraging that, as a first step in the war against terrorism, the United States government put enormous pressure on both sides to end hostilities and return to negotiation. But what next? How can the war on terrorism bring about a compromise that will satisfy both sides sufficiently that they will end the use of terror against each other?

Consider the problem more broadly. The powers that be have multiple weapons at their disposal. Although they frequently resort to terrorist methods, they often have alternatives. But the oppressed have fewer choices. They have no soldiers and police to employ against the oppressing powers. They have little if any access to the media that shape public opinion. If they lash out against their oppressors, their actions will almost always be terrorist in nature. It is these actions of the oppressed that most often come to mind when the word *terrorism* is used.

For this reason, there is danger that the war against terrorism will be a war against the oppressed. The acts of governments in suppressing opposition will not be the object of criticism. Indeed, these acts, however calculated to inspire terror among the oppressed, will be justified by the need to prevent acts of terrorism that threaten the ruling classes. This approach will increase the number of people who live in regimes of terror. It may reduce their terrorist acts by removing from them the last glimmer of hope. But it is more likely to drive many of them to ever more desperate acts of terror against their ever more violent oppressors.

There is another danger of the war against terrorism. It could lead us to think that the greatest evils in the world today are the result of the overt violence this term identifies. There is no doubt about its importance, but even more suffering is engendered in other ways.

An economic embargo does not come under the heading of terrorism. But the suffering it generates may be more terrible. Consider Iraq. We imposed an embargo for the purpose of forcing Iraq to end its efforts to produce weapons of mass destruction. The hope was that the desire to end the embargo and get back to normal economic life would make the government of Iraq cooperative. If this had happened, we could all celebrate.

It did not happen. Instead, the government of Iraq, headed by another of our U.S.-trained terrorists, has allowed the common people to feel the full brunt of the embargo, using their suffering to generate greater and greater hatred toward us. Its military might and its weapons programs have been little affected. Hence, the actual result of the embargo has been the death of hundreds of thousands of people, perhaps millions, many of them children. This supposedly more humane instrument of foreign policy has had consequences considerably more horrible than any terrorist act to date. Is it more important to end terrorism than to end the weekly dying of thousands of Iraqi children?

Many of us believe that an even more important cause of suffering in our world lies in the methods of corporate globalization to which the United States government, along with most governments, is committed. Despite criticism of details, most Americans of good will continue to support these basic policies, believing that global economic growth is the solution to the problem of poverty. Others believe that top-down development, which destroys existing communities and means of livelihood for the sake of increasing corporate investment, exacerbates the problem of poverty and reduces the capacity of the Earth to support even its present population. This is not the place to debate this issue. But it is the place to question whether the war on terrorism should take precedence over continuing the debate about economic globalization and the worldwide dominance of corporations.

There is a clear connection between these two issues. The terrorists singled out the greatest symbol of global corporate power, the World Trade Center, for their primary attack. Clearly, from their point of view, the corporate globalism that dominates the world is an enemy, perhaps the greatest enemy. There are hundreds of millions of people, perhaps billions, who agree. Many of them think that the loss of life and wealth involved in this act of terror is less horrible than the decades-long suffering and growing hopelessness that is their lot. To end acts of terrorism without addressing the reasons that they are directed against global corporate rule may not be a blessing to the world as a whole, even if it restores the sense of innocent security to the American public.

In this connection it will be important to watch the response to future protests against globalization. At Seattle, police were generally restrained in their responses. Since then police have become steadily more violent. At Genoa they attacked and beat up sleeping protestors, presumably to inspire terror so as to deter them from continuing their protests. The prospects for police response to the planned (and subsequently called off) protests in Washington, D.C. in late September were disturbing. The danger is that the use of terror against nonviolent protestors will accelerate dramatically, with the threat of terrorism as its justification.

The hope is that governments dedicated to reducing terrorism will allow peaceful protests to proceed and arrest only those protestors who are violent. Governments could shift from treating protestors as a threatening enemy toward engaging them in genuine dialogue. The media could send representatives to the impressive teach-ins that accompany these protests and report the profound thinking that accompanies them. We could encourage an honest national debate. But this would require that governments and the media attain some independence from corporate control. In the absence of such independence, peaceful protest will be met with terror, and serious argument will be kept out of both the mass media and electoral campaigns.

Do Christians Have Anything Distinctive to Say?

To a large extent Christianity functions much as any ideology. It strengthens ties among Christian believers just as Islam strengthens ties among Muslims and Judaism, among Jews. Christians are more likely to go to the defense of other Christians than of others, and Muslims are more likely to go to the defense of other Muslims. Belief in God leads to the conviction that those of the true faith are especially valued and cared for.

This binding together has great value. It tends to weaken barriers erected within each community toward other members who disagree about correct interpretations. It works against individual selfishness and religious nationalism. It reduces tendencies to racism. It contributes to the mutual support that we all so critically need. It provides an identity that gives meaning and purpose to life.

In the present instance the tendency is to associate ourselves as victims and as part of Christian civilization and our attackers as representative of Muslim civilization. Fortunately, many American Christians have accepted the idea that the United States is a religiously pluralistic nation, and that it is important, from a Christian point of view, that Muslims as Muslims not be blamed or assigned second-class status in the United States. Despite many incidents of abuse and destruction against Muslims, Christian and governmental leadership have spoken well on this subject. We have denied that those who attacked us represent true Islam. We have recognized that all our monotheistic traditions have the danger of absolutizing themselves in the name of the one God and defaming all others. We repudiate this tendency in the Christian tradition.

As Christians, we love our country, and we recognize a special obligation to relieve the suffering of other Americans. We understand that a healthy world requires healthy societies in which people take special responsibility for one another's needs. A cosmopolitanism that regards our responsibilities as directed equally to all works against the need for effective community. One Christian objection to globalization is that it breaks down healthy local and national communities.

Nevertheless, we repudiate nationalism. Although we have a special responsibility to our nation, we cannot view the world in terms of what advances the causes of just this one nation. We must recognize that the perspectives of other nations may be just as valid as our own. The suffering of people in other parts of the world grieves the heart of God as much as our suffering. Our task is to view world events dispassionately and neutrally, not in terms of their bearing upon us. While we seek to bind up the wounds especially of fellow Americans, we need to view our national actions both present and past as objectively as we can.

This is where we affirm our heritage from the prophets of ancient Israel. We find a culmination of that prophetic tradition in Jesus. Just for that reason, the fact that we worship God, as we know God in Jesus Christ, does not mean that God loves us more than others. It does not justify our lack of concern for people in other parts of the world with other beliefs. It certainly does not justify our support of policies that harm them for our gain. On the contrary, it means that we should strive for a greater obedience to God's call for love than we expect of others.

This prophetic tradition is present in all three of the great monotheistic faiths. Sadly, it does not shape the responses of most believers to crises. But there are exceptions. There are Jews who transcend communal Jewish feeling in order to call for real justice for Palestinians. They pay a great price, as prophets have always paid, in terms of the hatred they arouse among other Jews. In response to the terrorist attacks on New York and Washington, a few Christians have called for our national recognition of the terror we have inflicted on others. Their voices have as yet been too muted to attract much attention. But when and if they are widely heard, we can expect that most of their fellow Christians will denounce them. There is a great emotional need for both Jews and Christians to feel righteous in their anger. The prophetic challenge to that self-righteousness is most unwelcome, especially at the time of crisis.

Yet it is precisely that kind of self-righteousness that underlies the acts of terror against us. The depth of conviction of what constitutes righteousness that led to willingness to die in the process of inflicting a wound upon us is based on just that same unwillingness to see oneself in the inclusive context. If we respond by justifying ourselves in inflicting a larger wound on others somehow related to our attackers, our religious psychology is just like theirs. If Christians fail to offer the prophetic witness against our sins, we will have used our faith simply to sanction the normal reactions of sinful humanity rather than to offer a distinctive contribution.

No one has made the distinctive point clearer than Jesus. "You have heard that it was said, 'You shall love your neighbor and hate your enemy.' But I say to you, Love your enemies and pray for those who persecute you." (Mt. 5:43–44). If we love bin Laden, we will try to see the world through his eyes. That does not mean that we will agree with him. It does not mean that we will fail to undertake to bring him to justice. It does mean that once we have seen ourselves though his eyes, we will no longer be able to act self-righteously. We, too, collectively and individually, are sinners. While we hold others accountable for their crimes against humanity, we will recognize that we too have committed and are committing crimes against humanity. That is not a comfortable recognition, but our faith calls us to live in the light of painful truth.

2

Subversion, Body-Politic, Scripture
A Question on the Limits of Power

Creston C. Davis

German fascism is not the twin of American capitalism. But it is its older brother.

DANIEL GUERIN

For our struggle is…against the rulers, against the authorities, against the cosmic power of this present darkness.

SAINT PAUL

Every theory of the state is theological. Revolution has hitherto only perfected the state; the point, however, is to destroy it.

ANTONIO NEGRI

The shocking events on September 11 in New York and Washington, D. C., have, among other things, mobilized complex networks ranging from the most abstract global and national levels to the microcosmically particular local level. This movement includes mobilization of military troops, state and local police, intelligence and security agencies, and major shifts in energy, economic, and monetary policies. Indeed, the whole range of international, national, regional, and local policies have already shifted dramatically as a result of these acts of terror. The contention before us is this: To what extent have these

10

mobilizations at all levels affected the relationship between these newly formed institutions of power and the form of the democratic liberal state? We must, in other words, provide an answer to this question: Through the rapid development of military and security policies associated with the events of September 11, have there been substantial modifications, both in the normative and in constitutional and political terms, such as to affect the nature of the legitimization of the state? The basic form of this question was first developed and expressed by Antonio Negri more than fifteen years ago in a 1986 essay called "Some notes concerning the concept of the 'nuclear state'."[1] I want to canvass the seminal points of Negri's argument with the hope of identifying and characterizing how these rapidly shifting times—and the newly articulated organization of power associated with them—open a new discursive space between the Christian community and the liberal-democratic state. Could it be true, I ask, that these rapid shifts in policies suggest a movement into fascism unawares, and that the only way to identify such a movement is through scripture and the communities that faithfully interpret them? My thesis is that not only is the liberal state, as Negri points out, illegitimate, but the myth of liberalism is grounded in nothing other than its self-constitution of absolute power as such—an immanent domain. Furthermore, the sovereign power of the state cannot on its own terms identify its immanent limits and so can only be exposed for what it is through the habits and practices of a counter-cite that resists its self-legitimization within the secular—the Church. I will show this by focusing on the logic of scripture as embodied in its leaders—which opens the possibility of identifying the impossible within the immanent field of power itself. In this way, the secular logic of immanence is constituted not on its own terms—the myth of absolute power—nor is it subsumed within a counterlogic of a totalizing utopian flight without remainder. Rather, in identifying and characterizing the secular as a contingent intensity of power, the logic of scripture[2] is at once constituted by the secular—but not wholly absorbed within itself—and by scriptural communities whose practices and habits shape how to read against the grain of a prosaic semantic "realism" of secular immanence.[3] In this sense, the logic of scripture becomes a counterlogic (a theo-logic), the participation of which is necessarily subversive, or so I shall argue.

Given the fact that there now exist production cycles in the provision of nuclear energy and atomic weapons, Negri's inquiry is an attempt to see if the state form is one that is describable as a technical-theoretical entity called the "nuclear state." He begins by showing that, with the dawning of nuclear energy, there has taken hold a fundamental shift in a series of specific policies, and that shift is always already related to the formation of the liberal state. Moreover, it is wrong to conceive of two separate domains: one that deals strictly with the military and the other solely with energy. This is because nuclear energy and nuclear arms are intimately related through their modes of production (i.e., nuclear reactors) and the ways in which these modes of production influence the development and implementation of economic, security, and energy policies. Furthermore, these national, regional, and local policies affect what people actually can and cannot do and by extension, the possibilities of thinking that is not affected, to some degree, by the brute existence of the nuclear. Therefore, Negri attempts to apprehend a particular relational concept, one that specifically describes the relationship between the type of energy and the form of the state. Crucial here is the question of whether the transition from electrical power to nuclear power has substantially modified the means by which the legitimization of the state is established and sustained, to the extent to which the state's legitimization is called into question.

Negri asks: "What is involved in the concept of legitimacy in a democratic state?" He rejoins, "[L]egitimacy is a constitutionally guaranteed relationship between the legal exercise of violence on the one hand, and on the other, the consensual and democratic formation of both political directives and the organizations retaining a monopoly over the use of violence."[4] In theoretical terms there must necessarily exist a dialogical symmetry established and maintained between the dual levels of power expression mediated through organizations possessing constitutional jurisdiction. On the first base level, there is an organization of the collective subjects that gives rise to the popular will. This expression of the popular will further gives rise to the second hierarchical level, whose existence is justified through a representational correspondence of that popular will. The form of the state is legitimated, insofar as there is a certain balance between these two levels through which the popular will is derived and represented.

So we return to the question at hand: to what extent does the development of nuclear energy and the manufacture, stockpiling, and possible use of nuclear weapons affect the concept of democratic legitimacy and its constitutional implementation? Central to Negri here is the modification of the relationship between the formation of the popular will—or more strictly the conscious preformation of the popular will itself—and the legal exercise of violence. Negri's argument reveals that the democratic processes and constitutional relationships are fundamentally and irreversibly altered with the development of policies of nuclear defense. Why? He says, "because the latter [nuclear arms and the eminent threat of war] remove all limits on the potential effects of the legal use of violence and render the relationship between it and the mechanisms of the formation of the political will, a highly unequal one."[5] In other words, the pure might and brutal dimensions of the absolute power of nuclear armaments are totally controlled by those whose actions of violence are legally secured, which necessarily frustrates the conditions of possibility (consciously or otherwise) within which the political will can take hold. If one removes the conditions of possibility through which the political will emerges—through the absolute force of fear—and if the state is legitimated only through the actualization of such a process, then whatever prevents the former necessarily occludes the possibility for the latter.

Assuming Negri's thesis is right, namely that the introduction of nuclear power annuls any democratic means by which that power can be used, how can we apply it to our situation? This moment in history is one that cannot be reduced to a singularity of meaning–despite all attempts by the U.S. media to do so[6] – around which all things are explained in some prosaic, moral vacuum. The horrifying events in New York City and Washington, D.C., are thereby flattened out onto a surface of immediate and intoxicating passions, and that articulates a binary mapping on which options and choices are severely limited: either bomb or be bombed, either commit acts of terror or be terrorized. It is true, of course, that the constitution of this event operates only within a specific imaginative social geography. The point here is that our geography in the affluent West is one usurped by a semantics of vulgar realism inherited by a bourgeois cultural revolution[7] and sustained through the isomorphic flux of monopolistic capital.[8] Thus, the very possibility to situate this event, to interpret it and engage it on another non-immanent or theological level (a semiotic and not a semantic level) is occluded. There is here then a straightforward link between a flat and depthless linguistic[9] and conceptual geography that results in a crude binary logic of terror and Negri's argument. The fear of war (or of the terrorist) quicksands the possibilities of thought and social organization and cultural communication such that the formidable foe of fear (actualized in war or terror) wielded by a select few and seen in the absolute sovereignty of the state, cannot be circumvented. Fear is the exacting mechanism of social control and disciplines and determines language and practice within a homogeneous and ominous immanence. The logic of this fear–the reified "fear of fear itself," or a simulacrum of fear–is one that cannot think outside its own force and blocks off all exits constitutive upon any social, political, and linguistic bodies, the existence of which do not presuppose fear for its own existence.

Negri helps us to see that the absolutist state is not, as a matter of fact, absolute in any foundational or historical sense at all. In fact, the liberal state is no longer legitimate on its own terms. The absolute nature of the state is therefore only absolute in a strictly rhetorical fashion motored by the ability to saturate fear into all things–that is, to narrate this fear through a complex network of communication that necessarily presents itself as a universal self-generated discourse. For the hibernating Christian community, Negri becomes, in a sense, an alarm that alerts us to the fact that the state is not, as has been widely believed by Christians for far too long, part of divine creation.

On another level, however, Negri's argument is helpful, but not necessary, for the church to identify the contingency of the sovereign secular state vis-à-vis God's self-givenness in creation. Nevertheless, as John Howard Yoder argues, a traditional tendency within Western Christianity (Roman Catholicism and Protestantism alike) is to interpret the "institution of government ordained by God," as a "specific providential action of God." Yoder concludes, "Government exists by revelation"–that is, by necessity.[10] Yoder shows that if this be so, then the German state ruled by Adolf Hitler was just such an ordained institution against which Christians should not have resisted–which is sadly what happened in the 1930s. This conclusion seems straightforwardly absurd to our modern minds, not only because Hitler's Germany was so obviously diabolical, seen especially in the systematic torture and extermination of more than six million Jews, but also because it was a state not ruled by a democratic and liberal means. An absolute power ruled Germany. To the extent that our "modern minds" associate Hitler's Germany with an intrinsic evil, we may too often fail to see why Nazi Germany was wrong from an ecclesial and biblical point of view.

From scripture, it is clear that whatever is—that is, whatever is "real" or constituted on a strictly secular, semantic plain—does not entail its necessity. Once again the notion of "realism" is a complex social and political construction organized by multiple and contingent power determinations, which saturate language, practices, and cultural relations. Thus, there is no historical determinism (or even an ahistorical determinism) sealed by the connection between God's revelation and the institution of secular rule. This belief in a secular mechanical determinism ordained by God often emerges when modern, liberal Christians read Romans, chapter 13, in isolation from chapter 12 and the overall scope of Paul's letter. Such as liberal reading of scripture makes the word of God a seamless extension of secular authority. This is dangerous exactly because the logic of scripture is subsumed by an immanent logic of secular power, and so scripture merely extends this worldly power through itself. It is plainly naive to suppose that the scriptures are a self-authenticating *(sola scriptura)* and apolitical body of divine texts that on their own accord possess the ability to resist a secular overcoding. On the contrary, scripture is read from a specific cultural location within which a political community of Christians (or Jews or Muslims) interpret and live into its dramatic script. From here the logic of scripture resists the imperialistic and scientific perversion and opens out a reality that supposes that secular power and authority are themselves contingent manifestations whose very nature forgets they are contingent bodies produced by the violence of fear and greed. Armed with this anti-liberal reading of scripture, namely, that all forms of governments are not by necessity ordained by God—that is, governments are contingent and not self-justifying institutions—we are now able to identify the basic problem with a liberal interpretation of the Holocaust, which, according to this view, places blame on the specific form of government and its ideological implications of tyrannical rule. This liberal interpretation fails to see that Christians were killing the Jews in the name of Germany exactly because the church was unable to read the scriptures against fascism but instead read them within their own socially determined context uninformed by the counter-logic of scripture. Without the ability to understand that secular authority is a contingent and not a necessary institution, Christians were conscripted into performing acts of terror if only because they failed to resist the policies and militarism of Nazi Germany, even at the risk of their own peril. In this manner, a demonic irony developed: Christians were responsible for killing that which they depend on for their own faithful existence, namely the Jews.

The liberal critique of Nazi Germany (and the Japanese Empire) is to some extent helpful in that it identifies a *type* of violence resulting from a non-liberal and non-democratic form of government, which was finally defeated by a "free" and democratic form of government seen in the allied forces (Britain, Canada, United States, and so forth). However, it is not uninteresting to note that World War II ended by the dawning of the development and deployment of weapons of mass destruction. The evil of the absolute power of Hitler was defeated by the emergence of yet another more potent and destructive absolute. And this is where Negri's argument helps identify the limits of a liberal absolutist state. Liberalism is able to identify when a certain form of the state (democratic, socialist, communist, fascist, etc.) is good or bad, but it is blind to its inability to identify the state's absolute contingency. Insofar as secular liberalism is unable to identify its own contingency, then it too will be unable to know when it has passed from liberalism to fascism—even with the judicial protection of a constitution (a constitution, like the scriptures, does not stand outside history but is shaped by the powers that determine history). This is because if state sovereignty is justified through its own immanent means, then when it comes under threat—either externally, as on September 11, or internally, by the people actualizing their own will—it must become neofascist for its own survival. Negri's argument shows that the liberal state is illegitimate on its own grounds, and because it is backed and justified by absolute power, only recourse to an "outside" or theo-logic can possibly show this power what it is not. This "outside" is the body politic of the nonviolent church that reads and embodies the scriptures and can identify and creatively undermine this absolute and illegitimate power through the practice of reading itself. If it is true that the liberal democratic state is on a theoretical level illegitimate, and only appears now to be legitimate because it possesses on a rhetorical level the means of instilling fear mediated through a semantic lineage of "realism," then what remains is the ability to outflank this immanent force of fear through locating a semiotics that is not reducible to absolute secular authority. Ken Surin traces this movement out in the following way:

> The traditional wielders of power have increasingly to resort to domination and war (particularly the preparation for war) to halt the social revolution that is taking place, while their subjects, the carriers of this social revolution, have (in the "core" industrial nations at any rate) more and more to further this revolution through strategies of stabilization, and especially the struggle for peace. The resisting subject, always here a collective subject, deterritorializes the domain of the state by organizing a new kind of social power which cannot be mobilized by war and the fear of war.[11]

This word is indeed strange, but its strangeness is such by the overdetermined juncture crystallized through God's inexhaustible gift to the church—and the church's ability to hear God's word—mediated through the differential mundane language (determined by power relations). This diffusive juncture is pronounced especially when mundane language conflicts with itself by paradoxically being reduced onto a strictly semantic surface. When secular language contradicts itself–when it attempts to occupy a non-differential space with two conflicting and impermeable concepts–a rupture takes hold. One such moment is Negri's theoretical analysis of the state form, by which he opens a cleavage between appearance (the force of fear) and its root (illegitimate state) secured by absolute secular and diabolical power of nuclear armaments. The dynamic and dialectical liberal and democratic legacy, which reached its height in the 1960s civil rights movement, has waned to a virtual halt, as seen in the 2000 U.S. presidential election.[12] That is why the only option left is for the church to relearn what it means to read the Bible and to read it knowing that the liberal Western state is not an absolute *Ding an Sich* sustained by the simulacrum of fear. This means also, and perhaps most importantly, that reading the Bible–which by extension means one is participating in the life of the church–and being shaped by it are necessarily subversive acts.

To the extent that the secular powers justify themselves by allowing a degree of subversion to take hold only to be reabsorbed or overcoded by eradicating and neutralizing the conditions in which subversion is articulated, then acts of subversion and resistance, such as forgiveness, hospitality, charity, reading the scriptures, and celebrating the sacraments within a faithful, Christian community, seem to, in the last analysis, only feed the hegemony of secular power all the more. But this challenge supposes that subversive acts rely upon that power against which the acts are directed. Yet as I have already argued, the logic of contingency–informed by a faithful reading of scripture– can always be applied to secular power even if the application of this logic is judged to be blinded to ideological factors within which the application is expressed. The notion of *contingency* is coherent, not on universally objective grounds, but on scriptural grounds interpreted by a specific body politic. This notion of contingency allows the possibility of a resistance that cannot be fully reduced to being contingent, even in the face of immanent power. If this be true, then acts of subversion possess the germs of a body politic that are in fact coming to actualization in a peaceful revolution. It is this peaceful revolution of the ecclesial body politic that remains the only hope left for the survival of the world.

There is finally a second more serious challenge to this notion of secular "contingency," which maintains that the descriptive judgment about secular authority–being a contingent and not necessary authority–must derive its force from an absolutist and necessary ground. It is therefore in light of this absolutist ecclesial and scriptural ground that the notion of secular contingency is so constituted. This challenge is misplaced precisely because it fails to understand that contingency can be coherent within an analogical and participatory movement, within which immanent power can be called into question inasmuch as that power fails to participate in the flow of the divine (a flow that is not reducible to a flat or realist epistemological foundation).[13] The ecclesial and scriptural terrain remains always subject to the possibility of a non-necessary movement–the negation of the good–that annuls the capacity to identify the conditions of contingency in the world. In other words, the very ability to identify the limits of immanent power from a body politic disciplined by the sacraments and reading scripture always presupposes the possibility of losing that ability. The question before the church today then is this: have we lost this ability to name the world in a way that does not evade the real possibility that the church too is a contingent institution fully dependent on the Spirit of God and its tradition for its own existence? The ability to judge the world thus assumes that one also must be judged in the judging.[14]

3

"I Have Been through This Before"

Ariel Dorfman

I have been through this before. During the last twenty-eight years, Tuesday, September 11, has been a date of mourning for me and millions of others, ever since that day in 1973 when Chile lost its democracy in a military coup, that day when death irrevocably entered our lives and changed us forever. And now, almost three decades later, the malignant gods of random history have wanted to impose upon another country that dreadful date, again a Tuesday, once again an 11th of September filled with death.

The differences and distances that separate the Chilean date from the American are, one must admit, considerable. The depraved terrorist attack against the most powerful nation on Earth has had and will have consequences that affect all humanity. It is possible that it may constitute, as President Bush has stated, the start of the Third World War, and it is probable that it will be branded in the manuals of the future as the day when the planet's history shifted forever. Whereas very few of the eight billion people alive today could remember or would be able to identify what happened in Chile.

And yet, from the moment when, transfigured, I watched on our television screen here in North Carolina that second plane exploding into the World Trade Center's South Tower, I have been haunted by the need to understand and extract the hidden meaning of the juxtaposition and coincidence of these two September 11th's, which in my case becomes even more enigmatic and personal because it is a violation that conjoins the two foundational cities of my existence, the New York that gave me refuge and joy during ten years of my infancy and the Santiago that protected my adolescence under its mountains and made me into a man, the two cities that offered me my two languages, English and Spanish. Breathing slowly to overcome the emotional shock; making every effort not to look again and again at the contaminating photo of the man who falls vertically, so straight, so straight, from the heights of that building; trying to stop thinking about the last seconds of those plane passengers who know that their imminent doom will also kill thousands of their own innocent compatriots; and frantically making phone calls that should tell me if my friends in Manhattan are well and that nobody answers—it is in the middle of all this turmoil that I yield myself to the gradual realization that there is something horribly familiar, even recognizable, in this experience that (North) Americans are now passing through.

The resemblance I am evoking goes well beyond a facile and superficial comparison, for instance that both in Chile in 1973 and in the States today, terror descended from the sky to destroy the symbols of national identity, the Palace of the Presidents in Santiago, the icons of financial and military power in New York and Washington. No, what I recognize is something deeper, a parallel suffering, a similar pain, a commensurate disorientation echoing what we lived through in Chile on that September 11. Its most extraordinary incarnation is that I still cannot believe what I am witnessing. On the screen I see hundreds of relatives wandering the streets of New York, clutching the photos of their sons, fathers, wives, lovers, daughters, begging for information, asking if they are alive or dead, the whole United States forced to look into the abyss of what it means to be *desaparecido*, with no certainty or funeral possible for those beloved men and women who are missing. And I also recognize and repeat that sensation of extreme unreality that invariably accompanies great disasters caused by human iniquity, so much more difficult to cope with than natural catastrophes. Over and over again I hear phrases that remind me of what people like me would mutter to themselves during the 1973 military coup and the days that followed: "This cannot be happening to us. This sort of excessive violence happens to other people and not to us. We have only known this form of destruction through movies and books and remote photographs. If it's a nightmare, why can't we awaken from it?" And words reiterated unceasingly twenty-eight years ago and now again in the year 2001: "We have lost our innocence. The world will never be the same."

What has come to an explosive conclusion, of course, is (North) America's famous exceptionalism, that attitude that allowed the citizens of this country to imagine themselves as beyond the sorrows and calamities that have plagued less fortunate peoples around the world. None of the great battles of the twentieth century touched the continental United States. Even the Pearl Harbor "Day of Infamy," which is being extricated from the past as the only possible analogous incident, occurred thousands of miles away. It is that complacent invulnerability that has been fractured forever. Life in these United States will have to share, from now on, the precariousness and uncertainty that is the daily lot of the enormous majority of this planet's other inhabitants. In spite of the tremendous pain and intolerable losses that this apocalyptic crime has visited upon the American public, I wonder if this trial does not constitute one of those opportunities for regeneration and self-knowledge that, from time to time, is given to certain nations. A crisis of this magnitude can lead to renewal or destruction; it can be used for good or for evil, for peace or for war, for aggression or for reconciliation, for vengeance or for justice, for the militarization of a society or for its humanization. One of the ways for Americans to overcome their trauma, to survive the fear and continue to live and thrive in the midst of the insecurity that has suddenly swallowed them, is to admit that their suffering is neither unique nor exclusive, that they are connected—as long as they are willing to look at themselves in the vast mirror of our common humanity—with so many other human beings who, in apparently faraway zones, have suffered similar situations of unanticipated and often protracted injury and fury.

Could this be the hidden and hardly conceivable reason that destiny has decided that the first contemporary attack on the essence and core of the United States would transpire precisely on the very anniversary that commemorates the military takeover in Chile that a government in Washington nourished and sustained in the name of the American people? Could it be a way to mark the immense challenge that awaits the citizens of this country, particularly its young, now that they know what it really means to be victimized, now that they can grasp the sort of collective hell survivors withstand when their loved ones have disappeared and they have no body to bury, now that they have been given the chance to draw closer to and comprehend the multiple variations of the many September 11ths that are scattered throughout the globe, the kindred sufferings that so many peoples and countries endure?

The terrorists have wanted to single out and isolate the United States as a satanic state. The rest of the planet, including many nations and men and women who have been the objects of American arrogance and intervention, reject, as I categorically do, this demonization. It is enough to see the almost unanimous outpouring of grief of most of the world, the offers of help, the expressions of solidarity, the determination to claim the dead of this mass murder as their dead.

It remains to be seen if this compassion shown to the mightiest power on this planet will be reciprocated. It is still not clear if the United States, a country formed in great measure by those who have themselves escaped vast catastrophes, famines, dictatorships, and persecution, will be able to feel that same empathy toward the other outcast members of our species. We will find out in the days and years to come if the new Americans forged in pain and resurrection are ready and open and willing to participate in the arduous process of repairing our shared and damaged humanity, creating, all of us together, a world in which we need never again lament another, not even one more, terrifying September 11.

4

Business as Un-usual
Reconstructing Divine Economy

Marion Grau

For a few days after 9/11, *The New York Times* Web site pulled all its advertising, presumably because it seemed inappropriate to run advertising after the horrors and deaths of September 11. But only a few days later Neiman-Marcus handbags and Tiffany & Co. ads reappeared next to *The New York Times* header. The colonization of the news media by business interests has resurfaced, invisible for mere days. The emporium—along with the empire—strikes back, or so it seems. Along with the reemergence of commercials go ubiquitous encouragements to return to "business as usual," declaring the "trip to the mall" a patriotic endeavor. Slowly it seems, following these urges to consume, a grieving people pull out their wallets again, investing, restarting the wheels of neoliberal capitalism that had ground to a halt for a few days.

Though various critics have denounced current hypercapitalism as "a world run riot with unrealities" such as paper money, inflation, fluctuations in currency, stock hypes, and balloons—after 9/11 nothing about capital seems virtual anymore. The Twin Towers, a proud symbol of capitalism and the location of countless business transactions have, quite literally, become a mass of stone, dust, and blood; and there is certainly nothing virtual about the "human capital" buried within the ruins. The perceived immateriality of capital in an age of digitized money movements was unveiled as a fiction. What seemed unreal, digital, ethereal is again bricks and mortar business, crushed to Ground Zero, its concrete bubbles busted, the market crashed.

But just three business days later, vestiges of virtuality were resurrected. The NYSE on Wall Street, a quick walk from Ground Zero, is powered by largely computerized money markets that can simply go back online, though weakened through a significant drop in morale. The slump in investor and consumer confidence also threatens the fallacious abstractions that sustain oft-criticized, yet stubbornly resilient neoliberal economic concepts, such as John Stuart Mill's *homo economicus,* the "self-interested, rational, and autonomous" ideal economic agent.[1]

The present piece attempts a critical genealogy of the figure of the *homo economicus,* as it may be discerned in "his" possible ancestor, the gospels' figure of the Rich Young Man. This genealogy, fictional no doubt, materializes uncanny links between the youth in conversation with Jesus and the construct of Economic Man. Although economic agency is no longer recognized only in white male subjects, the *homo* remains abstracted from such an exclusive subjectivity, and thus remains invested with traits traditionally described as Western and masculine.[2] Might one facet of "his" redemption lie in "queering" "his" gender? The following interdisciplinary reading explores this hypothesis by diagnosing the Rich Young Man and Economic Man as hysterics, and probes whether this traditionally feminine ailment can help us conceive of an alternate economic subjectivity. From this critical genealogy, a Holy Fool of divine madness, a counter-economic trickster emerges, invested in reconstructing a Divine Economy that reincarnates a web of economic and ecological relations of which most of us remain in habitual denial, as we are continually fed by aesthetically sanitized media sound bites of disembodied economic transactions.

Post-9/11 Business: "As Usual"?

The reverberations of two commercial airliners crashing into and collapsing the Twin Towers provided a merciless reality check for the virtual reality of stocks, funds, and similar money market investments, the statistical fluctuations in which have now become incarnate in job losses and in the increased visibility of relations such as that between Alaskan halibut fishers and floundering Manhattan fish markets. Whether we own a modem that allows us to participate in e-commerce or not, connected we surely all are, for better and for worse, tied to one another through multitudes of mysterious exchanges. In the wake of 9/11, the often unconscious links and transactions between people have become uncannily visible, as if Adam Smith's "invisible hand" had suddenly materialized "in the flesh."

The economy, so we are told as we feel the echoes of economic chain-reactions, must be stimulated, and to stimulate it we need to do our duty as consumers—and consume. Behavioral psychology has increasingly been employed by economists to predict and divine future market trends, recognizing that people's psychological setup, their trust and willingess to invest, is crucial to the rise and fall of economic fortunes. Consequently, a depressive mood is not conducive to the needed crank to an economy that is headed toward recession. In order to prod the listless and frightened post-9/11 consumers, a new line of commercials is quickly developed, suggesting the patriotic duty of Americans lies in spending away grief, anger, and depression. The *homo economicus* should not hang "his" collective head, but should get on with life. A journalist paraphrases the sickening seductions hidden in the advertisements:

> Forget all the pain and loss of life. Forget the countless kind and selfless deeds performed without thought of recompense. It's time to get back to "normal." It's time to get back to business...This is still America...and we can still buy our way out of anything! Feeling lost and confused? Purchase a new car! Feeling vulnerable? Get a ThighMaster! Is travel down? Bail out the airlines. Are tourists staying away? Ratchet up the advertising. Buy, buy, buy, spend, spend, spend. It's worked for generations.[3]

The message: National, if not global, redemption will come from getting back to "business as usual." Forget the victims, forget the dead, forget the questions, the complexities, the layers of pain and anger and simply consume your anger in a rage of bombing and a rage of spending. Both will surely raise the GNP–and that, after all, is the bottom line!

As we see the ties that bind us economically and question how we might react to this new sense of economic interrelatedness, however, the old answers need to be newly questioned. Do we in the wealthy West want, do we need, and lastly can we *afford* and will the planet survive a return to "business as usual," or might it rather lead us to further intimations of apocalypse? Can we pin the events of 9/11 on a few deranged extremist religious fundamentalists and remain in a communal denial of the history, the context, and the reverberations of our own habits, locations, and lives? Instead, we may need to ponder whether "business as usual," though in many ways it helped to shrink the globe and connect distant locations to one another, has also, more tragically, helped to polarize West against East, North against South, and Western-style capitalism against those who would rather do business otherwise. Does "business as usual" mean that we will continue to regard our (trans)actions and investments as if disconnected from the others impacted by our money moves?

There are some signs that perspectives have shifted, as if adjusting to a new and expanded worldview. Thus, a *New York Times* journalist, feeling the pulse of the Wall Street traders who have returned to buildings surrounding the site of death and destruction, reports that many traders are not having "fun playing the game" anymore. One trader comments: "People who really make money in this business love the game. A lot of that love of the game has been lost."[4] Might there somewhere in our "merchants of the earth" as they "weep and mourn for her, since no one buys their cargo anymore" (Rev. 18:11), emerge a recognition or at least an unconscious realization that "business as usual" never was a "game"? And might, similarly, our metaphorical economic agent in the encounter with the Rich Young Man in Matthew's gospel be unveiled as rather "un-usual," and might we tease out of the cracks of his persona counter-economic possibilities for a trickster-like Divine Economy that does "business as un-usual"?

Defined by Lack: The Hysteric Economic Male

> Then someone came to him and said, "Teacher, what good deed must I do to have eternal life?" And he said to him, "Why do you ask me about what is good? There is only one who is good. If you wish to enter into life, keep the commandments." He said to him, "Which ones?" And Jesus said, "You shall not murder; You shall not commit adultery; You shall not steal; You shall not bear false witness; Honor your father and mother; also, You shall love your neighbor as yourself." The young man said to him, "I have kept all these; what do I still lack?" Jesus said to him, "If you wish to be perfect, go, sell your possessions, and give the money to the poor, and you will have treasure in heaven; then come, follow me." When the young man heard this word, he went away grieving, for he had many possessions. (Mt. 19:16–22)

The Rich Young Man's story concretely demonstrates, so W. D. Davies and Dale C. Allison say, "the impossibility of serving both God and Mammon (Mt. 6:24),"[5] perched as it is within the tensions of both powers. The young man approaches Jesus with a desire that knows no limits.[6] How can I have *zoon aionon,* life without end? An inscrutable Jesus offers a rather obvious answer—"keep the commandments." Asked whether he could specify which commandments, Jesus recites the second set of the Mosaic tablets, stressing a man's commitment to his neighbors.[7] The youth senses that the prize is not yet his, that there is something he lacks. *Ti eti hustero*–what did I miss, what did I fail to obtain, what do I lack?–he asks, knowingly, it seems. Exposing lack, Matthew's hysterical youth finds himself hollow, and thereby feminized. *Ti eti hustero?* What do I lack? Indeed, what does he lack? interpreters have puzzled. Has he not played by the rules that Jesus specified? The audience is left in suspense. We are never quite sure what is amiss. "Would Matthew" ask Davies and Allison, "have supposed Zaccheus deficient because he gave away only half of his goods?"[8]

Though imagined as a rational animal, guided by reason in the marketplace, *homo economicus* demonstrates his own sense of deficiency by engaging in frantic behaviors that appear at the margins of "his" psychological profile. In fact, "he" may be a hysteric! This experience of lack–or hysteria–exposes the intersections of theological, sexual, and material economies and the desire for divine and/or economic redemption. Hysteria–according to most antique medical writers a condition assumed to exclusively befall women–renders the composite figure of the Rich Young Man/*homo economicus* a feminized, possibly feminist figure.[9]

Hysteria is a cognate of *hustera,* signifying a woman's womb. The adjectival form of the root from which the word derives carries with it notions of "following, next," or "later, subsequent." The verb *hustereo* literally means "to be behind, come late," or in its metaphorical use to "lag behind, be inferior to," to "fall short," and "be wanting."[10] In a woman, this womb-related lack would have been thought to be caused by the lack of insemination in a young virgin or a widow and was believed to result in the dislocation of the womb. The womb was thought to then wander around the body in search of moisture, and it might attach itself to various organs. The result was suffocation, if it moved to the throat, as well as various other symptoms and ailments of the female body. Hysteria was considered a serious disease that, if left untreated, could lead to death.[11] Though the notion of male hysteria experienced a bout of attention only through Freud's work, one rare doctor in antiquity, Aretaeus of Cappadocia, observed that there was a form of hysteria unconnected with the uterus that could also affect men.[12]

Daniel Boyarin has argued that Freud eventually diagnosed male hysteria as "the sexual passivity of the male that feminizes (and paradoxically homosexualizes)" the "gender of the active subject."[13] This passivity of desire, or feminization, can also occur in nonsexual relations that frustrate a man's sense of masculinity and give him a sense of being acted upon without being able or willing to resist. Thus, Boyarin argues that "[h]ysteria, in short, while gendered as paradigmatically feminine, is not exclusively about women, but involves both women and 'feminized' men."[14] Whereas female hysteria was thought to be caused by the lack of insemination with a male penis, male hysteria appears to have to do with a lack of masculinity, and remains thus in a sense, a "feminine" problem, since it occurs in "effeminate" or "feminized" men.

Jean Baudrillard provides a similar interpretation of hysteria, as the abject feminine side of the *homo economicus* in capitalist modernity. Thus,

> Baudrillard's account of the hysteria of late capitalism would, in many respects, have made perfect sense to Freud and all the other eminent *fin de siècle* diagnosticians of civilization and its discontents.[15]

Ray Porter highlights Baudrillard's account of the resemblance between hysteria and capitalism as both evoke

> an intense, slippery, baffling network of fleeting, volatile manifestations...which possibly serves as teasing surrogates for the underlying reality, or more likely mask an absence, a void, beneath and within.[16]

This void lacks the claimed rationality, the cool calculations, the pretense of precision, predictability, security. Thus, the dense masculinity claimed for scientific economics falls apart and unfolds the void, the lack of ratio as hysteria, that most stereotypically feminine of all disorders. Porter further argues that for Baudrillard hysteria was the sly imp that thumbed its nose and poked out its tongue at the neat Cartesian mind-body dualism; hysteria mocked the formally clear-cut boundaries delineating soma from psyche, the physical from the moral, malady from malevolence.[17]

Hysteria, sometimes called mysteria, is unveiled as a trickster that unveils the gendered, rationalist pretenses of Western capitalism. Likewise, the hysterical male can become a trickster mocking the supposed masculine rationality of scarcity, by unveiling it as irrational, and as queerly gendered. Might we even, like Porter, find that "Homo oeconomicus was always also the *le malade imaginaire,* Homo hystericus."[18] Imagined, hyped, psychologized economics?

Baudrillard suggests that meaning in the consumerist emporium of late capitalism "is produced by endless, symbolic exchanges within a dominant code, whose rhetoric is entirely self-referential."[19] Might this narcissistic self-referentiality of neoliberal economic reasoning account for at least part of the perplexed queries of "Why do they hate us so much?" in the wake of September 11? It seems to me that the self-referentiality of Western-style market economy, its hysterical and hypochondriac mentality as described by Baudrillard, and the denial or inability to see the larger connections, ramifications, the history, and contextuality of that same economic approach are closely related.

Reconstructing a Hysterical Economic Subjectivity in the Context of a Divine Economy

When the young man heard this word, he went away grieving, for he had many possessions. (Mt. 19:22)

Will we return to "business as usual" as the Rich Young Man walks away from Ground Zero, his head lowered, grieving as he is unable to give up his wealth or his hysterical habits in pursuing redemption through asset growth, even though holding on to it has now been cashed in at such a high price? I hear echoes of the Rich Young Man and the *homo economicus* in the voice of a futures broker on Wall Street who stepped out of the subway that September morning and saw the towers aflame. He ran for his life, escaped with thousands of others across the Hudson in a cruise ferry, and hung his head, terrified, sad, confused. Later, he asked me: "Why do they hate us so much?" and I could not answer a question that is at once so obvious for those who have learned to visualize the Western market's "invisible hand" and the blood that drips from it, but hardly obvious in the context of the loudly proclaimed salvific dispensations of a divinized neoliberal economics as we continue to abstract our actions and deny that they are always embedded in a tight web of relations that includes all the inhabitants of this planet.

And the merchants of the earth weep and mourn for her, since no one buys their cargo anymore...The merchants of these wares, who gained wealth from her, will stand far off, in fear of her torment,

weeping and mourning aloud,
> "Alas, alas, the great city,
>> clothed in fine linen,
>>> in purple and scarlet,
>> adorned with gold,
>>> with jewels, and with
>>>> pearls!
> For in one hour all this
>> wealth has been laid
>> waste!" (Rev. 18:11, 15–17).

When I read Revelation 18 in the aftermath of 9/11, I see in it a resemblance to the mix of feelings that has been with me ever since that day. Disbelief at the extreme actions and the reverberations of the actions of a few minds committed to death and destruction, regardless of who the victims were. Frustration and anger at the longstanding colonial and neocolonial exploitations that have resulted in the denial of responsibility of relationality and community with those not willing or able to be or become part of "one Market under God," at the refusal to engage in forging alliances and conversations that prevent hate, resentment, and alienation. Grief and horror at the downfall of so many, at the terrible impact on a complex and complicated city that I have come to love. What to do with this mass of confusion, the conflicted emotions that have assailed us since 9/11?

Catherine Keller's "guide to the end of the world" may offer us some help here. In her reading of John of Patmos' text, Keller describes the ambivalent, explosive mix of hopeful prophecy and valid protestations against exploitation and domination with vindictive and often misogynist calls for revenge and purist identifications of the innocent and the guilty. Keller finds that she can neither simply dismiss nor ever feel smugly at home with John's Apocalypse, a text that has formed much of the Western consciousness, but must rather relate through a "counter-apocalypse" that holds in tension an admiration for the text's "intensity, its drive for justice, its courage in the face of impossible odds" and a rejection of its vengeful, bloodthirsty, and misogynist rhetoric.[20]

I propose to translate this counter-apocalyptic, ambivalent hermeneutic energy into what I call a counter-economic approach to Divine Economy, a hermeneutic that recognizes the Western Christian tradition's problematic stance on issues of economy as the egalitarian impetus of the prophets and Jesus stands in tension with the oppression of women, slaves, and others embedded in many biblical texts. And yet, as such a counter-economic subjectivity attempts to locate itself in the Divine Economy, it finds one possible figural incarnation in an unlikely and contested ancient ascetic, the "Holy Fool" Symeon. Symeon's behavior, while considered obscene and anything but holy by most of his contemporaries, is portrayed by Leontius as more saintly than that of any other previous saint.[21] While Symeon may appear to run with prostitutes, defecate in places of commerce such as the marketplace, and run naked into a women's bath, these "miracles" are—to the knowing clerical eye—witness to Symeon's incredible restraint and control of his body and desires.[22] While he seems to the public a lecher and glutton, his true strength and restraint emerge even more starkly as he seeks out these temptations, but stays miraculously untainted. Whether Leontius' somewhat strained sanitizing of a publicly defecating saint convinces us entirely or not, Symeon's public performance is certainly instructive. His concealed sanctity allows him to unveil the absurdities of urban economic life. He functions as a critic of his environment, mimicking and thereby exposing the excesses of the city. Thus, "Symeon's profaning actions in the marketplace comment on society's hypocrisy, iniquity, and economic injustice."[23] Leontius' Symeon is a Holy Fool who mimics Jesus—his model for holy foolishness—like a true disciple. While Krueger asks, "Is it possible that early Christians had a sense of humor? And to what use did they put this humor?"[24] we might ask ourselves what the counter-economic reconstruction of the figure of a Holy Fool might contribute to a contemporary trickster-like counter-economic theology.

Perhaps, today, Holy Fools might be discerned in similar "saints" who defy our expectations, such as the satirist Michael Moore, who "was religious" and attended "the seminary in high school to become a Catholic priest," yet ended up exposing the "economic terrorism" of corporate downsizing and its disastrous consequences on people and land.[25] A muckraker in the tradition of H. L. Mencken, he has debunked

> all this news about the "great economic miracle" [as the] best propaganda that's been fed to the American people since Ronald Reagan declared ketchup a vegetable.

A trickster and "holy fool," Moore pokes fun at the dead-serious causes of public ignorance and apathy when it comes to economics and politics:

> How stupid do they think we are? Really stupid, I guess. I wrote this book basically to show that I'm not *that* stupid.[26]

Relentlessly, Moore castigates by mixing hyperbole with shocking facts, inventing hoaxes to demonstrate the real poverty hidden from the public by a toothless media, identifying "big welfare mamas" and "corporate crooks" among the CEO's of the Fortune 500 in the form of fake trading cards.[27]

We might encounter another wordly saint in the design trickster Kalle Lasn, whose magazine *Adbusters* includes a graphic designer's "vow of chastity," describing the convictions of those that resist consumer culture by "jamming" it: "From now on I'll put truth and beauty in all my designs. If I have to lie, I'll lie for myself. No more grids, gimmicks, mindfucks, clients-haha."[28] Lasn's manifesto on "culture jamming" emerges from a "loose global network of media activists" who see themselves as the "advance shock troops of the most significant social movement of the next twenty years."[29] These culture jammers regularly interfere with the slick trades of "daily business…by getting consumer culture to bite its own tail."[30] Part of Lasn's thesis is that human consumers have been separated from their natural environment. He writes: "Abandon nature and you abandon your sense of the divine. More than that, you lose track of who you are."[31] This holy foolery, vowing public relations chastity, embodies another, if unusual, form of neo-asceticism that inhabits counter-economic space as it subverts, while it employs, the form and function of advertising media.

The alternate economic subjectivity of the Holy Fool attempts to subvert the powerful habits of hysterical consumption in late Western capitalism in the hope for counter-economic incarnations of redemptive exchanges that will have to be embodied globally, locally, personally, and communally. In the awareness of a location within and potential complicity with exploitative exchanges, the Holy Fool's counter-economic strategies strive to avoid purist denunciations and glorifications of business as usual, but rather engage in plotting un-usual business, mindful of our embodied relations to persons and to planet. Un-usual business practices question the primacy of consumption at any cost and reject the exploitation of grief and solidarity that result from an unreflected continuation of the highly problematic practices of "business as usual." Business as un-usual no longer buys into tired claims as to the redemptive powers of a spread of capitalism across the world to bring the world all-consuming peace. Rather, counter-economic Holy Fools must ask how we can develop creative facets of a Divine Economy at the "edge of chaos"[32] into which we have been thrown, and out of which new strategies of just trading and of un-usually co-redemptive business can emerge.

5

Civil War, Civil Rights, World Trade Center

Cheryl A. Kirk-Duggan

Guerilla warfare, terrorism, violence, and global economics integrally forged the growth of the United States before and after the signing of the Declaration of Independence and the ratification of the United States Constitution. War, usually a state of open and declared armed antagonistic conflict between states or nations, is a condition of hostility, conflict, or aggression, a struggle or competition between opposing forces or for a particular end. Guerilla warfare is an engagement in irregular warfare by independent units carrying out harassment and sabotage. Terrorism is the systematic use of terror, that is, of intense fear and violence, to effect coercion. Violence involves injurious physical, emotional, mental, spiritual, or psychological action. Violence, the culprit that manipulated these North American lands, seizing them from native peoples, has affected every immigrant and descendant of immigrants, all of us, who have made these shores our home—by desire or by force. War, terrorism, and violence are central to the infrastructure and aegis of the sociocultural and historical ethos of the United States. Our arrogance and vanity caused us to be surprised at the attacks on the World Trade Center twin towers and the Pentagon. One need hardly be surprised about terrorism meted out to us, when historically we have meted out terrorism on the soils of other shores. That conquering mentality is part of the United States' specific 100-year-old Manifest Destiny stratagem that has pushed us to subjugate other territories on Earth and in space. There is no way to justify what happened in New York City and Washington, D.C., on September 11, 2001, but one cannot help but hear the echoes of two adages: (1) What goes around comes around; (2) Malcolm X's, "The chickens have come home to roost." What happened to the United States that startling 9/11 day is daily fare for a large portion of the world's population.

Most children in the world live at the intersection of terrorism and violence, on the avenues of pain, in the province of war. Being orphaned or having to carry tiny coffins, when coffins are available, to their final repose is commonplace. This essay explores the theological, ethical, and global economic forces that have allowed the perpetration of terrorism and war in the United States of America, toward framing a prolegomenon for an appropriate response in the twenty-first century. After providing an overview of my methodology and terms, I situate the sociohistorical heinous acts of war and terrorism through the settings of the Civil War, the civil rights movement, and the World Trade Center attacks. I engage the voices of Hannah Arendt and Martin Luther King, Jr., to ascertain a philosophical and theological response to war and terrorism from twentieth-century voices, and I use an economic analysis to examine the connections of war to oil. I conclude by describing options for combating domestic and global terrorism that reject revenge and vengeance as improper and unworthy motives and suggest the alternative of justice as an option for a response to terrorism.

Revealing Tyranny: Seeing through a Womanist Lens

The term *womanist* derives from the use of the term "*womanish*" in African American communities, and refers to a black feminist who takes seriously the experience and oppression due to class, gender, race, age, sexual orientation, and able-bodiedness. Alice Walker's definition of womanist is complex and copious as a foundational rubric for doing analytical, critical research and listening. In addition to the components of survival, of loving, of taking charge, the term womanist also conveys a vitality of life, a quest for knowledge, and the paradox of youthful wisdom. Womanist sensibilities foster the freedom of being able to love all people, sexually and nonsexually, and sanction the manifestation of woman's culture and life. To be womanist invites holistic health and loving the spectrum of colors of blackness. Womanist theory is aesthetic, physical, spiritual, emotional, and creative.[1] Womanist evokes a plethora of variegated realities, yielding passion, love, hope, and change. Womanist theory, midst a faith-based curiosity, seeks to discover, analyze, and honor the lives and gifts of the forgotten and dismissed.

Womanist theorists facilitate us in focusing the eyes of women of African descent on and toward the transformation of themselves, of other persons of African descent, and of society, of the complex, violent, pathological institutions and communities that are sick and hurt: empowerment rather than negation and destruction. Cloaked by oppression, my Christian womanist stance involves: theology (dialogue, identity, sacrality, spirituality, and power); Bible and narratives (authority, characters, rituals, language, and history); ethics (value, behavior, visibility, integrity, and praxis); and context (autobiography, culture, aesthetics, ecology, and community). This interdisciplinary, relational system embodies a God who cares and a God who abhors the dismissal of a person made in *Imago Dei*–the Divine Image. Womanist theory provides the rubric for interrogating the context, content, contradictions, and catalysts at work in societal destruction of the self and of the other. The context for war and terrorism today is that of many states on a global stage.

Sociohistorical Excursions into Violence, War, Protest, and Terrorism

Among the properties of the modern state is that of extraordinary power, a property suggested by Hobbes, where he viewed the state as the "great Leviathan," the most powerful entity that he could imagine. What happened during the time of increasing commercial capitalism to make this Leviathan so powerful? Some scholars suggest that the Leviathan became gargantuan via the gradual emergence of a "military-capitalist" complex. A number of interrelated institutions permitted the accumulation of capital by commercial capitalists in civil society to increase the accumulation of violent force in government and vice versa. The Leviathan developed and became so powerful because the military-capitalist complex made the accumulation of profits and militaries mutually reinforcing. This process accelerated the accumulation of capital and of violent force. Such a concentration and intensifying of additional amounts of these forces within the state made it a powerful, commanding behemoth, a Leviathan beyond even Hobbes's imagination. During the seventeenth century, England successfully created such a military-capitalist complex, one better than its French, Portuguese, Dutch, or Spanish competitors. By 1763, England had enough power to exercise global domination. England's emancipated, gauche stepchild, the United States, by the twenty-first century was doing the same.[2] Osama bin Laden decided to put a chink in the armor of Western capitalist consumerism–the infidel-Leviathan was a threat to his image of a pure Islam. Like other rebels, clansmen, and hatemongers before him, bin Laden used the pretext of faith to justify evil.

That more than 200 million people died during the twentieth century as a direct result of war and war-related sanctions signals the universal capacity for human-engineered evil. Within the continuum of evil, one can go from minor or trivial infractions (someone cuts off another in traffic) to greater evils of prejudicial acts, to massive evils of serial killers and gang-rape-murders. All human beings have the capacity to commit evil. In the wake of the twentieth century's unutterable atrocities, including Stalin's purges and gulags that killed 20 million, Hitler's massacre of 6 million Jews, Orthodox and Christian, and the 1.7 million lives decimated in the killing fields of Pol Pot's Cambodia, if everyone has the capability for evil, why do only a particular group of people actually commit evil?[3] From a psychiatric perspective, evil probably involves intent to terrorize, to inflict emotional trauma, to pursue the helpless, and/or to protract suffering, and gain fulfillment from the practice of evil. Exercising true evil seems to require substituting emptiness in lieu of compassion, for dehumanizing and grossly objectifying others. Extreme self-centeredness or narcissism seems to express a lack of empathy and compassion, which disintegrates into unmitigated evil. Such extreme self-centeredness gives ordinary people implicit, and often explicit, permission to commit heinous, evil deeds, to the point of playing God, deciding who shall die toward the completion of one's narcissistic goals. Extreme self-hatred also allows that person to project inward revulsion onto others, killing or torturing others as a result. Some sociopaths, sadists, and heartless killers manifest no response to stress; the killers of others enact cruelty based on cognition; that is, the killers of others have been taught an ideology wherein particular people become subject to their hate because of a particular political, ethnic, or religious identity. Those who have participated in mob evils of ethnic cleansings and genocidal carnage and mayhem are "righteous conformists" who believe in the justice of their cause and who accept peer pressure as a helmsman for their moral identity. Often it is the ordinary, patriotic, religious, good citizen and devoted family member who has the capacity to demonize and dehumanize others; in the words of Hannah Arendt, this is what makes the banality of evil so horrific.[4] Whether acts of evil stem from abusive childhoods, skewed ideologies, or the desire for personal aggrandizement, offering psychological and/or cultural apologetics and rationalizations to justify the motives of evildoers is dangerous. Sometimes it seems that these apologetics and rationalizations acquiesce in the inevitability of an evil act. "Explanation becomes exculpation, and volition gets eclipsed. To understand all should not be to forgive all."[5] To begin to understand what is at stake in the continuum of evil means examining ordinary ways in which human beings perpetrate evil on one another, through the vales and volcanoes of violence.

Violence–injurious physical, emotional, mental, spiritual, or psychological action or treatment–stains the American flag, our halls of justice, our lands, our places of worship, our entire sociocultural and historical ethos. The United States was founded in violence and has used violence to become the alleged "greatest, wealthiest, most powerful country" in the world. This conquering, subjugating mentality, incarnated as Manifest Destiny, has caused tremendous oppression and is so commonplace that few recognize it as violence: such activity is deemed the American way. As opposed to the unofficial credo of the American civil religion of "Mom, the flag, and apple pie," one of the prevailing metanarratives of these United States, founded on the brokerage of human lives, land, and power, is the actual civil faith statement of the United States, that of manifest destiny, violence, and the counterfeit of freedom for those deemed other. Such warped political identity and manipulation of natural and human resources have forged the path toward terrorism and war.

War is the practice of organized violence executed by institutions within states. International or global war pertains to war between the military institutions of the governments of different states. Wars within states are internal wars: civil wars occur when a government's military institutions fight against different institutions within that same state's civil society. Civil society war occurs when different entities in a civil society fight each other without government intervention.[6] A nation's economic life relates to war in three basic ways. First, war develops out of an economic milieu of trade and financial preferences, imperialism, and global rivalries. Second, to wage war requires economic resources, whether one is situated as offensive or defensive. Third, the different sides or factions that are engaged in fighting the war have economic aspirations. When a nation wages war, a "total" war, then its economic system is framed according to the military need. Depending on the type of government, the economics can fall under dictatorial rule, or the nation can engage market and pricing systems to secure the needs of the war–for example, wage and price controls by all participants during World War II. The failings of a global economic equilibrium, the desire to acquire alleged additional living space (Hitler's *Lebensraum*) for one's nation under the hidden guise of conquering lesser powers, a desire to create a new defense-based economy, and a commitment to and preparation for war by a nation intimately tie economics to war. Such a totalitarian approach to war as demonstrated by Germany during World War II also leads to economic aggression, which caused great socioeconomic instability throughout Europe. Such a shift also affects foreign trade and foreign exchange policies, further exacerbating the instability of global economics.[7]

Economic issues related to war include the finances framing the war, the economic restructuring that needs to occur to equip a nation for war, and the economic restructuring needed within an industrial system at the end of a particular conflict. Thus, many factors converge to serve as a catalyst for war, including the particular psychological matrix, the commercial rivalries, imperial exploitation, concessions, and the belief by some that war is a sound, profitable business venture. During times of war, the economic and industrial system supports the war effort, being subservient to military needs (the Vietnam War being the exception that proves the rule). This protocol emerges–both for those countries where everything serves military ends and for those countries who do not so focus on the military, but emphasize meeting the needs of the people rather than the appetite of the military while at peace. After a war is completed, the question is not simply how the country gets back to business as normal, but how to view the related vast complexity of a country after the war, which will involve many problems of restructuring toward permanence.[8] In examining economics and war as related to the United States, one can readily see how war participation increased the economy in certain areas: more planes, uniforms, and military armaments, along with the need for more sophisticated technology, has boosted various financial coffers more than once. A recent extension, in which heads of government rationalize the calling up of troops, more equipment, and the need to declare war, is the newly articulated urgency to combat terrorism.

Defining terrorism is a complex issue. Not only are the lines between terrorism and organized crime blurred, but the time frame in which one explores terrorism affects how one constructs the definition. Heightened nationalism, extremists who adapt religious ideology for their purposes, the connection between history and contemporary conflict, access to information, and terrorist tactics employed by states shape how one views terrorism. Many scholars have not come to a universal sense of the meaning of this term. Terrorism, as a vehicle of mass destruction, involves chemical, nuclear, and biological warfare. Terrorism is an act of violence (e.g., bombing), causing intense fear and anxiety, committed by groups to intimidate a population or government into granting their demands for recognition, whether through insurrection or revolution.[9]

From a social science perspective, terrorism is an anxiety-inspiring technique of repeated violent action used by a semi-clandestine individual, group, or state for political, idiosyncratic, or criminal reasons. Terrorism is distinct from assassination in so far as the direct targets of violence are not the main targets. The immediate victims of violence are usually chosen arbitrarily (targets of opportunity) or selectively (symbolic or representative targets) from a target population. The violence is meant to send messages. Threat- and violence-based communication processes between a terrorist organization, the at-risk victims, and main targets are used to control the main target, the audience(s), creating a target of terror, a target of demands, or a target of attention. The strategy depends on whether the agenda is that of coercion, intimidation, or propaganda. The organizational methods of terrorists, as well as their choices regarding weapons and the type of conflict, are shaped by the communities of the terrorists and their victims, especially by their ease of mobility, technology, virtuality, and attitudes toward oppression.[10]

Terrorism ensues when people shift from civil disobedience and nonviolent protest into violence. General civil disobedience does not make one an outlaw. Building pipe bombs, robbing, or kidnapping does. Some people become fugitives as their priorities change. During the 1960s civil rights protests, nonviolence mattered, and the major focus was the cause; with terrorism, life revolves around survival and staying out of prison. If a group chooses to be terrorists, its members usually target mostly civilian, noncombatant, symbolic targets: airliners, cruise ships, embassies, the World Trade Center, the U.S. Capitol, and the Pentagon. Their goal is to function outside the law and to craft indirect, attention-getting ways to influence specific audiences.[11] One of the tools of violence, war, and terrorism is scapegoating. In life and literature, scapegoating has helped resolve the angst of tragedies through ritual sacrifices, that is, by the identification and killing of a victim. The death of the victim provides a catharsis and produces a type of heightened social collegiality where the crowd or perpetrators begin to understand the experience religiously. For French literary critic and cultural anthropologist René Girard, the scapegoat is part of a larger system he names mimesis, particularly mimetic rivalry, which he locates in his "Violence and the Sacred" theory.[12] Mimesis, to imitate, is pivotal for our epistemology, the way we know and learn. Mimetic desire is that experience where two or more people desire the same thing, same person, same place, or status. This desire leads to rivalry: several parties want the same object. For Girard, mimetic desire, and its ensuing ritualized conflict, is the process of resolving and containing the resulting violence. The scapegoat becomes the culprit, which allows the saturation of lust and thirst for calm, moving the given group of persons from a violent cataclysm into peaceful unification. This substitution allows for the invoking of a sacred structure, rooted in a sacrificial altar, the locus of creating and recreating communal, social solidarity. The success of the scapegoating process often hinges on the invisibility of the victim. As we face the victim, our rage often blinds us to our own complicity. In life and film, a cautionary tale emerges that warns us of making victims of perpetrators and the accompanying false innocence within ourselves. At issue is how to resolve the conflict.[13]

For Girard, extensive or collective persecutions of scapegoats are an ordinary kind of violence that can be "legalized," particularly when motivated or supported by public opinion. Individuals and groups need these objects of persecution because they need to define themselves comparatively over against another, identifying a susceptible group as "other" or "outside." Arab Americans became scapegoats for many throughout the United States after September 11. They were "other" because they were quite visible and often vulnerable. Heightened violence happens when one cannot name someone other. Girard refers to these conflictual rivals as monstrous doubles, which then shift the social order. Anthropologically, Girard argues that human beings imitate the desire of another, because when they converge around the same object, they use one another as models, and begin to parallel one another. Human beings learn through mimesis, an imitation that can produce pathological greed. Someone who looks, acts, or thinks differently, and is vulnerable, often ends up being the focus of a group's consolidated effort to define themselves and those deemed other by turning their own pursuit of power against those who cannot react. September 11 created a milieu of us "patriots" against them "foreign aliens." Thus, a group (the really "real" Americans) established itself by psychologically or physically eliminating or ousting the ones who are different (Arab Americans, including darker-skinned non-Arabs who wore turbans and were Hindu). Lynching (or stoning to death in the ancient world) and acts of terrorism are classic acts of collective violence,[14] of scapegoating–familiar fare during World Wars I and II.

The fire raids on Dresden, Coventry, and Tokyo, where the bombings were directly intended to kill and thus scapegoat "innocent" civilians, echo the fighting at Guernica, immortalized in Picasso's painting of the same name, when civilians were first targeted. The same occurred at Hiroshima and Nagasaki: both of these later targets had been untouched previously so that the United States could get good "data" on what atomic weapons would do to civilians and their structures. The whole purpose of the so-called "neutron" or "clean" bomb is to kill civilians by radiation and leave the structures standing: the reverse of the World Trade Center attacks. Osama bin Laden's aim in the World Trade Center, the Pentagon, and the U.S. Capitol attacks was not to kill civilians: his aim was to destroy the symbols of America, that is, of the United States. The civilian casualties were only "collateral damage," as the U.S. has used the term in Vietnam, Desert Storm, and now the present Afghan war. Just as the United States is no stranger to participating in wars and skirmishes across the seas, it is no stranger to scapegoating others nor to domestic acts of war and terrorism, particularly during the Civil War, the 1960s civil rights movement, and in the recent terrorism at the World Trade Center. Interestingly, the United States' reciprocal response was that of "state governmental terrorist acts" against the Taliban.

Mapping the Particular Acts of War and Terrorism

I received a phone call from my sister, Dedurie, who lives in Texas, before dawn on September 11, 2001. She told me to turn on the television, that an airplane had just hit the World Trade Center. I was incredulous when I turned on the television to watch a tape of the first plane hitting the WTC, only to see the second plane hit the other twin tower. Almost half an hour later, both towers imploded and collapsed. So much has been written and uttered over the tragic events of that "9/11," (the irony not lost in "911" being the universal telephonic SOS in the United States), that I need not repeat all the details here. What is significant is that this was not the first time that lives were lost in terrorist attacks and war on these shores. The violence and terrorism of the Civil War and the 1960s civil rights movement also brought terror and death. The Civil War battle at Antietam cost about 12,500 Union lives and about 10,500 Confederate casualties. With fighting so fierce and the casualties so high, Antietam was the bloodiest one-day battle of the Civil War. The bombing of the Murrah building in Oklahoma took more than 200 lives. Lynchings of men, women, and children of African descent, with suspect cases as late as 1999, have taken the lives of thousands. Lynching was a major public "entertainment" long before the emergence of professional sports. In the 1890s, 2,000 people rode a train from Atlanta to see a lynching.

As horrific as the World Trade Center attacks were—estimates are that as many as 3,000 plus lives were lost—more than 25,000 persons were able to escape from the massive funerary caldron of stone and steel before the two towers collapsed. Osama bin Laden wanted to make a symbolic point, and he was successful. United States foreign policy has been a case of playing both ends against the middle. We swap sides and oftentimes do not understand the long-term consequences. The U.S. made a strategic error in leaving Afghanistan to hold the bag with no help to provide the necessary infrastructure to regain its well-being after the Taliban fought for the U.S. toward the most successful goal of bankrupting Russia. The U.S. has an active military base in Saudi Arabia near two of the most holy sites of Islam, Medina and Mecca. These facts in no way condone bin Laden's terrorist tactics, nor is this about discounting the thousands of lives lost. I simply want to hold up a mirror to U.S. policy and trouble the waters a bit so that we let go of our insular, provincial, parochial mind-set when it comes to who has the power. Our arrogance and denial had convinced us that though we might help create war and terrorism on the shores of others, others would not wreak such devastation on us. In this instance, "you reap what you sow" implies that the rhetoric and actions of U.S. foreign policy have come back and indicted us. The voices of Hannah Arendt and Martin Luther King, Jr., provide some insight for these deliberations.

Revolution, Rhetoric, Resistance: Musings of Arendt and King

Hannah Arendt (1906–1975)–a political theorist, cultivated intellectual, and author–was born in Germany, of Russian-Jewish heritage with an entrepreneurial spirit. Arendt, knew grief and terror: as a child, her father's death, and warfare between Russia and Germany. Arendt completed her doctorate, became a political activist, and helped to publicize the plight of the victims of Nazism. A product of Weimar culture, her Jewishness was central to her experience. She also researched anti-Semitic propaganda, for which she was arrested by the Gestapo. But when she won the sympathy of a Berlin jailer, she was released and escaped to Paris, where she remained for the rest of the decade. Arendt helped rescue Jewish children from the Third Reich and brought them to Palestine. Arendt was sent to the British detention camp of Gurs, from which she escaped. She soon joined her husband, and in May 1941, both went to America. While living in New York during the rest of World War II, Arendt envisioned the book that became *The Origins of Totalitarianism,* published in 1951, the year she gained United States citizenship.

The Origins of Totalitarianism traces the steps of the idiosyncratic twentieth-century tyrannies of Hitler and Stalin, and chronicles the depths of how fatally wounded Western civilization and the human condition had become. Arendt shows the embedded nature of late nineteenth-century racism in Central and Western European societies, and how imperialism experimented with the potential of unspeakable cruelty and mass murder. She also unmasks the operations and activities of "radical evil," where heinous discontinuity within European history surfaces in the gross number of death camp prisoners. Totalitarianism lays out what had previously only been imagined in the medieval depictions of hell. Arendt argues that the Third Reich actually conducted two wars, one against the Allies and one against the Jews. In her coverage of the 1960 trial of Eichmann, the lieutenant colonel responsible for creating the bureaucracy that efficiently transported Jews to the concentration death camps, she portrayed Eichmann as "the banality of evil" instead of as a lunatic, a demonic anti-Semitic, or the embodiment of "radical evil." She further argued that such sociopolitical distinctiveness could not be limited to the Third Reich. Arendt also critiqued the Jewish councils for trying to negotiate with Nazis like Eichmann. Since Eichmann had not wanted to live on the same planet with the Jews, then Jews and the Jewish state did not need to share the planet with him–which was her own justification for endorsing the death penalty for Eichmann. For Arendt, Eichmann ultimately did evil because he had not critically analyzed what he was doing. That is, he did heinous acts because he was thoughtless, not because he was horribly racist or sadistic.[15] Like Martin Luther King, Jr., Arendt also criticized military activity in Vietnam and the abusive nature of an imperialistic Kennedy-Johnson-Nixon presidency. Like King, Arendt also addressed matters of violence, war, and terrorism.

Arendt says we need and justify violence. We do not rebel against this need out of a quest for liberation or freedom, nor out of a kind of pious resignation. Rather, we worship this need faithfully, to force liberation on people, as the hallmark of successful revolutions in the twentieth century. There are more civil liberties and a better maintenance of freedom in countries where no revolution has occurred. At the same time, Arendt notes that the absolute rule of violence requires that everybody and everything must become silent, which creates a kind of ethos of totalitarianism as played out in the concentration camps. Such silent absolutism is not the norm in revolutions.[16]

Arendt posits that revolutions and wars are two key political issues in our world. The only remaining cause for such activity is the struggle of freedom versus tyranny. Interestingly, the word *freedom* itself, she argues, has disappeared from the vocabulary of revolution. Rarely is war concerned with freedom. In searching for the justification of war, Arendt notes that the politics of power in war dictates that there be legitimate reasons for war. The notion of dealing with aggression as criminal intent, where one can only justify war to either prevent or deflect war, gained theoretical import only after World War I, with the noticeable absence of the question of freedom. Freedom enters the discussion after the world had achieved a certain level of technical advance; that is, the possibility for total annihilation of the planet. What one can see in the history of warfare is that (1) armies can no longer protect civilian populations; and (2) politically, war has become a matter of life and death, showing that most if not all governments have existed on borrowed time. In addition, the goal of warfare has evolved to the point where one seeks to develop such weapons that ultimately make war impossible. (Note the end of the Cold War and the ongoing negotiations between the United States and Russia and the reduction in nuclear warheads stockpiled.) Arendt also links her conversation about revolution with terrorism.

Arendt sees a two-sided compulsion of ideology and terror, coercing humanity internally and externally. Such a tension explains the way in which some countries with a meek attitude are doomed. Those who study revolution know the way the revolution must unfold.[17] Terror and terrorism, as institutional devices, came on the scene during the Russian revolution. Arendt exposes the absurdity, banality, and commonality of evil and its constituents of violence, war, and terrorism. She also helps us to see the kinds of tensions and dialectics that ensue in the great dramas and tensions of politics and the revolution. She shifts the role, even the centrality of freedom for most revolutions and wants us to be brutally honest when engaging in assessment of our own complicity in violence and the demise of our world and ourselves. Certainly Arendt reminds us of the connection between ideology and terrorism, part of the play enacted on September 11. Both Arendt and King, American citizens—one naturalized, one native born—as philosophers who moved to a different drummer can also provide insight for our reflections on contemporary war and terrorism.

Martin Luther King, Jr. (1929–1968)–preacher, philosopher, civil rights activist, ethicist, charismatic political leader, theologian, and orator–was born in the bowels of white supremacy, an African American with Irish and Native American lineage, rooted in the Black Baptist church. The revolutionary prospects of the gospel and the liberation and deliverance motifs of the Hebrew Bible shaped King's use of black cultural artifacts such as the spirituals, black Southern mores, morality, and faith. For King, his call to ministry was critical to healing the United States. He championed a priestly, covenantal experience of freedom. In the last years of his ministry, he explored the necessity of inclusiveness and how exclusion leads to destruction of the body politic. He spoke less of redemptive suffering and sacrifice during his last years of ministry, and became filled with anger, tempered by his practice of nonviolent resistance. King exercised prophetic rage, became militant, and gave authority only to God. He continued to espouse the American dream of justice, liberty, and the common good for all in his own writing, teaching, preaching, and faith journey. Consequently, he changed his strategy in 1968 for two reasons.[18]

King changed his goals, strategy, and philosophy because blacks were tired of being harassed, terrorized, beaten, and jailed for trying to exercise their constitutional rights. Second, the civil rights victories did not trickle down to the black masses, to the poor, to the underclass. His ministry of nonviolent direct action moved from the Southern pulpits to the northern pool room. King moved to Chicago, drank beer, and played pool with hustlers. He adapted to the sociocultural context and milieu of his constituency. When his children became hostile and distorted by the ghetto malaise of despair and hopelessness, he sent them to live with their grandparents in the South. The malaise his children experienced was thick as the fog wafting off Lake Michigan. Having read Franz Fanon, a black psychiatrist, and from his experience with black power advocates, King knew that when hope dwindles, hate usually turns most harshly on those who first fostered hope. Up against the combined forces of exploitative merchants, corrupt politicians, amoral gangsters, and black politicians strongly immersed in the white power structure, King returned to Atlanta, cognizant that his strategy had not addressed the socioeconomic problems. He now shifted to address race and class issues.[19]

King's commitment to a critique of race and class grew out of his ethics and theology that embraced populism, civil religion, religious fundamentalism, and the creed of self-improvement. King did not separate who he was as a preacher from who he was as an activist; he incorporated his civil religion, his Christian faith, and his political activism. From his nonviolent personal, social, and theological ethics, King worked for human rights and economic justice in accordance with his teleological sense of responsibility. The limits of his moralistic Christian nonviolent ethic transpired when his constituency was non-Christian, as it lacked particular psychological needs of the oppressed, and overlooked matters of gender justice. Even so, King saw nonviolence as the absolute modus operandi and rejected violence as an ethic or a tool for social change. When his nonviolence became more confrontative, it remained tempered by his middle-class status and his evangelical, liberalistic view of the Social Gospel. King enhanced his ethic by using his theology of a personal God, amid a faith of justice, power, and love that supported his belief in nonviolence, and aimed toward preserving human life and redeeming human personality. Nevertheless, violence played a part in King's nonviolent strategy as his key triumphs occurred when protesters experienced violent reactions, which generated public support. Ironically, the strategy often failed when the threat of violence was not apparent. Thus, in studying an ethic's *telos,* means and ends, one must build in enough flexibility and know that many gray areas exist when moving to universalize a particular ethical strategy.[20] King's focus was not his flexibility, but his faith.

The 1960s civil rights movement grassroots protesters came from a contextualized Christian faith to participate in the movement. These freedom fighters called King to lead them, and he connected his Christian idea of love, from the Sermon on the Mount, to Gandhi's nonviolence teachings and the promises of the Declaration of Independence for freedom and equality, to identify with other developing countries of color in overcoming white supremacy and racism. King became aware of the interconnectedness of global liberation struggles when he attended the ceremonies marking Ghana's becoming an independent nation state, ritualizing a universal quest for morality and justice. Part of this quest included the class issue of economic injustice, the poverty meted out because of exclusionary practices against all people of color. When King did confront poverty in the United States and the war in Vietnam, his prophetic journey moved from the center, the locus of power, to the periphery. He obsessed about a huge movement triumph and about his own death, given the fifty FBI-investigated assassination plots and the hate mail he received daily. King argued that the United States' presence in Vietnam was an indictment of war crimes. He posited that reenvisioning a success ethic meant a shift in focus to social and community success and service to others, against poverty, war, terrorism, racism, and exploitation.[21] One year from the day Martin Luther King, Jr., proclaimed at the Riverside Church, New York, that if violence was wrong in the United States, it was wrong in Vietnam, he was assassinated. This drum major for justice took a hit for preaching a consistent truth.

King could preach this truth because of his own vision of a beloved community. Relying on Howard Thurman's interrelatedness of love, forgiveness, and reconciliation, King created this metaphor where black people are redemptive participants in a vision of black messianic hope. He felt blacks had the unique historical, spiritual place in Western civilization to help transform the world because of their power based on love, goodwill, understanding, and nonviolence. King's vision of messianic hope pertained to the black commitment to Christianity, the biblical notion of a messianic people and nation. Where other black scholars have posited this notion of messianic hope, King was the only one to yoke love and violence closely to this ideal. He understood the shortcomings of black folk and the black church, but he believed blacks were uniquely suited, morally and spiritually, to help lead a movement to effect a new humanity.[22] What did King teach us that relates to September 11 and the United States' "War on Terrorism"?

King declared that amid the "terrible midnight of war" people ask for "the bread of peace," but the church usually has disappointed them. The church is usually silent, or goes along with the party line, often becoming irrelevant in its witness to the world amid times of terrorism and war. President Bush, America's secular high priest, droned the gospel according to patriotic retaliation from the hallowed, consecrated pulpit of the Cathedral of St. Peter and St. Paul. By contrast,King noted that the church ought to be an arbiter of justice, not in collusion with injustice or the dominant party line: the church is to call for peace in the throes of "a world gone mad with arms buildups, chauvinistic passions, and imperialistic exploitation."[23] King noted the tendency of the church to be either deadly silent or a fervent endorser of war, sanctioning destruction and orchestrated death as moral and noble. King noted the anemic response of the church when it often buys into the status quo and middle-class trappings. So too historic black churches also fail to answer the call for justice and balance because they are either enraptured with emotionalism or ensnared by classism and bogus dignity.

King placed faith and justice over vengeance and revenge, particularly in his early ministry. He argued for nonviolence and made it clear that no violence was acceptable. Interestingly, the more he protested and fought, the more militant he became. Toward the close of his life he grew closer to Malcolm X, and Malcolm X similarly grew close to King in thought. One cannot help but recall Malcolm X's powerful rhetoric: How does one accomplish change? "By any means necessary." What happens when one plays both ends against the middle? "The chickens come home to roost." King would have wanted us to have empathy with the great loss of lives connected to the September 11 tragedy, and he would have wanted to find something redemptive in the suffering, the problematic of such redemption notwithstanding. He would have rallied for negotiation instead of retaliation. As winner of the Nobel Peace Prize, he would have wanted to find other means before going to bomb Afghanistan in search of Osama bin Laden. As of this writing, December 2, 2001, Afghanistan is in even greater rubble; more lives have been lost; the Taliban has been ousted, to be replaced by the Northern Alliance, who have been gracious to Afghanistan Taliban rebels, but who have also mercilessly slaughtered foreign émigré Taliban zealots. We do not yet know what will come of this new regime, or even if there will be a regime, or a collective of warlords such as was present in the pre-Taliban rule of Afghanistan. Western paradigms that think of nation-states based on geographic or ethnic boundaries are problematic when thinking of groups that relate not in terms of geography, but in terms of racial-ethnic and religious affiliations, which traverse boundaries. Can violence that is regulated, governmental, technologically superior, nevertheless be a violence that can exact peace? Some claim it did in Japan. Can it exact peace in Afghanistan?

It Ain't Necessarily So: War and Terrorism Revisited

Like most wars, this "war on terrorism" being waged by the United States, like Operation Desert Storm, concerns oil. No surprises here really, if we learned one of the key lessons of Watergate: *follow the money.* Kazakhstan sits on about 50 billion barrels of oil; Saudi Arabia has about 30 billion barrels of oil left. Kazakhstan's economy collapsed after they declared independence in 1991 from the former Soviet Union. The gross poverty of Kazakhstan has led to the deaths of most elderly citizens, marked aging, and destitution. President Nursultan Nazarbayev has tried for almost a decade to get the landlocked oil to Western buyers. The problems are many, the options few. Kazakhstan's close alliance with the United States precludes the use of the shortest route through Iran. Sending the oil across Russia would probably result in the latter's deflecting the oil and using it without paying for it. To send a pipeline across China would be too costly given the needed pipeline length. The most logical option would be to extend Turkmenistan's current system to the Kazak field on the Caspian Sea, southeast of Pakistan, on the Arabian Sea, to run via Afghanistan. In 1994, Pakistan and the United States decided to stop Afghanistan's civil war by putting in a government that could also protect the Unocal pipeline project. The United States' State Department and Pakistan's Inter-Services Intelligence agency decided to back the then up-and-coming, ruthless Taliban. The two agencies provided arms and money to the Taliban as they waged war against the Tajik Northern Alliance. As late as 1999, United States taxpayers paid the complete salaries of every Taliban governmental official. The motive was oil, the hope to get enough oil to drop the price of gasoline. The Taliban, with its unholy coalition with Osama bin Laden and his al Qaeda terrorists, seemed not to be logical partners with the desired oil deal. While the 1998 cruise missile attack on Afghanistan momentarily squelched Taliban terrorist activity, on September 11, 2001, Saudi terrorist suicide bombers, trained in Afghanistan, not only hijacked four domestic passenger planes, but used these jetliners as live bombs to destroy American symbols, killing thousands of people as "collateral damage." This tragedy gave the Bush White House the perfect reason to do what it had wanted to do for a while: invade Afghanistan and/or place a new puppet government in Kabul. At the end of the day, the real issue is not the thousands dead or the horribly oppressed women of Afghanistan, but economics: "This ersatz war by a phony president is solely about getting the Unocal deal done without interference from annoying local middlemen."[24] Interestingly, the politics of the region are so unstable that the Northern Alliance needs U.S. occupation troops to hold Afghanistan in the wake of resistance from Pakistan, who do not want their Taliban Pashtun brothers replaced by Northern Alliance Tajiks. There is no way the oil will be gotten out to a Western market without Pakistan's cooperation.[25]

Along this same vein, Chevron Texaco Corporation and others in the Caspian Pipeline Consortium on November 25, 2001, opened their $2.6 billion pipeline, stretching 987 miles, with the capacity to pump 560,000 barrels of oil from Kazakhstan to the Russian port on the Black Sea. Both the United States and Russia back this project. The U.S. wants to sway Russia's sphere of influence over those on the Caspian Sea. Russia wants to collect more than $20 billion in taxes over the next forty years.[26] What comes after Cold War and bankruptcy? New alliances of old enemies!

Part of what is at stake in dealing with war, terrorism, and economics is the question of ethics, of behavior and values. Levinas upsets the typical understanding of ethics that places great regard on the self as an actor with power toward the other, by claiming that for the self to act ethically, it must be deposed from its position of totality. "Neither possession nor the unity of number nor the unity of concepts link me to the Stranger [l'Etranger], the Stranger who disturbs the being at home with oneself [le chez soi]. But the stranger also means the free one. Over him [*sic*] I have no power."[27] Displaced from power, the self has no ground on which to appeal, no power. This displacement from power is critical for ethics. "Infinity presents itself as a face in the ethical resistance that paralyses my powers and from the depths of defenseless eyes rises firm and absolute in nudity and destitution."[28] This infinity of the other makes the self incapable of movement. The other is present to the self as nude, defenseless. and destitute; the other is the orphan, the widow, the homeless. The other's face calls the self to responsibility. Yet, that the other's infinity flows into the rupture of the self's totality is devastating: "To contain more than one's capacity is to shatter at every moment the framework of a content that is thought, to cross the barriers of immanence– but without this descent into being reducing itself anew to a concept of descent."[29] As the infinity of the other pours into the capacity of the thought of the self for the other, that other explodes the thought. The self's totality is shattered, and in that shattering, the self is shattered. All conceptions are called into question. The self, in its displacement and shattering, is thrust into a position of hospitality and openness toward the other.[30] When are we capable of seeing bin Laden as the other? Is he never the other? Are we the other and we do not know it yet? As Rabbi Kushner muses, are we about justice, or do we want vengeance? What do we want? What do we need? What is really real for us since September 11?

Derrida calls us to a reality check, and to an awareness of *Globalatinization*. It is significant that we use the language of global and not world. This says a lot about how we in the United States have a conquering mentality; for we can hold a globe in our hands, but can only view the world from a satellite.

That is, religion in the West is Latin, of Rome, of Euro/Anglo/American ethos. Theology refers to discourse on faith or revelation and God. *Theo-logy* concerns being divine, the divinity of the divine, and relating of the essence. The experience of the saved, the holy, or the sacred concerns being the unscathed. Religion, then, is response. Globalatinization occurs as the world mostly speaks in Latin through Anglo-American discourse. In the new "wars of religion," what attacks or defends in the name of religion (such as extremist, fundamentalist faith) kills itself and kills another. Thus, today we have telecommunications, techno-science, and for many a return to the religious, by no means a simple undertaking. For the return to the religious requires "a radical destruction of the religious...like everything that incarnates the European political or juridical order against which all non-Christian 'fundamentalisms' or 'integrisms' are waging war...but also certain forms of Protestant or even Catholic orthodoxy)...that in face of them, another self-destructive affirmation of religion . . [the] autoimmune, could be at work in all the projects known as 'pacifist' and economic."[31] Allegedly in the name of peace, globalatinization is imposed, within the European-Anglo-American milieu, bringing together "indissociable religion and tele-technoscientific reason," reacting to itself, producing its own power of autoimmunity and its own antidote. That is, the unscathed or the holy must defend itself against its own protection, against its own immunity. There is no incongruity in the return to the religious between the fundamentalisms, the "integrisms" or their "politics"; and, otherwise, rationality holds the tele-techno-capitalistico-scientific trust. Given that the fundamentalism can be hypercritical, we can see how when bin Laden creates a war, and the United States retaliates, then the U.S. de facto is attacking Islam, and thus the United States has helped bin Laden figure out who is pure, who is not pure, and who will side with the United States, the Great Satan, and globalatinization. Similarly, women must wear burkas to protect men from their own male desires. With the machine-like nature of religion, we see parallels in telecommunications and teletechnology, where autoimmunity requires that the holy remain pure. Through rituals in religion, the pure and unscathed becomes human-scathed, and has to purify itself by attacking itself: the women and others oppressed under Taliban rule for the sake of the faith.[32] Now that the Taliban has been defeated in Afghanistan, and we have seen some initial hostile, sadistic behavior by the Northern Alliance, one wonders if we have jumped from the frying pan to an equally hot skillet.

The historical events of the Civil War, the 1960s civil rights movement, and the World Trade Center and Pentagon tragedies share many things in common. These events provide a venue for seeing the connections between religion, economics, and violence—albeit religion of the secular or sacred type. These examples also make plain the culpability of our own alleged innocence in matters of complex intrigue that affect national and global security. Religion and violence dance a mean dance together; they form a dark alliance, they scapegoat, as the violence and terrorism become ritualized public performance.

Terrorism is not an integral part of a political strategy. Terrorists often use religion to provide the warped moral agency needed for killing people en masse and for viewing these executions as collateral damage. Terrorist rhetoric is performance, drama, the symbolic statements needed to evoke a sense of empowerment to those who are hopeless, wretched, pathological persons and communities.[33] Similarly, the lives of those in New York, Washington, D.C., and Afghanistan are all unfolding dramas, for some of which we merely have a ticket in the balcony that requires binoculars, as in the political decisions made by our government. But even then, we are not fully innocent. We elect officials. They do not attain office by osmosis. We elected Presidents and they appointed others who helped set up the deal between the Taliban and the CIA. We, as in the United States of America, helped to train bin Laden. We helped to create the person whom some would see as a monster. Arendt reminds us not to be too quick to demonize before we listen to the person's case. In bin Laden's mind, for example, our military presence in Saudi Arabia desecrates holy Islamic space. King reminds us that war and violence, including retaliation, is wrong. If he were alive, he would ask, "Where do we go from here?"

My answer: Before we rush to judgment and demonize others, we need to acknowledge our arrogance and get our own house in order. I am intrigued that when Timothy McVeigh, David Koresh, and Jim Jones committed their heinous deeds, there was no public hue and cry to kill off or engage in racial profiling of twenty-to forty-year-old Euro-American men. When Susan Smith murdered her baby boys by securing them in their baby carriers in the back seat of her car and then drove that car into the river, no one said that we should persecute all twenty-or thirty-something distraught mothers. We have made idols of the flag, and our new hymn of celebration and mourning is "God Bless America." Until we can begin to see somewhat clearly through the lens of our own egotistical, Manifest Destiny, number-one status, our history will repeat itself yet again. We will grow newer and more sophisticated Unabombers. We must acknowledge our own terrorist activities and assess our own governmental and domestic realities. If not now, when? How many have to die before we realize that we have been contributing to their deaths? Prophetic voices are rarely welcomed, but their words must be uttered.[34]

6

"For This the Earth Shall Mourn"
(Jer. 4:28)

Fumitaka Matsuoka

Two forms of political religion have become starkly discernible in the wake of the September 11 events. One is morally secure but is subject to vulnerability; the other is morally insecure but its quality enduring. The former is rooted in Frederick Jackson Turner's vision of a society that regards the availability of free land and unconstrained mobility as coupled with an equality of opportunity. These are seen to be crucial determinants of American character and the source of American democracy. The essence of America consists in freedom, in both a physical and a spiritual sense. But this is a particular notion of freedom, progressive and extravagant. The other is exemplified by Carlos Bulosan's notion in *America Is in the Heart.* Here the displaced and dispossessed state is not the negation of freedom, but a realization of it in the midst of the tenuous state of life. For Bulosan, mobility is associated with subjugation, coercion, and the impossibility of fulfillment for self or community. But in such a state of being there is a home that is a movement, an equality of relationship where people seek to be their own and, at the same time, be increasingly responsible for the world.

That these two forms of political religion exist as undercurrents in our society is one of the most instructive aspects of our troubling situation today. The contrast of the two can be understood from the standpoint of a Christian interpretation of life and history. From this standpoint it is possible to see how quickly human virtue turns to evil when we forget that often corruption becomes expressed though human interest, but equally and unexpectedly, pain and vicissitude can become the seedbed of a reconciled relationship and community-building.

The ostentatious display of patriotism in the aftermath of the horrific criminal acts inflicted on the surface tranquility of our society, which had not had any experience of a direct foreign invasion save the attack on Pearl Harbor, is indeed an expected reaction. Flag-waving accompanied by the poignant singing of "God Bless America" and "America the Beautiful" are consistent with the mainstream view of America and what it holds to be sacred: independence, freedom, and the opportunity for individual actualization and societal renewal. These foundations that have reflected the Turner orientation of society for all these years are suddenly under assault. But there is another way of understanding the events of September 11 and their meaning. These events and the troubling occurrences following that tragic day have triggered in many Americans an opportunity to reexamine our basic worldviews, values, and social conventions that we hold to be sacred.

From Hawthorne's *The Scarlet Letter,* Melville's *Moby Dick,* Twain's *The Adventures of Huckleberry Finn,* and Steinbeck's *The Grapes of Wrath,* the controlling influence in American literature has been the perception of an open continent and limitless opportunities. The Puritan "errand into the wilderness" is predicated on the possibility of movement, however charged with ambivalence, between "civilization" and "nature." The dominant intellectual tradition that has emerged out of this unmitigated freedom of movement is a tradition of an order that seeks to discern, understand, decipher, know, and if possible, master and control the conquered. It is true that the price of extravagance behind these abundant opportunities often generates a gnawing sense of dissatisfaction with the realized freedom. Often this results in the fragmentation of human relatedness through radical individualism. Nevertheless, in the wake of the September 11 attacks, we Americans, explicitly or intuitively, have realized an assault on this very notion of freedom. A symbol of economic freedom, the World Trade Center, was destroyed by a symbol of our mobility, planes of United and American Airlines. Literally overnight, we have found ourselves in a strange and insecure place, a place of chaos. The very sacred conventions that we have long cherished and taken for granted—security, self-confidence, certitude, and optimism—are suddenly under assault. The commercial airlines were grounded for a while, and travel has become increasingly difficult since then. Our mobility has become questionable. The nation's Capitol, the citadel of democracy, is no longer a safe place because of the anthrax scare. Government officials are quoted as saying "I don't know" to the questions posed to them about public safety. An act of defiance against these assaults takes the form of the display of the national flag, the symbol of all national symbols. The military campaign against the Taliban regime in Afghanistan is an overt acting out of our defiance.

But this is only a partial story. Another reading of our current chaotic and uncertain situation is reflected in the work of such American literature as Carlos Bulosan's classic work *America Is in the Heart,* Ruthanne Lum McCunn's *Thousand Pieces of Gold,* and Peter Wang's film *A Great Wall.* Bulosan's work is about the failure of home-founding and the permanent state of dispossession for the early Filipino immigrants in the U.S. The book's theme is the exilic and dispossessed state of the Pinoys in the U.S. The "America" in Bulosan's heart is the unrealized potential, the unfulfilled dream of a democratic America, which might come into being through the labor of Filipino immigrants and other Americans. But there is no guarantee of such an outcome. In reality his actual life experiences involve constant displacement. Under displacement life becomes strenuous, chronically directionless, and dependent on external factors over which the individual has little control. These experiences of Bulosan belie his passionate tribute to American ideals. Home for Bulosan is a tenuous existence in perpetual dislocation.

Bulosan's experience reflects the permanent state of dispossession and displacement that marked the limits of the early Filipino immigrants' world. The "iron cage" of dispossession and displacement signals not only the dictates of nature (the labor demands of seasonal crops) but also the political and economic constraints placed on the Pinoys, making them constantly threatened by erasure from the white consciousness. Often they have been accused of savagery, immorality, and shiftlessness. In the world of the Americans represented by Bulosan, McCunn, and Wang, the events of September 11 reconfirm their own experiences of the "heart of America," that is, exclusion, displacement, the sense of tragedy, and mobility born not out of the luxury of freedom, but of necessity. The jarring surprise attacks of September 11 that reveal the presence of these two forms of American political religion prompt a theological interpretation and response from Christians.

The dominant Christian culture bears a large measure of responsibility for the "frontier" form of political religion. In today's charged societal climate, an impulse to achieve justice through the exertion of extravagant freedom and unmitigated mobility in the form of military power corresponds with this brand of the Christian faith with its idea of history. Our society has been founded on the principle of free, responsible human activity. What made "America" was not a new vision of humanity only, but a new idea of history. As Reinhold Niebuhr wrote, "The dominant note in modern culture is not so much confidence in reason as faith in history." The conception of a redemptive history informs the most diverse forms of modern culture.[1]

There is, however, another Christian culture today lurking in our midst. Its texture is exilic and sees our history through another kind of mobility, usually associated with subjugation, coercion, and impossibility of fulfillment for self or community. It is the theological motif of Israel's exile in the Old Testament and the realism of the cross in the New Testament. The central motif of faith according to this reading of reality is not emancipatory freedom but rootage, not the pursuit of happiness but belonging, not separation from community but location within it, not limitless opportunity but life amidst pain even in the current generation of optimism about what can be. This alternate Christian culture echoes the perspective of Bulosan, McCunn, and Wang to an extent. They have a keen awareness of mobility as a historical given rather than a private frustration or temporary setback. The central learning from history in this reading of life is that grasping for home leads to homelessness and risking homelessness yields the gift of home, but in an unanticipated fashion. Immobility is not the negation of freedom but a realization of it. The mainstream and exilic Christian cultures intersect at the point of political interpretations currently taking place in society, the exilic in danger of being overshadowed by the dominant discourse in the heat of patriotic rhetoric.

However, one common experience is equally shared among Americans as a result of the September 11 horrors, the subsequent anthrax scare, and the uncertain future of our military intrusion in Afghanistan. Our faith in the history of extravagant freedom can no longer be taken for granted. There is an air of precariousness and uncertainty about life among us. Threats come from both within and without. Suddenly, we have become aware of our own vulnerability, finitude, and limitations. Invincibility and invulnerability are no more. We are in a state of contradiction, because our expectations and our experience no longer meet and inform each other. Sadly, there is little in the operative traditions of our "officially optimistic" culture, to use the expression of Douglas John Hall, to enable us as a people to encounter at the level of conscious reflection a prolonged experience of negation.[2] The popularized Christian political religion that endorses and reinforces Frederick Jackson Turner's reading of history has not prepared us to face the current situation of uncertainty. Our expectations have been overwhelmingly positivistic and forward-looking; our experiences of today are increasingly and profoundly negative, bewildering, and chaotic.

To respond to this contradiction we face, we hear a repeated comment in the media: "America has lost its innocence," as though the events of September 11 were *sui generis*. We choose to ignore other tragic events in our history: slavery, the Civil War, the Great Depression, the cold war, Vietnam, Watergate, and countless other events. This lost "innocence" is a state devoid of collective memories. It is the absence of the memory of tragedy in our collective life. No wonder the conversation between expectation and experience upon which this society depends has been stifled for a want of courage to confront this discrepancy openly. Memory is a passion no less powerful than love. To remember is to live in a multiple world, to prevent the past from fading, and to call upon the future to illuminate it. It is to revive fragments of existence and to rescue lost beings. The question is whether we Americans will discover healthy ways of facing the experience of our finitude, of valuing our painful past, including the recognition of the negative and indeed nihilistic factors implicit in our own expectations.

It is instructive that George Semann, editor of the London-based Arabic-language newspaper *Al Hayal,* warns that the U.S. will not be able to uproot terrorism "unless it changes its perspective on how it builds its interests and how it defends them, by building a network of relationships that takes into consideration the interests of others who are weak and who have rights but are incapable of imposing these interests or these rights.[3] This is a time for us Americans to acknowledge the presence of negation, the recovery of our collective painful memory, and the possibility of reordering how we view the world. The question that the current situation raises for Christians is whether Christianity in some political form offers clues that might contribute to a meeting point for expectation and experience. The question is, can Christianity provide a means for navigating our deeply held mainstream values of independence, freedom, opportunity for individual actualization and societal renewal on the one hand, and the actuality of our life that is uncertain, tragic, bewildering, and chaotic on the other?

Unfortunately, we are not yet in a position to consider Christianity's potential for providing clues for reordering how we view the world out of our painful experiences. So far as a Christian articulation of the limits of human certitude is concerned, American Christians have not been able to state adequately the "thin" tradition of our faith because of our positivistic reading of history.[4] For so long our individual and collective lives have been shaped by the myth of a secure, self-confident, and forward-looking outlook on life. We have just begun to feel at our gut level what finitude might look like in the wake of the terrorists' attacks. The truth of the matter is that the America of Bulosan has not been a valued political and cultural view or discourse of history for this society. It has been neglected, ignored, and negated. The mobility out of necessity, not out of luxury, has never been acknowledged as being constitutive of our society. The positivistic notion of history that has been endorsed by dominant forces of Christianity, furthermore, has sanctioned a luxurious freedom that contributes to our difficulty in valuing any alternate reading of our history. It has also led to devaluing the central symbol of the Christian faith, the realism of the cross. The very faith toward which we look for redemptive possibilities has been established in such a way in this society as to make it inaccessible to us for reordering the way we relate with the rest of the world. Seen in this way, the real terrorist assaults are indeed upon the deeply held values and conventions that prevail in our society. At the depths of our social relationships and cultural assumptions is a particular brand of Christianity with its discourse about history that intrinsically binds us together. America is indeed under attack. The attack is upon our popular notion of certitude, unmitigated freedom, and optimism. Where should we go from here?

Though our future is uncertain and precarious, one thing that is sure is that we are in deep mourning today. A large number of lives were lost in the powerful cities of New York and Washington, D.C. Lives were sacrificed through the terrorist attacks by mail, another symbol of the freedom of expression. Countless lives are being lost in the war in Afghanistan, American and others. The cry of pain and the expression of sorrow are the seedbed of the formation of a new society and of a different way of relating with one another around an alternative perception of reality. A powerful source for such a counter form of society is to trust one's pain and to trust the pain of one's neighbor that is very much like our own. The task of the Christian church is to interpret our sorrows and distresses, the agonies and pains through which the world is passing, and to recognize the hand of God in them. "For this the earth shall mourn, and the heavens above be black; for I have spoken, I have purposed; I have not relented nor will I turn back" (Jer. 4:28, RSV). A temptation for Christians is to fall into either complacency by evading the gravity of our experience or despair and destructive anger by interpreting the distress of our day as merely an evil act inflicted upon us by an outside enemy. Surely, God's faithfulness to people prevails in this travail of the nation, in this shaking of historic stabilities and traditions. However, the Christian faith heritage reminds us that the relinquishment of the old order always comes before the embrace of the Holy One. The rock bottom of faith formation is the recognition and communal articulation of pain that belongs inevitably to the social process, where our faithlessness is both evoked and crushed. The crucial hinge in this faith formation is the foundational power of an awareness of finitude and its associated experience of pain.

But today our collective experiences of pain have found their outlet in the military intervention of the U.S. and its European allies and have moved the discussion of justice to a dangerous confrontation between the opposing views of "way of life." A continuing military campaign by our government threatens the fragile but constructive path toward justice that began following the attacks of September 11 through an international cooperation to combat terrorism through legal measures. We have yielded to a desire to punish the Taliban regime through vengeance. But the question is, what are we hoping to achieve? Do we engage in violent acts so that we can recover the "innocence," the lost vision of extravagant freedom, mastery, and control over the world's wealth? If that is what we are doing, the Christian "thin" tradition of the realism of the cross, as well as the political religion rooted in Carlos Bulosan's America with its sensitivity toward those who are at the margins of life, are once again being submerged in the military aggression of the U.S. and its allies in a faraway country and in the jingoistic patriotic fervor at home.

How do Christians embrace the Holy on the cross in the current precarious and uncertain state of our society? Surely justice in the face of the violence inflicted upon the innocent should shape our response. But God's justice is not operative merely in the act of punishment of an evil deed. While we inevitably must make careful and considerate judgments upon the perpetrators according to the relative degree of justice and community that we embody, Christians cannot afford to make such judgments final. The Christian church is called upon to mediate divine justice and grace upon all people and upon itself, the justice rooted in God's compassion and tempered by mercy and forgiveness. However terrible the "evils" that the terrorists perpetrated against innocent people, our resentment against them surely should not obscure the common sin and guilt of all, out of which this specific criminal act emerged. This is the time for Christians in America to ask the question about the root of the anger of the perpetrators of the violence. How do people reach this level of anger, hatred, and frustration? Is it possible that their anger is generated over time through a myriad of historical injuries, poverty, a deep sense of threat to their identity, and experiences of sustained exclusion? Anger seeks recognition. Out of anger the perpetrator of violence expects the powerful to lash out in counter-violence, a greater degree of violence, against the powerless. Military actions on the part of the U.S. simply meet the expectations of the perpetrators of the September 11 events.

George Semann's warning once again needs to be heeded: that the U.S. will not be able to uproot terrorism unless we change our perspective on how we build our interests and how we defend them, by reordering a network of relationships that takes into consideration the interests of others who are on the margin of the world and who have rights but are incapable of imposing these interests or these rights. Semann's warning is a call for Americans to reexamine what this nation stands for and how we order our lives. It is a call to reexamine the U.S.' foundational approaches to nations of the world; to invest in economic development, education, a broad social agenda in the poverty-stricken nations, and to cooperate with them to meet the fundamental needs of their people; to pursue a sustainable peace process in the Israel and Palestinian conflict by working toward the mutual affirmation of each (which means the recognition that the authentic security for Israel is through justice to the Palestinians). This reorientation is a radical and risky call. Can this level of collective self-reflection and examination of America's soul realistically be embraced by us? This seems to be a tall order. But not to answer this call may well be too costly. The possibility is so great for the continuing loss of innocent lives at home and abroad, and for the escalation of international tension whose magnitude we have not seen in history.

This is a time for Christians in America to be reminded that the redemptive power of mourning that comes from the loss of certitude is indeed an opportunity in our midst. A window of opportunity exists during this difficult time for a shift in the collective societal consciousness of our sacred conventions. It exists in our current communal mourning of the loss of lives, in our expression of pain in the face of the injustice that defies our language, and in our experience of threat that comes from within our society. When the question Why do these things happen? defies an answer, and we find ourselves able only to express pain, suffering, and the questioning in our hearts, then we are involved in a strange sort of alchemy where we become connected with the lives of our opponents. Our soul touches the souls of those who instigated the violence and chaos. The connection lies in a common sharing of an exilic state of being, "a mind of winter" as Wallace Stevens calls it, or a place of critical distance from all identities and a restless opposition to all orthodoxies. Thus, being in exile is not a geographical fact. It is a very special way of seeing things around us and in us. Understood in this way, exile, though painful, is also a morally valuable condition. "It is part of morality not to be at home in one's home," as German-Jewish philosopher Theodor Adorno reminds us.[5] It can generate a generous imagination and sympathetic understanding. Being in exile can accord us a position from which to speak from an awareness of finitude of life without succumbing to the temptation of power and prestige. The Bible addresses this central human condition of homelessness (*anomie*) and seeks to respond to this reality in terms of grasp and gift.[6] Exile is not the negation of freedom, but indeed the realization of it. Correspondingly, the notion of unconstrained mobile freedom coupled with limitless opportunity leads to an erosion of mutual relatedness and the aggravation of an adversarial posture toward other human beings. The oppositional dynamic of relationship that is operative in the frontier spirit and its notion of "life, liberty, and the pursuit of happiness" is pernicious, just as when we demonize "enemies." Such fixed differences of ideology constitute impenetrable barriers to generous imagination and sympathetic understanding.

Soon after the events of September 11, an insightful article appeared in the *San Francisco Chronicle*. The article was written by a mother who reflected on the current resurgence of patriotism:

> My town, Tucson, Ariz., has become famous for a simple gesture in which some 8,000 people wearing red, white or blue T-shirts assembled themselves in the shape of a flag on a baseball field and had their photograph taken from above…My teenage daughter, who has a quick mind for numbers and a sensitive heart, did an interesting thing. She laid her hand over a quarter of the picture, leaving visible more or less 6,000 people, and said, 'That many are dead.' We stared at what that looked like—all those innocent souls, multi-colored and packed into a conjoined destiny—and shuddered at the one simple truth behind all the noise, which is that so many beloved people have suddenly gone from us. That is my flag, and that's what it means: We're all just people together.[7]

This is a powerful image of the exilic state of our society, the sudden loss of beloved people from what seemed to be a secure home of ours that unexpectedly yields the gift of home; that is, in the very midst of this grief we affirm "We'are all just people together."

We Americans stand at an intersection of our history. As Jose Ortega y Gasset reminds us, decisive historical changes really do not arise from wars, cataclysms, or some ingenious inventions, but come out of the human heart that "inclines its sensitive crown to one side or the other of the horizon, toward optimism or toward pessimism, toward heroism or toward utility, toward combat or toward peace."[8] The Christian church, too, lives at such an intersection of the human heart. The church is at once a human institution and God's covenant community that prompts such a swaying of the human heart with its rituals and sacraments, practices that make our beliefs tangible and physical. And with the powerful symbols and narratives that resonate with those rituals and sacraments, the fundamental truth of social ontology is expressed in community. In these acts we are made aware that we did not create ourselves *ex nihilo,* that we are not the only form of reality, with an unmitigated freedom of behavior and choice. Rather, as Christians we live by the fragile nudging of the cross, in the image of the one who is deprived of dominion and power, deprived of possessing, with only a capacity to receive and to share what he receives. America's pain is deep and intense in the current turmoil that has put our world upside down. Can Christians in America be an ally to the America of the "thin" reading of its history by Bulosan, McCunn, and Wang by reclaiming the Christian "thin" tradition incarnated in our communal practice of faith? In our response to this question may indeed lie a clue to the future of our collective life called the United States of America and our relationship to our world neighbors.

7

Roots of the Taliban

Judith Mayotte

Getting at roots is not simple. The Taliban emerged and grew out of a multitude of circumstances and events that came together—out of history, tradition, and geography; out of patriarchy, tribal loyalty, and Islam; out of local, national, regional, and international strategic interests. The lens through which I watched the climate for a group such as the Taliban to grow was through a refugee lens –particularly through the eyes of refugee women and children, who make up 80 percent of most refugee populations. During the mid-eighties, I spent considerable time among the Afghan refugees as I gathered material for my book *Disposable People? The Plight of Refugees.*[1] For the peoples of Afghanistan this period of enormous change in their lives opened the way for the Taliban.

On a sunny day in 1988, as our small Foraker plane started its descent into Peshawar, tears began to stream down the face of my friend and colleague Sima Wali. For the first time since she fled her Afghan homeland eight years earlier, she sighted in the distance the mountains that border Pakistan and Afghanistan. She could see the edge of her homeland, but she could not yet step foot on Afghan soil.

For Sima and all Afghans, April 27, 1978, might be called their September 11. This was the day of the Saur Revolution. Sima describes the surprise and the horror of that day. In her words:

> We had no warning that a coup was imminent. The previous evening, people had gone about their normal routines. My family had been to a ball where many members of the extensive Mohammadzai clan were present.

56

The coup began early Thursday morning with many Afghans going to work as if on a normal day. Around noon action intensified. Tanks began to cause traffic jams, as people returned home for the half-day holiday. Traffic police directed tanks to the side so that buses filled with passengers could continue on their normal route.

Suddenly, about midmorning, planes began flying over the city. We thought the planes were on military maneuvers until we realized they were all headed to the heart of the city, close to the palace and the surrounding government buildings. When bombardments began, we turned on the radio, but there was no news, only music.

Later in the day, we learned what had happened. Daoud [the president] had sent word to his family, members of the royal family, and families of other officials to come to the palace, where he felt they would best be protected. But the palace was the first target of the coup and was seized very early...

The soldiers lined up Daoud and his family, members of the royal family, and other government officials and their families. When the soldiers began firing, they aimed very low at the children, a ploy to terrorize the parents. The children were the first victims of the massacre. Over fifty members of the royal family were present. All were killed save one. Some of the men who were in the palace and who had guns realized before they were lined up that they and their families would not be spared. They began killing their wives and themselves so that they would not die by a firing squad or be taken to prison where they would undergo torture and horrible deaths.

The only survivor of the palace coup was the wife of one of President Daoud's sons. She was a friend of mine. Two of her teenage daughters and her husband were killed in front of her. The poor woman had the brains and blood of her children splattered on her skirt. She sustained several bullet wounds and was left for dead...

On the same day, soldiers began to round up other members of the extended royal family and Mohammadzai closely related to the branch ruling at the time...Women and children were not spared. Intellectuals, student activists, and religious leaders became victims of the coup.

Members of more distantly related Mohammadzai, families like mine, were placed under house arrest. Domestics were placed in our homes who reported our conversations and activities to the authorities.

People began to leave Kabul with minimal possessions and often with return tickets so that they would not be denied exit visas or have their passports absconded [sic]. Neighborhood monitoring groups reported those who sold their homes, jewelry, and other valuables as suspects. Often monitors were children trained in school to betray their parents, many of whom were imprisoned and killed based on what the children said.[2]

April 27, 1978, will serve as the day for us to look backward and forward in time to reflect on some of the influences that gave rise to the Taliban.

In looking back, since September 11, we are now more aware that Afghanistan is a rugged land where geography has played a significant role in the shape the nation has taken. This is a part of the world where the Karakoram, Himalayas, and Hindu Kush come together. The Hindu Kush, "killer of Hindus," stride into Afghanistan like a skeletal foot from the edge of China, heel to toes across the central core of this harsh, rugged land. Many would-be conquerors in search of crossroads and buffers have marched into this forbidding land only to be repulsed or exhausted by the terrain as much as by its tireless warriors –Alexander the Great, Genghis Khan (described by Afghan expert Louis Dupree as the "atom bomb of his day"[3]), British and Russians, and the Soviets. Resistance and revival are hallmarks of Afghan history.

The Afghans are tribal, patriarchal, and basically rural peoples–divisive, yet fiercely loyal to the land. The male is the provider and the defender of the honor of the family. Women symbolize the honor of the family.

The Afghans are also people of Islam, since the seventh century. *Purdah* is the means of defending a woman's honor. The veil is the curtain that safeguards her purity, and the walls of the home compound protect her from the eyes of strangers. Afghans, who are mostly moderate Muslims, were always less rigid in their interpretation and observance of traditions, including *purdah,* than more radical Muslims. In fact, prior to the Soviet invasion, someone dubbed them "the southern California of Islam."

As tribal, patriarchal, Islamic, and fiercely independent peoples, Afghans moved forward and accepted change, but at their pace, not at the pace of rulers or outsiders. Amanullah Khan, who was king at the end of the third Anglo/Afghan War, in the early years of the twentieth century, was determined to rule over a unified nation, as did his grandfather, as well as over an independent Afghanistan. And he was going to bring the nation into the twentieth century. Amanullah wanted to do away with what he considered outmoded tribal customs and bring Afghanistan into the stream of Western modernization. He plunged headlong into initiating change, failing utterly to be sensitive to the established tribal and religious traditions of his people. The reforms that rankled hit at conservative Islamic customs–for example, the removal of the veil from women, the introduction of Western dress for all, imposition of coeducation. Religious revolts brought him down.

Moving closer to the present, when King Nadir Shah was murdered in 1933, his young son and heir Zahir Shah was only fifteen. Uncles ruled in his name for twenty years. In 1954, Zahir Shah took the throne for himself, and his cousin Daoud Khan held the office of prime minister. Both Zahir Shah and Daoud sought moderate reform and development. At this time, following World War II, when boundaries, alliances, and the balance of power had changed throughout the world, foreign aid became inextricably bound to the foreign policy of those powers embroiled in the Cold War. Both the king and the prime minister were willing recipients of aid from both the East and the

West. The U.S. and USSR vied to finance large-scale infrastructural projects, and in the end, rather than the projects benefiting Afghanistan, the country became a pawn of the U.S.-USSR competition. Ultimately, when Afghanistan tried to remain neutral and benefit from both, the U.S. began to construe Afghanistan as procommunist, and cut aid. The same, of course, happened with Sihanouk in Cambodia. Neutrality does not seem to fit well with U.S. foreign policy. Afghanistan, subsequently, moved closer to the USSR for aid and armaments.

In addition, Daoud began to press for greater social reforms, which caught the ire of more conservative tribal and religious leaders. These leaders decried him as a traitor to Islam when he pressed for an end to *purdah,* as well as for mainstreaming women in educational development and the work force. He tested the waters one day in 1959 during the festival commemorating Afghanistan's independence. On the second day of the festival, Daoud and his entourage stepped into the boxes of the stadium grandstand. The women, dressed in colorful Western garments, had shed every vestige of the veil. Daoud was accused of cozying too closely to both Soviet and Western ways. As Zahir Shah became increasingly aware that real power rested with Daoud, in 1963, the King asked Daoud to step down. Zahir Shah formed a constitutional monarchy and continued more gradually with reform.

The constitution, however, opened the door to political parties, including the far left of the educated minority. The players of the April 1978 revolution-to-come now stepped forward, and in 1965, the People's Democratic Party of Afghanistan (PDPA) was born. The most significant players then and in the future were Babrak Karmal, Nur Mohammad Taraki, Hafizullah Amin, and Najibullah Khan.

Before the radicals took control, Daoud returned to the scene. On July 17, 1973, in a bloodless coup, the reign of King Zahir Shah and the age of monarchy in Afghanistan ceased. Daoud Khan, brother-in-law, first cousin, and former prime minister to the king, declared himself President of the Republic of Afghanistan while Zahir Shah was in Europe.

Finally, on April 27, 1978, the PDPA was able to come forward and bring about the Great Saur Revolution. On this day, the massacre in the palace, recounted earlier in Sima Wali's words, took place.

The more radical members of the PDPA, led by Taraki, held reign. These radical revolutionaries implemented extreme reforms that flew in the face of tradition and religion. The flag was changed, and the name of Allah was no longer invoked. Radical land reforms turned rural society upside down. The age-old *jirga* (or people's assembly) was banished. Women's issues were dealt with without foresight or understanding of cultural traditions, especially among rural people. Mullahs and elders reacted vehemently against young urban party workers who came to the countryside insisting on coeducation and demanding that *purdah* and the bride price be abandoned. The PDPA denounced reaction by mullahs and elders and imprisoned and killed many. The Soviets decided to act as resistance grew in the countryside, as thousands fled the country, as thousands more were imprisoned or killed, and as Amin sabotaged a Soviet plan to have the more moderate Karmal (living in the Soviet Union) rule alongside the more radical Taraki, and unleashed a ruthless three months' rule.

On December 27, 1979, Soviet troops invaded Afghanistan and Babrak Karmal took control. In practice, he made clear that "the prophet Mohammed would have to coexist with the prophet Marx," as Arthur Bonner noted.[4] But as a prophet of an outside invader, Karmal would never be able to rally the people behind him. The conflict was no longer internal. For Afghans it was time for *jihad* to rid the country of the invading "infidel," approximately 150,000 Soviet troops. Seven years later Najibullah replaced Karmal and remained in control until he and the Soviets were worn down.

Among a population then estimated at between sixteen and twenty million (no formal census has taken place in Afghanistan), the decade-long war generated at least 5.5 million refugees (3 million in Pakistan, 2 million in Iran), another 2 million internally displaced civilians, between 1 and 2 million dead, and the destruction of 20,000–25,000 villages among the estimated 30,000 Afghan villages.

Symbolically, the question of the veil was an issue in this war and in this society. Its place and its meaning had tumbled a king more than fifty years earlier. It had to do with the past and the future, with tradition and development, with progression and regression, with independence and its lack thereof. It had to do with a way of life that was giving way to the twentieth century. The invasion pitched questions and visions onto the battlefield rather than around tables of peaceful discourse.

When people are forced into exile, leaving all they have known behind and without material support, they frequently become bound to exaggerated expressions of traditions and suffocate under the weight. In the case of the Afghans, when the Soviets came and bombed their villages and belittled their customs, traditions, and religion, the Afghans withdrew into a protective, defensive siege mentality. They retreated into what they knew best, the family and religion. Rather than act moderately as they had in Kabul or in their villages, the dispersed Afghans tended to become more conservative. Longing for the familiar in an unfamiliar place, they radicalized their cultural and religious traditions, believing that in doing so, they might sense the familiar.

In addition, no matter where they are, Afghans are governed by a set of cultural norms, the unwritten Pushtunwali–"the way of the Afghans." The code is sacred. *Nang* (honor) and *badal* (revenge) are the heart of this tribal code–particularly in regard to *zar* (gold), *zan* (women), and *zamin* (land). Following the Soviet invasion and the flight into exile, *namus* (defending the honor of women) became a critical test of an Afghan male's ability to protect the family, the tribe, and the Afghan nation and culture. Protecting their honor by protecting the women gave stature to Afghan men. Observing a mixture of culture and religion, men began to wear long beards and prayer caps, while the women observed a strict *purdah.* Bearing these symbols, many refugees began to live intensely the fundamentalism signified by the symbols, religiously, politically, and culturally. A particular mix of war, culture, politics, and religion coalesced, placing the lives of all Afghans, particularly the women, on hold in exile and in their homes through an extreme enforcement of *purdah*. Ordinary Afghans found themselves caught up in the political machinations of their leaders, the leaders of Pakistan, the leaders of the U.S. and the USSR, donors with strong Islamic fundamentalist convictions, and communists who controlled Afghanistan. Each wanted to influence the creation of a new government in Afghanistan once the war was over. Each had a desire to control and reshape a battered nation. The climate was fertile for the emergence of the Taliban.

In regard to their own leaders, we look both inside Afghanistan and to the places of exile, particularly to those exiled in Pakistan. Early on, what became known as the Seven Party Alliance was formed among Afghan leaders in Pakistan. They were not the chosen leaders of Afghans at home, or really of those living in exile. But commanders at home, fighting against the Soviets, as well as mullahs and elders within and outside Afghanistan, had to align themselves with and profess loyalty to one if they were to be adequately equipped and fortified to fight against the intruders as well as be a part of the food distribution to the refugees in the camps. The parties ranged from the most fundamentalist Muslims and most conservative tribal leaders to the most moderate of both. They ranged from Pushtuns, to Tajiks, to Hazaras, to Uzbecks. Through the commanders and the elders, each held sway over a particular group of people and a particular geographic area.

The government of Pakistan funneled money, arms, and influence from those backing and supporting the mujahideen–particularly the U.S. and Saudi Arabia. Pakistan favored the extreme fundamentalist Gulbuddin Hekmatyar and his Hezb-I-Islami party over other less fundamentalist or more moderate parties and their leaders. With money, arms, and support, influence grew among those who adhered to and interpreted more rigidly the tenets of Islam. In 1988, toward the end of the war, when the Soviet military withdrew from Afghanistan, the Seven Party Alliance, backed by the U.S. and others, formed what became known as the Afghan Interim Government or AIG. Many Afghans thought the AIG to be another foreign-installed government. Rather than returning to Afghanistan to govern from within the liberated areas of Paktika, Paktia, and Nangarhar Provinces, they chose to govern from Pakistan. This did not sit well with commanders, who felt they had remained on the front lines and should have more control over the peoples and areas under their influence. Many set up what might be called mini-states in the areas they controlled. In Kabul, the Najibullah government remained in place–in fact for four years following the Soviet pullout.

In the countryside, commanders became more and more independent from the party leaders in Pakistan, and the sharp differences between them were evident. The internal war continued to fragment Afghans. Conflict increased among leaders of the AIG and between AIG leaders and the commanders, who became increasingly independent, but also among the various ethnic, tribal, and religious groups, even at the village level–Tajiks against Pushtuns, tribal chieftain against tribal chieftain, clan against clan, resistance group against resistance group, Sunni against Shi'a, fundamentalist against moderate.

The United States government, Pakistan, and Saudi Arabia, backing away from conciliatory overtures from Gorbachev to form a coalition government consisting of Najibullah and the AIG and believing that the Kabul government, without Soviet financial backing, would fall, urged the rebel forces to begin to attack the cities. But the *mujahideen* could not form a united front. The Soviets felt that if they let go of Najibullah, an extreme Islamic government would form in Afghanistan and pose a threat to the then Soviet Union's Islamic States (Uzbekistan, Turkmenistan, Tajikistan, etc.).

In late January 1992, Pakistan cut off all military aid to the *mujahideen,* and Najibullah had already lost Soviet military support. In March 1992, Najibullah agreed to step down. However, Najibullah made a grave strategic mistake when he dismissed his most loyal and strategically adept general– Rashid Dostam, an Uzbek we are now reading about in the news. Dostam defected to the *mujahideen* Ahmed Shah Masud, who we know was killed September 9, 2001. When Najibullah tried to flee the country, Dostam blocked him. He took refuge in the UN offices and remained there until the Taliban took control of Kabul. The Taliban hanged Najibullah in a public hanging.

Sebghatullah Mojadiddi, a theological scholar from the mystic Sufi branch of Islam and a moderate in his religious thinking, was chosen to head a government formed by the Seven Party Alliance (the AIG) in 1989. On the fourteenth anniversary of the bloody Saur Revolution, April 27, 1992, Mojaddidi left Peshawar, Pakistan, for Kabul. Burhanuddin Rabbani, a Tajik who now heads the remnant Northern Alliance, followed Mojaddidi. The parties and the factions proceeded to engage in a bloody war among themselves, leaving cities such as Kabul in ruin. Afghans became appalled with the inability of the parties and commanders to bring a peaceful and stable government to Kabul. It was then that the Taliban were ready to act.

It was not as though the Taliban were waiting in the wings, but circumstances opened the way for their ultimate march to Kabul. Youth in the refugee camps proved to be fertile ground for spreading their vision of a strict Islamic state. In this war, as in most conflicts, children learn early the concepts of war and the enemy. Much less of a child's mental and emotional energies are expended on thoughts of peace and friendship. Through ideological training, all sides to a conflict vie for the minds and hearts of children, for they, after all, are the future.

During this time throughout Afghanistan, Soviets spirited young boys out of their classrooms and transported them by the planeloads to the Soviet Union for a Soviet education in which birth language, traditions, and ideals were discredited and disavowed.

In the Afghan refugee camps, tented schools run by the parties schooled young boys not only in the teachings of the Koran, but also in the ways of *jihad.* I watched boys as young as five leading their schoolmates in chanted phrases raised to fever pitch of the glories of *jihad.* Party schools were not the only ones that appeared among the Afghans in Pakistan. Some that more directly influenced the rise of the Taliban proliferated throughout the Northwest

Frontier Province and in the Quetta area where most of the Afghan refugees lived. Saudi money poured in not only in the form of arms and military hardware but also as humanitarian assistance. I saw magnificent mosques and *Koranic* schools or *madrassas* that some of the Saudi Wahabbi money built. The Wahabbi creed promotes a strict and austere adherence to Islamic teaching and law and has been embraced by the Saudi royal family. Young males who attended these *madrassas* received little in the way of a regular academic curriculum, but more in the study of Islam according to Wahabbi interpretation.

In Pakistan another Islamic movement, The Deoband, had already been introduced and *madrassas* were thriving. Originating in India to serve Muslims living in a non-Muslim state, the Deobandis believed in a broad education for Muslim youth, who in turn would live Islamic values in a changing and more diversely integrated world. However, the Deobandis believed in restricting women in their movement, dress, education, and incorporation into the mainstream of society. They ruled out any form of hierarchy in the Muslim community, and rejected Shi'a Islam. Many Afghan and Pakistani youth were schooled in Deobond *madrassas.* The Taliban embraced and exaggerated the restrictive, narrow aspects of the Deobandis and rejected their broader educational vision.[5] As the young boys became young men and returned to Afghanistan, many aligned themselves with those who interpreted Islam in its most radical and restrictive forms. The Taliban found these young men ideal recruits. We are all well aware of Taliban social restrictions in women's dress, in men's beards, in negating entertainment—musical, kite flying, dancing, and so forth.

The education of young girls and women also became an issue in the camps. In Afghanistan before the war, more women were beginning to receive not only rudimentary education, but advanced studies as well. It was mainly urban women who were given the latter opportunity. Once in exile, as *purdah* was more strictly enforced, strong women who believed in the need for educated women in postwar Afghanistan struggled to create educational opportunities for young women. There are two situations in which I was involved. Two highly educated, young Afghan women created the Women's Center to help Afghan women become literate and provide the poorest women with skills for self-sufficiency. The two women, loyal to their Islamic tradition, believed that if the women could read the *Koran,* they could better understand the true place of women in Islam. Like the founders of the Women's Center, Tajwar Kakar, formerly a teacher in Afghanistan and imprisoned and tortured for her political activities, struggled for the right of Afghan women to live according to the tenets of Islam and the cultural code of Afghans. Tajwar became indefatigable in her search for a political party or humanitarian organization to sponsor a secondary school for Afghan female refugees. In the end she succeeded, but at a price. Tajwar and the school were never withour their detractors. The school was always in danger of being closed, or worse, destroyed. Tajwar's life was threatened more than once.

Little, really, is known about those who organized the Taliban and became its leaders, even though they held 90–95 percent of Afghanistan, harbored and received support from Osama bin Laden, and were recognized as the legitimate government of Afghanistan by only three of the nearly 200 nations of the world. Of the three, Saudi Arabia, the United Arab Emirates recalled their diplomats after the September 11, 2001, attacks on the World Trade Center and the Pentagon, while Pakistan continued for a time to recognize them as a communications conduit. We know the Taliban are composed mainly of Pushtuns, the majority ethnic group in Afghanistan; are Sunni Muslims who reject Shi'a Muslims; are little schooled in economic, political, or cultural matters; created little governmental structure; ruled more by consensus among themselves; dictated their decrees without advice or consent from the population; and strove through force to bring about a strict Islamic nation. Their one-eyed leader, Mohammad Omar, fought against the Soviets, as did others who were of fighting age during the Soviet invasion of Afghanistan. He remained reclusive to the end of the Taliban regime and let others speak for the Taliban.

As Ahmed Rashid and Peter Marsden relate in their excellent books on the Taliban, Pakistan, during the time Benazir Bhutto was prime minister, looked to southern Afghanistan as a likely trade route into Central Asia. Central and northern Afghanistan were racked by the civil wars among the parties and commanders. Kandahar, while riven with corruption, banditry, and strife, was less involved in the ongoing conflict than the north. The story goes that bandits held up a thirty-truck convoy from Pakistan as it was making its way across southern Afghanistan. A small group of Islamic militants came to their rescue. No longer bankrolling the former *mujahideen,* and, needing to bolster its flagging economy through opening trade, following the assistance given to its trade convoy, Pakistan's interior minister created the Afghan Trade Development Cell. While overtly commissioned to promote trade routes to Central Asia, it funneled money to the Taliban to help rebuild infrastructure in the southern regions and to give military and general financial support.[6] Emboldened and with provisions, the Taliban began their march across the land, taking countryside, villages, and cities and imposing on a war- and corruption-weary population a law and order that became more and more extreme. The Taliban, in its efforts to control the country and impose its brand of Islam, became as brutal as its predecessors.

Now, we have come to today. And we will have to meet tomorrow in this troubled and devastated land. How will it all come out on the other side of the present conflict? None of us possess crystal balls. I will only say that there are things we must and must not do if Afghanistan is to become a stable and peaceful nation under a rule of law. One is that no outsider should try to impose a government on the Afghan people. We have seen what that has done in the ancient and recent past. Second, for Afghanistan to become stable and peaceful, those of us who have interfered in that land have a responsibility to help Afghans help themselves rebuild their battered nation. We did not have the moral or political will to take on this responsibility in 1989. Do we have such will today?

8

Sovereignty, Empire, Capital, and Terror

John Milbank

The question that one should ask in response to the immediate aftermath of the events of September 11 is this: Why was there outrage on such a gigantic scale? After all, people are killed in large numbers all the time, by terror, politics, and economic oppression. Within a matter of days after the attack on the World Trade Center, the United States already may have killed more people in response than died in New York, through increased and tightened sanctions in the Near East. So why this unprecedented outrage? There may be two answers here.

The first answer is the threat to sovereign power that is involved. It is, after all, sovereign power that is supposed to have the right over life and death, whether in Islam or in the West. The sovereign state can execute people. It can pass laws that increase the lives of some and decrease the lives of others. It can fight wars. It can impose sanctions that kill. Individuals who take upon themselves this right of life and death are considered to be criminals. But to kill on this scale throws everything into confusion. Is this a crime? No, it seems, because killing on this kind of scale is something only the State is supposed to be capable of. Is it then an act of war? Well, if so, then it is a different kind of war, because only sovereign States can wage war. It actually seems to be worse than normal war waged by a State because it's a threat to the very idea of the State itself, and sovereignty itself.

Ignore the pieties about the dreadfulness of terrorism. The West and Israel itself engage in many acts of terror. The terrorism that is seen here as being uniquely evil is the terrorism that assumes a power that is supposed to belong to States alone. I'm not at all saying that the people who blew up the World Trade Center buildings were anarchists. No, they were perhaps indeed a species of Islamic fascist–who themselves wish to establish tyrannical sovereign States. But their *mode of action* threatens the very idea of the State. So that's my first answer.

But answer two is that there was a hidden glee in the official outrage on the part at least of some, though certainly not of others. The attack seemed to give an opportunity to do things that some factions in the West have wanted for a long time. What are these things? An assault on so-called "rogue states"; a continuous war against terrorists everywhere; a policing of world markets to ensure that free market exchange processes are not exploited by the enemies of capitalism. But, above all the attack provided an opportunity to reinscribe State sovereignty.

The modern secular State rests on no substantive values. It exists to uphold the market system, that is an ordered competition between wills to power– the idol of "liberty" that we are supposed to worship. And this State itself creams off and piles up this power in the name of a people. Every modern state therefore is inherently semi-racist, because it gathers around the notion of a people. This semi-racist holding together of a people requires an exterior –a potential enemy. As Carl Schmitt argued, the occasional emergency of war is crucial for a state's legitimacy.[1] But globalization puts the modern State into crisis. There is now the prospect of no more exterior, no more real foes. Sovereign power is consequently threatened. If it remains merely domestic, it will wither away in the face of multiple loyalties. If it exports itself and drives toward the global State, then it still needs an enemy who is other. Without an external enemy, the enemy must now be internal, lurking everywhere. Without the possibility of the occasional emergency of war, there must be perpetual war against an internal danger.

Because of its history of expanding frontiers–its internal wars against native Americans, African Americans, British loyalists, Spaniards in the South and West, the dissenting Confederate states, Southern and Central America, dealers in alcohol and drugs, and Communists in the 1950s–the United States has in a sense been long preparing for this new sort of global conflict. As Michael Hardt and Antonio Negri have argued in their *Empire,*[2] American neo-Roman imperialism works by a constant subsumption and inclusion of "others," such that difference is apparently welcomed, yet actually subordinated to an unremitting uniformity. This subsumption coincides with an obliteration of the older distinction between colonies as the extra-capitalist sources of "primary accumulation" and the fully capitalized home markets. Now all comes to be within the unrestricted one world market.

This contrasts with older European imperialism, which held the other at a subordinated distance, permitting its otherness, even while subordinating it for the sake of an exploitation of natural and human resources. And one should, I think, add to Hardt and Negri that, in the case of Britain and France, there were also many utopian imperialist schemes that went even beyond this subordination, and tended to deploy the peripheries and "savage" to mock the center and "civilized."[3] Such nuances are shockingly overlooked in pseudo-left-wing American "post-colonial" discourses, which actually assist the ideology of the American Right by implying the original "innocence" of the United States as a once colonized nation and its natural solidarity with all the colonized.

These implications tend to conceal the fact that American neo-colonialism is far more insidious than the older variety. It does not attend to cultural difference (like, for example, the British law code for India, assisted by the historicist and comparativist work of Henry Maine); it pursues no substantive goals of the political and social good (however deluded the ones of old empires may often have been); and seeks instead both for pure economic exploitation and for the absolute imposition of American signifiers. (Even foreign English-language films in the U.S.—such as *Harry Potter*—have to be doctored to conform with American English; the reverse never applies.) Under French and British colonial law child labor was outlawed; now within the "American Empire," but of course with total European connivance, it is everywhere rife.

While Hardt and Negri concede that neo-empire outdoes old empire in vileness, they still subscribe to a dialectical myth that renders this more nakedly capitalist phase of empire somehow a necessary staging post on the way to socialist utopia. Surely we need instead more sober reflections on the temporary need for some sort of more benignly parentalist assistance for the South from the North—given that so much of the South is devastated in its internal resources and in any case so bound up with the North that only global solutions will be viable. Tony Blair at times has such a vision: unfortunately those times are utterly vitiated by his continuing devotion to the market.

Instead, any enactment of this vision would require a withdrawal by the North from its unqualifiedly capitalist commitments. But what we now see is the very opposite: a fearful extension of American Republican Imperialism, in terms of a logic that is impeccably Machiavellian. The unity of the Republic, snatched by fate out of time for the sake of its own negative freedom (and the negative freedom of its citizens insofar as this is secured through their absolute submission to the Republic), can only be secured through constant reunification in the face of a threat to this freedom. Given that the Republic is isolationist, and has no interest other than its own freedom, it is not able to mediate with the other, even in an old-European hierarchical fashion. Instead it can only withstand by subsuming, by expanding at least its frontiers of cultural reach. Commentators who tend to think that Bush has been now jolted out of isolationism by the catastrophe tend to miss the point that isolation and hysterical expansion are two halves of the American Republican dialectic.

Moreover, the American sense that what is isolated and expanded is unquestionably the *acme* of human political achievement, frozen forever in an ideal constitution, tends to disallow the self-denying ordinances, the sense of temporariness, of passing expediency, and of fearful desire to avoid *hubris* that is expressed, for example, in Kipling's poem *Recessional*. American imperialism never supposes that the Captains and the Kings must one day depart.

This is why, in an emergency that tends to release the unspoken truth, there is so much apparently insane language concerning "infinite" processes: an infinite war, infinite justice, infinite retribution. This was sustained in George Bush's terrifying address to the Congress. There he declared, for the first time perhaps since Hitler's announcement of the Third Reich, a kind of state of perpetual emergency. He announced a new sort of war without aims or a foreseeable end, often to be fought in secret. Those not with the United States and Britain in the War were declared to be against them and allied with terrorists. This is a license for totalitarianism, and already, for the sake of fighting a vague conflict explicitly projected to last almost forever, it has become unquestionable that basic legal procedures and respect for people's privacy should be suspended.

How does this unspeakably bizarre turn of events relate to the idea of a war of civilizations, which has also been in the air?

Within the post-Hunsinger perspective, Islam has been seen as the other, outside the Western legacy and somewhat immune to Western post-enlightenment values. However, Islam should be rather thought of as both other and yet not other.

Revived Islamic civilization is in some ways a challenge to the Western secular state, but it is also much more like a rival twin than we care to imagine. Recent scholarship is showing just how Islamic the West itself has been ever since the twelfth century. When the University of Oxford was founded in the late twelfth century, some scholars there took over an essentially Islamic project for the experimental control of nature that was at first to do with optics and alchemy. The Cartesian turn to the subject, the idea of knowledge as detached representation of spatialized objects, the exposition of being as univocal, all have their long-term origin in, ironically, the oriental thought of Avicenna (Ibn Sina). To say, as many do, that Islam was only accidentally, and for only a time, the bearer of a Mediterranean civilization to which it was essentially alien is quite untrue. Even though philosophy was less easily assimilated within Islam than in Christendom, Avicenna and other philosophers were still concerned with "prophetology," or the nature of inspiration, and this profoundly inflected their rendering of Aristotelian and neoplatonic understandings of the soul. In this crucible, proto-modern ideas concerning subjectivity were forged and then handed over to the West.

In the year 1277, the Christian West reached its crisis: certain drastic edicts issued by the archbishops of Paris and Canterbury meant that it decided more or less to outlaw the common Hellenistic legacy of Aristotle fused with Neo-Platonism and blended with allegorical readings of the Hebrew Bible, which it shared with Islam, Judaism, and Byzantine. A common culture of mystical philosophy and theology, focused around analogy and ontological participation—which has tended to favor also social participation—was rendered impossible. The West went in one direction and Islam in another, since Islam too tended in this period further to outlaw this perspective. From now on Islam became a doctrinally orthodox, scriptural, and legalistic civilization to the exclusion of dialectics and mystical theology (apart from newly enhanced Sufistic tendencies).

The conventional view is that from then onward, the West became secular and Islam became theocratic. But that seems to me to be a half-truth. In fact, by abandoning the shared mystical outlook, Western Christian theology started to look more and more itself like Islamic orthodoxy; it started to read the Bible more like the Quran, allowing only the literal meaning, and construing that more narrowly than hitherto. The new stress in the fourteenth century that only God's will makes things true and right echoed earlier Islamic Kalam theology and some of the ideas of Al Ghazali. The West's attitude to evil, with, ironically, the Cathars safely defeated, started to become more Manichean, again taking over the unfortunate Iranian contamination of Islam and the primordial Zoroastrian tradition. But above all, in the political domain, the Islamic alliance of the absolute will of the Caliph linked to the will of Allah, and with the right to fight holy wars, is taken over by Christian thought. As earlier in Islam, so now also in the West, a merely *de facto* grounding of State sovereignty in absolute right to do what it likes is linked to its mediation of the will of God. Thus, the early Western nation-state started to fight holy wars within Christendom itself. Modern Islam and Christianity are not, after all, so dissimilar in certain ways.

What I want to suggest here is that theocratic notions of sovereignty are not simply something archaic within Islam that stands over against our Western modernity. In many ways theocratic notions are specifically modern in their positivity and formality (as Carl Schmitt indicated). Bush in a crisis has appealed to the supposed divine destiny of America, and it is modern Judaism that has lapsed into a statist, Zionist form.

There is now a terrible symbiosis arising between Zionism and the American Protestant and un-Christian literalistic reading of the Old Testament in the Puritan tradition, which equates Anglo-Saxondom with Israel. There is also an unfortunate tendency within contemporary theology to play down the Christian going beyond the law, which incoherently and anachronistically seeks a kind of alignment with post-biblical rabbinic law, as if this somehow had obviously more status for Christianity than Islamic law (even if we may well often find it to be nearer to Christian charity).

Meanwhile, Islamics of the Wahabist tendency to which bin Laden and his group belong, are themselves in some ways very modern. They are opposed to all iconic images and all aural manifestations of religion; they are urban, middle-class, fanatically puritanical; they are prepared to compromise the Islamic tradition insofar as it stands firmly against usury; and they are thoroughly in love with technology. Bin Laden in the desert with his gun is surely an American anti-hero: perhaps a sectarian first cousin to Joseph Smith. For it is not an accident that the Mormons—that archetypal American sect, according to Harold Bloom—express such explicit kinship with Islam.

But of course the West and Islam have construed the legacy of theocratic sovereignty in very different ways. The West has invented a secular sphere that is neutral and unmystical: the sphere of a pure balance of power, whose control is still, nevertheless, in the last analysis divinely sanctioned. Strict Islam knows only an expression of sovereignty through sacred laws. I don't much care for either variant. But on what basis can one decide that an Islamic sacral state, especially if it took a more sophisticated form than that envisaged by the Taliban, is not permissible? And in reality our apparent concern for women and others persecuted by these unpleasant people is fantastically hypocritical: as recently as 1998 the Californian oil giant UNOCAL, with the backing of the United States, was trying to enlist Taliban support in building an oil pipeline through Afghanistan from the former Soviet territories to the north.

The only possible basis for refusing the legitimacy of an Islamic state would be if Islamic men, and especially Islamic women, themselves decide that they no longer want such a thing. This decision would amount, though, to a new construal of Islam, and a redefinition of Islamic community apart from the sanction of coercive law. Islam would perhaps then have to proceed in a more Sufistic direction. It is certainly not in principle up to the West to decide, but I don't think that the West as it is presently constituted can tolerate this forbearance and all its implications.

Yet properly speaking, this is a debate that Islam should be able to conduct with itself without external impediment. Such a debate could even help us in the West to realize that genuine religious pluralism and tolerance means far more than merely respecting the private beliefs of the individual. Communities also are collective realities that we should respect, within certain bounds of discrimination.

A perpetual war against terrorism can be seen as an effort to resolve the crisis of State sovereignty in the face of globalization. Since in a real sense both the Western and the different Islamic state forms face the same crisis, one can go further and say that both terrorism and counter-terrorism, which are already commingled and indistinguishable, are attempts to resolve this crisis.

But there is also another aspect to the crisis of globalization. This is economic rather than political. The West, especially the United States, has expanded its economic hegemony since the end of the Cold War. Once there was no longer any need to pander to Third World regimes in order to counter Soviet influence, the United States, mostly supported by Europe, proceeded to set up economic structures that operated entirely in the West's own selfish interests more than ever before, with the result that global inequality has vastly increased, as has environmental damage, which is sometimes the direct result of U.S. intervention, as in Colombia at the present moment. These structures have included the liberalization of markets and the removal of all inhibitions on stock exchange speculation.

But now these hegemonic economic structures show signs of starting to implode. Supply has been outrunning demand; there has been overinvestment in computer technology, a possibly rash selling off of Western interests in older manufacturing, and an allowing of domestic shares and economically crucial information to get into the hands of people who are potentially enemies. The United States and Europe are consequently faced with a need to implement more internal regulation—but also with the specter of having already let things slip beyond their control.

The assumption has been that the market simply lines up with Western dominance. Now, however, we are beginning to see how a small number of hostile, politically motivated investors can reap devastating effects. September 11 was like a kind of chiasmus—a crossing over and reversal. During the 1990s, Western power became more and more abstracted and virtual in character, dominating the pathetically real and material lives of people in the South. Now suddenly the West is reduced to the Paleolithic. We saw that the abstract was still partly stored in two fragile standing totems with less resilience even than Neolithic standing stones. This still-fixed capital was simply knocked over. But meanwhile, in the face of the failure of Western information to stop this catastrophe, the terrorists, whoever they are, were manipulating information in order to seize the maximum abstract advantage.

Given the sheer convenience of war and military emergency to forces wishing to resolve the twin crises of Western sovereignty and Western capitalism, one has to ask to what extent these forces were, subconsciously or consciously, urging war before September 11? The current war is a war against terrorism we are told, which has suddenly become a global and immediate threat, though we were not generally told this before the catastrophe. And in fact there is much evidence that global terrorism has been recently in decline rather than to the contrary. Therefore, there is every reason to suspect that this war is not really a war against terrorism, but is rather a war potentially against multiple targets that is designed to ensure the continued legitimacy of the American State and the perpetuation of the neo-capitalist revolution of the 1980s.

Ever since January 2001 at the very least, crisis has surely been in the air. Bush withdrew from international agreements on ecology, weaponry, debt, and the pursuit of justice. Most ironically of all, he refused to acknowledge that any American could ever be a war criminal, thereby undercutting the legitimacy of international juridical procedures against someone like bin Laden. Meanwhile, communism in the East has been reemerging, anti-capitalism is reasserting itself in Western Europe, and under the banner of anti-globalization it is starting to coalesce with resistance movements in the South. Right along the Atlantic seaboard from Britain to Portugal there has been fury at America in the face of economically disastrous flooding probably linked with global warming and scarcely reported in the United States at all. In Great Britain the

Conservative Party faces extinction, and public opinion, moving to the left of Tony Blair, now favors more state intervention and action to drastically reduce corporate greed.

More seriously still, the socialist President of Venezuela (and friend of Fidel Castro), Hugo Chavez, has been flexing considerable political muscle as against the general failure of neoliberal regimes in his subcontinent. In the face of American and European opposition, he has encouraged the OPEC countries to sustain a middling level of oil prices where market demand would have forced a drop. This, obviously, has implications for Middle Eastern politics, and for the United States hegemony in that region.

Suddenly then, American and capitalist hegemony looks surprisingly fragile—although of course this should not be exaggerated. But it must appear fragile enough to powerful right-wing think tanks, who are in any case prone to apocalyptic scenarios. There will seem to them to be a frightening possible convergence of a protesting South America, Islamic nations rich in oil, revivified communism, and a Europe more wobbly and more prone to anti-U.S. sentiment than at any time since World War II.

Finally, the United States is itself an increasingly unstable polity. Cultural and political shifts in South America would have ripple effects among Latino populations in the U.S.; low election turnouts reveal a vastly indifferent and often alienated population; an eighteenth century constitution produces constant stasis and deadlock that cannot even deliver normal modern state infrastructures and welfare provisions that form a buffer against dangerous discontents of the underprivileged; the cultural gap between coastal and middle America could erupt into something serious; edgy rival oligarchies do not trust democracy to deliver security, but believe they have to manipulate the outcome of elections (as occurred in November 2000).

In the face of this potential hydra, it is clear that the U.S. establishment and the Bush administration are deeply divided and inconsistent. Isolationism has been one response, yet it has been clear to many that this is a very risky course. Those advocating a more aggressive and interventionist strategy on the assumption that American supreme power must never be challenged (a doctrine initiated by Madeleine Albright: the Democratic Party is as guilty as anyone else in all this) were delivered, by good fortune or otherwise, a supreme present on September 11.

Not only could national security from henceforward override democracy without question, but also the immediate threat of terror for the moment pulled Europe, Russia, South America, moderate Arab States, and China in line behind the United States. They have been enlisted with varying degrees of enthusiasm and begrudgingness behind a military action that will assault all those who resist the sway of the global market allied to police deployments to ensure that the free market and flow of information are not themselves used against the market and against this flow. In addition, a new unity of Americans, rich and poor, behind a ludicrously sentimental and inappropriately personalized patriotism, has been put into place. The fractures lurking ever since November 2000 are for the moment sealed, although any manifest failure of "the War" (as is more or less inevitable) will cause them to appear again with a vengeance.

There can be no doubt that at the very center of this strange and multiple conflict stands oil. Detailed and objective analyses by *Le Monde* and others show that what is currently being played out in Afghanistan is not a war against terrorism, nor a response to the attack upon the twin towers, but *le nouveau grand jeu de Kipling*. Multiple interests are trying to seize control of one of the largest pools of natural resources in the world in the former Soviet and largely Islamic territories to the north around the Caspian Sea. There is also an attempt by the gulf States to reestablish the ancient silk route to China, which would link these states all the way to Islamic Chinese communities. Hence, the economic-political stakes are enormous and also deeply confused. I have already mentioned that the U.S. initially sought to cooperate with the Taliban in building oil pipelines. But they proved far too unreliable partners; in particular, they could not control bin Laden.

It has become instead imperative for the U.S. to lay oil and gas pipelines through a more manipulable Afghanistan. In the face of a rebellious OPEC, the U.S. badly needs a new pool of tame oil suppliers besides the increasingly edgy Saudis (whose own Islamic brutality goes unmentioned by the U.S.). At the same time, this new North-South resource-route will cut through the middle of the potential Islamic East-West trade and political axis.

Oil therefore is the clear focus of a crisis that has nonetheless wider political and economic dimensions of the kind that I have described. It is certain that war in Afghanistan was already planned before September 11, which may even have been a preemptive strike by some Islamic forces or other. There are also unanswered questions about the somewhat implausible tardiness of the U.S. reaction to the terror-strike at every level.

One does not, however, need to suppose any sort of conspiracy theory for my main thesis to stand, even if this cannot as yet be ruled out. Reactions to September 11 in the United States government were various and variously motivated: even George Bush kept on changing his tune, especially as between a police and a military response. However, one does have to ask why so universally and immediately this was compared to Pearl Harbor, when, after all, it was only a terrorist attack, albeit a horrendously successful one. One man destroying New York with a nuclear bomb would still be a criminal and not a warrior. One treats all warriors with more respect than criminals. Usually one avoids seeing terrorists as engaged in war, because that is just how they want to be seen, and starting a war is generally their aim. In the annals of terrorism, al Qaeda has now been uniquely successful: the West has played their game at every turn, even if it is also a game they *wish* to play.

Supposedly a war is being pursued against bin Laden, and yet it doesn't seem likely that if he were ever caught he would be treated in accord with the Geneva conventions. If terrorism were *really* the issue, then much the safer thing would be to stick to the discourse of crime and the practice of regular policing and due juridical process. Anything else, as the bitter experience of the French and British shows, only tends to increase the support of terrorist groups and legitimate their operations. As Ken Surin has pointed out, the ethical evil of terrorism is that, more than certain modes of conventional warfare, it directly instrumentalizes human life. But this means that any response that tends to do the same thing is uniquely ineffective: in losing the ethical high ground, it *also* tends to lose the strategic high ground. This, as we see, has already happened to America in Afghanistan where, as elsewhere ever since 1945 (and even before), it has deliberately used the massacre and the disabling of civilians (e.g., the use of cluster bombs) as a primary military weapon. This is not even collateral damage; it is the state terror of a secular liberalism, cumulatively on a par with the Holocaust and the Gulag.

The oft-repeated analogy here with medieval wars against pirates is not really right. Pirates in the Middle Ages were in many cases treated like criminals in a period in which war itself was seen as a kind of police action—at least justified war. And because pirates were mostly afloat, they were a kind of isolatable anti-state in any case. Terrorists, by contrast, live like criminals in the pores of society and cannot readily be reached by military means. There cannot be a just war against terrorists, because they are neither a sovereign state, nor do they necessarily represent a true rebel cause that will justify talking about civil war in some sense. The U.S. in effect admits this, since "terrorist suspects" are not to be treated as prisoners of war. Yet, as the enemies of sovereignty, they are not to be accorded criminal proceedings *either*. Instead, they can be shot in secret, watched by "relatives of victims." This is barbarism well beyond public execution that witnesses to the pure objectivity of law. This is state-sanctioned blood-feuding. And to deny the categories of either warrior or criminal is to reduce suspects to sub-humanity; it is to deny the *imago dei* in them.

Were this a war against terrorists, it would not be a just one. This is primarily because it would be an insanely "disproportionate" action *and* because mainly those not responsible for September 11 have been attacked. But it is hard to believe that this is not evident to the powers that be. So one must rather assume that the "war against terrorism" is a cover for other operations and purposes of the kind that I have described.

Unfortunately, the chance for the Western state and the Western market to ensure its continued hegemony in the face of dire threat is also the chance of specifically modern Islamic fanaticism. Bin Laden's followers, among them those who in other circumstances would deplore him, now increase by the hour. Soon he may be a hero for more than simply Islam.

A war against a civilization cannot be won. And Islam could prove to be more united, less decadent, and more resilient than the West. Prophecy is perilous, but we may have reached the point where the only way out of a catastrophe that could potentially destroy the West is to abandon our global idolatrous worship of sacralized absolute sovereignty and its empty pursuit of power, in West and East alike.

Both empty secular power and arbitrary theocratic power, in their secret complicity, show us no way forward. Neither enlightenment nor "fundamentalism" can assist us in our new plight. Instead we need to consider again the biblical and Platonic-Aristotelian metaphysical legacy common to Christianity, Judaism, and Islam. We should ponder ways in which this legacy may provide us with a certain area of common vision and practice, while at the same time respecting social and cultural spaces for exercised difference.

Such a common vision would eschew all idolization of formal power, whether in the case of individual "rights" or of absolute State sovereignty. Instead it would trust that human wisdom can imitate, imperfectly but truly, something of an eternal order of justice. A shared overarching global polity would embody this imitation in continually revisable structures dedicated to promoting the common good insofar as this can be agreed upon. It would also embody this imperfection through the maximum possible dispersal and deflection of human power.

9

September 11 and the Ethics of Violence

Jorge Secada

I

On September 11 thousands of innocent human beings were murdered; they were culpably and cruelly killed. Those murders were particularly abhorrent because they manifested a willingness to unjustifiably instrumentalize other human beings, to use their actual or threatened suffering and death as a means to further ends. This repugnant disposition is essential to terrorism. However, the willingness to unjustifiably use or excuse human suffering by appeal to further ends is something common to many more people than to just those usually and rightly called terrorists.

Some seek to justify the acts of September 11 by appealing to laudable ends they help bring about. Others might not go all the way and justify the acts, but think rather that somehow that appeal makes them less culpable. This latter reaction is more common across the world than many in the U.S. seem to realize.

Some ends are clearly better than others. Punishing the United States for its foreign policies, helping to ensure the purity of Islam, and subverting globalization are among the ends cited with reference to the World Trade Center massacre. Terrorists both here and elsewhere in the world have appealed to various utopias, to justice, individual freedom, collective liberty, democracy, or other such goods, as ends that justify the slaughter and suffering they have caused. And these same ends are constantly appealed to by those who act in the name of states carrying out monstrous acts of violence against the innocent.

The connection between the means and the end, and the evidence with which that connection is known are of course morally relevant. But this should not obscure the fact that the slaughter and suffering of the innocent is an evil, an evil for which those who freely cause it are responsible. And this responsibility will need to be discharged, under pain of moral guilt.

Appeals to ends and to greater goods have to take into account the magnitude of the wrong committed, the connection between it and the justifying good, and the certainty with which this connection is known. To put it concisely, it must be inevitable that either the evil considered as means or a clearly greater evil resulting from the failure to enact these means will occur, and this must be known to be so with the utmost practical certainty. This is particularly the case when we are talking about the monstrous evil of slaying an innocent child. The horrors of war are such that this demand can only be met after the most careful, clearheaded, and humble reflection.

Differences in the ends with which terrorists and other criminals and evildoers seek to justify their doings might in fact have bearing on the moral worth of these agents. Some may be deemed perverse through and through, while others are rightly deemed to be misguided and morally confused. But the evil actions will gain no justification *solely* from appeal to a great good.

Consequential reasoning does have a place in moral deliberation. Sometimes one is confronted by inevitable evil, whatever one does. In those circumstances one must of course opt for the lesser evil. And though the killing of an innocent child is an evil, it is clear that the death of two children is worse than the death of one. However, before one embarks on a course of action that one knows will lead to the death of an innocent child, one had better be certain that there is a clearly worse outcome one is thereby stopping.

In the plane that fell over Pennsylvania on September 11, three passengers decided to confront their hijackers. By doing so they probably brought about the immediate death of some innocent hostage, a defenseless child or flight attendant, and caused in fact the crash of the plane and the death of all the other passengers. We know that one of these passengers agonized over his decision, a decision that required enormous courage, not so much I believe on account of the physical dangers he faced but rather on account of the monstrous ethical situation in which he found himself. Once he knew what the facts were, he and his companions chose to stop the terrorists from carrying out their designs. Over Pennsylvania courageous and clearheaded persons recognized the inevitability of certain outcomes, all monstrous but one clearly much more so than the others, and then successfully acted to stop the worse one. They did not bring about the situation that confronted them, nor were they in the end at all to blame for any of those deaths.

Some actions have both good and bad consequences, and they may sometimes be justified. Some justified actions can be described in ways that are morally contradictory: the saving of a child may be the killing of a child, when we are referring to surgery required to separate twins who if not separated will both die. Nonetheless, the moral demands on those who deliberate with a view to pursuing such actions are clear: the inevitability of some evil outcome and the commensurabilty between the contemplated evil and the good it brings about must be known clearly and with as much certainty as is demanded by the moral risks that one is confronting. And one must always bear in mind in such deliberation that it is incomparably better to be the victim of an injustice than to be the one who perpetrates it.

It is easy to fail to see the force of these constraints when we dehumanize the victims of our actions and refer to them as casualties or the untargeted victims of collateral damage. Terrorists might consider their victims martyrs, contributors to the greater good.

Unfortunately, I cannot have solidarity with people who speak of "us" being hit on September 11 and the "us" being referred to is the United States of America. This collective entity, the U.S., is pretty low on the list of entities that suffered that day. It comes after all the persons who were killed, all the persons who were left orphans or who lost a brother, and after all the widows, bereaved parents, and mourning friends. It even comes after much more significant groups who were victimized that day: humanity, civilization. I cannot have solidarity with a manner of speech that has as a direct consequence the dehumanizing of those events, and that, not surprisingly, therefore paves the road for easy and culpable reactions in reply to them.

Reference to states and other groups might be important when we analyze those events, when we try to explain them. But we must bear in mind that speaking in those terms covers up the moral facts, that 4,000 innocent people were killed, that many, many thousands more have been left to suffer.

The frame of mind disposed to contemplate the undertaking of great evil without the strenuous deliberation that it demands is common to terrorists, many who act in the name of states, and many more who irresponsibly go along with them.

II

Let us now move on to consider one other way in which the events of September 11 are characterized: they were not simple murders; they were instead acts of war. This is the way officials of the United States government have chosen to characterize those events and, consequently, their response to them.

Perhaps the members of the U.S. government are unwitting in their offer of a moral justification for at least some terrorists who can now claim to be exonerated from blame as combatants in a war following the orders of their leaders. Even if a war is unjustified, as most are for all the participating states and certainly all are for at least one of them, we should not treat the combatants as simple murderers. Plain combatants are not criminals.

Officials of the U.S. government are certainly not unwitting in the power this characterization gives them when dealing with their targets, who, it has been suggested by the U.S. Attorney General, do not deserve the protections afforded by the U.S. Constitution. Their enemies can now be treated as war criminals engaged in crimes against humanity. They can be held without the proper protections of law and tried summarily by military courts. What is needed in order to generalize this treatment to all terrorists, in spite of the fact that in war simple combatants benefit from protections not afforded to murderers, is easy enough: deny all of them the status of plain combatants and treat them all as instigators, planners, and leaders.

It is appropriate here to note an equivocation in the way the word "war" is used. We speak of a war against drugs or crime. Mary Baldwin College or the University of Virginia may decide to engage in a war against laziness and sloth. And it is not uncommon for nutritionists to fight wars against fat, salt, and sugar. In this sense, war is any struggle between opposing principles or against something undesirable.

This warring is to be distinguished from the use of armed force by a state against another state, or by organized and effective parties within a state, all of which claim to act with the legitimacy and purpose of states, against each other. It is of course only war in this second sense that could justify the acts of September 11, mitigate their evil, or justify responding to them with the armed violence that characterizes war, as opposed to, for instance, the use of force called for in the pursuit of common criminals.

The reference to states is crucial. Wars can be carried out only by those who reasonably claim to act with the legitimacy of states and who can, by and large, muster the support of at least some sizeable portion of those who are that state. Individuals as such, the citizens of a state, whether acting alone or in gangs, do not have the authority to promulgate laws, to enforce them, to collect taxes, to wage wars, or to do any of the things that can be legitimately done only by states. An individual, however powerful, cannot engage in war solely on his or her authority: neither a bank robber who robs a bank using an atom bomb, nor a mobster who imposes his will on the population at large using a gang of thousands, are engaging in war. And the reason is that they do not have nor can even claim with any semblance of plausibility the mantle of legitimacy that belongs only to states.

It is precisely the usurping of such authority when carrying out grossly unjust wars that is thought to justify the harsh and special treatment of those who commit such crimes against humanity. Turning a criminal into a war criminal cannot therefore be a mere matter of expediency or semantics. It needs to be justified.

Things in the world are very different now than they were just a few decades ago. It may be that nations are in the process of evolving into something else or disappearing altogether. It may be that humanity is moving toward very different forms of social organization. However, what is not in any danger of extinction is the authority that nature bestows on a commonwealth so that it can aim at the common good. And war, insofar as it might be relevant in this context, is something that happens only under such authority, whether legitimate or merely plausibly claimed.

Attending only to this minimal but necessary condition, I do not see how the acts we are talking about could be deemed acts of war. The alleged perpetrators, Osama bin Laden and his gang, have not even presumed to act under such authority, nor could they claim it with any plausibility. Some of them have made reference to a "holy war," though only in response to attacks by the U.S., not as justification for the slaughter of September 11. Moreover, it is unclear that there is plausibility to their claim to have authority to declare holy war in the name of Islam against the U.S. and the Western powers. Nor is it even clear that such holy war carried out without the authority of states is in fact war.

On the other hand, the Taliban government of Afghanistan has not even been accused of being the perpetrator of those acts, but of giving shelter to criminals who did bring them about.

So it appears that the criminal acts of September 11 were just that and not acts of war. They were not acts carried out, either in fact or even just allegedly, under the authority of a commonwealth or state.

In any case, for a war to be justified, certain conditions must be met. I propose that those include the following:

1. the war must be carried out under the authority of a legitimate government;
2. it has to be in pursuance of a just objective (such as, for example, self-defense, the aiding of the innocent, the assisting of allies engaged in just wars), and it must be pursued only to the extent of securing its just objective;
3. it has to be waged so as to restrict the harm it brings about (that is, the suffering and killing that it causes, regardless of who is the target) to the minimum required to secure its just objective;
4. it has to originate in the most certain knowledge of the facts, including those that refer to the connection between the means (the use of armed force) and the end (the just objective), and also those that refer to the causes and objectives themselves; and
5. it has to be undertaken only after all peaceful alternatives have been explored for as long as they may have a reasonable chance of making war unnecessary, and so long as the objectives that justify the war do not thereby become impossible to attain, or the harm of not waging war outweighs the harm of waging it.

Soldiers may be justified in their acts even though the state for which they fight is unjustified in its war and their rulers are in fact guilty of murder. Soldiers and citizens may reasonably trust their leaders. Though we all have a duty to establish the justice of the wars we collectively undertake, still we cannot be blamed for relying on the judgment of our legitimate rulers, particularly when there is the appearance of justice, the issues are complex, and the facts are difficult for us to determine directly.

Justified war is inevitable evil, evil that is justified on account of a greater good. When deliberating about whether to engage in war or not, rulers must keep in mind that "what is done in war is most cruel and atrocious—slaughter, burning, devastation" so that "it is not lawful to start war on account of just any injury" nor to do so recklessly and without certain knowledge of the relevant facts.[1] And again, they must also bear in mind that it is always better to suffer an injustice than to commit it.

States that shelter criminals might give cause for a just war against them. The just objectives of that war would be to capture the criminals or perhaps to stop the offending states from sheltering other criminals in the future. But in order for the war to be just, one would have to not only know the facts, but also be fairly certain of the connection between the use of armed violence and these just ends, that the benefits derived from attaining these ends clearly outweigh the suffering that will be inevitably caused by war, and that there is a necessity to pursue them under pain of allowing a greater evil.

Having heard Secretary Powell maintain that one of the objectives of the bombing of Afghanistan was to make the supporters of the Taliban regime understand that such support would only bring suffering to them, and President Bush say that the time for negotiating was long past as the bombing was underway, one is reasonably inclined to view these acts of violence as illegitimate and criminal responses to criminal terrorist acts, even if one does distinguish between the moral worth of the agents involved. There appears to be reliable indication that the duty to deliberate was not discharged by those who decided the U.S. response to the events of September 11.

III

One consequence of viewing the acts of September 11 as simple murder is that the motivations, the worldview of those who committed them, are seen to be unimportant when it comes to evaluating the morality of the acts themselves. They may, of course, be criminally important. They may be useful in order to stop those who engage in these crimes from engaging in other similar acts, or in order to apprehend them and bring them to justice. Or they may be of interest to those who wish to explore the psychology of evil.

It is important to note here that there is no common motivation for terrorism, just as there is no common motivation for crime and murder.

I am Peruvian. Particularly since this was for a very long time the only piece of news from Peru to reach the U.S., some of you may know that roughly between 1980 and 1995 Peruvians were the victims of terrorism. I will simplify a bit here and concentrate on the most effective of the terrorist groups that were active in my country during those years, the Shining Path, the Partido Comunista del Perú-Sendero Luminoso, a criminal gang with its own brand of Marxist-inspired thought.

The Shining Path carried out a campaign of terror in which more than 30,000 people died in their hands or in the hands of the state forces who were combating them. Shining Path members would go into villages, small villages of just a few hundred inhabitants, where they would round up the mayor and other public officials, take them to the village square, try them, and then execute them in horrible and very cruel ways, forcing all the villagers, including the relatives and friends of their victims, to watch. They did this over and over again.

Eventually the Shining Path took its terror to the cities. The peak of this part of their campaign came with a large bomb explosion in a densely populated commercial area of Lima. Many people were killed in that explosion, many were maimed, and many more suffered the loss of loved ones.

The terrorists never had the support of Peruvians, and they were never more than a small band of a few thousand activists and supporters. But as a result of their activities, hundreds of thousands of Peruvians suffered. Many left their Andean villages and went to the big cities, terrified of the Shining Path and of the forces of the state. In the early 1980s the army would go into areas where the terrorists were active and kill everybody there because they thought that was the only way to get rid of the Shining Path. It did not take the Shining Path very long to decide to be most active in the places where the population most resisted them.

What do the Shining Path terrorists have in common with the terrorists that we are talking about today? The brief answer is not a lot.

Unlike most Islamic terrorists, many members of the Shining Path were women, young women. In fact women were the most active and belligerent terrorists in Peru.

If you planted a Shining Path cell in Fort Lauderdale and gave its members $10,000 a month to live there with their families so that in two years' time they would carry out their mission and kill themselves flying into a building, I am sure that one year, eleven months and twenty-nine days after they had been planted, they would go underground and start rationalizing why the "objective historical conditions" were not quite ripe for their mission yet. They would not fly a plane into a building.

Members of the Shining Path were mostly lower middle-class Peruvians driven to criminal despair by their unyielding misery and poverty. Though fanatical, their fanaticism was not religious. Their motivations were very different from those of the men who flew into the Pentagon or the World Trade Center. Their aims were also different. They believed in a quasi-Marxist science of history, in social Darwinism and social engineering.

They did have, however, one thing in common with the terrorists of September 11. They had a justificatory rationale that was part of their motivation: the instrumentalization of the innocent in pursuit of higher goals. Some good end justified using people, their lives, and their suffering, as means. They engaged in a calculus of enormous moral risk without the minimal consideration for their victims.

Another thing that the Shining Path terrorists shared with Osama bin Laden and al Qaeda is a hatred for the United States government and many of its policies, and perhaps also for much of U.S. society. In fact, this is connected to how they justified many of their murdering activities: as retribution or punishment for the wrongdoing of the United States. U.S. citizens should reflect on the sources of this common hatred. For it is a hatred that, widely differing in degree and kind, extends well beyond those who are terrorists or who support terrorists, and is a source of much of the basic moral confusion expressed by those who are inclined to view the events of September 11 as less or more understandable responses to U.S. foreign policy.

Some people in California and in Sweden and other places in the U.S. and Europe described the Shining Path criminals as carrying out a war of liberation in Peru. And they supported them financially. Some well-meaning persons may still believe they were right to do so. Lori Berenson, a confused and pathetic young woman from New York, went to join one of those groups and persists to this day in speaking of the racial and social differences in Peru in the context of her activities and the activities of other terrorists. She is the very image of ignorant and arrogant U.S. citizens in the eyes of many Peruvians, both poor and wealthy.

IV

Those acting in the name of states can of course commit acts that are morally analogous to those committed by the terrorists in New York, Washington, and over Pennsylvania. People acting in the name of states can instrumentalize human beings and use their threatened or actual suffering in the pursuit of laudable goals. Secretary Powell has provided us with an example in the context of the events that we are now examining. And we know that people acting in the name of states can murder and that they can be accomplices to murder.

Reflecting on the events of September 11 and state terrorism, and being Peruvian, I cannot ignore that this date is indeed infamous and not just on account of those recent monstrous acts. All my life I will remember what I was doing on September 11, 1973. Just as I will also remember what I was doing on that date in 2001.

It is disturbing that so few even among intelligent and informed persons in the U.S. knew of the infamy of that date before the recent events. On September 11, 1973, the Chilean military, with the backing of the U.S. government, killed President Salvador Allende. That is the day that Allende died defending democracy in Chile.

One of President Allende's murderers, at least as much a murderer himself as the Taliban share in the responsibility for the slaughter in Manhattan, walks to this day the streets of Washington, D.C., and New York City. He is interviewed on television and asked to give advice about what the U.S. should do in response to the recent bombings.

This is outrageous, because it makes us, insofar as we are willing to accept it and not denounce it, either with knowledge of the facts or through culpable and comfortable ignorance, share in the dehumanizing mentality of murder and terrorism. Thousands of innocents were killed in Chile. Thousands were tortured and disappeared, leaving innocent children behind never to know for certain the fate of their parents. So what? A communist government was stopped. What if General Pinochet made fun of common graves, citing the efficiency of the state? What if he had Minister Letelier and his secretary, a U.S. citizen, killed with a car bomb in Dupont Circle? That probably served the interests of the U.S. And maybe if that communist government hadn't been stopped, more people would have died. And so on.

For a utilitarian calculus of this sort to go through, one has to examine carefully countless possible alternatives and their probabilities; one has to be fairly certain of the truth of numerous counterfactuals. It is obvious that those acting in the name of the U.S. government and of the Chilean military only had the certainty and concern of criminals.

A factory in Sudan is bombed, and eventually and quietly it is admitted that it was not a chemical weapons factory and that a mistake had been made. This happened not very long ago. And I recall having heard colleagues, academics with informed and critical minds, state that they trusted that their government knew what it was doing and that the German engineers who were denying that that was a weapons factory almost immediately after the bombing were not to be trusted.

Was a lesson learned then? How long can one go on pleading ignorance? Can one continue to give those acting on behalf of the government the benefit of the doubt when so much is at stake, when one is running the risk of being the negligent accomplice to murder? Track records are very important here, and they are not at all encouraging.

Over the years I have become very distrustful of the media, and also of people speaking on behalf of governments. I do not at this time truly know who is alive and responsible for the murders of September 11. I am not willing to trust those in power when, given their track record, they are not themselves willing to make evidence available and rest content with an appeal to the fact that they are on the right side, that their goals and ends are my own (supposing they were). No, we will have to wait. Perhaps after a few years, we will start to know what was truly going on here.

The desire to understand others who do not share our points of view, to learn about how we are perceived by those who are distant in mind and space from us, is a healthy and encouraging desire. It should neither confuse us about the nature of the events of September 11, nor make us lose sight of the duty we have as citizens of states that carry out acts of monstrous violence and evil to find out the facts as best we can, to think carefully through the arguments and the reasoning, and then to do what is in our legitimate power to stop injustice and to discharge our own individual responsibility for the acts of our governments.

And it should also serve as an opportunity for self-examination, for self-criticism, and for humility. Moral deliberation is not best served by pride and self-affirmation. When the stakes are so high, the risk of culpable arrogance should be strenuously avoided. Again, it is far better to be the victim of terrorism than to be a murderer, just as it is better to err on the side of generosity and love than to share in the instrumentalizing and dehumanizing mentality of terrorists.

As human beings alive in these dark and enlightened times, we should do our best so that the cost of learning to accept and live with one another will not be counted in the thousands and millions of lives and in the terrible suffering of the innocent. Here in the U.S. we should ensure that healthy confidence in one's own beliefs goes along with true respect for those who believe differently. Among states none is so much better than the other that it only has to teach and guide but not to learn and follow. When it comes to deciding the future of humanity, we are all equal partners in a common journey.[2]

10

"Dealing in Straight Power Concepts"
Justice and the Use of Force

Kenneth Surin

> *We have 50 percent of the world's wealth, but only 6.3 percent of its population...In this situation we cannot fail to be the object of envy and resentment...Our real task in the coming period is to devise a pattern of relationships which will allow us to maintain this position of disparity...We should cease to talk about the raising of the living standards, human rights, and democratization. The day is not far off when we are going to have to deal in straight power concepts. The less we are then hampered by idealistic slogans, the better.*
>
> U.S. STATESMAN GEORGE KENNAN, IN 1948[1]

How do we respond to the acts of those who, by virtue of their perpetration of these actions, seemingly belong to a political, religious, or moral universe that is starkly incompatible with ours? How do we respond to the intolerable, given that the crime that took place on September 11 was monstrous and irrational? The hallmark of terrorism is that its agents signal by what they do their resolve to have no limits placed on their conduct. As Dostoyevsky noted, the terrorist's *raison d'etre* is encompassed in that most succinct of formulas: "Everything is possible." Nothing is beyond the pale for the terrorist, and while grief, sadness, and indignation are inextricable parts of any response to the events of September 11, an act so palpably unjust necessarily poses the question of how justice is to confront injustice, of how justice is to confront the intolerable.

Justice can be neutralized or subverted in the circumstances of its dispensation, and while these circumstances can be ignored and overlooked, the claim of justice itself is absolute and unnegotiable. For if any negation of the claims of justice is rendered absolute, and justice is thereby forced to absent itself, then truth can only witness to injustice, to fanaticism and irrationality.[2] Truth therefore calls for the irreducible presence of justice. So the question necessarily presents itself: How is justice to be embodied in our responses to the crime of September 11? If justice were not fundamentally embodied in these responses, our responses would themselves partake of the disorder that defines the initial situation of injustice. By not being in justice, these responses would not be in the truth.[3] Truth is thus the force that counters the constitutive nondecidability that lies at the heart of falsity and injustice. If this nondecidability should prevail on a decisive enough scale, the person engaged in the pursuit of truth and justice would not know which processes, constitutive of this pursuit, he or she would have to be involved in precisely as a condition of living in truth and in justice. As such, truth is the *sine qua non* of any materialization of the principles of justice. To live in truth is to live in justice, and vice versa.

But justice is not an abstract ideal order, an order of the kind implicit in the viewpoint (say) of those American constitutionalists of the so-called "original intent" school who would have us believe that any constitutionally enshrined principles of justice are timeless and immutable.[4] Nor is justice, in its more tangible dimensions, the exclusive province of police officers and judges. Bringing any principles of justice to their point of realization requires that attention be given to political circumstances. Politics is something like an irremovable condition for justice's constitution as *this* or *that* event of justice. For the truth of justice, if it is to be embodied, can only be manifested in a context indelibly marked by the particularities of power, and these particularities are perforce always political. The truth of justice is therefore irreducibly the possible truth of a political standpoint.[5] Truth cannot be separated from politics. However, when truth is applied to a political standpoint, it always has to be qualified by the prefix "possible." For truth is what breaks into and interrupts the seemingly undifferentiated continuity of life (a continuity permeated by the nondecidability that is falsity's defining mark, and that *a fortiori* conduces to the absence of justice), just as it disrupts the collective fantasies that underlie and make possible the seamless continuity of everyday life.

The truth, as the event of this disruption of the (politically inaugurated) continuity of life, as the power that counters life's (politically sustained) nondecidability, is always a "point of exception" (the phrase is Alain Badiou's). Truth is an always-specific series of operations on (political) reality's pervasive nondecidability, or where the question of justice is involved, on reality's propensity to render undecidable the basis for distinguishing adequately between justice and injustice. The quality that defines truth–and this is a quality that *eo ipso* also characterizes justice–is thus the quality of a singularity, a singularity that does not cohere with the (politically instituted) continuity of life.[6] This is a singularity in which a specific operation or amalgam of operations establishes the basis for an event of justice by bringing to the point of decidability a particular historical or political process that hitherto had eluded, or been bypassed by, the political forces that make effective the various structures of decidability. Politics thus establishes the "beingness" of truth and justice, if one wants to put it in a Heideggerian idiom.

This operation or set of operations, whose name is truth, does not produce automatically, and hence cannot guarantee, its own mode of actualization, that is, it cannot of itself banish the historical and political conditions, whatever they may be, that serve to preempt its realization as a truth-operator. When this happens, and these preemptive political and historical conditions are active, nondecidability comes to prevail. Untruth prevails, and justice is absent. The truth-operator and its encompassing regime therefore require a politics capable of activating and sustaining them–quite simply, there is justice only when there is a politics able to banish the forces of nondecidability. This is why law and justice are inseparable from politics.

The politics of justice thus has to supervene the functioning of legal and political institutions: as indicated, the material interests, forms of power, and structures of governance lodged in these institutions and their agents, and the kinds of information and principles of understanding used to guide their decisions and actions, all affect the various regimes of decidability and nondecidability in ways that are crucially important for determining if an event of justice is to take place. In which case, the pursuit of justice after the atrocities of September 11 will involve a particular and distinctive configuration of political forces, one capable of weakening any regime of nondecidability that is perforce the negation of a real quest for justice. More about this later.[7]

But if the truth of justice is the truth of an always particular event, and there can be many such events of truth and justice, what then of a truth that is taken to be all-encompassing, and possessing the ambition to be of the widest possible generality? The aftermath of September 11 has been full of these all-embracing generalizations, not just in the saturation coverage provided by the media, or in George W. Bush's vapid declamations about "the evildoers," but also in Samuel Huntington's harebrained vision of a cataclysmic battle between the Christian West and Islam, as well as in bin Laden's curiously inverted "Huntingtonism," in which the clash is still very much one involving religious cultures, with an embattled Islam taking on the "crusader" West.[8] Truth that is taken to be comprehensive and insusceptible of pluralization, as opposed to being unreservedly singular, necessarily becomes the ground of terror. Terror exists when political agents and subjects act deliberately in ways that involve a renunciation of this perspective of singularity, in which truth (if it is truth) necessarily resides, and extend this perspective into one of a monolithic coherence, a monolithic conformity that silences or annihilates other perspectives (and the possible truths that inhere in them). The demands of the terrorists are precisely that–nonnegotiable. The nonnegotiability of the terrorists' demands, whether explicit or tacit in their actions, in turn elicits a parallel nonnegotiability in the responses to these actions (again something very evident in the reactions of the Bush administration to the attacks of September 11). This, if one thinks about it at a certain level of abstraction, is exactly the metaphysical core of the crime that took place on September 11. And this metaphysical core will *not* be present in any event in which a true and effective justice counters the injustice of the hijackers. Quite the opposite: the just response will have the quality of an absolute singularity, and it will *not* seek to possess the despotic coherence that marks the perspective of the terrorist. This despotic coherence is not, however, confined to the outlook of the terrorist. As has just been pointed out, a striking feature of the American media coverage of the response to the attacks of September 11 has been the unceasing orchestration of American patriotic sentiment. This dragooning of public opinion, in which the public has admittedly been a more than willing colluder (as my colleague Fredric Jameson pointed out in a teach-in, the war on Afghanistan *is* America's therapy after the catastrophe of September 11), has imposed a blanket uniformity of perspective on the brutal bombing of Afghanistan now taking place. The ensuing conformity has meant that the overwhelming majority of Americans these days no longer possess the capacity to be in the truth. The media-instigated fueling of the narcissism of any figure wearing the insignia of authority (so that even a Mick Jagger or Michael Jordan, celebrities though they may be, now have to genuflect before anyone appearing onstage in a fireman's uniform at a charity rock concert or pregame show); the erosion of any collective capacity to discern evasions of the truth palpably evident in the utterances of the politicians and their "spin doctors"; the effective impoverishment of the available forms of general response (nowhere more evident than in Bush's inability to characterize events except by resorting to such banalities as "the evildoers hate us good American folks," etc.)–all these have created a situation in which the real possibility of creating an event of justice has been greatly minimized if not eliminated altogether.

So what is the typical political orientation of a response whose form is that of an event of justice? What precisely is its quality as a singularity? Here it has to be acknowledged that the just response will achieve its singularity by recognizing the unavoidable particularity of interests that defines the initial situation in which justice is being sought. But while it grants the force and centrality of this unavoidable particularity of interests, the just response will embody as its principle of action the axiom that the just judgment gives no preference to any particular interest. If one is a humanist, this eschewing of the particularity of interest will involve judging an action from a horizon whose essential basis is that of a rigorously common humanity.[9] Hence, the perspective from which we judge Osama bin Laden will not be qualitatively different from the perspective used by us to judge Mother Teresa, and vice versa. To insert a materially significant qualitative difference into the respective perspectives from which a Mother Teresa and an Osama bin Laden are judged would be to incorporate the particularity of interests into the heart of our judgment-making, in this way rendering the ensuing judgments unjust. And even if one is not a humanist (and the argument of this paper does not presume any commitment to such a humanism), a perspective that eschews the particularity of interests will at the very least be one that engages subjects from the standpoint of a collectivity whose constitutive principle is that of a strict equality among all participants. Or more practically: from the standpoint of the requirements of justice, it would be unacceptable if the taking of an innocent Afghanistani life is not judged in terms of exactly the same principles as the murder of an innocent person who worked in the World Trade Center. To violate without justification this rigorous symmetry between the innocent Afghanistani and the innocent victim of the World Trade Center bombings is perforce to violate the equalitarian axiom that underlies any event of justice. It is to sanction an injustice. A putative quest for justice that uses means and instruments that are themselves unjust is self-vitiating. Innocent civilians killed and injured in the American and British bombings of Afghanistan because they happen to be "collateral damage" (in the dreadful nomenclature of the military spokesman) are willy-nilly victims of an injustice, unless there is some other absolutely compelling principle that overrides the above-mentioned equalitarian axiom. Is there such an overriding principle that permits the killing of innocent Afghanis in the U.S. government's quest for justice after the events of September 11?[10]

Philosophers of law may be exercised by the question of whether the hijackers (and their affiliates in al Qaeda and the Taliban) believed themselves to be fighting a total war in which there are no innocent parties, with the United States, having sustained an attack, now committing itself in retaliation to an equally total war against al Qaeda and the Taliban, and in so doing thinking itself permitted to kill civilians, as long as the latter deaths are the "unintended consequences" of military actions that have to be taken if this war of retaliation is to be won, and so forth.[11] It also could be argued by supporters of the U.S.'s military campaign that this campaign is not simply to be understood as an attempt to bring to justice those responsible for the atrocities of September 11 (though it is certainly that), but is, rather, an attempt, wide and enduring in scope, to diminish the possibility of a repetition of such acts of terrorism. If this were so, then the aim of the attacks on Afghanistan would be deterrence and prevention, a kind of anticipatory self-defense, and not the pursuit of justice purely and simply.

The appropriate reply to this claim—viz., the war in Afghanistan is an act of anticipatory self-defense and is not just an attempt to bring to justice those responsible for the attacks of September 11—is that any actions taken in the name of anticipatory self-defense, no matter how tenuously or firmly these measures may be tied to the events of September 11, are nonetheless themselves subject to the principles of justice. In fact, if the attacks of September 11 come under the remit of an event of justice in the sense specified here, then any military action taken to prevent a repetition of these attacks will itself come under the purview of that particular event of justice: If the attacks of September 11 are deemed to be criminal, and constitute the *prima facie* basis for an event of justice, then any measures taken to prevent a repetition of similar crimes will necessarily fall within the purview of that event of justice, the original crime constituting the specific occasion ("the cause") for the subsequent need to engage in this particular form of deterrence. Furthermore, these military measures, whether undertaken in the name of anticipatory self-defense or not, have *already* involved the slaughter of innocent Afghani civilians. This raises the necessary question, a question read *jus in bello,* of the legality and justice of the military campaign in Afghanistan.[12] Is the military campaign undertaken in response to the crimes of September 11 a response employing methods and instruments accordant with the principles of justice? In addition, the recourse to war in the name of deterrence and the pursuit of anticipatory self-defense poses a fundamental question, a question here read *jus ad bello,* namely, Who is entitled to determine whether a wrong, this or any other wrong, is so grievous as to warrant a resort to the use of force?[13] Who, here, is entitled to be in the legally and morally authoritative position of being able to determine what the just ends and means are in any response to the events of September 11?

A wide-ranging and complex debate, extending over many centuries, has taken place over these questions, typically under the rubric of just war theory. One of the positions in this debate–called "absolutism" in surveys of the array of the various positions taken in the debate–maintains that the deliberate killing of innocent civilians or noncombatants is never justified, even in anticipatory self-defense.[14] The U.S. government and its allies have had to resort to a consequentialist justification for their actions in Afghanistan. The massive aerial bombardment, involving the widespread use of cluster and "daisy cutter" incineration bombs, along with the displacement of civilian populations now facing starvation and severe winter hardships, are justified by the U.S. government on the grounds that the long-term consequences of "failing to defeat terrorism" clearly outweigh the destruction and harm caused by the war in Afghanistan. For the U.S. government and its supporters "the defeat of the evildoers" somehow makes the killing of unarmed Afghani civilians worthwhile, regrettable though the latter obviously is. For the U.S. government, therefore, there can be no plausible sense in which the killing of innocent noncombatants is impermissible *in itself,* since the U.S. clearly believes that the killing of innocent civilians is acceptable, morally and politically, as long as "the defeat of the evildoers" is one of the outcomes of the military campaign in Afghanistan. But what if it is a principle of justice that these military means cannot be justified by *any* putative consequences?[15] All this is rather abstract, so let me turn to the practical context in which the quest for justice on behalf of the victims of the attacks on the Pentagon and the World Trade Towers is to be undertaken.

In most reckonings of the motivations of the hijackers, and by extension those of the al Qaeda organization, there has been a pervasive tendency on the part of the media pundits and the politicians to single out one or two sources for the resentfulness that purportedly drove the hijackers to do what they did. So some take this source to be "America and all that it stands for–freedom, goodness, etc."; for others it is "the situation between Israel and Palestine"; for still others it is "the clash of civilizations"; and even "globalization" has been canvassed as a possible root-cause of the hijackers' rage and cruelty.

Certainly, U.S. policy toward Israel has been deeply flawed for decades, and the term "blowback" has appropriately been used to characterize the unintended consequences of the Reagan administration's decision to give military and financial support to the mujahedeen, thereby enabling the Taliban's rise to power. America has been conducting itself as an imperial power since the end of the Second World War, toppling democratically elected leaders and bombing the peoples of three continents in that time, and while there is no scope here for a detailed discussion of the political consequences of post-World War II American statecraft, the following passage from Chalmers Johnson's book *Blowback: The Costs and Consequences of American Empire* is strikingly prescient:

> Terrorism by definition strikes at the innocent in order to draw attention to the sins of the invulnerable. The innocent of the twenty-first century are going to harvest unexpected blowback disasters from the imperialist escapades of recent decades. Although most Americans may be largely ignorant of what was, and still is, being done in their names, all are likely to pay a steep price– individually and collectively– for their nation's continued efforts to dominate the global scene. Before the damage of heedless triumphalist acts and the triumphalist rhetoric and propaganda that goes with them becomes irreversible, it is important to open a new discussion of our global role during and after the Cold War.[16]

Johnson goes on to say:

> "Blowback" is shorthand for saying that a nation reaps what it sows, even if it does not fully know or understand what it has sown. Given its wealth and power, the United States will be a prime recipient in the foreseeable future of all the more expectable forms of blowback, particularly terrorist attacks against Americans in and out of the armed forces anywhere on earth, including within the United States. But it is blowback in its larger aspect–the tangible costs of empire–that truly threatens it. Empires are costly operations, and they become more costly by the year. The hollowing out of American industry, for instance, is a form of blowback–an unintended negative consequence of American policy–even though it is seldom recognized as such.

The growth of militarism in a once democratic society is another example of blowback. Empire is the problem. Even though the United States has a strong sense of invulnerability and substantial military and economic tools to make such a feeling credible, the fact of its imperial pretensions means that a crisis is inevitable. More imperialist projects simply generate more blowback.[17]

I agree with Johnson that it is crucial for anyone thinking about the events of September 11 to analyze the United States's global role during and after the Cold War. From such an analysis, we can begin to construct the rudiments of a political orientation that is within justice, using justice in the sense specified in the first part of my remarks. This political orientation within justice can then be used as a guiding framework for determining the acceptability or otherwise of the responses made by the United States and its allies to the attacks of September 11. But let's be clear that such an analysis of the American imperium, and the opposition provoked by that imperial order, does not provide the basis for any kind of justification of the attacks. To account for the motivations of the hijackers, and to identify the context in which such motivations were able to become so catastrophically effective, is not to imply that there is a justification for the hijackers' actions: there is a necessary and salutary distinction to be made between justificatory and motivational reasons, and accepting that a particular reason is one that motivates an agent is not thereby to imply that this reason is a justification for what that agent did. That said, any quest for justice after the events of September 11 involving military action has to acknowledge the fact that hostility, whether directed at combatants or noncombatants, always has the form of a social and political relationship (the political being the basis of the social) between those who perpetrate the hostile act in question and those who are subjected to such acts.[18] Any response to the hostile acts of the hijackers that resorts to a counter-hostility inevitably involves one in political and social relationship with those who are the objects of this counter-hostility: justice, no matter how it is pursued, is necessarily social and political. Let me conclude by saying, in an admittedly programmatic way, what this political orientation should be for those seeking justice after the events of September 11.

First, there has to be the beginnings of a profound longer-term reorientation of American policy, especially in regard to Israel, where a whole succession of agents of the Israeli state, Ariel Sharon being only the most recent among them, have been for the Palestinian people the instruments of a scarcely remitting violence and injustice.[19] The United States has supported despotic regimes in Saudi Arabia, Egypt, Iran, and Oman for decades, and routinely has used military interventions to bolster the American hegemony in the Middle East. A quest for global justice has to involve significant measures to address the long-term causes of the pain and despair of the peoples of the Middle East, and not simply take the form of this or that *ad hoc* operation against America's enemies, let alone a few thousand so-called Islamic fundamentalists in Afghanistan. And where Afghanistan is concerned, the quest for justice on behalf of the victims of the attacks on the World Trade Center and the Pentagon has to be concordant with the requirements of a commensurate justice for the noncombatant civilians of Afghanistan, now suffering at the hands of both the Taliban and the American military forces.

Geopolitically, the United States is also going to have to find ways of no longer conducting itself as an imperial power, and to show that it is much more willing than it has been up to now to treat all people right (not just the citizens of its client states), instead of submitting countless numbers of people, especially those in the nations of the South, to the deleterious impact of American policies. These policies, and the American-dominated international order sustained by them, have brought to many in the South nothing but increased hunger, environmental despoliation, indebtedness, growing social inequality, and higher levels of disease and mortality. The United States, in constructing and consolidating this international order, has of course itself been a major sponsor of state-terrorism, as is known by anyone familiar with the post-1945 histories of Argentina, Bolivia, Brazil, Cambodia, Chile, Colombia, the Congo, Cuba, El Salvador, Greece, Guatemala, Haiti, Indonesia, Iran, Iraq, Nicaragua, Panama, Vietnam, and elsewhere. The nature and scope of this American-led international regime are characterized thus by Peter Gowan:

> Although the United States and other Pacific Union governments publicly stress the need for the global spread of liberal rights and regimes, their policies actually obey a double derogation. In "strategic backwaters," such as most of sub-Saharan Africa today, even real genocide can be casually covered or countenanced, as the experience of Rwanda has shown. Where delinquent states are pivotal to American strategic interests, on the other hand, they are vigilantly shielded from human rights pressures, as the cases of Saudi Arabia, Israel, Turkey or Indonesia, to name only the most flagrant examples, have long made clear.[20]

In short: this geopolitical regime enables the United States to promise and provide rewards for client states while putting a lid on (or turning the proverbial blind eye to) the disgruntlement and misery of those who resist. It would, of course, be misleading to hold this flawed American-dominated order directly responsible for the attacks on September 11. But the wretchedness of much of the South creates conditions in which those with enough rage and despair can be motivated to become terrorists, and to direct their venom at the principal sponsor and beneficiary of this inequitable global order. The United States has to become a much more effective protagonist in the pursuit of global justice if it is to win any "war against terrorism." Without a real and effective commitment to global justice on the part of the United States and the wealthier nations of the North/West, the conditions and forces that fuel the growth of terrorism are simply not going to be weakened. The United

States and the other wealthy countries of the North/West ("the rule-makers" of this international order) have so far shown themselves to be unwilling to take significant steps to alter the fundamentally asymmetrical character of this order, even though it is becoming increasingly clear that this order has been singularly ineffective in overcoming the impasses and shortcomings that bear disproportionately on the less privileged nations of the South (the "rule-takers" of this order).[21]

Second, and more immediately, the principles for meting out justice to the perpetrators of the attacks on September 11 should be entrusted to an international body embodying the widest generality of human interests (I have in mind here an organization like the United Nations, unsatisfactory though the United Nations is in many ways). The same applies to the military action now being undertaken in Afghanistan or elsewhere (Iraq is looking more and more like a potential next target): this action should be placed under the auspices of a paranational body as soon as possible, since only an international system of adjudication will be able in principle to ensure that the interests of the United States and its allies do not ride roughshod over those of groups in Afghanistan who want al Qaeda and the Taliban to be removed, but who have no wish at the same time to be ruled by the coalition of warlords that is the Northern Alliance (who, turbans and beards aside, are hardly distinguishable from the Taliban in the unprincipled ferocity of their contribution to Afghanistan's two-decade-long civil war). The fall of Kabul to the forces of the Northern Alliance demonstrated all the more clearly the need for a political solution to Afghanistan's problems, as the summary executions of prisoners have begun. As things stand, the capture of bin Laden and his associates does not yet seem to be in sight, and there is a dangerous power vacuum in Kabul (and the rest of Afghanistan) that not even the triumphant Northern Alliance progress can conceal. Justice has still to be dispensed, and there is no convincing evidence that what is transpiring is likely to conform in any remotely significant way to the conception of justice sketched out here. For one thing, some of the Northern Alliance warlords are criminals by the terms of all the legal protocols governing the conduct of war, having massacred civilian populations in their previous campaigns (even CNN announces this), and so we now have the irony of a United States government seeking "justice" for bin Laden and his supporters in concert with known criminals and terrorists, whose proper place should be in the dock at the Hague rather than in the parliament building in Kabul.

The state's primary function in the current international order is the effective neutralization of those forces that, if unchecked, would weaken and supplant the apparatuses that constitute the state. Above all, the state exists to promote economic and ancillary interests organized according to the logic of capital. Justice for the state can therefore only take the form of a harmonization of the multiplicity of interests. The state in this order can never transcend the confines of interest; at best it can only thread a way through these confines (e.g., by orchestrating patriotic campaigns, promoting a sham humanitarianism, etc.). There is no more pertinent illustration of this than the sight of a Bush administration that had been dissociating itself strenuously from several international treaties and agreements in the months before September 11–the Kyoto Accord on global warming, the international agreement on land mines, the international agreement on chemical weapons (the withdrawal a result of pressure from U.S. pharmaceutical companies who feared that scrutiny by international regulators would reveal their commercial secrets), the international agreement on limiting the use of small arms (the dissociation a result of pressure from U.S. small arms manufacturers and the National Rifle Association), the international court on crimes against humanity and war crimes, multilateral agreements to regulate offshore banking and tax havens, and the 1972 ABM treaty–now wanting the rest of the world to give a damn for the United States by joining George Bush's coalition to save "civilization." The Bush administration has of course done a recent U-turn on some of these decisions, almost certainly prompted by the needs of a short-term expediency rather than by any enduring principle.

The state in the current geopolitical dispensation cannot create an event of justice because its fundamental propensity is to confuse and conflate the events of (a real) justice with the subjugation of its opponents. Those responsible for the attacks of September 11 have of course to be apprehended as criminals, and punished as criminals if found guilty.[22] But, as we have seen, the event of this quest for justice requires an appropriate political orientation for its realization, and this political orientation's essential structure, to put it a little too cursorily, is the structure of a concerted and well-organized pursuit of global justice. So how is global justice, the sine qua non of the required political orientation, to be promoted? And promoted not just by the smaller and less wealthy nations, and the usual plethora of well-meaning individuals and NGOs, but above all by the United States and the nations of the North/West?

The quest for global justice is inextricably bound up with the pursuit of policies that promote the flourishing of the mass of human beings, especially those living in the less-developed nations. The inequities of the prevailing international system can only be redressed by a concerted program of redistribution from the richer to the poorer countries.[23] The only way to begin to secure this redistribution is for there to be a framework of international institutions who will aid the nations of the South in their quest for development. The goal of such institutions would be to mount the equivalent of a Marshall Plan for the world's poorer nations, somewhat along the lines of a Leibnizian universal jurisprudence, with the aim of reducing levels of malnutrition, poverty, and disease in these countries. These institutions for economic development will parallel the work of the politico-legal regimes and protocols by seeking to ensure that the asymmetries of power that are a pervasive feature of the current international system are minimized and ultimately removed. In this way, measures can be taken to reform the currently inadequate system of regulation of global economic and financial systems, to promote transparency and accountability in the international organizations that steer this international order, and to reinforce and safeguard the legal, political, and social prerogatives of the disadvantaged nations of the South.[24] This, of course, will require the curtailment of American power, since American supremacy is the *raison d'etre* and driving force behind the organization of this currently inequitable global system. American power with its built-in "unipolar" propensities is simply not compatible with the existence of the egalitarian and welfare-based political orientation necessary for the dispensation of justice after the events of September 11.

The military campaign in Afghanistan was given its name by those who rule us. The egregious title "Infinite Justice" was tried for a very short time and found wanting. "Enduring Freedom" was the subsequently preferred nomenclature. The politics that is in truth and in justice has to begin by naming this brutal fight for what it is–namely, a massive and concerted attempt to find a new and revived form for American exceptionalism. If they really are responsible for the attacks of September 11, then al Qaeda and the Taliban deserve to be punished. But the noncombatant inhabitants of Afghanistan do not deserve punishment. Least of all do they deserve to receive this punishment from the Leviathan who is the architect of the baneful order that consigns an overwhelming number of human beings throughout the world to lives of unrelieved poverty and misery. The fight against terrorism may only be won when the power of this Leviathan is subdued.

11

Errant Concepts in an Age of Terror

Edith Wyschogrod

Is it possible to describe what might be called the semantic spaces of Terror? Is Terror a condition that requires radically new thinking by those of us who think about religion? After 9/11 can anything remain the same? It is Kierkegaard who, in a theological context, draws attention to delimiting the before and after of a decisive happening. What divides earlier from later is the Moment, not any moment, but for him, the entry of eternity into time, an instant that alters the character of the believer's life. Like Kierkegaard's believer, we are confronted with an event that separates past and present, an instant at which a new state of affairs has come about.

Yes, 9/11 has changed things radically. But ought we in haste to jettison approaches already developed for encountering historical change? Consider first the analytic strategies of continental thinkers in the period from the 1960s through the 1980s, designed to cope with its own species of turmoil that may remain relevant: Foucault's archeological exhuming of meaning constellations; Derrida's epistemic tentativeness, his alertness to the spectral (or ghostly) re-arising of concepts; Deleuze's analyses of identity formations as contingent upon difference and replication and his construing of the real in terms of plateaus and desiring machines; Levinas' privileging of the Other in ethics. These are sites (some of which I shall turn to) that offer no solid ground but rather a cluster of tactics, of propositions about the world that are not intended to stand fast for us but constitute a non-place, a ground zero in a landscape of concepts.

In what follows I shall consider numerous conceptual schemes, moving errantly from one to another. I shall touch upon how conditions of disclosure enter into the configuring of the nihil; how recent anthropological inquiry might assist in interpreting the spread of Terror; how the genes and memes of our biological and cultural inheritance may provide the metaphors for the conscious and subliminal ways in which we encounter bioterrorism; how new non-totalizing interpretive models of complexity understood as interacting mini-systems may help to penetrate antecedent modes of rationality and their collapse. The event may lie beyond our reach, yet as we stand both inside and outside it, Terror demands questioning.

Conditions of Disclosure

Consider first the prephilosophical terrain upon which concepts stand through which we may attempt to approach Terror. It is by now no longer to be taken for granted that thinking remains bound exclusively by formal requirements, that is, arguments whose truth conditions can be stipulated. Although the presuppositions of analysis in the sciences, politics, and economics, not to speak of the multiple ways in which information is modeled, may differ, many philosophers of otherwise conflicting perspectives agree on the importance of interrogating the conditions of disclosure of a claim or argument. Not only who says what, when, and under what circumstances, but also what could be said under specifiable conditions, no longer lie outside inquiry but are part of what must be brought within its purview. The unstated rules and protocols that govern discursive possibilities change when they collide with new cognitive perspectives or are impacted by events. Has Terror now become a prior condition, the sine qua non, of our current thinking and speaking?

Long before the Terror, Foucault-inspired archeological tendencies, bringing to light the pretheoretical conditions of a discipline or thought structure, affected the way many philosophers thought about thinking, about what has standardly been called the history of Western philosophy. It is by now no longer startling to read that the way the self is envisioned conforms to constellations of power that inhere in language itself. The study of non-Western beliefs and practices as well as issues of gender called for attentiveness to the conditions that allowed for their expression. In conformity with this view, it will not do simply to examine claims about the meanings of Terror but rather to exhume the ways in which Terror enters into the semantic grid through which our acts of questioning must pass.

Prior to the Terror, inquiry into the conditions of disclosure of what were alleged to be the attentuated religious beliefs and practices of modernity led some theologians to click on the delete icon: delete the modernity that these analyses have disclosed, then delete the postmodern strategies that enabled one to delete in the first place and return to a default position of some version of premodernity. Can those who think about religion in a time of Terror endorse the recent attempts at repristinization attempted by some radical orthodox theologians? Can they, for example, subscribe to John Milbank's claim that explanations of social phenomena are to be ruled by theology as the alleged queen of the social sciences? In his terms, "the central theological framework of radical orthodoxy is 'participation' as developed by Plato and reworked by Christianity, because any alternative configuration perforce reserves a territory independent of God…[q.e.d.] every discipline must be framed by theological perspective" or it is grounded in nothing.[1] Such efforts ignore the conditions of their own emergence as well as the ineliminable Enlightenment residues that they may wish to retain. How can one otherwise speak to those with whom one may be compelled to speak in this time of Terror? Must we not include (at least as regulative ideals) a level playing field for the conflicting views of interreligious conversation and tolerance for alterity?

What is more—here the work of Gilles Deleuze may help—one who holds a particular philosophical position can be interpreted as what Deleuze calls a "conceptual persona." Her proper name is not a referring term in the usual sense, but the envelope, as it were, into which her concepts are folded, the sum of the concepts themselves. Deleuze has no objection to knowledge by way of concepts, so long as one is mindful of the field or plane they inhabit, a ground that must not be confused with them but that shelters them. "Concepts pave, occupy, or populate the plane bit by bit, whereas the plane itself is the indivisible milieu in which concepts are distributed."[2] The self as thinker is dismantled, dissolving into a structure of related concepts. With the advent of Terror have we not come to know viscerally what the dissolution of the sheltering ground of concepts that stood fast for us, that enabled us to be who we are, has become: an absence of ground, a non-ground, ground zero?

The Anthropological Perspective: The Matter of Culture

If all that was heretofore solid has melted away, should those who think about religion abandon standard questions such as, "What counts as a tradition?" and "How are traditions transmitted?" Or are answers to such questions useful to the extent that they may help to account for our responses to the event? Consider Pierre Bourdieu's idea of the *habitus*. Contrary to the biases of intellectual idealism, "*habitus* are constituted in practice… oriented to practical functions," whose principle is that of "a system of structured structuring dispositions" that organize practices without a conscious aiming at ends.[3] While the *habitus* imposes constraints and limits on thought, Bourdieu hopes to overcome the dyadic biases of freedom/determinism, conditioning/creativity, and individual/society. Might we not gain from this account an explanation for practices that preceded the Terror whose residues persist in such practices as the spontaneous efforts to rescue as well as in responses of violence?

Other insights might be expected from the radically materialist perspective of other anthropologists. Brain-based models could earn summary dismissal as reductive when accounting for complex beliefs and practices, but nevertheless might help to illustrate the dilemmas opened by Terror. Pascal Boyer, who is concerned with the oral transmission of traditions, insists that the processes involved in such transmission must be in conformity with the findings of cognitive psychology. Not only should the constraints of transmission be naturalized but the strategies that have proven fruitful in dealing with the natural world should be extended to explaining social differences. The strong claim for naturalization is used by Boyer to account for cross-cultural similarities in that the recurrence of religious phenomena requires explanation. "Experimental psychology shows that a number of universal richly structured, early developed conceptual principles organize our understandings of particular natural and social environments. [The] claim is that the latter provide to a certain extent an explanation for cultural recurrence."[4] But what are we to make of a Terror that cannot be folded into patterns of recurrence, patterns of war or economic malaise? How are we to appropriate a sequence of events that continue to arrive in no particular order yet threaten total annihilation?

Materialist anthropologist Dan Sperber maintains that brains are inhabited by ideas and that some of these ideas are contagious. An account of culture is contingent on the explanation of why and how ideas, like disease, are spread. Humans, he argues, have a disposition to develop concepts, some of which are infectious. Thus, culture can be explained in terms of "a true epidemiology of representations" that are stored and tested against further experience.[5] Sperber writes:

> What psychology is to epidemiology of diseases, psychology of thought should be to epidemiology of representations. [The latter], the causal explanation of cultural facts,…and the psychology of thought…stand in a relationship of partial interpenetration and mutual relevance.[6]

Even if we can give an account of its cultural outcomes, how are we to configure a Terror that disfigures representation itself? In a world of infopolitics, where images, speech, and writing attempt to tame Terror, how are we to compare conflicting images of Terror that arise in diverse contexts and that appear to share a certain semantic space? Consider these images: a photograph of the skeletal remains, the steel remnants of a towering structure, tilted against an urban skyline; a photograph of the opening of a cave against the backdrop of a vast and empty landscape. Are such comparisons tendentious from the start, each image "falsifying" and colonizing the terrain of the other? Or are we, on the contrary, creating new meaning constellations, new units of complexity? Ought one to see the way in which one responds to the constructions in space I have described as deriving from common biologically grounded fears and constraints? Or rather do such instances reflect an unrepresentable real as Lacan might call it? Are such multiple perspectives useful or reciprocally nullifying? These new spaces and the ethical dilemmas they present can be seen as calling for an expanded rationality, one in which absence and negation figure, rather than a return to an uncritical positivism in which meaning is determined by reference to a prior reality.[7]

It is a truism that those who think about religion have been confronted with unfamilar stretches of cognitive terrain, the discourses of genetics, sociobiology, cognitive science, shifting semantic fields that might bear upon the ways in which religious traditions can be construed. If students of religion fail to respond to the new epistemic and ethical challenges these perspectives pose, their interpretation is effectively handed over to the media and to experts in the special sciences.

Speaking about What We Do Not Understand: Venturing Discourse

Can "my death" still be seen as "ecstasis towards the end" as death is described by Heidegger, or is it encompassed in a movement toward an end that is the termination of everything? Whether one thinks of oneself as a being-in-the world among other beings or as a sequence of memory states or as gendered corporeality, some evolutionary biologists counter these differing views by redesigning the body as code. What some biologists envisage is not merely that the body in the everyday sense, the body as a living entity, is subject to genetic programming but, more radically, that the form of the organism, the phenomenological body, can be severed from the genetic code that is to count as self. Richard Dawkins, who famously refers to the selfishness of genes, offers no disclaimer to the view that "any animal form can be transformed into a related form by a mathematical transformation although... the translation may not be a simple one."[8] Thus, code is privileged over the vulnerable gendered body of flesh.

We may indeed ask whether code trembles before the nihil, before the interruption in being that explodes as Terror. It could be argued that phenomenologists of an earlier generation who spoke of the lived body, the body as experienced, were well placed to counter such claims. But the idea of the lived body was not developed as a response to the body as code but rather to the body as envisaged by a positivism influenced by early modern science, the body as object that is subject to the laws of motion as other physical objects are. To perceive the body as object is for Merleau-Ponty and other phenomenologists of the period a misreading of self-world transactions, a construing of the body in terms of matter, motion, and force. In fact, it was argued, one's body is not an object among others but the subject of experience. Does the body as code revise one's relation to a mathematized universe whose laws demand a new reading of corporeality? Or, in the light of Terror, can the body be read as William James put the matter earlier: "The body is the storm center, the origin of coordinates, the constant place of stress"?[9]

Before turning to the matter of code, consider first the gene's eye view that sees evolution as taking place not on behalf of the organism as the indivisible unit of biological individuality but rather in the interest of the gene, "that little bit of chromosome that lasts for many generations." For Dawkins "all life survives by the differential survival of replicating entities," genes, that little molecule of DNA, the bearer of immortality for which the organism is merely its means of transport.[10] What is radical in Dawkins' description is his minimizing the importance of the phenotype, the organism's perceptible attributes resulting from the interaction of organism and environment, and his claim that gene activity can lie outside the bodies in which the genes are lodged.[11] Thus, an individual entity made up of genes is extended beyond the organism they inhabit so that genes constitute a new entity. Genes are replicators with lives of their own. Even cultural units of transmission, ideas, not those of the philosophers, but memes, entities such as the wheel, the wearing of clothes, or the movement of a symphony, are viewed as replicators. In an age of bioterrorism, disease-bearing organisms are spread as copies of themselves passing through bodies that die while they persist. It is crucial to see the power of replicators, anything of which copies can be made. Information-bearing DNA molecules, gene strings, are active when their effects lead to their being copied, passive when they die out. The gene is the "unit of heredity" that is to be retained in the evolutionary process. Only those likely to be copied survive, while passive replicators become extinct. What remains clear is that although the phenotype continues to be "the all important instrument of preservation, it is not that which is preserved,"[12] or, as Dawkins also avers more graphically, a body is the gene's way of preserving the genes unaltered.[13]

How, in the wake of the Terror, might we usefully appropriate Dawkins's further claim that he is "not trying to convince anyone of the truth of any factual proposition" but rather to open "a way of looking at new facts and ideas, and a way of asking new questions about them?"[14] Only if we recognize that it is not the explanatory power of gene replication in evolutionary theory that is of interest, but rather the fact of replication itself. According to his version of neo-Darwinism, as we have seen, the telos or purpose of replication is neither the perpetuation of the species nor of the individual organism as the unit of natural selection, but rather that of the active germ replicator, the "ancestor of an indefinitely long line of descendents." What is more, replicants serve to expand power either through deception, a technique not foreign to intruder genes, or by virtue of a sheer increase in the number of copies. Although some germ lines may die out, "any germ line replicator is potentially immortal."[15] Disease-causing organisms are replicants, copies that go on to make more copies, and inhabit a space within and outside bodies. Thus, whether factually true or not, the spores, viruses, and bacteria, the bearers of anthrax, smallpox, and other diseases that can be released in acts of Terror are seen as immortal.

It can be argued that Derridean conceptions of liminality, of inside and outside, expands the descriptive horizons of the relation of genotype and phenotype in ways yet to be explored. Baudrillard's postmodern notion of the "precession of the simulacra," copies without originals, may be relevant to thinking about the meaning of the "originary status" of genes.[16] Bioterrorism demands a rethinking of replication as a quest for immortality in light of philosophical accounts of the meaning of repetition. Bioterrorism can now be seen in the light of an unstoppable increase in quantity. The magnitude of the Terror's power is dependent upon a potentially vast number of replicants, upon excess and superabundance rather than upon the concentrated power of a single unit.

Whose Life Is It Anyway? Terror and Artificial Life

How are we to envision the subjects of Terror, not those who are seen but those who are invisible, removed from us? Are they not configured as virtualized agents, coded ciphers that act upon real bodies? The biologist's view, the interpretation of the body as code, lends itself readily to transmutation into an image of artificial life, life that is humanly contrived. In turning to computational paradigms for understanding biological life, artificial life theorist Christopher Langton asserts that life is not a property of matter but rather of its organization, for which computational models are eminently suited, so that now research can be directed away from "the mechanics of life to the logic of life."[17] It could be argued that the creation of artificial life would be served most effectively by relying upon the organic chemicals of carbon-chain chemistry. Apart from the practical difficulties inherent in this effort, Langton contends that more can be learned from the "creation of life *in silico*" in that it opens up the "space of *possible* life."[18]

In essence what is being sought is the generating of behavior through the creation of computational automata, de-realized life that is at once terrifying, beyond one's control, yet, as code, manipulable. The effort to devise robotic forms through the use of available technologies has a long history, including the development of such humanoid replicas as clockwork automata.[19] By contrast, present models see the genotype as a bag of instructions that specifies behaviors or modifies structures that are activated through it. What is crucial is that computers, not human agents, are now the breeders who are engaged in the process of natural selection.

In one simulation system, the Tierra, even the earlier proxies for the human agent, the algorithmic breeding agents, are eliminated. The computer programs themselves compete for CPU (computer processing unit) time and memory space. Programs piggyback upon themselves: to be reproduced they simply require the act of self-reproduction. "The programs reproduce themselves and the ones that are better at this task take over the population,"[20] Thomas S. Ray, the developer of Tierra, contends. "There is no connection between the Tierran world and the real physical world. I have created a virtual universe that is self-contained."[21] The subject of bioterrorism can now be envisioned as de-realized, virtualized, faceless, inhabiting a network of computational cells to whose code one has no access and who is known only through the disease and death that are delivered.

It might be thought that Terror thus understood can be constrained in that, it is assumed, computers can only do what they are programmed to do but cannot generate mutations or novel animal behavior. Thus, the other can somehow be brought under one's control. But artificial life theorist Langton maintains that, if sufficiently powerful, computers may be unpredictable. He writes, "It is impossible to determine any non-trivial property of the future behavior of a sufficiently powerful computer from a mere inspection of its program and it initial state."[22] The only way to determine phenotype changes is to run the program. The other as agent of Terror is seen as a computational construct, as a virtual subject that spins beyond one's control.

Expanding the Conversation: New Modes of Rationality

Poststructuralist discourse does not end with its "grand figures." Consider the context of a global economy or, in journalist Tom Friedman's language, the world of the Lexus and the olive tree. The work of Eric Alliez in *Capital Times* (despite its Francophone density) is an interesting foray in this direction. Alliez considers the relation of time to economy and sees the history of philosophy as a history of the conquest of time, in which "quantity conquers everything." According to Deleuze, the force of Alliez's work is in "discovering and analyzing the processes of extension, intensification, capitalization, subjectivation, that become something like the conditions for a history of time."[23] Can Terror not be seen as an implosion of the conquest of time understood as quantity? The student of religion must ask whether this implosion will take shape not only as a collapse of economic and cultural systems of rationality but as an incursion of a terrifying and uncontrollable sacred.

I cannot hope briefly to summarize Dominique Janicaud's arguments in this regard as they are laid out in his analysis of the relation of Power to rationality. Power, born not from rationality as such but from a particular mode of excessive rationality, is "an upheaval in rationality."[24] Is there no egress from the planetary expansion of what he sees as the technology-science composite? The sacred has been lost but, in a complex analysis of time, Janicaud argues that the dimension of future time opens the power of the rational to the possible. He contends that "the future is the sacred in time" that unfolds in the spheres of the ethical, the political, and the poetic.[25] But, it may be asked, can such incursions of the sacred not manifest themselves as Terror?

Finally, to further understand the possibilities for the implosions of Terror, it may help to consider complexity theory, an account of the interaction of components in self-developing wholes. There is no need to explain such wholes by recourse to external teleology, to a principle outside the system. Open wholes resist inclusion in totalizing structures and metanarratives, issues considered in works as different as those of Nicholas Rescher, Paul Cilliers, and the forthcoming work of Mark C. Taylor. Rescher claims that complexity is a feature of the real and that a system's complexity is a "a matter of the quantity and variety of its constituent elements and of the interrelational elaborateness of their organization and operational make-up...As a system's complexity increases, so do the cognitive requisites for its adequate comprehension." Rescher adds significantly: "Complexity can in principle make itself felt in any domain whatsoever."[26] Grappling with complexity involves "the devising of cognitive instrumentalities for coming to grips with it" in sociocultural contexts that are in "in the process of giving rise to a new instrumentality."[27] Rescher concludes optimistically that complex systems need not elude cognitive grasp if only appropriate instruments are devised. He maintains, however, that developments in the sciences are "outside the range of our present day [postmodern theorists] so that the facts of life about the complex natural world in which they live are something they neither can nor wish to understand."[28] Leaving the polemical thrust of the remark aside, Rescher could not have imagined the profound slippages of meaning in propositions that once held fast for us, in the so-called "facts of life" and in the instrumentalities in the domains in which they were reputed to hold.

Contrary to Rescher's rejection of the usefulness of postmodern strategy, research engineer turned philosopher Paul Cilliers claims that complexity as involving the behavior of systems without fixed structures is, as such, amenable to postmodern interpretation. Complex systems are usually associated with living things from bacteria to brains and language and are made up of multiple elements in dynamic interaction. "There are loops in the interactions" that feed back on one another. Such systems have a history. But each component is "ignorant of the behavior of the system as a whole" and each is responsive only "to local information."[29] Each system is self-organizing and has the capacity to store information.[30] Cilliers shows that the postmodern stress upon a multiplicity of discourses in constant interaction struggling for territory, and upon "the distributed nature of the society as a connectionist network" is itself an example of complexity. "Self-organized criticality," a mark of postmodern discourse, "is the mechanism by which networks diversify their internal structures maximally."[31] But what are the consequences of radical diversification in the structure of a single system within the network of systems? Complexity is the result of the interaction of a system's components. Systems are permeable to one another and as such vulnerable to implosion, to a nihil that is itself refractory to explanation.

In/conclusions

Ceaseless talk—talk about genes as the retrieval bins of memory, about DNA as storage space for a world of self-replicating genes that serve as metaphors for the terror we feel before the nihilatory power of incurable disease. Talk about the commonalities of culture as linked to the materiality of brain states, about the epidemiology of beliefs and practices, both of which transmit residual meanings, traces of a past that cannot be made present. Talk about systems as open non-totalizable wholes and their permeability to one another allowing them to implode in a nihil that is refractory to conceptual grasp. Before the event, the relation of non-philosophy, the conceptual spaces in which philosophy unfolded, shed light on the concepts of philosophy itself. How are those of us who think about religion to interpret pleasure and pain, flesh and spirit, God and revelation, now that everything is different?

Yet the Terror does not preclude attentiveness to the past. Some of the banalities that pass for interpretation in the infoculture we inhabit attest to this need: an ahistorical account becomes empty assertion. In calling attention to thinkers that before the event had marked pathways through the trackless beliefs and practices of religion, I have not tried to draw a map that, in postmodern language, precedes the territory, but rather to move from island to island through an archipelago of concepts.

PART 2

Visions

12

Fragments of a Vision in a September 11 World

Teresa Berger

In the year 2001, on the brilliantly clear morning of Tuesday, September 11, I saw the divine presence.

She was squatting in the midst of billowing smoke and raging fire, of mountains of twisted steel and broken glass. An apocalypse of destruction and terror engulfed her. Her face, bearing the serene features of an indigenous woman of this continent, was covered with a thick layer of ash. But the ashen face seemed strangely glistening. The divine presence wept.

And then I saw: in her strong brown arms she was gathering the remains of her beautiful creation, all the maimed and the burnt, the dying and the dead, the unborn, the orphaned, the lost, and those who inflicted loss. I saw her gather, passionately and gently, the lives of all. With tears trickling down her ashen face, she caught in her arms those who jumped from great heights, and she cradled in the palm of her hand a dying priest.

And the divine presence whispered, Holy, holy, holy is every human life. Heaven and earth and the very heart of God mourn when death so violently overcomes life. Then I said, Woe is me! Why do my eyes have to see the divine presence mourning, gathering her torn creation in her arms? Why can I not see God sitting on a throne, high and lofty, with the train of his garment filling the temple and seraphs in attendance above him, each with six wings? I am lost.

Then one of the living dead came to me and touched my eyes. Look again, he said. And I saw the divine presence, groaning, crouched amid the heaps of rubble, her belly

110

large and full of life. And I saw that she was a woman in travail, desperate to birth new life, a child of peace. And as every mother since the first, the divine presence also birthed amid waves of pain, and in fear of futility.

Then I heard the voice of the divine presence saying, Who will labor with me, and who will be midwife to life? Here I am, I said, I want to birth life with you. And the divine presence said, Come, take your place beside me.

In the year 2001, on the brilliantly clear morning of Tuesday, September 11

Yes, I did see the divine presence. But was it really on September 11? It took days before I was able to see anything resembling a divine presence. On the brilliantly clear morning of September 11, I saw only billowing smoke and raging fire, mountains of twisted steel and broken glass, an apocalypse of destruction and terror. The images were everywhere, stark and powerful, replayed again and again, within ourselves and all around us. Soon, another powerful icon appeared, superimposing itself on the rubble of the Twin Towers: the American flag, raised over the rubble, then swiftly transubstantiating itself into lapel pins on business suits, T-shirts of all imaginable sizes, bumper stickers on Jaguars and pickup trucks, and, with the beginning of November(!), patriotic Christmas tree ornaments, "premiering at only $9.99 each." The icon became a totalizing presence, holding captive our eyes.

Where is there space to see our culture's complicity with the roots of the hatred behind September 11? Where is there room to remember the 30,000 children who died of hunger and hunger-related causes on September 11, and the 30,000 more who died on September 12, and every day since then? Who will fill National Cathedrals for them and their loved ones? What is the meaning of our daily indifference?

United we stand? I have no desire to. Broken, I want to kneel.

I saw the divine presence

Like Hagar in the desert, I yearn to see and to name God and to live. Instead, the towers, and the flag. And then the words, endlessly…those of the reporters and of the politicians, and, above all, a sudden multitude of experts. Heaps of words on heaps of rubble. The religious leaders also are in high demand, the archbishops and rabbis on CNN, and even a theologian on Oprah. It will not last.

But who will help us see the face of God? As a deer longs for flowing streams, so my soul longs to see the Word of Life stand against all idols of death. My soul thirsts for the profound silence of the Unnameable. When shall I come and see the face of God? I am tired of the fine-tuning of words: will this be the beginning of a war, a just war, an armed intervention, or plain murder? What are the prerequisites for a just war? The carefully crafted theological arguments of the professional theologians—of whom I am one—do not seem to reach the depth of my soul. Deep calls to deep. I yearn to see the face of God and live.

The divine presence wept

Where are the seers and the sages, the visionaries and the wise, the ones who have learned to see the face of God in billowing smoke and raging fire?

It is time to learn from the people of Chile. Their September 11 came in 1973. The pictures from Santiago on September 11, 1973, no longer look "foreign": billowing smoke and raging fire, an apocalypse of destruction and terror, airplanes overhead attacking the Moneda, the symbol of Chilean democracy. And after the airplanes and the fire and the destruction came the disappearances and the tortures, the disbelief and the despair, the unspeakable:

> And then, they took our children –
> And they took their scissors –
> And then they took the hands of our children.[1]

It is time to learn from the everyday terror in women's lives, from a survivor of rape who wrestles with a psalm:

> **do not give me over to the will of my tormentors**
> You already did.
>   maybe you cried too...

It is time to learn from the Christian Palestinian women in Bethlehem:

> Even now as we write this, tank shells are exploding around the Bethlehem area and a young girl and a young woman in Beit Jala have just been killed... There is no time to feel, to weep, death comes upon death, destruction follows destruction. As the shelling becomes louder and nearer, as we listen to the wailing of the ambulance sirens going nearby, we urge you not to leave us "orphans." Do not forget us in our time of trial.[2]

I want to learn from these and other witnesses to suffering and resistance to evil in crafting a response to September 11 beyond finely tuned arguments. "All thought must be interrupted by the great counter experiences of suffering";[3] "theology begins with God's heartache."[4] I long to see God's real presence, but only if it can be a presence for and with the abused, the tortured, and the dead. I cannot imagine God's presence without the gift of tears–why would the giver of all gifts not claim this one as God's very own?

Holy, holy, holy is every human life

Are there words that sustain, after all? Are there God-sustained words? I can barely entrust myself to the shortest of prayers, two or three words. *Kyrie eleison.* Sustain the dying. Deliver us from evil. Comfort those who mourn. *Dona nobis pacem.* Be Thou my vision. *Holy, holy, holy is every human life,* **every human life.**

Fragments of a theological tradition emerge from deep within that have nurtured faith in the past. None but the briefest ones remain. *Gloria Dei vivens homo.* "God is the beyond in the midst of life." *Solo Dios basta.* I repeat them to myself as if they are confessions of faith. They are. "Just to be is a blessing, just to live is holy."

I saw her gather, passionately and gently, the lives of all

"We have gathered here as Americans, and as Christians." The priest opens the first liturgy I attend after September 11 with these words. I turn to leave. I am a resident alien, my citizenship is not from this continent. As I turn, I suddenly see. In the midst of this liturgy that does not speak to me, I see: *in her strong brown arms she was gathering the remains of her beautiful creation, all the maimed and the burnt, the dying and the dead, the unborn, the orphaned, the lost, and those who inflicted loss. I saw her gather, passionately and gently, the lives of all.* The liturgy continues, but within me, finally, there is only silence, the brilliant eloquence of silence.[5] I see. She gathers the lives of all.

Where are those who can teach us to pray for "the enemy," to do good to those who hate us, to bless those who curse us, to bless and not to curse? I need a distant language to respond to this stark demand of the gospel. I wrestle with strange words:

Almighty and eternal God
Who alone art infinite justice and sovereign judge of all
Though who art of purer eyes than to behold evil:
Deliver us when we draw nigh to Thee
from hateful and vengeful hearts.
Forgive us our trespasses, and teach us to forgive others.
Help us to pray, even and especially for our enemies.
Grant to all the grace to turn from evil.
Draw nigh unto the souls of those who have gone astray
and turn the wicked from their ways.
Deliver us and all from evil
that we may persevere in the path of Thy justice.
To the honor of thy holy name.

She cradled in the palm of her hand a dying priest

The vision of another man superimposes itself over that of the priest dying among the New York firefighters, a man who also died within the rubble of a world violently crashing all around him. Dietrich Bonhoeffer was hanged in Flossenbürg concentration camp on April 9, 1945, just days before the end of the Second World War. He knew that he was being walked to the gallows when he entrusted these words to a fellow prisoner: "This is the end, for me the beginning of life." Bonhoeffer must have seen what I saw on the brilliantly clear morning of Tuesday, September 11, when Franciscan Father Mychal Judge died in the rubble of the WTC: a Life beyond all Life opening up in his ending, ready to cradle him in the palm of Her hand.

Still, the fragmentation of lives ended by violence remains real. For Bonhoeffer, the fragmentation itself became a pointer to an ultimate wholeness that we cannot give but only receive as gift: "there are some fragments...

whose importance lasts for centuries, because their completion can only be a matter for God, and so they are fragments that must be fragments."[6] For Father Mychal, who in his own words had "always wanted to be a priest and a fireman,"[7] there seems to be nothing but perfect meaning in the final fragmentation of his life, because it also embodied a final fusion of his disparate passions, the blending of the dying priest with the dying firefighters of whom he was one. Would that all our dyings held such clarity and wholeness, in the very midst of the violent fragmentations all around us.

And I saw the divine presence, groaning, crouched amid the heaps of rubble

The brilliance of this autumn is real, almost too real. I kneel in front of a golden tabernacle knowing that it holds pure life. Or does it hold a broken body, for a fragmented world? Or is it the one only because it dared to become the other? What do I do with my deep yearning for wholeness, for redemption, for life abundant, for bread **and** roses? My hunger for life only increases with every piece of broken bread I eat and every sip of wine I taste.

In the end, the questions dissolve in the golden brilliance of the tabernacle. There is silence, and in the silence, presence, real presence. I open my eyes to see.

And I saw that she was a woman in travail, desperate to birth new life, a child of peace

Yes, I did see. But I knew, deep down in my heart, that this one would be stillborn. The womb would become a tomb for this child, peace. No matter how many protective symbols I sewed onto the birth-shirt, the "child-eater" would ravish this one, for sure.[8] What was more painful? That simple knowledge, or the knowledge that I could not pretend to be an uncompromising midwife of peace anyway? I knew, deep down in my heart, that for most hours of the day, I was not a pacifist. Granted, September 11 almost made me one again. But ever since the birth of my child, I had known that I would defend this vulnerable life entrusted to my care, and I would defend it violently. This realization was painful—more painful than the marks of violence my child's long and hard birth had imprinted on my body for the rest of my life.

I want to birth life with you

Since I bear on my body the marks of having given birth amidst violence, maybe I can learn to midwife amidst heaps of rubble? How can I be anything but midwife—"with-woman"—to one in travail, desperate to birth new life?

A theologian as midwife? I need to learn from Shiphrah and Puah, the Hebrew midwives who defied Pharaoh, how to conspire and co-labor in bringing forth new life.[9] I need to learn with feminist theologians how to engage in the mending of creation.[10] I do know how to recycle my household trash and sign petitions protesting the treatment of Afghan women. But what about bioterrorism and poisoned mail? What about the richest country on

Earth relentlessly bombing the (almost) poorest one, and that for weeks without end? I thought there were no targets…And then the cluster bombs have the same color and size as the food aid packages, and Afghan children pick up both. I desperately need to learn more about the Jewish notion of *tikkun olam,* the repairing of the world. I do not know how to repair a world in which hungry children pick up unexploded cluster bombs instead of food. Does God know?

Will anything help me find words that my little son will not be ashamed of when he is grown? Can I find something to sustain us in the face of television images of people with smallpox? I stare at the archival material in disbelief.

Come, take your place beside me

There is no other way: broken I kneel. I will learn to practice midwifery crouched amidst heaps of rubble.

Postscript

I pledge allegiance to this vision of the divine presence
and to the vision of the world for which it stands,
one world
in which violence and fragmentation are real
yet in which God labors to bring forth life.
I am called to kneel beside Her
in Her labor.

13

The Armageddon of 9/11
A Counter-Apocalyptic Meditation

Catherine Keller

"Hallelujah! The smoke goes up from her forever and ever."
(REV. 19:3)

*The wind must be blowing north today. As I step out on my twentieth-floor balcony
for a breath of sunny autumnal stimulation, two months after and ninety blocks up, I
am startled to smell it again: that unmistakable, acrid aroma of roasted chemicals.
"The smoke of her burning." Nothing collapses distance like the sense of smell. This
"she" of Revelation 18 and 19–the "great city," her people, her "flutists and trumpeters,"
her "artisans," her "merchants" who "were the magnates of the earth," the pale arrogant
elite, the workers of many hues and sixty nationalities, those who died, those who live–
I breathe them in as I write. "Alas, alas, the great city."*

Pardon my apocalypse. But bear with it. It is not my own.

Apocalypse is going around. I write late in the year 2001. As though on
cue, we are enacting our entrapment in its narratives: Christian, Jewish, Muslim,
and secular.

Apocalypse has been cycling through for centuries.[1] But still it is not very
often that one can quote its primary text with such acuity:

The merchants of these wares, who gained wealth from
her, will stand far off, in fear of her torment, weeping and

116

mourning aloud.
"Alas, alas, the great city,
clothed in fine linen,
in purple and scarlet,
adorned with gold,
with jewels, and with pearls!
For in one hour all this wealth has been laid waste!"

(Rev. 18:15–17)

So in the wake of that single hour an already unsustainable global economy, long wasteful of the earth and its poor, shudders toward collapse. And consider the fourth seal–the pale horse, sickly green, whose "rider's name was Death, and Hades followed with him; they were given authority over a fourth of the earth, to kill with sword, famine, and pestilence" (Rev. 6:7). So as our military claims authority over far reaches of the earth, mass starvation threatens an Afghanistan already plagued with drought. The pestilence of anthrax filters (all too *liter*ally, Lat. "of the letter") through our letters. With theatrical flair, Manhattan Island throws in a very rare earthquake, and a plane falls from the Long Island sky. Osama "I love death" bin Laden announces his capacity to send forth the nuclear horse. This is a good moment for religious literalists.

As an amplifying feedback loop of dread encircles the planet, it is crucial that religious leaders face, name, and personify the mythic scale of such a moment. We who do not pretend to decode the present meaning of history from biblical signs and portents need nonetheless to read, and to read *theologically* if not literally, the "signs of the times." How else shall we discern within the fluctuations of fear and denial an alternative frequency of hope? Hope may mean precisely *not* the expectation of a final omnipotent intervention from above, but the inspiration of a just and sustainable peace process. But for now, we are in a war process, one unlike any before in its sinister unpredictability–and so paradoxically more open to the phantasmagoria of apocalyptic prediction. The literalizing script requires total war: only then, in the end, comes the *pax apocalyptica*. A counterapocalypse confronts the power of these self-realizing prophecies in our history.[2] It faces them in order to make them conscious, to disarm their dangerous oblivion, to make peace in whatever piecemeal fashion is possible already and always.

Does the realistic way to a just peace run through a "just war"? And even if it sometimes might, does the present war qualify? Christians have two strong traditions of response open to them: that of the pacifism of the early Christian community, in which John's apocalypse formed; and that of the just war doctrine, which evolved as an ideal of constraint for the subsequent Christian empires. I leave more abstract discussion of these ethical options to fellow essayists and will let the question of "just war" arise from within the spiral of this meditation on the loop of competing apocalypses. But the current moment can only be read within a dense haze of politico-religious history. Nothing defuses the high-strung dualism of apocalypse like historical understanding. Otherwise, as Edward Said has recently written, we are left with gimmicks like "the clash of civilizations," or "Islam vs. the West"–"better for reinforcing defensive self-pride than for critical understanding of the bewildering interdependence of our time."[3]

In the meantime, many are the voices crying "Hallelujah!"

Islam and Apocalypse

The terrorists have effectively targeted the U.S., long-time Great Satan of Islamic fundamentalism, as the primary cause of Muslim suffering and humiliation. Exploding the economic power stacked in the Twin Towers, they enacted an apocalyptic judgment on "the great whore" of obscene greed. Yet the representatives of bin Laden have not even hinted at an economic analysis or strategy. However one parses their motives, they embrace death as martyrs for a final war of pure good versus pure evil. Hence, their stunning achievement has inspired–even from a sober, progressive analyst to whom we will return– the label "apocalyptic terrorism." They represent the most extreme form so far of what is called, for lack of a better term, Muslim fundamentalism.[4] In their extremity they could be compared, but for their infinitely superior organization, to the Branch Davidians or to David Koresh, who was inspired by the latter.

What about the apocalypticism of Islam, however? Certainly in its Christian forms, fundamentalism is by definition apocalyptic, oriented to a final confrontation of absolute good and absolute evil, privileging martyrs among the saved and bringing the world as we know it to an end. But the sort of literalism that characterizes fundamentalist exegesis is foreign to the elliptical poetry of the Koran itself and to the highly evolved disciplines of its interpretive traditions. At least as late and foreign is premillennialist dispensationalism to its Christian sources. As within the Christian Bible, the apocalyptic symbolism of a final judgment of the just and the unjust pervades the Quran. Indeed, its discourse of doom emits resonances as potent as those of John's Revelation. Yet Islam eschews the sort of time line of creation-to-apocalypse that developed early within Christianity and drives toward historical realization. "The Koran is not like the Bible, historical, running from Genesis to Apocalypse," writes Norman O. Brown, in appreciation of the Koran. "The Koran is altogether apocalyptic. The Koran backs off from that linear organization of time, revelation, and history which became the backbone of orthodox Christianity, and remains the backbone of Western culture."[5]

Permit me to cite a bit of Sura LXX, not that it "translates," not that I could interpret it, but to give a taste of the Quranic apocalypse. It is–as in every passage of the Quran–"Allah, the Merciful, the Compassionate" who speaks:

> Upon the day when heaven shall be as molten copper
> and the mountains shall be as plucked wool-tufts,

no loyal friend shall question loyal friend...
Nay verily it is a furnace
snatching away the scalp,
calling him who drew back and turned away,
who amassed and hoarded.

Surely man was created fretful,
when evil visits him impatient,
when good visits him, grudging,
save those that pray,
and continue at their prayers,
those in whose wealth is a right known
for the beggar and the outcast,
who confirm the Day of Doom
and go in fear of the chastisement of the Lord...
And guard their private parts
save from their wives and what their right hand owns
then not being blameworthy...Those shall be in gardens, high-honored.[6]

As in biblical prophecy, economic injustice figures prominently as doomworthy; what counts as virtue in capitalism—amassing wealth—is a supreme vice. Likewise, both traditions feature the attempt to contain sexuality, male as well as female, within an intensified patriarchal propriety. Moreover, as in the Bible, the Day of Doom comes at no predictable point, no end of a line: "To Allah belong the secrets of the heavens and the earth, and the matter of the Hour is as the twinkling of an eye, or it is nearer still."[7] Also, both books remain consistent as to the *agency* of final judgment: the punishment of the evildoer is a divine prerogative—"so their Lord crushed them for their sin, and leveled them."[8] Such punishment is *not* to be exercised by Allah's followers.

Surely upon Us rests the guidance, and to Us belong the Last and the First. No, I have warned you of a Fire that flames.[9]

Islam and Modernity

Deep dissatisfaction with historical injustice boils throughout the prophetic traditions, usually demanding not Armageddon but active application to human social orders. Indeed, Mohammed himself (unlike Jesus, who did not live long enough) conducted a wondrously successful experiment in socially just, spiritually attuned living during his last ten years of life. That was al-Medina.[10] And that memory and its texts give rise in Islam—more consistently than in Christianity, which tends to postpone justice to final judgment—to endless attempts to bring about social justice within human political forms. The concern for the poor, the widow, the orphan never falls silent in the Quran. The *zakat*, or "alms tax," is to be paid every year to help the poor and is the third of the five pillars of Islam.[11] The stunning success of Islam within one century of the prophet's death—becoming an empire extending through Northern Africa, the Spanish Pyrenees, and the Himalayas—was the product of both religious energy and pragmatic expansion. "Western people often assume that Islam is a violent, militaristic faith which imposed itself on its subject peoples at sword-point. This is an inaccurate interpretation of the Muslim wars of expansion."[12] Its success must also be attributed to its relatively moderate practices, requiring obedience to its laws but not conversion to its religion. The conquering Arabs often were met with little resistance.[13]

For almost a millennium, medieval Muslim empires hugely surpassed Western European achievements in trade, social organization, and military conquest. But through what we call the birth of the modern nation-state, beginning in Spain five hundred years ago with its ethnic cleansing (the mass expulsion of Jews and the Muslim Moors) and its aggressive colonial drive, Europe reinvented itself.[14] Still, only two centuries ago did the tables of power turn: first with the British colonization of Mogul India, in the economic plundering and then political domination of Muslim Bengal. Then in 1798 Napoleon, admirer of both the European crusaders and of Islam, attacked Egypt brutally and efficiently.[15] Scientists, Orientalists, and an Enlightenment ideology of freedom accompanied Napoleon's modern occupation army. The Muslim world naturally mutated in response to wave after wave of the aggressions of Western modernity. Muslim leaders had little choice but to modernize in self-defense. They follow the example of Mehmet Ali, who responded to the encounter with Napoleon by seizing power in Egypt in 1805 and superimposing a European and secularizing modernity.[16] The ruthless impositions of these alien forms on local cultures—both by regional leaders and by Europeans—were profoundly disorienting. Modernization was experienced by many Muslims as its own day of doom: "major battles; formidable happenings; calamitous occurrences; terrible catastrophes; the multiplication of evils...the disruption of time, the inversion of the natural order."[17] The modernization process systematically targeted Muslim traditions and institutions, portrayed by indigenous and colonial leaders as obstacles to progress.

Islamic protest movements arose. From 1929 on, the Society of Muslim Brothers—from which hail many al Qaeda brothers and principles—worked to fill the vacuum. It developed a network of social, educational, and economic services, Quranically inspired, for the poor of Egypt. It was too popular to be tolerated by the secular Arab state and only became a militant underground movement in response to vicious persecution—especially by the secularizing nationalist Nasser.[18] A similar process transpired in Iran under the ruthless secularizing rule of Reza Shah Pahlavi. When clergy and students protested, he had them murdered. In 1920 the young Ruholla Mussaui Khomeini (1902–1989) came into this scene, a Shiite mystic, not a "fundamentalist" until much later. In the aftermath of Reza Shah and World War II the U.S. begins to play a new role in the region. Through a CIA-engineered 1953 coup, the popular and democratically elected Mussadiq, who had nationalized the oil industry, was replaced by the deposed son of Reza Shah. "For the hundreds of millions of dollars that the American colonialist imperialists will gain in oil, the oppressed nation will lose all hope of liberty and will have a negative opinion about all the Western world," predicted Ayatollah Kashani.[19]

By necessity the Islamic movements militarized, attempting to defend the integrity of Muslim society both spiritually and socially. Yet this reaction strained Islam. The ruling Shiite theocracy of Iran, for instance, represents a bizarre transmutation of the subtle mysticism and deferred messianism of the Shiite tradition. Fundamentalism began to appear, for instance, in the influential ideology of the Pakistani Mawdudi, who called for a universal jihad against the encroaching Western secularism. He argued that "jihad was the central tenet of Islam. This was an innovation."[20] But only with Sayyid Qutb (1906–1966) does the founder of Islamic fundamentalism in the Sunni world appear. Witnessing Nasser's torture and execution of his fellow Egyptian Brothers, Qutb called for a violent jihad for the political victory of Islam.[21] His innovative Islam provided the main inspiration of the Taliban. That the militant fundamentalisms, contrary to Western stereotype, hardly pose a unified picture is suggested by the fact that in the 1990s the Taliban murdered thousands of Shiite Muslims.

A picture: under Reza Shah, who forbade Islamic dress, the soldiers would use their bayonets to tear off women's veils. The veil had become a symbol of the obstacle to progress–a progress not understood as women's equality, but as Westernization. No wonder many Muslim women voluntarily wear the veil as a symbol of resistance to Western cultural dominance.[22] Juxtapose this current picture: women's faces bared and smiling on the streets of Kabul. "Apocalypse"–the "unveiling"? Who will give it a single face?

Christian Endtimes

While all fundamentalisms offer return to the true origin of the religion, they can only be contextualized as modern phenomena, that is, as radical reactions against modern aggression. But of the three monotheistic religions, Islam was the last to develop its fundamentalist strain, "when modern culture began to take root in the Muslim world in the late 1960's and 1970's."[23] Unlike Christian fundamentalism, the Muslim analogue stresses the prophetic social justice tradition. It must defend against the economic and military aggressions as well as the secularism of Western modernity. The point is that if we want to understand rather than demonize all who resonate with al Qaeda, we will have to understand ourselves better. And "we" are also partly constituted by the tensions of modern secularization and fundamentalist reaction. I cannot detail this more familiar history here, but only point to a peculiar symmetry.

Our own fundamentalists sound strangely like "theirs." Instantaneous was Jerry Falwell's response to 9/11. He said he would point a figurative finger at those "who have tried to secularize America" and say, "you helped this happen." It was the feminists, abortionists, homosexuals, and defenders of civil liberty who got the finger. Added Pat Robertson, "I totally concur." Yet they are loath to identify God with the cause of Islamic terror. So "He" didn't directly will it. "He lifted the curtain of protection."[24] Yet another "unveiling"! Thus, the U.S., with its sinful secularism, attested to flagrantly in gender equality and sexual immorality, is getting its comeuppance. Christian and Muslim absolutists are one in blaming secular America for 9/11.

A more moderate fundamentalist approach, intent on displaying its patriotism, runs like this: "Colin Powell said it well, 'We will go after the branch and root to get at these terrorists.' For it is the soil that yields the plant. If it is Osama bin Laden, he can only exist as an evil terrorist because of the country that harbored and supported him."[25] This writer takes Powell's justification of a war against Afghanistan and turns it into a call for our repentance: "As Christians, it is also now our job to go after the branch and root as well, and even to the soil, to create the kind of environment that will please God for the fruit that will be produced. In our own country, we have not done that well. The devastation of these days is a wake up call."[26] I would concur, as would most progressive commentators, with that latter point. After much biblical prooftexting, he gets down to his point—no call to deal justly with Islamic peoples or our own ethnically vulnerable populations, but rather, the familiar agenda: to correct all of our above sexual deviancies or else we will become like bin Laden. The author again fails to note that his problem with secularism echoes theirs, that the Taliban sexual ethos resembles his own ideal.The main difference between fundamentalisms (apart from the divinization of a prophet as God) seems to be the lack of interest in economic and social injustice among the born again.

However much we oppose their agendas—and certainly their violence—shall we scorn the antimodern apocalypses? The project of modern "progress" has won its indubitable advances in science, standard of life, democracy, and finally even the rights of women. But at what cost? Repeated acts of ethnic cleansing, conquest, and genocide; an economic hegemony that keeps most of the world's populations, human and nonhuman, dependent, subject to our markets and, if need be, to extinction. So the hope for a just and sustainable peace arises within a theological *post*modernism, predicated on a steadfast excavation of the systematic violence of the modern project of the last five hundred years.[27]

Is the whole modern complex fatally flawed? Should the apocalyptic reverberations of that question be ignored just now? Neither Christian nor Islamic fundamentalists will join the (too secular) struggle of environmentalists and workers against globalization. But they all know how to map the economy of the Beast. While always locating Armageddon in the Middle East, U.S. fundamentalists have long identified Manhattan as Babylon: "the nations have drunk of the wine of the wrath of her fornication…and the merchants of the earth have grown rich from the power of her luxury" (Rev. 18:3). Even this feminist pro-choice New Yorker unhappily appreciates the fit.

The Empire Strikes Back

In Christianity the prophetic social-justice tradition, along with its anti-imperialist apocalypse, was marginalized from the time of the Christianization of the Roman Empire. The U.S. is the only present candidate for world empire; more specifically, it is what is dubbed our economic neo-imperialism that, with the backup of our military hypertechnology, maintains our global dominance. Apocalypse in the biblical text and in the 9/11 strike is directed *against* Rome/Babylon, against all empire. Of course the empire retaliates. Our government sends forth the powers of state-authorized terror, legalized as war. But being the government of a nation born and born again from the narratives of millennialist messianism, it cannot resist the rhetoric of apocalypse: our mission, our moment; "they" are evil, and we fight pure evil; if our bombs cause "collateral damage," that too is "the enemy's" fault for hiding behind women and children; if children starve there, if freedom is compromised here, that is too bad; we will not stop until evil has been annihilated. Yet if our aggression only spawns martyrs for Islam, does this mean that we will never stop, that this final war will spiral on—until the End?

The logic of apocalyptic overdetermination need not prevail. The "spiral of violence" can be broken.[28] But we may have a difficult time imagining a realistic alternative. The unknowable gains daily in endtimes density: Can we prevent the humanitarian catastrophe that we are causing? Do the terrorists have nuclear weapons? smallpox? Can our assault yield the capture of the culpable parties or only unify more Muslims against us, Israel, and their own hated governments? Will all the issues that matter unconditionally to the future of a sustainable planet, such as global warming, the ozone hole, the economy, racial justice, education—already on the back burner—be ignored until truly it is too late? The uncertainty lurches at moments toward the unbearable. Yet it is precisely the tone of *certainty* that rings apocalyptic, the certainty of what is evil. And so we are certain of "our" goodness. Fundamentalism has reacted not only against the arrogance of modernity but against its growth toward pluralism, ambiguity, and indeterminacy. Yet who does not grasp at straws of certainty when so much is at risk?

Apocalypse Left

Even the progressive U.S. response gets caught in the apocalyptic mirror game. Chickens come home to roost; the *real* cause is our policy in the Middle East, especially in Israel; or the *real* cause is the global economy. While I heard myself in the initial shock laying these propositions on my students, and heard them echoing through my theological community, their indignant certainties rang hollow at ground zero. I needed something more difficult and honest than the monocausal explanations, the warmed-over and misfitting Vietnam-era slogans, the I-told-you-so's that did tell the truth.[29] The construal of Islam as a mere third world victim of an omnipotent U.S. suggests a kind of negative grandiosity that may satisfy our conventions of protest but ill serves its own cause—that of peace with justice. Not just because it is heard as "justifying" the terrorists but also because it reinscribes the orientalist stereotype of the helpless, feminized, and dangerously homogenized Other. Moreover, it reduces the long history of aggressive interactions between Islamic empires and the crusading powers of the West, as well as of internecine battles within Islam itself, to a faded leftist messianism: evil U.S. versus oppressed innocence.

Might we instead confess that the U.S. has been multiply culpable in the Middle East: in donning during the Cold War the old mantle of the European imperial aggressions; in our economically determinative, ecologically devastating oil addiction; in our support of the Israeli state's immoral policies toward the Palestinians; in our patronage of unpopular Arab governments. These legitimate grievances against us ferment a bitter, transgenerational rage—rife for manipulation by propagandists and terrorists. But they do not collapse into a single explanation of 9/11. Indeed, the very model of a monocausal explanation, with its linear predictability and its indignant certainty, echoes with the hoofbeats of secular apocalypse.

A nonlinear model will better serve understanding. It requires multiple causal paths, many but not all derived from U.S. neo-imperialism. These paths wind through the oldest internecine minefields of the Middle East, and therefore of Western civilization: that of the sibling rivals of the patrilineage of Abraham. In other words there are multiple causes that at every juncture require a complex analysis. For us to take *responsibility* for our own arrogant and unjust history in the Middle East is not to accept *blame* for the terrorist attack. We did not "cause" it. We can acknowledge that we have done much to make such an attack likely and that until we shift course in policies vastly exceeding the matter of our own security, but essential to it, we will continue to lend terrorism a wide base of respect among Muslims of many perspectives. *Responsible action* is based on continued work to understand and thus *respond* to—not just *react* to—those who act as our enemies. A strategy of responsible action would not grant moral credibility to terrorists; on the contrary, it remains the only way to maintain moral credibility for the U.S. among our allies and at home. It is therefore the only way for the U.S. to meet our legitimate objective, that of self-defense. This is the pragmatic argument that Christians can make loudly and clearly—whether or not we think that this or any war is *justifiable*.

Apocalyptic Terror and Just War

So to the question of a "just war." Self-defense against an aggressor has traditionally counted as a just cause for the use of force. To my nonviolently set ears, the phrase "just war" remains an oxymoron. But I recognize that the Christian basis for pacifism arises within the context of a colonized people, quite the opposite of my own context, which more resembles the Constantinian empire. Christianity in its mainline forms has accepted the inevitability of some wars (as Jesus seems to have done) and so—at its better moments, when it is not itself fostering war—attempts to impose realistic constraints. In this, and not in its pacifist heritage, it overlaps with Judaism and Islam. I also confess that as a Christian who has practiced solidarity with some insurgencies who used violence (such as the African National Congress) and who thinks it is better that the U.S. entered World War II than had it not, I have implicitly accepted a form of just war ethos.

Might the discourse of a just war at present have more power than that of pacifism to advance the process of a just peace? I found eye-opening a succinct article on "Ends and Means: Defining a Just War" by Richard Falk, a leading scholar of international law and an antiwar activist since Vietnam who has never "supported a shooting war in which the United States was involved."[30] It appeared shortly after the bombing had begun, and so reflects an already past moment. Nonetheless I cite his strong position:

> The war in Afghanistan against *apocalyptic terrorism* qualifies in my understanding as the first truly just war since World War II. But the justice of the cause and of the limited ends is in danger of being negated by the injustice of improper means and excessive ends. Unlike World War II and prior just wars, this one can be won only if tactics adhere to legal and moral constraints on the means used to conduct it, and to limited ends.[31]

"Apocalyptic terrorism"? Has Falk also gotten sucked into the mirror game of apocalypses? He argues that the label is useful in that it places the "extremist political vision held by Osama bin Laden...outside any framework of potential reconciliation" for several reasons:

> Its genocidal intent is directed generically against Americans and Jews; its proclaimed goal is waging an unconditional civilizational war–Islam against the West–without drawing any distinction between civilian and military targets; it has demonstrated a capacity and a willingness to inflict massive and traumatizing damage on our country and a tactical ingenuity and ability to carry out its missions of destruction by reliance on the suicidal devotion of its adherents.[32]

This strong characterization clearly distinguishes bin Laden from other Islamic militants. Yet Falk is just as clear that the U.S. response was already in mid-October beginning to violate the constraints of a just war. He warns that many in the White House "seem to regard the attacks as an occasion to implement their own vision of a new world, one that proposes to rid the world of 'evil' and advances its own apocalyptic vision."[33]

By the time this volume appears, our use of violence in self-defense may or may not have already liquidated the restraints that just war doctrine–an amalgam of mutually reinforcing traditions of international law and all major religions–demands.[34] At best, the formulae of just war remain subject to hugely divergent applications. Our government's apocalyptic propensity, however, "to approach war as a matter of confronting evil" may preclude even a relatively just war. "In such a view, victory can be achieved only by the total defeat of the other, and with it, the triumph of the good."[35] Falk seems, in other words, to recognize the threat of competing apocalypses. In the terse rhetoric of international law, the "apocalyptic terrorism" recognizes the novel threat of this new and intentional enactment of politico-religious messianism. But then the point is precisely not to respond in kind. And that is the cool logic of this moment: to mirror the apocalyptic terrorists with our own total war is to hand them final victory. In the face of apocalyptic terrorism, the win/lose logic of apocalypse cannot be played by a nation-state anymore—without assuring our own loss.

Historically, Armageddon and just war represent opposites on the Christian continuum: apocalyptic communities, envisioning total war and final utopia, were in practice pacifist; just war arises as an ideal within the context of a Christian empire, in which apocalypse with its revolutionary hopes was repressed, its End endlessly deferred. The religious organizations of the U.S. operate willy-nilly, and hopefully with eyes open, within that latter context. Of course the "realistic" idea of just war remains, ironically, almost as utopian with regard to the rarity of its practice as pacifism. Does this mean that our pacifist heritage is irrelevant? Not at all. Even from Falk's strategic perspective, "the spiritually motivated pacifist witness can be both inspirational and instructive, and help to mitigate and interrogate militarist postures."[36] Standing on the fluid border of that pacifist witness, I suggest that religious leaders can be most effective in our mitigation of militarism if we also *respect* the just war strategy as a regulative ethical discourse and *use it as rhetorically needed to mitigate violence*—whether or not we believe that such a thing as a just war has ever existed and however badly our military may commit "the injustice of improper means and excessive ends." But as religious leaders, we speak a different language than political analysts. It is our task not to condone even limited uses of violence but to deplore the causes, the effects, and the spiral of violence. Walter Wink's concept of a "militant nonviolence," modeled on "Jesus' third way," well supports the churches' needed strength of witness.[37] Yet at this moment nonviolence seems reactive as a construct, the negation of a negation; I would subsume it under the wider category of *responsible action*.[38]

Love Whom?

For a U.S. Christian leader at this moment, apocalyptic certainty—with its aura of political purity—is not only unnecessary but illusory. But this much seems clear to me: we must make clear that all rhetoric of Christian virtue or heritage is disqualified if we do not espouse a Christian view of the enemy. Does this mean to "love" Osama and company? Love the enemy was an imperative of the gospel, not the apocalypse. It has held up poorly under the least historic pressure. It may not have been directed at distant political enemies anyway. But for this reason we had better keep trying it: on an interdependent and indeterminate planet it may be the path of greatest realism. But the love imperative does not call me to "love" any mass murderer. It does not imagine reconciliation with apocalyptic terrorists. I do not even believe it calls me to "forgive" anyone who does not repent, that is, cease to act as enemy—except in his or her potentiality to do so. I love that potentiality in any terrorist, if it is not dead. I love it as I love my own potentiality to outgrow fear and respond in love. This love is not meant in any sentimentalized, personalized, and unbiblical sense. But the inscrutably all-embracing love of God demands from followers of Jesus–the Jewish radical, prophet among Muslims, incarnation of Love itself among Christians–some unexceptionable version of the golden rule.

We must demand from any Christians, including a born-again president, what Islam also demands of its followers: *that we treat all enemies as human beings,* that is as creatures capable of responsibility and only therefore culpable. We hold them responsible for their inhumanities precisely because we are willing to take responsibility for our own. The Christian principle does not read: Do unto others what they would do unto us. Their violence against noncombatants will never justify ours. Their ethnocentrism, hatred, or aggression no more justifies our own than our own prior ethnocentrism, hatred, and aggression has justified theirs. Rather, it is only our adherence to a just standard that justifies our condemnation of their violence. And *justice* means *acting in consciousness of the relationships that bind us together, relations of fragile, global interdependence.*

That interdependence expresses the nonlinear, multicausal history that binds us all–and that can amplify chaotically out of control at any time. But chaos is not answered–responsibly–by dominance but by wisdom. Uncertainty will not go away. But our fear of the others with whom we are globally interdependent could dissipate. For it is our interdependence–even of "Islam" and "the West," "Christian" and "secular"–that can, and for Christians must, reveal the difficult universality of divine love.

This is not Sunday school. This is the world hanging, as it sometimes does, in the balance. In our risky interdependence roots the ability to love the other–even the Muslim extremist–as myself: for we are not seperate. Minimally, responsibility to ourselves and to the world dictates that we recognize our specific interdependence with the Afghan people. We entered this war by appeal to the precedent of World War II; therefore, we can only responsibly exit after having realized an analogue of the Marshall Plan, with the help of the nations of the world funding and facilitating a just and sustainable peace. Responsibility would also mean a persistent renegotiation of the terms of our friendship with Israel. Christians must see through the apocalyptic mirror game of the new Muslim anti-Semitism and the Israeli anti-Palestinianism. Israel has been a comfortable, Western-style ally, but Israel's own secular modernism, a thorn in the flesh of embattled Islam, is ironically belied by the fundamentalist messianism of its own ultra-orthodox constituency.

Religious leaders in the present crisis must insist upon *at least* a tri-faith, nonlinear model for peacemaking. We do this confessing our part in the "many-sided contest among these three followers–not one of them by any means a monolithic, unified camp–of the most jealous of all gods."[39] We must insist on the participation of the daughters of Sarah and of Hagar at every negotiating table–how else should the fratricide cease? We support not the goal of the "end" of terrorism but of "the healing of the nations" (Rev. 22:2). We will not stop remembering the deep history and envisioning the open future: the alpha and the omega not of a final war but of a counterapocalypse.

Epilogue

My cab is stuck in heavy evening traffic (too many of us afraid of subways this month). Fortunately the driver is an interesting man, articulate and kind. He plunges right in: Of course we must make someone pay for the attack. But the bombs won't do it. We can't ignore everything else, especially the economy. He says he was a Marine in Vietnam, and he recognizes the quagmire we are quickly sinking into. He says he was drafted, and he should have taken his father's advice and resisted or fled to Canada. He fears that our president is a religious fanatic. He tells me of clients rehearsing World Trade Center–relevant verses of Nostradamus. After we have stopped and I have paid, he turns his full face to me, handsome and dark. He says he does not want to depress me, but the aurora up by the Eskimos has been brilliantly red this month. This only happens before terrible world crises. And the Bible refers to the two towers. He says this war may really be the beginning of the end. You know, the End of Time.

I have so liked this thoughtful cabby. I can't just negate or nod. I say, "Don't you think the apocalypse could be a warning, not a foregone conclusion?" "It may not have anything to do with our response," he says. "It may be a matter of forces we have no control over." "Yes. But you seem to live like such a free person. You think hard. You make responsible choices. What if God is one who inspires that freedom, not one who works us like puppets?" He laughs out loud, "You may be right." He drives off chuckling. I stand in the darkness for a moment. I am grateful for his uncertainty.[40]

IN THE NAME OF GOD, THE MERCIFUL, THE COMPASSIONATE.

NOVEMBER 2001

Part 3

Responses of Theology

14

"Make Them as Tumbleweed"

David R. Blumenthal

Disclosure

I write as a Jew. I also write as a rabbi and senior academic whose field is theology, and as a heterosexual and upper middle-class, married, male with a family. Two of our sons, a daughter-in-law, and some students are living in Jerusalem. I write, too, as a long-time supporter of peace in the Middle East. As a college student in the late 1950s at the Hebrew University, I visited a classmate in an Israeli Arab village and I witnessed their humiliation. I regretted this, for them as well as for the Jewish state, though I also saw their enthusiasm as they listened to Nasser's speeches urging that the Jews be pushed into the sea. Later, I supported peace movements in Israel and America, speaking up clearly in favor of a Palestinian state long before Oslo. I also write as a scholar of Judaism under Islam where I have worked with Judaeo-Arabic texts pointing out the deep interrelationship between these two cultures.

I write, too, as an American, born and raised in this country, accustomed to the freedom of movement and speech that characterize this great democracy. I have studied and taught abroad and always been proud to bear my American passport and to see Old Glory flying. I also deeply appreciate the openness of American society, the freedom to construct one's economic and social life, and the lack of suspicion, indeed one might say naive openness, of Americans as a people.

What you are about to read may contain historical errors in this or that detail but it is, nonetheless, true in the broad strokes it sketches. It is how I, one American Jew, feel; and I feel it deeply. I know from discussions with others that it is also how many Jews and Americans feel. What I am about to say will not be popular in academic and Christian religious circles; many Jews will disagree with it too. But it needs to be said.

Finally, this is written on October 28, 2001. It may be woefully out of date by the time you read it. History may have proven me wrong, or right; I, of course, cannot know. But we, Americans and Jews, stand at an ethical and political crossroad. As we choose our way, we must examine where we have come from, know who we are, and turn toward our God with the clearest vision we can muster.

Accusation

Psalm 120

¹A song of the steps.
To the Lord I called when I was in trouble
and God answered me.
  ²Lord, save my very being from lips which lie,
  from tongues which deceive.
    ³What will it do for you? What will it add to you? –
    a tongue which deceives.
    ⁴The sharp arrows of the fighter
    and the burning coals of the juniper tree.
⁵Woe unto me, for I have lived among the peoples of Asia Minor
and dwelled in the tents of the Arabs.
⁶For too long have I let myself dwell
with those who hate peace.
⁷I am for peace.
But when I speak, they are for war.¹

EXPLICATION

This is the first of the fifteen songs that were sung on the steps of the temple in Jerusalem. In verse 1, the psalmist begins his soliloquy, for which we are the audience, by telling us that it is to the Lord that he has called and that God has answered him in the past. This enables us, as we pray this psalm, to follow the path of the psalmist and to turn to God in prayer in times of trouble.

In verse 2, the psalmist gives us the text of his prayer: a pleading that God save him from liars. In verses 3 and 4, in an aside within his soliloquy, the psalmist turns to his enemies to ask what good lying will do them. He also answers his own rhetorical question: Lying will surely bring them punishment.

In verses 5–7, the psalmist returns to his soliloquy, conveying to us the full sense of his anguish at his failed mission of peace.

Three linguistic notes: In verse 2, "my very being" renders the Hebrew *nefesh;* so does "myself" in verse 6. This term came to mean "soul," but only in later Hebrew. In the Tanakh, it means "me" or "my very being." In verse 5, "peoples of Asia Minor" renders the Hebrew *meshekh.* According to the genealogy of Genesis 10:2 and elsewhere (Ezek. 27:13, etc.), this refers to the people of Asia Minor. Similarly, "the Arabs" renders the Hebrew *kedar* which, according to Genesis 28:13 and elsewhere (Song 1:5, etc.), refers to the Arabs.

INTERPRETATION

Could any text express the anguish of the current situation better? Our enemies speak with "lips that lie and tongues which deceive."

They call out the purity of their cause, but calmly kill 6000 innocent people. They proclaim the holiness of their faith, but deliberately assassinate two opposition leaders. They declare their righteousness, but commit acts of terror and support terrorists on a global basis. They announce their rectitude, but they appropriate the cause of other terrorists. They don't even make political demands; they just label us "Satan" and promise death and destruction. They proclaim their dedication to justice, but protect terrorists when they are their own and resist any attempt on our part to fight terrorism as an "attack on their religion." They proclaim the sanctity of their holy places and their love of their people, but they place their arms caches and headquarters in mosques, schools, and hospitals, using those sanctuaries as places from which to fire on us. They assert the rights of civilians, but coopt young men into forced military service. They claim we conspire against them, but it is they who maintain a subtle worldwide network of terror.

They tell the West that they will control terrorists, but they don't. They promise security, but don't deliver it. They commit themselves to cease-fire agreements in their public pronouncements, but their taped telephone conversations show them giving orders to continue the drive-by shootings of ordinary citizens traveling home. They pronounce loudly their regret at suicide bombings that kill religious children in a pizza shop, but they put up a public museum dedicated to exactly that attack which makes a hero of the suicide bomber. They condemn the killing of innocent and secular teenagers in a seaside café, but they refuse to arrest the known perpetrators of such atrocities and even call them heroes. They give interviews to the Western press about the need for peace, but the second in command is recorded giving the order to assassinate a cabinet minister. They make known their political demands, but their actions show that their true goal is not an agreement but our elimination. They say to the West that they want a state, but in their mosques, schools, marketplaces, and media, they see statehood as only a step toward our annihilation. They vaunt their love of children, yet send them to the front lines of conflict. What father would urge his child to be killed? What mother would wish martyrdom for her child? All this, while proclaiming children sacrosanct. "You shall not allow any of your offspring to be offered up to Molech" (Lev. 18:21).

We Americans are just too naive. We are too open, too honest, to believe that there are people who really hate us. We want to trust the world; indeed, we do trust it. We leave our society open and terrorists come in. We do not—or did not—have guards at our public places. We do not check the identity of strangers; we welcome them and do not permit ourselves to discriminate against them, much less to persecute and kill them. We open our airwaves, our malls, our press, and our means of transportation to all. We believe in the Constitution, in the right of every person, even non-citizens, to a life of physical security, economic opportunity, and political freedom.

But hate knows no boundaries. Hate comes from the depths, from the dark places of the human soul. It consumes. Hate makes one speak with "lips which lie and tongues which deceive." It is very hard for us to realize that our enemies consciously lie and deceive. We, in our openness, instinctively trust their assurances of goodness, and we close our ears and minds to the hatred that emanates from them.

This is very dangerous, for hate, when combined with power, can only lead to extermination. Hate strives for power and, when it achieves power, hate annihilates. Lying is a means to achieve power; it is a means to an end. Lying is a prelude to destruction. If these liars ever get power over us, they will try to convert us and, if we refuse, they will exterminate us.

And yet, how long have we tried to make peace with them? How long have we kowtowed to Saudi Arabia, even when they did not allow the Christian and Jewish American soldiers who were defending them to pray on American bases in Saudi Arabia? How long have we accepted the legitimacy of the bin Laden family, while they gave him money and provided channels for moving his funds and businesses to cover his activities? How often have we received Yasir Arafat at the White House, even though we knew that it was he, personally, who gave the orders to shoot down civilian airplanes in the 1970s and even though we have recorded tapes of his instructions to increase the violence of the intifada even as he assured us that he was trying to reduce the violence? How often have we closed our eyes to Iraqi and Syrian terrorism, accepting at face value their protestations of innocence and their corrupt expression of Islamic solidarity? And, how often have we been too tolerant of anti-Zionist polemic in international forums, accepting it as something less than what it really is: an expression of Jew-hatred spewed into the realm of public discourse?

I do not claim for a moment that the policies of the American or Israeli governments are without blame. I am a student of the biblical prophets and have been active in a number of protest movements against those policies that I consider unjust. It is my duty as an heir to the prophets, as a citizen of the United States, and as a member of the Jewish people to protest when the authorities do wrong; and I have. Yes, our country has supported dictatorial regimes that have oppressed the Arab masses. Yes, the military-industrial complex has kept us dependent on Arab oil and made a great deal of money for the already-rich at the expense of the common person in much of the world. Yes, American culture with all its openness has its faults, its vulgarity, its violence, its racism, and its exploitation of the poor. And I understand that others do not even want to swallow the whole pill of freedom. Much of what we have done is wrong and must be fought, but America is not "Satan."

And yes, the Israeli government has oppressed Palestinians, punishing the innocent together with the wicked. Yes, they have set up settlements on Arab land and deprived many of their basic civil rights. Yes, they have not treated even Israeli Palestinians with equality. Yes, they have their own form of racism and sexism. And, yes, the occupation is wrong and innocent people have been killed. All of this is wrong and must be fought, but Israel is not the evil empire, vermin to be eradicated.

On the matter of religion, things are not much different. They proclaim their religion as one of equality, but they practice extreme forms of sexism. They declare their religion is humanitarian, but in some places, they actually run the slave trade and, in others, they control the opium trade, funneling opium to us with the conscious intention of corrupting us. They say their religion teaches tolerance, but their basic doctrine preaches uncompromising proselytization. They say their religion encourages coexistence, but their basic doctrine teaches that any territory once conquered by them is forever sacred and can never again be yielded to an unbeliever. They see the crusades as a temporary distortion in their dominance which they gloriously rectified by force; this serves as an example for the present and the future. No one can have sovereignty over land that once belonged to them, though they talk peaceful global politics when they are in the West. They say their religion values education, but their schools fill their students with hatred and exclusivist intolerance. And they proclaim the high value of charity, but use those charities to support murder.

To be sure, Islam has its moments of sublime vision as well as its moments of terror. So do Judaism, Christianity, Hinduism, and other world religions. To be sure, Muslims, too, are varied. Not all Muslims are fundamentalists, nationalists, or terrorists, just as not all Jews are nationalist fanatics and not all Christians are exploitative imperialists. But the extremist elements have gained the upper hand in the world of Islam and, perhaps worse, the voice of self-criticism has been all but silenced by the rhetoric of solidarity and the threat of reprisal. A few critical voices exist in western Islam; almost none in the heartland because ethnic and religious solidarity trumps universal ethics and morality, and because death awaits the dissenter.

And we, in our naivete, believe them. We, in our desire for openness and peace, trust what they tell us when they talk to us. We do not even hear the religious roots of their hatred for us. We engage them in interreligious dialogue, but that is part of the "lips which lie and tongues which deceive." We, in our naivete, want to believe that there are "moderates" and "dialogue partners," so we hear selectively, and they continue to lie because it serves to cover their true intentions. We, in our political correctness, hesitate to criticize our "allies" and their religion, so they continue to talk peace to us while practicing hatred against us and teaching hatred of us to their own.

"I am for peace. But, when I speak, they are for war."

The time has come to turn to God and ask for God's help in defeating our enemies.

Prayer

Psalm 83

¹A psalm of Asaf
²God, do not You be silent.
Do not be still.
Do not be quiet, God.
³For, indeed, Your enemies roar.
Those who hate You have lifted up their heads.
⁴They connive in secret against Your people.
They take counsel against Your treasure.
⁵They say, "Let us go and wipe them out from being a nation
so that the name of Israel never be mentioned again."
⁶Indeed they have put their hearts together.
They have cut a covenant even against You. –
⁷The tents of Syrians and the Saudis,
Yemenis and Iranians,
⁸Hamas, Islamic Jihad, and Tanzim,
the Palestinian Authority and the dwellers of Lebanon.
⁹The Iraqis too have joined them;
they are the arm of the sons of Lot. Selah.
　¹⁰Do to them as You did to Midian,
　to Sisera and Yavin at the stream of Kishon.
　¹¹They were destroyed at Ein Dor.
　They were dung for the land.
　¹²Make their leaders as Orev and Ze'ev.
　all their chiefs as Zevah and Tsalmuna.
　¹³For they have said,
　"We shall inherit for ourselves the gardens of God."

¹⁴Oh, God
make them as tumbleweed!
as straw blown before the wind!
¹⁵As fire burns a forest,
as flames cause a mountainside to blaze,
¹⁶so should You pursue them in Your windstorm
and confound them in Your tempest!
¹⁷Fill their faces with humiliation
so that they seek Your Name, Lord!
¹⁸Let them be ashamed and confounded forever!
And let them be disgraced and destroyed!
¹⁹So that they know that You, Your Name, Lord, are alone,
far above all creation.

EXPLICATION AND INTERPRETATION

This psalm is divided into two parts, divided by the word "selah": the first describes the situation of enemies that surround the people and plot openly their total annihilation; the second is the psalmist's prayer that God thoroughly defeat them, politically and morally.

Note the perfectly clear rhetoric of the enemy in verses 5 and 13; an à propos summary of what is said against us today in the Arab media, even if we don't want to hear it.

In verses 7–9, I have substituted modern names for the traditional text which, written in biblical times, reads as follows: "The tents of Edom and the Ishmaelites, Moab and the Hagarites. Geval, Amon, and Amalek; Philistia and the residents of Tyre. Assyria, too, has joined them; they are the arm of the sons of Lot. Selah." Hagarites is a synonym for Ishmaelites. The nations of Geval, Amon, and Amalek occupied what is now Jordan. Philistia was located in what is now the Gaza Strip though it covered more territory to the north. Tyre is still in Lebanon. Assyria was northwest of what is now Iraq. The modern names give the sense of contemporary reality rather than that of ancient history.

By contrast, I have left the biblical names of the defeated foes in verses 10–12 precisely in order to invoke history and the covenant with God that governs history. Midian is soundly defeated by Gideon (Judg. 7–8). Yavin, king of Hazor, and his general, Sisera, are soundly defeated by Deborah, Barak, and Yael (Judg. 5–6). The battle of Ein Dor is not directly recorded in connection with the war against Yavin and Sisera, but Ein Dor is close to Taànakh (Josh. 17:11), which is the location of the crucial battle in Deborah's war. Orev and Ze'ev are Midianite commanders killed in the battle (Judg. 7:25). Zevah and Tsalmuna are Midianite kings killed in battle (Judg. 8:12–21). The sons of Lot, by incestuous relationship with his daughters, were Moab and Amon (Gen. 19: 29–38). The historical references, thus, were quite real and serve as a powerful precedent for invoking God's protection. Note, too, the clear statement of intent by these enemies in verse 13: they intend to displace and disinherit the people.

Verses 14–19 are part of the psalmist's prayer, but I have set them apart because they can apply to any enemy in any time. The metaphors are very powerful: tumbleweed, straw in the wind, and a raging forest fire. The proper punishment is also strong: humiliation, shame, confounding, and disgrace, followed by destruction. The ultimate purpose, however, is not revenge but the acknowledgment of God's sovereignty over all God's creation. (The "they" in the last verse may refer to the destroyed enemies, or to the surviving enemies and bystanders.)[2]

Point/Counterpoint

"There is a time to plant, and a time to uproot that which is planted; a time to kill, and a time to heal; a time to break down, and a time to build up…a time to love, and a time to hate; a time of war, and a time of peace." (Eccl. 3:2–8)

As Americans, who are optimistic and agreeable in our national character, we like to think that it is always a time to plant, to heal, and to build up. As Westerners, perhaps under the influence of the motif of Christian love, we like to think that it is always a time of love and peace. But it is not so. There truly is a time to uproot that which is planted, to kill, and to break down. There really is a time to hate and to make war. This is because there truly are people who hate us; we really do have enemies.

As Jews, universally hated and persecuted over centuries, we like to think that peace and coexistence is possible. We yearn for the time when we will not have to fight to justify our simple existence, when the nations of the world will say, "Here are the Jews. They, too, deserve a homeland. They, too, deserve physical security, peace, and freedom; a place among us." But this has not come yet. The Arab and Muslim nations resent our very existence in their midst, wish and work hard for our destruction, and would annihilate us if they could. And the West, while sometimes affirming us, sees us more as a thorn in the side of international peace. This is an illusion for the West, but it is so. Jew hatred really is a permanent fixture of human civilization, even among nations who do not know Jews or Jewish history. Jew hatred truly is an existential fact.

Of course, we (myself included) will try to keep the door of dialogue open with those who also desire to build and to make peace. We will continue to talk to those who talk to us in truth and sincerity, and there are people like that. In the end, there is no other way but dialogue. Of course, we will continue to work toward coexistence, tolerance, and interhuman understanding, linking hands and effort with men and women of goodwill everywhere. However, we will do this with a certain degree of reserve, even of suspicion. When trust is shaken, one cannot abandon trust, but one must be careful in offering it yet again. Still, we (I) will try.

But I will also, insofar as I can, work toward the defeat of my enemies and support those who share that goal. And I will pray that God utterly defeat my enemies; thoroughly and completely. In so doing, I will keep alive not only the integrity of my own personal and national existence, but also the hope of all people for a world in which coexistence, tolerance, and interhuman understanding are basic values of all men and women everywhere. "You who would love the Lord, hate evil" (Ps. 97:10).

15

Truth-telling Comfort

Walter Brueggemann

The events of September 11, 2001 (the airplane attacks in New York City and Washington, D.C.), evoke for me the sobering verdict of Karl Barth:

> As ministers we ought to speak of God. We are human, however, and so cannot speak of God. We ought therefore to recognize both our obligation and our inability and by that very recognition give God the glory.[1]

This surely is the perplexity in which pastors of the church find ourselves always, but intensely so in the face of that ominous happening. Of course I have no warrant to speak beyond that of every sister and brother in ministry to speak when we cannot; but like every brother and sister in ministry, I have some obligation to try.

I.

The first word to be spoken in and by the church of course concerns *grief and comfort* over the insane loss of life that is, in the countless concrete cases, completely nonsensical. The grief is about loss, more so about meaningless, violent loss, and it must be uttered deep and loud and long, and not quenched soon. I suspect that the church will be driven to texts of sadness such as it has not "needed" for a long time. The grief surely concerns personal loss. For this, a series of lament psalms provide a powerful script.

But the loss, beyond the personal, is a systemic shattering, a new public sense of vulnerability and outrage, an abrupt subverting of our shared sense that we in the U.S. are somehow immune from the rage of the world. There is currently great attention to "lament psalms" as they function in "pastoral care," an immense gain in church practice. Not so much noticed, however, are "communal laments"(such as Ps. 74, 79) that bespeak the shattering of the most elemental public symbols of coherence and meaning, in the Old Testament embodied in the Jerusalem temple. This public dimension of grief is deep underneath personal loss, and for the most part, not easily articulated among us. But grief will not be worked through well or adequately until attention goes underneath the personal to the public and communal. My expectation is that pastors, liturgically and pastorally, most need to provide opportunity and script for lament and complaint and grief for a long time. No second maneuver after grief should be permitted to crowd in upon this raw, elemental requirement.

The full voice of grief is to be matched, in pastoral attentiveness, by the *enactment of comfort* that seeks to meet grief. That comfort of course begins in bodily contact; but eventually we must speak about the God of all comfort beyond our feeble but indispensable personal offer of comfort. I suspect that in our effort to speak credible comfort, we will be driven back to Easter seriousness, an Easter claim that has not been very serious or even credible in much of our bourgeois self-sufficiency. The claim on which everything rests for us, however, is that the God of the gospel has rendered impotent "the last enemy" who can no longer rob us of life with the God of whom Paul affirms:

> For I am convinced that neither death, nor life, nor angels, nor rulers, nor things present, nor things to come, nor powers, nor height, nor depth, nor anything else in all creation, will be able to separate us from the love of God in Christ Jesus our Lord. (Romans 8:38–39)

We pastors utter these words almost every time there is a funeral. But now, I suspect, we will be tested by this required Easter utterance. On the one hand we will be tested to see if we subscribe enough ourselves to say it; on the other, we are challenged to make sure that the affirmation is not glib in its failure to credit the durability of Friday and the permeability of Saturday, the power of which is not fully sated by Sunday morning. Church people will be helped by the affirmation that the anguish of Friday and Saturday persist, as we know in our own experience.

Grief and comfort come first, and are the peculiar work of the believing community. For it is the comfort out beyond our management, the reality of God, that makes grief without protective denial possible. It is now frequently said that the U.S. church is "theologically soft" on the things that count. Now we shall see. We shall variously find out for ourselves in the dark, silent hours of pastoral resolve.

II.

Beyond that obvious but urgent pastoral task that is entrusted peculiarly to such as we, we are drawn back to first questions by *the power of negation,* the kind of question that we often need not face. President Bush has said in response to the disaster, "Our nation has seen evil." He of course did not exposit his use of the word "evil," but his usage has given me pause. Most likely the President referred to the "evil persons" who committed these acts of brutality, and that dimension of evil is not to be discounted.

But for pastors, the term "evil" evokes more and is not easily contained in human explanations about particular sins enacted by human agents. For "evil" draws us beyond "bad deeds" to cosmic questions. Very much Christian triumphalism claims easily that God in Jesus—at Easter—has eliminated the cosmic power of negation. Barth, however, has written of the durable power of "Nothingness," and almost all of us are familiar with Cullman's suggestive notion about the continued threat of the enemy between D Day and V-E Day. More recently Jon Levenson, a Jewish interpreter, has shown that in the Hebrew Bible evil as a cosmic force persists, made visible in concrete acts, but not contained in or reduced to visible acts. Evil persists in a powerful way in defiance of the will of the Creator.

So what shall we tell our children? Perhaps we will have learned enough from the Jewish Holocaust to refrain from any glib triumphalism, in order to affirm that God's crucified way in the world continues to be vulnerable and at risk from the demonic forces that may be in a last gasp, but in a powerful last gasp. Our children, so protected and privileged, may need to be delivered from romantic innocence to recognize that we live in a profoundly contested world, contested all the way down between God's goodwill and the deathliness of evil. Our commitment in the thick contest, moreover, matters, so that when we sign on (in baptism), we join the contest as partisans of the Vulnerable One, and join the at-risk vocation that is the God-willed future of the world.

III.

Finally, of course, pastors with a cunning sense of good timing will eventually have to raise questions about U.S. policy and U.S. entanglement in the spiral of violence that continues to escalate. Much of popular opinion, reinforced by official posturing, acts as though Reinhold Niebuhr had never spoken about U.S. innocence and self-righteousness. The huge temptation for "Christian America" is to imagine that the U.S. is a righteous empire that endlessly does good around the world, comfortably portrayed in Manichean categories of good and evil. Such knee-jerk response to the crisis traffics in a combination of chauvinism and unreflective Christian triumphalism that refuses to think systemically about the U.S. as the international bully that continues to enact and embody the "Christian West" against non-Christian societies with its huge economic leverage, and with immense, unrivalled military power. And with the gospel of Western globalism, the U.S. is passionately committed to override the fabric of any other kind of culture.

The prophetic task surely has never been more problematic for us than in this issue. The old texts articulate the stunning claim that God can indeed critique and move against God's own chosen people. The simple prophetic articulation by itself is too raw and must be accompanied by patient education in systemic analysis of power. An analysis is known and implied in the prophetic texts, but seldom made explicit.

There will be, to be sure, little patience among us for such systemic analysis, and pastors should not, in my judgment, resort to this second task too soon. But if pastors eventually settle only for interpersonal "grief and comfort," the deep issues of U.S. militarism in the service of U.S. consumerism will go unexplored, because there is almost nobody else for such analysis and such utterance.

This is a moment in which the pastors of the church might together—liberal and conservative—move out of deathly intramural spats to face big questions about good and evil, and about our U.S. location in the midst of it all. Pastors who face such questions will be engaged in deep questions of their own faith. Pastors who face such questions will be beleaguered, because a triumphant society does not relish truth-telling.

It occurs to me that Paul's lyrical declaration about ministry, so popular in more-or-less innocent ordination sermons, is a moving resource for today:

> We are afflicted in every way, but not crushed; perplexed, but not driven to despair; persecuted, but not forsaken; struck down, but not destroyed; always carrying in the body the death of Jesus, so that the life of Jesus may also be made visible in our bodies. (2 Cor. 4:8–10)

As you know, Paul concludes: "So we do not lose heart" (v. 16). The heartless evils of September 11 could cause loss of heart. But our heart is set elsewhere in joy and freedom, in grace and in truth-telling about the God of all truth.

I suggest that there are a series of important pastoral tasks concerning (a) grief, (b) comfort, (c) cosmic evil, and (d) social analysis. The evils of yesterday create a new context for priority. The rawness will make for careful alternative listening, because the word the church has now to speak matters enormously. Having said that, I finish by insisting, yet again, that the first task is grief, grief to be done long and well before anything else.

16

The Theologian in the Twilight of American Culture

M. Shawn Copeland

I

Just before the 1992 election, in an effort to awaken us to the increasing drift in U.S. culture, politics, and economy, political scientist Manning Marable observed that we were living in the "age of Clarence Thomas and David Duke." Marable spied this gravitational pull not only in Thomas' sexist behavior and Duke's white privilege but in a cultural life lived in thin, nearly moral-less air and deprived of humanity's essential humanness.[1] The behavior and the privilege were concrete and concretely real; they were also symptomatic of grave breakdown, decline, and loss. Since then, Pierre Bourdieu, Barbara Ehrenreich, Susan Haack, bell hooks, Robert Kaplan, Charles Mills, Cornel West, Morris Berman, and most recently, Michael Hardt and Antonio Negri have gone on to expose the brutal intensity and scope of the effort of the socially (i.e., politically, economically, technologically) privileged few around the globe to thwart the aspirations, the hope, and the survival of marginated others.[2] And, on Berman's sobering account, we theologians find ourselves in the "twilight of American culture." That culture, *our* culture, a form of Western culture, Berman argues, is collapsing underneath,

142

accelerating social and economic inequality; declining marginal returns with regard to investment in organizational solutions to socioeconomic problems; rapidly dropping levels of literacy, critical understanding, and general intellectual awareness; and spiritual death—the emptying out of cultural content and the freezing or repackaging of it in formulas—kitsch, in short.[3]

If Berman is sobering, he is not fatalistic, makes no claim on prophecy, and distinguishes his analysis of the history of humankind from that posed by a certain Enlightenment. "Many of us," he states, "want to peer over the next horizon, to have a sense of how it will all come out." But we should not, he continues, be too distraught about the larger picture, about the future over which we have very little, if any, control; even if we did, "the long-term configuration is just going to be whatever it is."[4] Berman concludes his analysis by quoting British philosopher Stuart Hampshire, who declares: "If the supernatural claims about the Creator's intentions are dismissed, there remains no sufficient empirical reason to believe that there is such a thing as the historical development of [hu]mankind as a whole."[5]

But "[i]f the supernatural claims about the Creator's intentions are dismissed," what can we theologians offer to the struggle for an authentic human liberation from within late imperial culture? How shall we theologians speak of these times? How shall the next generation of theologians speak of us and of the age in which we have come of age? These are my questions as a Christian, as a political theologian, as a black woman living in the tremor—*the in-between time*—of late imperial culture. These questions take me to the border of political theology where the terrifying and terrible events of September 11 continue to impose themselves, to penetrate our daily living. How shall we speak of *our* times? How shall the next generation of theologians recall the age in which we have come of age? Must we confess that we despaired and surrendered our most cherished principles and values to expediency? Must we admit that our shoulders sagged in recognition of the cost of truth? that we averted our eyes as the struggle slipped from our hands? that the cost of personal moral and intellectual conversion and social transformation were too dear? What do our times call us to be, to become?

Such questions call us to forge new ways of dealing with our philosophic, scientific, and technological achievements as a people, as a culture; at bottom, they plead for new approaches, a new understanding of ourselves, new gestures toward God, a new hopeful sense of responsibility toward human 'others.' These questions emerge in the encounter between theological responsibility and encrusted social sin. And if they plead for new approaches, they push us to understand racism as one pervasive and vicious form of social or communal sin.

II

"The problem of the twentieth century," W. E. B. Du Bois wrote, "is the problem of the color-line—the relation of the darker to the lighter races of men [*sic*] in Asia and Africa, in America and the islands of the sea."⁶ Du Bois easily could have included Iraq, Pakistan, India, Egypt, and the countries carved from the land of the Middle East in his list. His incisive digest of five hundred years of white racist imperialism, colonialism, and supremacy is as precise today as it was nearly a century ago. First and foremost, *racism* is a complex structural or systemic phenomenon. James Boggs, a lifelong factory worker and an iconoclastic organic intellectual, gives us a good, comprehensive definition of structural or systemic racism:

> Racism is systematized oppression of one race of another. In other words, the various forms of oppression within every sphere of social relations–economic exploitation, military subjugation, political subordination, cultural devaluation, psychological violation, sexual degradation, verbal abuse, etc.–together make up a whole of interacting and developing processes which operate so normally and naturally and are so much a part of the existing institutions of society that the individuals involved are barely conscious of their operation.⁷

In the case of the United States, white racist supremacy does not rely on the choices or actions of a few individual white men; rather, it is structured or institutionalized. Thus, white racist supremacy goes well beyond prejudice or even bigotry and welds attitudes or feelings of superiority to the putatively legitimate and commonly sanctioned exercise of power.

Michael Omi and Howard Winant employ the term *racial formation* to denote the complex historically situated process in which human bodies and social structures are represented and organized, how race is linked to the way in which society is organized and ruled.⁸ It can be extended to comprise the "normal" and "natural" way white racist supremacy in the United States is carried forward through unquestioned acceptance and affirmation of standards, symbols, habits, reactions, and practices rooted in racial differentiation and racist privilege implicit in the creation and transmission of culture (education and access to it, literary and artistic expression, forms of communication, representation, and leisure); participation and contribution to basic aspects of the common human good (opportunities to work, to engage in meaningful political and economic activity); promotion of human flourishing (intellectual, psychological, sexual, and spiritual growth); and the embrace of religion (leadership, membership, ritual, doctrine, catechesis, and theology).

Structural or systemic white racism conditions and is conditioned by *racial formation*. The racial formation perspective clarifies the nature of racism, the relationship of race to other forms of difference–to sexism, to nationalism, and the dilemmas of racial identity. While this perspective grasps the brutality of racism on global and personal scales, it discredits any romanticization of race as essence as well as race's misrepresentation as illusion. Race is a constant in social structure, not a deviation; it is a dimension of human representation rather than an illusion.⁹

Racial formation as *large-scale social process* operates in two ways. Omi and Winant label one form of this social process *neo-conservative,* the other *liberal.* While these labels are overused and, often, misleading, they can serve us as functional distinctions. Large-scale *neo-conservative* social process promotes color blindness: In other words, while it is acceptable for us to notice someone's race, we cannot and ought not to act on that awareness. Race must play no role in the conception and enactment of legislation or the creation and formulation of social or educational policy. Large-scale *neo-conservative* social process handles race as an irregularity, an illusion: the merit of the individual defies her racial group, or she is swallowed up by racist reaction to the behavior and unpredictables that impinge on her group. The impact of this position on any schema for affirmative action ought to be obvious: we cannot redress centuries of black disenfranchisement and exploitation because to do so would recommend, even require, differential treatment.

Large-scale *liberal* social process often uncovers the ways in which race and racial attitudes are embedded in the conception and enactment of legislation, in the creation and formulation of social and educational policy. Moreover, large-scale *liberal* social process focuses attention on the historical role of government in crafting segregation and enforcing racial difference, as well as government's inclination "to reproduce those patterns of inequality in a new guise."[10] Because large-scale *liberal* social process often admits a hermeneutics of suspicion as well as the possibility of self-criticism (in theory, if not always in practice), it allows both a capacious understanding of equality and creativity in legislative, social, and educational response.

Racial formation on the micro-level permeates everyday experience. The most ordinary activities—grocery shopping, banking, registering for school, inquiring about church membership, riding public transportation, hailing a taxicab—are racially charged. We *see* race; it is one of the first things that we notice about people (along with their sex) when we meet them. *We see; we interpret.* The ability to accurately interpret race, to categorize people (black or white, red or brown) is crucial for social behavior and comfort; the inability to accurately identify a person's race provokes a crisis.

To put it another way: White racist supremacy thrives in an atmosphere of biased common sense. I use *bias* here in the sense of Bernard Lonergan's technical denotation to refer to the more or less conscious choice to be incorrect, to repress or deny the surfacing of further questions or insights.[11] Our interpretations of race and our reactions to race are conditioned by biased notions that require people to act in accord with the *stereotypes* of their racial identities: the Chicana attorney in casual clothes working on a Saturday is stopped at the elevator to her office; the East Indian physician is harassed by police while driving through his own upper-class suburban neighborhood; the gasp of white students is audible when the black professor enters the classroom on the first day; you instinctively assume that your black colleagues are less qualified and were hired to fulfill affirmative action guidelines in your university. The truth of this analysis has been brutally played out in the past few weeks when Sikhs have been murdered because someone thought they were *Arabs–as if Arab was the new synonym for terrorist.* Neither badges of American citizenship nor trappings of merit served to deter the enraged and biased individuals who murdered someone's lover or husband or son or father or brother or uncle or friend–misnaming revenge, retaliation, and fear as justice. *We see; we interpret; we react.* A racialized social structure shapes racial experience and expectation; it conditions racial meaning and racial response.

So far, much of what I have said has attended to the bipolar (white-black) typology of racial formation, but there are many, many 'other others' within the borders of the United States. These women, men, and children were and are the object of racist immigration policies, repressive government tactics, restricted naturalization, economic exploitation, racially motivated violence, illegal internment, and deportation. They are Sioux, Cherokee, Menomonee, Oneida, Mexican, Filipino, Puerto Rican, Lebanese, Iraqi, Chinese, Indian, Korean, Japanese, Hmong, Vietnamese, Jordanian. Under the press of (white) movements hostile to their being and to their cultures these people are coerced to act as racial groups and sometimes to stand in for "other" groups when the wider society engages in what Yen Le Espiritu calls "racial lumping" or "the inability to distinguish Mexican and Ecuadorian or Chinese and Korean."[12]

Such racial lumping and the crisis that results when racial identity is not clear have been brutally evident in the aftermath of the terrorist attacks of September 11. A day or so after the attacks, *The New York Times* reported an incident of mistaken identity. A young man using an ATM cash machine and wearing a knitted cap like those frequently worn by Muslim men was surrounded by a group of his fellow New Yorkers–U.S. citizens turned vigilantes. The young man was pushed and shoved, then beaten as police were summoned. Throughout this ordeal, he kept insisting, "I am a Puerto Rican Roman Catholic!" Police verified that he was. Racial arrogance and xenophobia renders American citizens frightened of one another: In Milwaukee, Wisconsin, the local television evening news program featured the story of a Chinese couple who own and operate a laundry and dry cleaners in the affluent suburb of Brookfield. Out of respect and sympathy for local firefighters and police officers, the couple offered to clean and press their uniforms without charge. In their televised interview, the woman said something like this: "We are Americans. We feel this pain. *We may not look like Americans, but we are 100 percent Americans.*" I shook my head in disbelief: What, I thought, do Americans look like? This incident exposes not only how racial arrogance, white privilege, and xenophobia shape our most cherished institutions, but also how these vices of nationalism pervert patriotism and impress themselves on immigrants, despite postmodernity's affirmation of culture diversity.

Although fighting words, threats, and hate-speech can and do terrorize, terrorism is not so much a speech-act as it is a vicious reduction of the human heart and voice to mute desperation, a wail that grabs our apathy by the throat. Terrorism strikes out for recognition, regard, respect. We in the United States are shocked and paralyzed even as we overreact. But it is not our democracy or our freedoms—already so perilously endangered by our acquisitive materialism—that the so-called third world envies to the point of hatred. Rather, it is our indifference and arrogance at their suffering and death. Writing in London's *Guardian,* Booker Prize winner Arundhati Roy courageously reminds us of an interview that then Secretary of State Madeleine Albright gave on a national television news program. When asked what she felt about the fact that 500,000 Iraqi children had died as a result of U.S. economic sanctions, Albright replied that it was a "very hard choice, but that all things considered, we think the price is worth it."[13]

How arrogant, how xenophobic of us to think that American lives are worth ending the lives of others! How arrogant, how xenophobic of us to think that *white* American lives are worth more than the lives of others of us! How tragic when other racially and culturally diverse groups and individuals believe this to be the case. For even as we strive to forge strategic alliances, we too see, interpret, and react. Competition for limited resources between and within these groups, along with the attendant frictions of gender and class, are sharp challenges to the creation of a common human good—that concrete, daily lived expression of what being human means as mediated through value-laden choices in which we in our collaborations and relationships constitute (or not) the conditions for authentic progress and embrace (or not) responsibility for our neighbors' flourishing as human persons. Have you read the nearly gloating newspaper report of an African American man who, when questioned about the racial profiling of Arab Americans, stated that he was not quite sure just how he felt? He himself had, the man said, been subjected to racial profiling, but perhaps this situation was different, he said. He admitted to being ashamed of himself, of his attempts to make sense of racial profiling in this case.

We are all living as Audre Lorde told us, in the "master's house"—a still stunning and stunningly accurate metaphor for the marriage of heterosexist white racial privilege and capitalism.[14] This domain of sin and evil is a house of disordered love: love of God become love of money, become love of whiteness, become self-hating love of the whiter, lighter, self. In this house, connections, not relations, matter: connections to power, to prestige, and to privilege. Moreover, these connections are assigned to "white" skin and to the skin of white *men* most especially. To win protection and affirmation in this house, white women resign themselves to the definitions and designs of white men; they learn and practice the ways of the fox and the ways of the lion or else take up an ornamental position from the sidelines. To stand at the door of the "master's house," we women and men of color (men especially) submit to representations and roles developed for us by whites; we learn and practice compliance and deference, or when the occasion prompts, studied, crafted anger. In this house built on race, white men and women trade all forms of repentance and amendment for sly acceptance of guilt and anxiety, the risks of pluralism and difference for the security of conformity, and collaboration and commitment for individualism and co-optation. We others huddle, wounded at the margin, through passive accommodation to racial contempt; we compromise our very being, dishonor our ancestors, and in tragic mimesis barter away our hope.[15]

Racism—in its various forms and guises—is a beam in the eye of our global village. Moreover, as global white privilege, racism poses a most dangerous threat to human life, to the creation and development of human community, to the realization of the body of Christ to the reign of God. Now inasmuch as theology seeks to understand, to interpret, and to impart the word of God and its meanings in various historical, cultural, and social contexts, it grapples with the conditions and state of culture and society. Racism is one such biased condition in the world order. But theology can meet its critical exigence only when theologians take up comprehensive analysis and reflection on society and its potential meaning for the realization of a common human good. Indeed, nearly fifty years ago, writing of the ineluctable relation between the social and the personal, Bernard Lonergan insisted that "the ascent of the soul towards God is not a merely private affair but rather a personal function of an objective common movement in that body of Christ which takes over, transforms, and elevates every aspect of human life."[16] In that body and for that body, in the twilight of American culture, the theologian has not only a role but a vocation.

III

With the word *vocation,* I want to suggest a calling and a response to a call. With the word *vocation,* I want to make a decided step away from notions of career and academic mobility. These may not be unimportant, but too often they crowd out the very One whom theologians are called to love, to cherish, to imitate—that is, the Truth who is the crucified Jesus—for theology also "rises from love and love's dynamism."[17] With the word *vocation,* I want to suggest an attentiveness, an intelligence, a reasonableness, an acceptance and embrace of responsibility and love.

In "Christian faith, knowledge and life, truth and existence" have been considered intrinsically connected.[18] The theologian is invited, under the inspiration of the Holy Spirit, to participate in the mission of the promulgation of "the mystery of salvation."[19] To carry out the command of the gospel effectively (Mt. 28:19ff.), the church is urged to insert itself fully into the circumstances of the various peoples just as "Christ by his incarnation committed himself to the particular social and cultural circumstances" of the women and men among whom he lived.[20] Contemporary Christian theological witness requires a thoroughgoing grasp of the social and cultural circumstances in which the gospel is to be preached and Christian faith lived. Theology offers responses to questions and problems that confront and prod faith. The work of theologians, our work, "constitutes an integral part of obedience to the command of Christ, for men [and women] cannot become disciples if the truth found in the word of faith is not presented to them."[21] We give full assent to requirements of our discipline, to the most rigorous standards of research and argumentation, to the "obligation to be critical"—to interrogate the presuppositions and conditions that account for our doctrinal or social or cultural findings.[22] Theology is about truth and truth-telling, however cauterizing those truths may be.

To speak about racism and this vocation of truth and truth-telling involves serious reading of the *"signs of the times."* In fact, nothing is more relevant to a theologian's exercise of her or his vocation than such a reading.

Consider this sampling of "signs" from the past two decades:

- Feeling threatened, Bernhard Goetz shot four young black men in a New York subway.
- Media manipulation of the story of Willie Horton, a black Massachusetts inmate, helped to elect George Herbert Walker Bush president of the United States.
- Racial confrontations and rebellions occurred in Forsyth County, Georgia, and in Miami City, Florida, in 1980, 1982, and 1989.
- In 1982 Chinese American Vincent Chin, who was mistakenly identified as Japanese by enraged unemployed Detroit automobile factory workers, was murdered by the workers.
- After fatally shooting his pregnant wife and wounding himself, Charles Stuart made up a story about a black man's committing the crime. Ray Flynn, then the mayor of Boston, has yet to apologize for the ensuing gross and vicious police treatment of African American males in the city's Roxbury section.
- Former Ku Klux Klan head David Duke was elected to the Louisiana state legislature.
- The war in the Persian Gulf provoked angry outbursts against Arab Americans. For example, in Blissfield, Michigan, a restaurant owned by a Palestinian American couple first was vandalized, then burned.[23]
- A car speeding through red lights on California Highway 210 was stopped, and twenty-five-year-old Rodney G. King, an African American, emerged to face twenty-one Los Angeles police officers; King's encounter with them left him with a "split inner lip, a partially paralyzed face, nine skull fractures, a broken cheek bone, a shattered eye socket, and a broken leg."[24]
- James Byrd, an African American, was dragged to death behind a truck in a small Texas town by a group of young white men, at least one of whom was acquainted with Byrd.
- Haitian immigrant Abner Louima was so brutally beaten by police that he required hospitalization and surgery.
- Amadou Diallo, an unarmed African immigrant was shot forty-one times as he reached for his wallet.
- In the course of twelve months, fifteen black men were fatally shot by Cincinnati police.

- A white gunman with a hate psychosis fired an automatic weapon at a day-care center for Jewish toddlers, then killed an Asian American postal carrier.

- Matthew Shepard, a young homosexual college student, was beaten to death in Wyoming.

To paraphrase Malcolm X: "What is looked upon as an American dream for white people has long been an American nightmare for [people of color]."[25]

What import do these nightmarish instances hold for us as theologians living, thinking, teaching, and writing in the world's lone and, most likely, last superpower? How does our theological vocation compel us to respond to men, women, and children who daily absorb the blows of white racist supremacy?

These "signs" impose on the exercise of our vocation as theologians, women and men of all races, in several ways. Here are four:

First, these "signs" call for theologians to give critical scholarly attention to understanding the reach and extent of white privilege. White Americans in particular have yet to discover the numerous doors that their skin privilege opens, even as they protest their commitment to meritocracy. The daily and ordinary activities that white Americans take for granted are the very ones that trip up people of color and for which, for the very sake of survival, people of color are on constant alert.

Second, these "signs" prompt us theologians to retune and refine our sensitivity to American public discourse about liberty, justice, and equality. How utterly remarkable that a nation founded on the backs of slaves and the rape of black women, sustained by the exploitation of conscripted prison and immigrant labor, and maintained at every level, even today, by segregation and racialized capitalism can so comfortably tout itself as egalitarian, committed to liberty and justice.[26] A counterdiscourse is sorely needed—one that supplants (uproots, plows under) the dominant discourse, which defines and promotes those acquisitive market and cultural (dis)values that devour the spirits and, hence, the lives of our people.[27] If we ourselves are unable to formulate such discourse, we must agitate for its development and support those political philosophers and scientists, sociologists and economists, who can. What we can do is contest the power-draped language of liberty, justice, and equality to which we too readily give mindless allegiance and which corrupts the virtue of patriotism.

Third, these "signs" oblige the renewal of scholarly attention on the part of Catholic theologians to Catholic social teaching, to the mounting of a critique of white racist supremacy, and to the integration of this critique into that social teaching. Our world, our nation, our church can no longer tolerate our neglect of the critical analysis of race, of racial formation, of white racist supremacy. Can we not make the twenty-first century challenge that James Cone put to black theology our own: "to develop an enduring race critique that is so comprehensively woven into Christian understanding that no one will be able to forget the horrible crimes of white supremacy in the modern world"?[28] Can we not all—white, red, yellow, brown, and black—work together to develop a sufficiently complex analysis of the structure of white racist supremacy, with its history, its *shape-shifting* as economic or political or cultural practices that foster counterfeit forms of equality or that seek to engineer or depreciate the humanity of our people and all others?[29] Then we could work *together* to spell out the ways in which racism "divides the human family, blots out the image of God among specific members [and] violates the fundamental dignity of those called to be children of the same Father,"[30] and "denies the reconciling and humanizing work of Christ."[31]

Four, these "signs" enjoin us to disciplines of prayer, fasting, and Christian hope. Many of us do Christian theology because we want to collaborate in a most fundamental way in bringing about a different kind of world in the here and now. Yet to do this, our contribution is to think about that here and now in light of the eschatological future that only God can give. We advocate for the reign of God. Our *ultimate* commitment can never be to system or structure, person or group, church or university, but to the God of Jesus Christ. His prophetic praxis, in the face of certain death, demonstrates the risk and meaning of a life lived in prayerful hope.

Prayer is reach and risk into the Unknown; it is passionate launch into a lifelong journey of discovery—discovery of the Divine, discovery of self, discovery of the only future worth hoping for and worth having. In prayer, the theologian seeks the One whose love redeems, whose sacrifice of life gives back our own. For the glory of the crucified Jesus we shoulder study, research, and writing. Outside of loving relationship with him, all that we write and speak is stale and withers. Prayer is no substitute for theology, the disciplined, critical reflection on ultimate meaning and value; but without prayer, theology is emptied of passion, of hope.

IV

One large context for this reflection is that of political theology. Theological reflection can go a long way to complementing individual and communal responses to situations of disgrace—exposing some of the ways in which structures and systems are disordered and deformed. However, political theology always must cast a light on the ultimate and transcendent solution to the problem of evil, to the realization of a common human good. And that solution is located only in the darkly luminous mystery of the cross and resurrection of Jesus of Nazareth. For if the prophetic praxis of Jesus reveals the transcendent passion of an eschatological imagination in the midst of a concrete human setup, the cross shows us its radical risk, love, and hope.

Morris Berman in *The Twilight of American Culture* and Michael Hardt and Antonio Negri in *Empire* conclude their respective analyses with exhortative possibilities drawn from Christianity. Berman suggests that there are individuals within our crumbling culture who represent what he terms the "monastic option."[32] Now Berman does not mean this literally, though literal withdrawal from the world is neither unimaginable nor improbable. More than a thousand years ago, monasteries participated in the preservation of culture; it can and may happen again. Rather, the monastic option refers to those persons who are not afraid of their creativity, their humanity's essential humanness. Berman's "new monastic individual" is one who "reflexively sees through his or her own cultural conditioning and refuses to be blindly driven any longer by the heroic program of power and achievement."[33] These individuals spark; their commitment, their integrity, their willingness to risk are unmistakable, and others join in–to save a school, to restore an old building for authentic cultural use, to tell the truth about our economic and psychological exploitation. These individuals choose to live simply and do not impose much on our resources. To put it differently, but familiarly: they act locally, think globally, and imagine and strive to realize solidarity. They may be writers, painters, disemployed longshoremen, carpenters, retirees, college professors, high school students, parents, or restaurant owners, all ordinary men and women, young and not so young, who act locally, think globally, and imagine and strive to realize solidarity

Hardt and Negri offer a similar option, but are quite specific. These authors set before us an account of the carefree son of an affluent twelfth-century merchant. At some point in his life, Francis Bernadone underwent a profound moral and religious conversion; he found himself transformed by a passionate love of Christ. To open his arms and heart to fully embrace the Beloved Jesus, Francis gave up everything. In order to "denounce the poverty of the multitude…[he] adopted [their] common condition and discovered [among them] the ontological power of a new society."[34] Hardt and Negri argue that we too are at a critical juncture; we too are presented with a choice: the joy of being or the misery of power. Love, simplicity, joy, and union of all creation– nature, sun, moon, stars, animals, poor exploited human creatures together– pose against the will to power and corruption, empire.

Both these options–Berman's and that of Hardt and Negri–entail sacrifice, difficulties, and struggle as well as making oneself available for religious, moral, and intellectual conversion. Paul Tillich wrote that grace "strikes us when we feel that our separation is deeper than usual…In the light of this grace we perceive the power of grace in our relation to others and to ourselves."[35] This grace is being offered to us now in our social location. It presents a unique opportunity to us as we stand at the crossroads and before the cross, to reach out to one another through the nightmare, to name and repudiate bias, to repent of our collusion in the other's marginalization and domination, to redress these wrongs, and to embrace one another and dwell in God's own love.

V

How will the next generation of theologians remember us and the age in which we have come of age? And what of the state of the tradition they will receive from us–broken, nearly illegible moral fragments; theological integrity compromised by expediency; a religion grown effete and commercial? Will they be ashamed of the way in which we stand as the profession, of the way we live out our calling? Will they be ashamed of us?

How will what we know and believe, the One whom we love, the One about whom we theologize, be communicated? Will other women and men perceive the radiation of God's self-transcending love in our lives? Will our students see Christ crucified in us? Let those of us who are theologians pose love and union over against the will to power and corruption; let us pose the reign of God over against empire. For is this not our vocation? Is this not our calling?

17

Faith, Ethics, and Evil

Robin W. Lovin

For pastors and theologians, one striking part of the experience of September 11 was the realization that suddenly everybody was looking to us to make sense of events. There was twenty-four hour news coverage complete with political commentary and historical observations, but what filled the churches for several Sundays afterward was the widespread feeling that what had happened called for something deeper—something that would be at once more personal and yet more transcendent than the news reports could be. The church's pastors, teachers, and theologians go about their work in these days after September 11 with an awareness of heightened expectations for what they will have to say.

That awareness is both gratifying and disturbing. Gratifying, of course, because we all like to think that what we do is important, but also disturbing, because we are aware that faith is both a source of comfort in the face of terror and uncertainty and in an important way also the starting point for the terror itself. Faith inspires hope and courage in the face of evil, but it is faith of a twisted and distorted sort that also inspires the terrorists. The challenge of religious leadership in these days is not only to speak with pastoral sensitivity to those who are angry, fearful, and grieving, but also to speak with theological and ethical integrity about the complex relations between faith and politics in the new world we live in after September 11. To do that, we have to be honest about the dangers that are inherent in faith commitments, as well as the redemptive possibilities.

Of course, the strange blend of religion and nationalism that makes up the ideology of terrorism has nothing to do with the genuine theology of Islam. We Christians have an obligation to remind ourselves of that and to repeat it publicly at every opportunity. The most basic reason for this obligation is historical accuracy. We need to avoid blaming Islam for terrorism, because what happened on September 11 is related to Islam only on the margins of history. It has nothing to do with what that faith is centrally about.

But we also need to avoid blaming Islam so that we may see an important and disturbing truth about all faith, including our own. While terrorism has nothing to do with Islam in particular, it does have something to do with faith in general. There are risks and dangers inherent in ultimate commitments, and people in our congregations and on the street who are struggling to make sense of events are newly aware of this. At least part of what they are asking is whether it is safe to answer an evil that was inspired by ultimate commitment with another call to faith.

The question has some bite, even if the faith we proclaim is quite different from the distorted Islamic fundamentalism of the terrorists. Indeed, the evidence of history is that Christians are every bit as capable as any other kind of fanatic of reducing other people to instruments in the service of their Christian commitments. We would like to say that extremism, intolerance, and persecution are not what real Christianity is about, and I think we would be right to say that. But there is a long line of people who have suffered through history from the effects of extremist Christianity who would say that that version of the faith looked real enough to them when they were staring it in the face.

No response to this moment in our history that overlooks the evils in Christian history can be an adequate Christian response. To treat extremism as if it were only a problem for other people's faiths calls our own honesty into question. Nor do we have to go back to the age of the crusades or to the Inquisition to confront the problem. It is present today in hate crimes, and there is more than a faint echo of Christian religious intolerance in our ethnocentrism and our ignorance of the rest of the world that allow us to ignore the needs of people who are sufficiently far away and sufficiently different from ourselves. Ways of being faithful that subtly put self in the place of God are a constant risk in Christianity, as in any other faith. If we are unable to admit that to ourselves and confess it before God and humanity, people of other faiths and of no faith will regard Christian calls to faith as a very dangerous response to the present problem.

It may be, then, that the more appropriate—and finally the more faithful—response begins with ethics rather than with belief. That is, we need to start with the ways in which people think about what it takes to live a good human life, and especially the ways that they think about it in communities where they may not agree on their ultimate commitments.

Such questions go back at least to Aristotle, and to his notion that politics is the whole community's effort to do ethics together. If that seems unlike politics as we have experienced it, perhaps the political questions that we have been raising in recent years have not been as basic as the ones Aristotle asked. Perhaps, too, the political questions that we have been raising are not as important as the ones that arise in the aftermath of the destruction of the World Trade Center. Our politics after September 11 may begin to look more like Aristotle's politics, because we are now forced to consider the most basic political questions about how to prevent future terrorism without creating in the process a kind of security state in which no one would choose to live.

The questions begin with those about the use of force. While there was an understandable outcry for retaliation, military leaders realized almost at once that the weapons of mass destruction alone could not produce lasting results. The discussion shifted to questions about what level of force would be justified in response to the hijackings, and what targets would be appropriate. The need to produce hard evidence against the likely suspects was acknowledged. Consensus grew around building an international coalition, instead of relying on a unilateral U.S. response. Everyone began to stress the need to avoid collateral damage and to minimize civilian casualties.

In short, politicians and the press quickly reinvented the language and logic of just war theory. When they found out that some traditions had been talking in those terms for a millennium and more, the phones started ringing in the ethicists' offices. Not all those involved in these discussions were theologians, to be sure. Some were political scientists and international lawyers. But the introduction of just war criteria into the public discussion of our response to September 11 was one important contribution that the church made in those first days of the crisis.

Since then the concepts have shifted somewhat. We initially took our lead from the President's statement that the assaults on the Pentagon and the World Trade Center were acts of war. We have since begun to question whether *war* correctly names this kind of conflict, and the just war theory has helped us formulate these questions too. A war, the just war tradition reminds us, requires a legitimate authority to declare it and wage it. A political authority may be justified in mobilizing its people and its resources to use force against an attack. Whether the ensuing conflict should be called a war in the full sense, however, depends in part on the nature of the power on the other side. No one would doubt the authority or the capacity of the United States to make war when attacked, but in a "war against terrorism" it is less clear what the other authority against whom the war is to be waged would be. So our thinking has begun to shift from an image of warfare to an image of crime and punishment—"bring our enemies to justice, or bring justice to our enemies," as the President put it in his address to the nation.

That hardly ends the ethical discussion, but it does move it to a more fundamental level. The question now is not just about the legitimate use of force, but about the basic purposes of the state. After a century in which the recurrent themes of political discussion have been about the relationships between government and markets and about social responsibility for individual welfare, we suddenly find ourselves at the beginning of the twenty-first century pitched back into a discussion of the nature and purpose of the state that dates back to the beginning of the modern era.

In the political confusion that surrounded the Reformation and the rise of new, more centralized powers of government, questions began to be asked about why people accept the authority of their rulers in the first place. The answer most philosophers had accepted by the end of the seventeenth century was that people accept the constraints of government to avoid the risks and dangers to which they are exposed when everyone uses force to achieve his or her own version of justice. People create governments, so the argument went, in order to enjoy the security that comes with order.

That was the idea behind the modern nation-state: Take the power to use force away from every petty landowner who can surround himself with a few horsemen and give it to a government that will exercise a monopoly over the use of force in a given territory. This has been so basic to our way of life in the ensuing three centuries that it is hard to remember what an achievement it was. The modern state creates an orderly society in which people can acquire, and plan, and even fight with one another in relative security, according to rules that they can know in advance, with outcomes that they can reasonably well predict.

That great idea lasted until September 11. What became all too clear as the towers of the World Trade Center collapsed was that under the conditions of modern commerce and technology, no state can unilaterally guarantee the security that it is its most basic function to provide.

We can and will give a great deal of public attention to the tactical questions of how we are going to identify and eliminate the particular terrorist network that is responsible for the hijacked aircraft, the ruin of lower Manhattan, and the death and destruction at the Pentagon. But the more important question, which deserves even wider discussion, is what we will do to restore the fundamental public security that was shattered on September 11. This is not just a matter of getting used to security measures in airports, or better regulation of hazardous materials, or any of the thousand other intrusions that we will have to live with, at least in the short run. The state itself will never be the same.

Suppose for a moment that it turns out that everybody who did or might have done some act of terror on or near September 11 is in fact part of a single organization that takes its orders from someone who happens to be at some place we can identify, and we eliminate him and his network. Suppose that we really do bring justice to our enemies or bring our enemies to justice or some combination of the two things, so that the people who were responsible for what happened on September 11 and whatever else they may have planned are just history. Suppose, in short, that the conflict that began on September 11 has an equally definitive ending date. Can you imagine that the world would simply go back to handling terrorism the way that it handled it before? Could we ever again, after September 11, treat the rise of some Taliban-like movement anywhere in the world as a purely internal matter for the people in that country to settle for themselves?

We are moving into an era when there cannot be any purely "domestic" politics, just as there has not been, for some time now, any such thing as a purely "domestic" economy. Governments are going to start asserting a legitimate interest in how other governments treat the opposition forces in their countries. They will begin to say that they have an interest in the life chances of youth in refugee camps or the employment prospects of peasant farmers on other continents, not because of some abstract commitment to human rights, but because of their basic obligation to protect the security of their own people. The globalization of economics is going to be followed by the globalization of politics, and the notion of what it means to be a state and to exercise the powers of government is going to change fundamentally in the process.

What marks these urgent questions of ethics is that they are questions we have to solve together, quite apart from our diversities of ethnic identity and religious commitment. The questions are universal, not in the sense that there's some international language of reason that we can use to resolve them, but in the sense that they are questions that we all must face. There may be a variety of perspectives and solutions. In a place as big as the planet, there is no reason to suppose that we all have to come to the same answers, at least not all at the same time; but we've all got to be involved in asking the questions, because every nation and group that is left out of the discussion becomes a very real threat to whatever conclusions are reached by those who do participate.

The questions as posed in this essay have strong links to Western philosophical, legal, and religious traditions; but we must be careful not to privilege those discourses. In fact, we must learn to raise the questions in Muslim, Hindu, Confucian, and indigenous African terms too, because any workable solution must presuppose that this diversity of languages and identities and commitments will continue under whatever new conditions we create to provide a form of security on which we can once again depend.

So I think that the questions that confront us first in the aftermath of September 11 are questions of ethics. Questions of religious ethics, probably, maybe even questions of comparative religious ethics, but questions in any case about how we are going to work together to create the conditions under which we can survive and thrive.

These are not new questions for Christian theology. We have been thinking and talking about these basic questions of politics for a long time. Christian traditions about politics and order are in fact older than the modern state. Theologians attended the birth of that institution and helped define its proper sphere of authority, in part to keep its rulers from the mistakes they were apt to make when they confused the authority to keep order with authority that resolves problems of morality and spirituality. We do not need to invite ourselves into the discussion about the state and its future. We have been participants in it from the beginning.

Interestingly enough, theologians do not need to remind the lawyers and political scientists and economists of that history. They often understand it better than the theologians do, and they are less likely to criticize the theologians for clumsy attempts to speak the languages of law and economics than they are to fault them for poor knowledge of their own traditions. Kenneth Anderson, a political scientist, describes in a recent issue of *The Times Literary Supplement* a worship service he attended at a United Methodist Church in Washington, D.C., on the Friday following the September 11 attacks:

> Pacifism is a coherent theological and moral position, but the preachers at the Friday night service I attended seemed to want it both ways, to maintain the moral purity of pacifism while still sounding relevant to the real world of conflict, sin, and death. They recognized the inevitability of armed retaliation, but elided the question of its legitimacy. They thus deprived themselves, it seemed to me, of the rich moral frameworks that Christianity, Judaism, and indeed Islam have developed over millennia, frameworks which simultaneously authorized but also morally limited armed force.[1]

Perhaps what the theologians need to do, especially the moral theologians among us, is not so much to master the variety of contemporary discussions as to master the history of our own discipline.

We may also need to remind ourselves that we have theological reasons for taking up these questions about war and politics. For complex historical reasons that have much to do with reactions to the incautious mixture of religion and nationalism on both sides of World War I, Christian theology in the twentieth century tended to assume that we had only two choices: to be truly theological in splendid isolation from the culture, or to participate in it in ways that would compromise the purity of the gospel and confuse our own culture with the kingdom of God.

In fact, the history of Christian participation in society is a much more complex story of critical distance and practical arrangements, of seizing the moment and withdrawing to fight another day, of creative construction of new institutions and creative misuses of old ones. It is a story that includes both prophetic judgments on the culture and moral appeals to the culture; and it goes back at least as far as the New Testament.

There were moments in twentieth- century Christian ethics that recognized that history. Emil Brunner's "orders of creation" and Dietrich Bonhoeffer's "divine mandates" both spoke to the ways that our understanding of God is tied up with thoughtful participation in the problems of society. The same could be said for the tradition of the Catholic Social Encyclicals that stretch from the work of Leo XIII through the social teachings of John Paul II.

We need to renew that part of the discipline of Christian ethics at the beginning of the twenty-first century, and the task gains urgency as we come to understand the limitations of the eschatological perspective that speaks its word of judgment from a prophetic distance. There is a risk, of course, that if we make a commitment to our own culture and society, we will confuse that culture with the kingdom of God, but we prevent that best by understanding the practical, political solutions that engage a broad spectrum of people in a search for the conditions of a good human life.

People who actually participate in politics are not likely to confuse it with the kingdom of God. Those who are apt to be confused are those who have withdrawn from the political community to live as aliens in the midst of it, and the specific confusion to which they are susceptible is the assumption that God is absent from the political community and only present with them in isolation.

The peculiar conditions of politics in the Islamic world—conditions for which the developed West bears a large responsibility—have encouraged the development of these eschatological religious communities to which we have now, belatedly, begun to pay attention. But we should not suppose that this brand of eschatological anti-politics is a distinctly Islamic phenomenon. It is a mistake to which every form of ultimate commitment is susceptible and which no religious community can entirely avoid.

One important part of our Christian theological task in the face of the new historical conditions in which we find ourselves after September 11 is to renew our Christian participation in ethics and politics. We need to do that because, as the historians, lawyers, and political scientists are reminding us, we have some important traditions to contribute to the political and ethical discussions. But we also need to do it for the theological reason that it is by participating in politics, and not by avoiding it, that we are most likely to keep clear the distinction between our own proximate ideas about what to do next and God's final judgment on human history.

The particular form that evil takes for us today is people who have lost sight of that distinction between their ideas and God's judgment, and who have made use of the available technical and economic means to inflict their confusion on the rest of us. In that context, to participate in moral and political discussions—discussions open to everyone who wants to participate in them— is not only a practical necessity but a religious obligation. It is part of what we must do in order that the faith we confess not be confused with those murderous distortions of religion that use human lives as instruments for limited human purposes.

That is the case for ethics. But what becomes of belief? Is there a place, too, for faith and for a call to commitment in this new situation? Some skeptical voices say "No," suggesting that any faith that makes demands or seeks decisions is a part of the problem. They will suggest that the only kind of belief we can welcome in the world after September 11 is a religion that offers comfort without challenge and accepts identity as it finds it. We would do well to expect that response, but we need not fear it. Such a religion of comfort without challenge would be too optimistic about human nature to hold up very well against the harsh realities of our recent experience, and it actually would expect too much from ethics.

Ethics holds out a realistic hope that if we measure our responses rightly and make our choices well, the world may be a better place for human habitation by the middle of the twenty-first century, however tragic the events that got the process started. But ethics does not promise that we will root out evil wherever it exists, and in whatever forms it takes. Ethics does not even promise that we will eliminate terrorism as a result of this effort, though we may very well come close to eliminating the particular network of persons and causes that brought this particular disaster upon us.

Terrorism itself is going to be an ongoing problem. Like nuclear weapons, terrorism will not go away, even though we may greatly reduce the threat it poses. Part of the new political and moral world we need to create will have to be a system of controls and interventions that identifies problems that are likely to turn into terrorist threats and redirects the energies before they get beyond the reach of the political and moral systems that the rest of us live by. We need to be devising a system that monitors political discontent and keeps it flowing in political channels–if necessary, by opening the channels in which it needs to flow. We need to make sure that no one has the means, and if possible to make sure that no one has the motivation, to seize other parts of our complex technical and economic systems and turn them into signs of rage and alienation. It is perhaps somewhat idealistic to think that such a political system could be built, but it is possible.

But we will not end evil, and we will not create a world in which a political system to restrain evil is no longer needed. The purpose of politics is not to end evil, but to cooperate on the possibilities for a good human life under the conditions of life as we find them. Part of the political task is to get straight which of the conditions of life are changeable so that we don't give up too soon in favor of the misquoted notion that the poor will always be with us. Part of the political task is to get straight which conditions are not changeable so that we don't slip into a political rhetoric that promises an end to evil.

For what we surely do know is that human beings will dream more than they can achieve, and their dreams will lead them to anxieties about what they have achieved, and their anxieties will lead them to make their achievements more important in their own minds than they can possibly be in reality. The impulse to realize our dreams by turning other people into mere instruments of our own purposes will always be with us, whether it finds expression in some new and dreadful kind of terrorism, or in the petty sins of which we find ourselves capable every day. Politics and ethics are about how we live with one another knowing these facts about ourselves. Politics and ethics are not about changing these facts, and a politics that promises that– even indirectly and rhetorically–promises too much.

Good politics understands these limits to politics and suggests a role for belief, even in the political and ethical task that is central to our response to September 11. Alongside the many political and ethical decisions that theology rightly holds up as meaningful and important, Christian theology also speaks of one central decision that sets parameters for all the rest.

Christian theology calls for a decision about a decision that God has already made. However dramatic the preacher and however real the stakes in this choice may be, nothing can erase the fact that God has already decisively chosen to redeem our fallen humanity. The decision is not about whether or not God is going to be gracious. The decision is about whether we will accept God's decision. If the proclamation on which the theology is based is the Christian gospel, that's the message, however difficult it may be to get it right and however easily it may be confused with other messages.

There are other ways to understand this decision. Dualistic faiths, whether they are gnostic religions or Christian heresies, call for a decision between good and evil, light and darkness, flesh and spirit—as if the poles of that choice were somehow equal contenders for our allegiance, as if the outcome of the choice were somehow still open. Milder, New Age versions of the same proclamation call for a choice between a true self and a false self, between a closed self and an open one—as if human nature were a matter of human choice.

In the aftermath of September 11, it is important to be clear about this decision that Christian theology calls for, because the temptation to confuse it with other decisions will grow more intense as the conflict that surely lies ahead of us intensifies. We will be told that the choice before us is a choice between life and death, good and evil, truth and falsehood, and we will be told that the fate of nations and the fate of humanity as a whole hangs on which choice we make. We will be told that the disaster that befell us on September 11 is actually an opportunity to become a new people and a new kind of society, that the crisis of terrorism allows us to choose for caring and giving against selfishness and greed, that the economic disaster is in fact a spiritual opportunity, and so on. We will be told these things about our choices by our political leaders, who will need to motivate us for the long conflict that may lie ahead. We will be told these things about our choices from our pulpits, by well-meaning clergy whose emotional awareness of the seriousness of the moment is greater than their intellectual understanding of it.

The dualistic message that tells us that history is in our hands and that we can become whoever we need to be to meet the challenge of the moment is exactly the message we do not need if we are in fact going to meet the challenge of the moment. The dualistic message promises total victory, even over ourselves. The real challenge of the moment is to recognize the tendency to evil that will not be eradicated from our human nature and to construct a realistic, limited politics that manages this human reality as well as it can be managed. No one would want to say that a president, politician, or preacher who is trying to rally a democratic society for a difficult struggle is on the same moral level as the terrorists against whom they speak, but there is an ever-present temptation, given the difficulty of the task, to offer people choices that they do not really have and to engage them in commitments that, taken seriously, would pitch us into that same war against human nature that the terrorists have undertaken.

That is why Christian faith is especially important at this point in our history, and why it is important to be clear about what that faith is: We are called to a decision about a decision that God has already made. The outcome of history is not in doubt. Only our place in it is open to question.

We can decide to accept God's choice of us, gladly acknowledging our fallen human nature and living in ways that are appropriate to repentant sinners. Or we can decide that being chosen by God is not good enough for us and that we will remake ourselves and our world until we are fit for the choice that we want to make. The temptation to the latter choice is understandable. It is, in fact, part of that fallen human nature that God has nonetheless chosen. But just for that reason, we need a clear and constant proclamation of what the real choice is.

A call to faith should not be our first word in the face of the evil we confront in the world after September 11. Making it the first word skips over the moral and political problems that we have to solve. Making it the first word ignores the possibilities for evil that are part of every ultimate commitment and that have become so apparent in the commitments of the terrorists. The first word needs to be the word of ethics and politics. But if ethics and politics are to serve their human purposes in this crisis, they will need the last word of a faith that announces the limits of all politics at the same time that it proclaims the good news of a choice that is not ours to make.

18

When Listening Is Not Enough
Pastoral Theology and Care in Turbulent Times

Joretta L. Marshall

A group of local church pastors, community resource leaders, students, and faculty gathered in the chapel of Eden Theological Seminary on the morning of September 11, 2001. The assembly was an annual event marking the start of the academic year's field education program. As the participants entered the sanctuary, it was clear that something was happening in the world around us, but the details and extent of the disaster were not yet evident. We did what many folks did at that moment—we stopped, we prayed, we tried to attend to our work, and we huddled around television monitors throughout the school. By the end of the morning many of the pastors and the leaders within our institutions were organizing prayer services for that afternoon and evening.

This scenario, I suspect, is not unique among those reading this volume. In church buildings around the world, people gathered to pray and to be with one another. In the middle of chaos and crisis, the church responds with rituals of care, listening to one another's fears, angers, and concerns. As we listen, we participate in shaping the context in which theological reflection and conversation occurs. What is clear is that immediately following a crisis, communities of faith often know how best to draw upon the resources of faith. The church becomes the embodied place in which people listen to one another with deep sensitivity and incredible care. We gather the people, we pray, we remind the community about the experience of the grace of God, and we listen for God's stirring in the narratives and stories of the lives that we encounter.

What is less clear, however, is how the same churches and pastoral leaders draw upon the resources of theological traditions as they move past the initial moments of grief, mourning, anger, hurt, fear, revenge, and chaos. Shortly after the dust begins to clear—and in this case before the fires even subside—we find ourselves at a loss for words, thoughts, and actions. After the first Sunday or two of attending to our communal numbness and shock, listening for underlying fears and concerns, we are uncertain about what to pray for or what message to offer in worship. After we listen, how do we concretely respond to the walking wounded or to the vulnerabilities of people's lives in the aftermath? It is precisely at these moments that we need a grounded pastoral theology to lead us in our reflections. Without such pastoral depth we are tempted to settle for simple listening or the offering of theological platitudes that inadequately reflect the depth of our experience or the wealth of God's grace.

This essay is an attempt to do two things. First, it affirms and names some of the significant ways that caring ministry takes place immediately after a crisis such as the one through which we are moving. Second, I want to challenge those of us involved in the caring ministry of the church to recognize the importance of a pastoral theology that moves beyond listening and comforting in the aftermath of events such as September 11. Public crises, I would suggest, offer pastoral theology the opportunity to think critically in ways that engage the depths of our faith and traditions. Acts of care require not only intentional listening, but also leadership that responds to such complex situations.

Responding Pastorally to Immediate Needs

Traditionally, there are four functions involved in the caring ministry of pastors and local churches: sustaining, healing, guiding, and reconciling. Every seminary course in pastoral care, at some point, notes the significance of these four historical functions of the church. Those connected to the church expect pastoral leaders to be able to offer prayers of healing for those experiencing physical or spiritual anguish and to sustain those caught in feelings of despair and hopelessness. Likewise, churches expect pastoral leaders to assist them in thinking about how best to guide the children, youth, young adults, and aging of their congregations, or how to offer reconciliation to faithful folks who sit on opposite sides of an issue as they gather around the table of fellowship.

It is, perhaps, the sustaining presence upon which many of us first depend in the days following a tragedy or disaster. As a result of the church's daily presence in the lives of individuals, families, and communities, people turn to the church and its pastoral leaders in the aftermath of a public crisis. The churches that offered sacred space for prayer were full as they opened their doors during the week of, and following, September 11. People needed somewhere to bring their vulnerabilities and their fears, and the church provided a sanctuary in which to receive them. We all needed someone to listen to the anxieties, questions, and fears that tugged at the depths of our souls and to have those concerns voiced in the context of a community of faith. The sustaining ministries of the church were immediately apparent not only in the efforts of persons located at the sites closest to the tragedy, but in churches around the world as well. The church found ways to reach out to its members, and also to move beyond itself, as it became a safe haven for persons who had not entered a church in years, if ever.

Inviting people toward healing is also one of the core functions of pastoral care. Several months later, as we meet colleagues and friends, many of us take time to recall where we were the morning of September 11 and how our particular church communities moved through the days that followed. This individual and communal ritual of remembering is not unusual after any public crisis; through such encounters we are able to participate in the ongoing process of coming to terms with such tragedy. We share the stories and we listen to one another's hurt, pain, despair, and fear. The elders among us remember where they were when bombs were dropped on Pearl Harbor or Hiroshima; some of us remember where we were when we heard about the shooting of John F. Kennedy, or the disintegration of the Challenger; many of us who lived in Colorado remember where we were when the young gunmen fired on students at Columbine High School. Gathering the people together, offering prayers on behalf of others and ourselves, remembering where we were when we first heard news of public crises, are all rituals of care. Such rituals provide steps toward healing as we seek to respond to, and to process, the chaotic public events of our lives.

In the weeks following September 11, denominations and local churches continued to respond to the needs of individuals and families. Whether it was providing the sacred space for funerals, offering workshops on crisis and grief, or creating opportunities for persons to pray for others, communities of faith responded with healing and sustaining presence. The church listens as people talk about their anger at those they feel are responsible, their fears of travel, their concerns about contracting anthrax, or their anxiety about going to war. We are the embodiment of God's presence in the midst of a hurting and fearful world.

Pastoral care that offers guidance is not something we immediately notice in the context of the church and its response to public crisis. Yet, many local churches took on the role of guides as they helped people sort through their initial feelings and responses. Pastoral leaders met with members who brought deep theological questions to their relationships with God. Because of the nature of trauma, events such as September 11 stirred up old wounds in new and sometimes incredible ways. Many ministers made referrals to appropriate pastoral counselors and mental health workers for those who needed work beyond what the pastor could offer. Sermons focused on helping people move beyond the primary feelings of helplessness, immobilization, and hopelessness. These are all pastoral acts of guidance.

Reconciliation has always been part of the church's struggle, particularly as we work with traditions, communities, and individuals that are different from our own. We have often let diversity divide us, instead of finding it to be a blessing. Recognizing the chasm that has developed among interfaith traditions, many churches have offered opportunities for dialogue and education. Leaders from the Islamic and Muslim communities became partners as faithful Christians tried to understand the complexities of our interfaith relationships. Indications of reconciliation began in some communities as persons recognized that the "other" may look different and worship in distinct ways, but may still reflect part of God's richness. Churches are reaching out in genuine and comforting ways to various faith traditions, recognizing our allegiances with one another.

It is clear that the church in many forms has been present in healing, guiding, reconciling, and sustaining ministries throughout the past several months. We have listened carefully and have responded to those whose pain and fear we can identify, and we have tried to be present for those who walk with the wounds of the day in the depths of their souls. People are theologically transformed through the activities of pastoral care in the context of congregations and communities.

A pastoral theology and care that has depth and substance must do more than respond to the immediate needs and feelings of persons who approach them for care. Without prolonged attention to the deeper issues, pastoral care becomes a benign form of offering soothing comfort in the moment and loses its ability to sustain, guide, reconcile, and heal at deeper and more meaningful levels. The activities of care are present immediately following and long after the crisis, but a deeper pastoral theological foundation is necessary for later stages of healing.

A Sustained Public Voice for Pastoral Theology and Care

After the initial crisis, I heard many pastoral leaders and church members asking, now what? We responded to the immediate needs of persons around us, but now what do we pray for and how do we lead our congregations? In particular, as we wage a public war with an enemy that is elusive in our thoughts and in real life, how do we frame theologically the nature of our ongoing public care, public prayers, and public responses? We have prayed for the victims, the survivors, their families, and the innocent people of Afghanistan. Now, how do we speak in deeply meaningful theological terms about such things as evil, suffering, retribution, justice, or peace?

Pastoral theology is transformative when it listens to people's stories, seeks to bring the resources of faith to our deepest concerns and dilemmas, and offers concrete responses to the questions of our lives. Sometimes such pastoral theology provides comfort and care; other times it is painful and disquieting as it moves beyond the confines of our individual lives to contemplate the broader and more complex realities of our communal living. In the midst of offering care to individuals, we dare not settle for the easing of people's pains without challenging inappropriate or inadequate theological claims. Indeed, the gift of pastoral theology is that it offers a framework for responding to human concerns because it draws upon the deepest resources of theology, scripture, faith traditions, behavioral and social sciences, and experience. Pastoral theology can lay the groundwork to contribute significantly to the public discourse of our faith.

Three dilemmas illustrate the need for such public pastoral theology and care: how do we challenge the use of simple theological platitudes in response to complex queries of faith and understanding; how do we offer comfort and challenge when our hurt and pain turn into threats of vindication and violence to others; how do we move beyond simple interfaith conversations to work at deeper and more genuine interfaith dialogue? The manner in which pastoral leaders respond to these dilemmas provides glimpses into the depth of pastoral theological commitments they bring to their work of care.

First, how do we challenge the use of simple theological platitudes in response to complex queries of faith and understanding? Public crises raise opportunities for broader theological reflection. It is true that we need pastors to listen to our hurts and pains; it is also true that we need pastoral leaders to help us clarify our questions and inform our responses. Who is God? Is God active in this public crisis? If so, how? If not, why not? Has God chosen a side? What do justice and forgiveness mean?

One important aspect of moving toward healing and wholeness is the wish for insight and understanding for the difficult and complex questions that arise from a crisis. Some of these questions were less clear to us before the crisis and have now become sharper in our recent reflections. Because of our human desire to find answers to our deepest questions, quick explanations come in many forms and from various sources. Yet, few interpretations are as damaging to the deep integrity of our faith as those simple theological platitudes that respond to our immediate needs for comfort but that are insufficient to respond to the depths of our souls or our world dilemmas. Several theological themes and questions are raised in the public discourse following a crisis, many of which have no simple answers.

For example, one of the theological themes that arises quickly relates to our understanding God and God's activity in the world. What is the nature of God? Does God provide grace and mercy for some, but not for all? While prayer was one of the early companions offering peace and comfort to people, it has more recently become a place for persons to voice their appreciation for a God who provides protection for those who are fighting the just war. But what does this say about the nature of God's inclusive or exclusive claim on the world? If God is the God of Afghanistan, Pakistan, India, the United States, and every other corner of the world, how do we interpret the activities of that God?

A second set of theological themes relates to notions of justice, revenge, atonement, and forgiveness. How are we to understand these dynamics in the complexity of our global situation? One might wonder, for example, if the rhetoric of Christians seeking revenge adequately reflects the gospel. When, if ever, is it appropriate to seek revenge? What does forgiveness mean in this context? It is too simple to state that the United States is justified in its revenge without also asking the question about how we have participated in the creation of a world where terrorism becomes the only way to get a response from a rich and powerful nation. Again, it is not the purpose of this essay to answer these theological questions; rather it is my purpose to note that we need to avoid moving toward simplistic theological answers to complex and difficult questions. I propose that this set of issues needs deep and provocative thinking if we are to assist our communities of faith as they consider how best to respond to the world around us.

A third theological theme focuses on questions of evil, theodicy, and suffering. What is evil and how do we recognize the forms and shapes of its existence? Is terrorism the only evil entity in the world against which the United States ought to take a stand? How does God participate in the creation of, or the eradication of evil? Again, good pastoral care requires that we offer opportunities for conversation and dialogue about these kinds of theological questions. Churches and communities of faith are steadfast in their care if they can sit in the ambiguity of not having all the answers and, at the same time, provide sanctuary for persons who bring questions of this nature.

Pastoral theologians are called to bring our public voice as we invite people to reflect on the content and meaning of our faith. Even when we are not able to provide answers sufficient in response to the multiplicity of questions, it is necessary and significant that the church and its pastoral leaders create the climate where deep theological issues are addressed and discussed.

The second dilemma for public pastoral theology is how best to offer comfort and challenge when our response to hurt and pain turns into threats of vindication and violence to others. When people are hurt and filled with pain and anguish, it is common to initially respond to the depths of our anguish in ways that are immediate and not always helpful in bringing justice or peace. When we experience deep hurt some of us withdraw, while others of us strike back without thinking about the consequence or meaning of such violence. Pastoral caregivers must find appropriate ways to offer comfort for the pain and the anguish, while prophetically challenging the destructive moves toward revenge and violence.

As I listen to the discourse in the churches around me, I am aware of the intense depth of feelings still present in our culture. We are a world that sits on the edges of our seats and wonders when the next crisis will strike and on whom it will be perpetrated. Will one of us contract anthrax, or will one of our children's lives be placed at risk? Will one of our grandchildren be sent to fight a war in a country far from our shores? We are rightly concerned with questions that relate to our individual lives. Yet, pastoral leaders must ask deeper questions about our public anxieties and fears. We must ask questions that sometimes will make faithful Christians feel disquieted.

Illustrative of the disquieting questions we must ask are those associated with the individual nationalism that has become prominent in the past several months. Once again people feel good about singing the "Star Spangled Banner" or "God Bless America," and we have come to appreciate flags flying in the breeze in front of our homes and businesses. A number of pastors with whom I have talked note that the national flag has been brought back into the center of the worshiping area, almost without conversation or thought. While it is important and vital to express support for our country, it is increasingly difficult to be the prophetic voice that challenges a nationalism that is self-serving in its promotion of vindication and violence rather than understanding and peace. By this I am not meaning to suggest that we should not bring justice to those who are responsible for the atrocities of September 11. What we ought to be perplexed about, however, is that our rage became apparent only when we felt personally attacked, while our public voice lacked anger against the violence the rest of the world experienced on a daily basis. The homicides, genocides, and violence of the world have come to visit us and finally we are enraged. A pastoral theologian might ask why we have not been invested in caring for others around the world when they have lived with this kind of violence on a daily basis.

In this time of our corporate lives it is important to listen and to comfort; yet it is just as important to challenge and confront the extreme nationalism that promotes self-interest. I would suggest that the issue is not whether one sings "God Bless America," or whether one flies the flag; rather the issue is how pastoral leaders listen for the deeper theological meanings about what such decisions reflect. Then, in the context of the community of faith, we offer thoughtful and appropriate ways to engage people around their feelings of fear and anxiety, hurt and pain, but never in the name of simple nationalism. The question, perhaps, is how do we begin to confront the violence and revenge that is cloaked in such words as justice and responsibility? How do we bring our best pastoral theology to what justice and responsibility mean for all the participants in the world, not just those whom we have targeted as enemies?

Pastoral theologians and caregivers always need to keep two realities in tension with one another. First, we must acknowledge and recognize that our feelings and fears are valid and real. Second, we must confront in prophetic and caring ways the destructive actions that arise from our fears and feelings. Too often we simply either dismiss people's feelings because we think their actions are inappropriate; or we dismiss the actions because we think they are unfeeling and unchristian people. Pastoral theology recognizes and affirms both feelings and appropriate actions.

Finally, a pastoral theology for our time must move beyond curiosity about interfaith communities toward a genuine and mutual conversation with various faith traditions and perspectives. We can no longer afford to be isolated Christians in a world that is increasingly diverse and complex. Just as we must recognize and be honest about the extreme differences that exist within our own faith traditions, we ought always to acknowledge the diversity of others. If we are honest about our differences, we will not ignore them or dismiss them; rather, we will find ways to talk about them and to come to terms with the complexity of belief and faith in the multiple realities of our world.

In a postmodern world, we know that faith traditions are not all the same and that they should not be collapsed into one another. One of the dangers of our time is that we will be tempted to collude in misappropriating and dismissing meaningful aspects of other faiths by pretending that we are all the same. We seem to be less willing to name those significant and meaningful differences that truly make our faith perspectives unique and distinct. A pastoral theology that allows us to honor and be in conversation with various traditions does not assume that we are all the same, nor does it try to find congruence where there is none.

If we want deeper understandings of the connections and differences between and among communities of faith, we must meaningfully engage each other. I have been deeply appreciative of the churches that have invited scholars, teachers, and leaders from the Islamic community into their buildings for education and conversation. This is, indeed, a piece of the good news. What seems less apparent as I watch and listen is whether the education is intended to deepen and foster mutual conversation over the course of the months and years to come or whether it simply helps us with our own feelings of discomfort. In other words, how will our church communities stay meaningfully engaged in the worldwide communion that they have now invited into being? Interfaith conversation must be something that encourages people to begin to look deeper and ask harder questions about others, our relationships, and ourselves.

In conclusion, pastoral theology responds to the needs and concerns of individuals, families, and communities even as it seeks to engage the world critically. Genuine pastoral care is not interested only in making people feel better in the moment, nor does it settle for responding to the first layer of pain, fear, and grief without moving toward the depths of relationships with self, others, and God. A community's deeper and more long-lasting anxieties, fears, depressions, and worries deserve as appropriate a pastoral response as do those whose wounds we can easily see in the first moments after a crisis.

19

Four Ways of Worship in a Time of National Trauma

Martin E. Marty

"God Bless America"

The sound of the song has been inescapable; the sight of its title bannered in red and white and blue has been unavoidable since September 11. Citizens for many reasons, beginning with the need to ritualize their grieving, moving through their common search for meaning, and climaxing for many in their celebration of hope, have been praying, gathering, worshiping.

All this is going on in a society that usually gets typed as "secular" and "pluralistic." Secular societies—some Western European nations are that—include so many citizens who have become indifferent to God and the godly that they do not ask God to bless them, do not have an instinct to pray, to gather, to worship.

The word "secular" comes from the Latin *saeculum*, which refers to "this age." In a secular order people make all decisions about personal and public life apart from any consciousness of being a transcendent order. The world "rounds itself off" without reference to such, and certainly without reference to God.

In many respects America will remain secular. Our market transactions, many aspects of political life, most of the world of entertainment, are of this

172

secular character. But we have seen anew how many dimensions of life do evoke the sense of the sacred in a majority of citizens.

Yes, and "pluralist" we certainly are. Pluralism, in colloquial terms, means: (1) any number can play; (2) great numbers do; (3) there are rules of the game; and (4) an ethos, a set of customs develop. Religious pluralism means that hundreds of denominations stake out their claims here. The U.S. Constitution sets forth in broad outline some "rules of the game." The American ethos calls for both devotion to one's own faith and tolerance of others and, on occasion, activity that crosses the boundaries of faith communities. "God Bless America" does not mean "God Bless American Presbyterians" or "Episcopalians" or "Pentecostals." We are presumed to have some things in common. So, in trauma and crisis, we search.

That common search leads to confusions and difficulties both for the anti-God or casually God-less minority—are its members less than full citizens?— and for people who take very seriously the particular ways of apprehending God's action and of worshiping God. They may at times seem to be stumbling and fumbling and at others unpatriotically standoffish. What to do?

The situations are too complex for any single response. But I do want to suggest one four-fold scheme for conceiving worship in this time when public, congregational, and personal approaches overlap and are all exposed to view.

We need names for these four. I will call the zones of worship (1) civil religion; (2) interfaith; (3) Christian; (4) confessional. Take them in order.

Civil Religion

Civil religion is most visible in a time when a scattered set of citizens faces a common threat or opportunity. American founders invoked Divine Providence, without special reference to, say, the God of Abraham, Isaac, and Jacob or the Father of Jesus Christ. Abraham Lincoln was the most profound theologian of this civil religion. For him it witnessed to "transcendent justice" and an Almighty who had "his own purposes." Edmund Wilson said that Lincoln treated the Union itself as "religious mysticism."

Such civil religion is most celebrated in times of war. Its icons are all red, white, and blue. Its rituals tend to find military symbolism congenial. God is invoked, but in a very general way.

The Jewish theologian and sociologist Will Herberg, who often commented on America's "civic faith," said two things about it. First, he thought that every complex society *did* generate such a faith, and must do so. "We hold these truths…" And, he noted, from the viewpoint of prophetic (as in biblical prophet-speak) language and viewpoint, all civil religion was idolatrous. That is, in our case, it is easy to arrogate to the United States the special status of ancient Israel as God's people, and to come to worship this captive God and these people and their symbols.

Christians are often called these days to be measured by such a civil religion. It would be bad manners, even offensive, to ask for theological precision when people gather at "Ground Zero" in New York or the thousands of town squares and courthouse lawns to grieve, to find resolve, to seek hope.

Participating and even leading such worship becomes a kind of civic duty. But from the prophetic and Christian angle, such leadership involves some uneasiness, some reserve, some need for caution. It is easy for the church to be "used" to justify everything a nation does or claims to be. An experiment: Try removing the flag from your church sanctuary if it was there September 11. You could remove the cross more easily, less controversially. That's a warning signal.

The Christian lay or clerical leader has to show that one can be reverent about patriotic rituals—I feel awed at the Vietnam War Memorial or the Tomb of the Unknown Soldier—and *still* find ways in prayer and message and choice of song to make clear that we do *not* believe that America is God's own chosen people and that it is justified in all it does. There is no way to set forth guidelines, since situations vary. But the Christian leader must find ways to show that God, and not the nation and its heroes, is the subject and object of worship, and not anything or anyone else.

Interfaith Worship

Some believers are so open to "the other" in religion that they put the highest premium on prayer and worship, in a time of crisis, at occasions when Protestant, Orthodox, Catholic, Jew, Muslim, Sikh, and more link arms and languages for common prayer. In some ways this is what we might call a form of "public religion," where communities and their leaders come out of their particularities for common witness.

Interfaith worship raises the stakes on both sides over civil religion. On the positive side, with the many faith representatives giving voice to prayer, there is less danger that worship will focus on the nation, and there is more readiness to reach for the sacred realm that transcends it. On the negative side, worshipers can give the impression that the religions, whose members have citizen parity and can be equally helpful in national causes, are themselves on a par, "different boats heading for the same shore."

What then results is confusion, muddling, the potential for wishy-washiness. One must be careful about what is being signaled. The morning after a national disaster is not the moment to stand off, to try to make extra points that are beside the point to the grievers and hopers. But I think there are ways for participants to make common cause with fellow citizens *and* be clear about their faith.

The most vivid and potentially abrasive point comes when Christians are confronted with the choice: either omit reference to Jesus Christ, through whom they believe they have access to the Father, *or* needlessly offend common worshipers for whom Christ is not that means of access and, in their view, may even block it, as in "stumbling-block."

No easy solutions are here. I resent the notion that Christian prayer is general prayer to which the name of Jesus Christ is tacked on. And I resent being taken for granted, as when a praying parson at a presidential inauguration invokes that part of the audience (not congregation) that follows Jesus Christ as being the specially chosen, the in-crowd. What to do?

On occasion and especially at short notice, brief worship occasions of interfaith character, I will advocate generalized rituals, so as not to cause needless offense—and find other ways, other days, to stress particularity in Christ. When there is more time, I might begin with a twenty-second introduction something like this: "In a moment I am going to lead a prayer. When I am at Muslim worship or when I hear a Jewish prayer, I want it to give voice to faiths other than mine, join as I can, and hold some assent in reserve. So with you: I am your guest, I welcome your presence, I know you don't all worship as I do; where my language and intention are particular—as when I pray 'in Jesus Christ,' I do not take for granted that you agree or assent or came for that. At such a moment, translate to your own language and I will be respectful when you are particular." And then pray. Most of the search for justice and hope can be of a sort that does not focus only on Christ, but the special character of Christian faith remains.

Christian Worship

In Christian worship, most of us expect prayer to be ecumenical in character. Even the most sectarian and self-isolated denominations use hymnbooks most of whose hymns and prayers and liturgies came from other than their own "sectarian" traditions. While the differences between denominations are of great importance, they do not have to be settled on the day of common Christian worship.

The values of Christian worship include the prophetic possibility that we keep God and not nation as our main focus and that we do not let the concern for earthly survival, victory in war, or national politics be matters of ultimate concern. The God beyond the nation, the "God beyond the gods" is the only fitting magnet for worship, and this is most clear in common Christian witness. Participants can return home and settle theological disputes in different venues, without cluttering Christian worship by distracting and, to mourners and hope-seeking people, momentarily beside-the-point accents.

Confessional Worship

Finally, there is what we might call "confessional" worship. This does not refer to confession of sins, though there will be plenty of that. It refers to "confessions of faith," creed-based, belief-centered communities that together make up the one, holy, catholic, and apostolic church. And it refers, therefore, especially to congregational worship. Such worship draws upon long memories and extravagant hopes, on clarified witness and evocative stories.

Thus, as a personal example: After September 11, I was often involved, though at television-distance, in observing civil religious ceremonies at football games and public memorials. On a couple of occasions I worshiped at (but was not called to lead) interfaith gatherings, but I have often been a leader at such when national crisis was not central. A Christian service that drew on diverse traditions was "home-plus," and enriched my understanding and offered a wider variety of options.

After the other worship services, nothing meant more than when my own "home" congregation gathered. It is Lutheran, and we draw on specific Lutheran understandings about time and eternity, sin and grace, divine vengeance and human caution. Down the block the Catholics are doing the same, and so are the Presbyterians and, a bit farther down the block, the Pentecostals and Baptists. This is *really* rich worship, at all such places. It allows for family-feeling and familiarity, though I hope never in an exclusivistic sense.

Two Christian Callings

James Fowler has written that in a pluralist society most believers feel that at times they are withholding the most helpful words and gestures, biting their lip and tongue, holding back. I sense that when called to speak at a service for former colleagues. On one occasion I attended the Resurrection Eucharist of a fellow Lutheran and was transported "above" by the chorales, the organ, the communion. Then I spoke at an academic-civil gathering at the University of Chicago for this same person, a trustee. We could eulogize him and celebrate his causes, but we did not reach so deeply as did the earlier service.

On another occasion, when a very prominent trustee died, his family asked me not to speak, but to preach at Rockefeller Chapel, a cathedral-sized sanctuary on our campus. "Chicago's powerful will be there," a family member said, "Protestant, Catholic, Jew, atheist. We want you to say, 'The family has asked me to pretend this is Mr. X's little white church in X, and I have been asked to preach a message of Christian resurrection hope." And I did. At the reception following, quite a number of Jews and nonbelievers said thanks, in informal words that I'll condense thus: "Now we know what holds you Christians together and gives you strength. We get to so many inter-faith gatherings that we hear only muffled versions, not witness to what animates you."

So the Christian is left with two callings: one, to participate on every level possible in speaking words of "transcendent justice" and human hopes to a grieving, not always repentant, groping citizenry. Worship there is not a theological forum where all the niceties get straightened out. And, second, to participate on profound levels in the language of Christ crucified and risen, of God's judgment upon all nations and God's word of hope to those who respond. Trauma time, crisis time, is not a time to resolve all issues connected with worship. It is a time when we can think through more clearly than before what are the purposes of worship and witness, of citizen life and profound expressions of Christian faith.

20

Hope in a Time of Arrogance and Terror

Jürgen Moltmann

The Beginning of Life: Christian Hope

If we ask whether our world has an end, we are asking a typically apocalyptic question. Some people talk about "the end of all things," others about "the end of the world," or "the end of history." Why do we ask about the end at all? Can't we endure the state of things as they are any longer? Have we had enough of this world? Or do we fear for the continued existence of things we love and cherish? Can't we get enough of this world? Is it only good if it ends good? Or is an end with terror better than this terror without end? Every thought about "the end" is ambivalent. It can fascinate us, but it can terrify us too.

In Christian theology, questions about "the end" are treated in eschatology, under the heading of "the final questions." Eschatology is called the doctrine of "the Last Things" (*ta eschata*). The End will bring the "final solution" of all unsolved problems in personal life, in human history, and in the cosmos. Apocalyptic imagination has always painted with tremendous passion God's great final judgment on the world's last day. The good will go to heaven, the wicked to hell, and the earth will be annihilated in a holocaust of fire. We know too the apocalyptic images of the final battle between God and the devils, Christ and Antichrist, the good and the evil in the valley of Armageddon (Rev. 16:12–16).

All these ideas and images are certainly soundly apocalyptic, but are they Christian? The authentic Christian expectation of the future has nothing at all to do with final solutions of this kind, for its focus is not *the end*, the end of life, the end of history, or the end of the world. Instead, the focus of truly Christian eschatology is *the beginning:* the beginning of true life, the beginning of the kingdom of God, and the beginning of the new creation of all things. When Dietrich Bonhoeffer was taken away to the place of execution in Flossenbürg concentration camp on April 9, 1945, he took leave of his fellow prisoners with the words: "This is the end—for me the beginning of life." One is reminded of T. S. Eliot's poem: "In the end is my beginning." Expectations of the end are only Christian if they conceive their future horizons out of the remembrance of Christ's death on the cross and the resurrection of the crucified Christ with the dead into the eternal life of the coming glory of God. For Christ's end, too, was and is, after all, his true beginning. Christian hope of the future does not prolong or extrapolate into the future the lines of the past and the present of world history, in order to postulate a good end or, as is more frequently the case, a bad one. Instead, Christian hope perceives in the cross of Christ the anticipation of the end of this world, which is a time of sin, death, and evil. This is because—yes, because—in Christ's resurrection, Christian hope recognizes the deliverance from evil that is present in the beginning of the new life and the new creation of all things. In the energies of the Spirit of Christ, we already experience that new beginning here and now, as we are being reborn to a living hope.

How does this work? Nobody is required to be perfect, but everyone must be able to start anew. All that matters in life and death is the new beginning. If a child falls down, it learns to stand up again. Failures and disappointments are not problems, but it is important to stand up and try again. Christian faith is in essence resurrection belief. This is grounded in Christ's resurrection from the dead and opens the expectation to eternal life. This resurrection belief is the present power to find the beginning of new and true life here and now. In our lifetimes, we may see only the beginnings and the first steps, but we trust that God sees the perfection. "I am confident of this," writes Paul to the Philippians (1:6), "that the one who began a good work among you will bring it to completion by the day of Jesus Christ." And no death can hinder God from doing this!

How are the end and the beginning, beginning and end, related to each other? Radical social critics in Germany like to quote the dictum of the philosopher Theodor W. Adorno of the Frankfurt School: "There is no true life in the life that is false." This seems to be self-evident. But for Christian hope, Christ (who has come into this false world) is the real beginning of true life in the very midst of this false life. This is why we feel, through Christian hope in the beginning of the new life, the end of the false life too. In the light of the resurrected Christ, we perceive the world under the cross. We see the world through the eyes of the dying Christ, with everything that is false in it, as well as everything that terrorizes and destroys. This falseness is what is to be brought to an end; it is what must disappear. Hope in the resurrection of life leads us to the realism of the cross.

It is not, however, that the end of the world brings a new creation. The very opposite is true: it is only God's new beginning that brings this perverted world to its deserved end. We first perceive the darkness of the night in the light of the new day. We recognize evil only in the light of the good, and we feel the deadliness of death only through our love for life. The annihilation of life, or of a whole world, has not in itself anything creative about it. Nobody can extort from God a new creation through the destruction of the present world. This is the fatal error of terrorists.

The true end of this world is only the side we see when God's new world begins. Just as we understand the resurrection of Christ as a divine process of transformation from mortality to immortality and from shame to glory, so we can also imagine the passing away of the old and the coming of the new world as a divine transformation process. Annihilation is not the end, but everything will be transformed. "Vita mutatur, non tollitur," as the Preface to the Roman Catholic requiem Mass says. The children in the concentration camp of Theresienstadt painted butterflies in the face of their death: when the poor caterpillar dies, the beautiful butterfly is born and will fly into freedom.

Christian expectation of the future answers apocalyptic questions about the end with the recollecting and making-present of the crucified and risen Christ. That is the only answer we can give with the assurance of faith and without uncertain speculations. It does not answer all the apocalyptic why-questions about God's justice and the when-questions about the coming of the end. After all, Christ himself died not with an answer but with the question: "My God, why have you forsaken me?" (Mt. 27:46). But in the fellowship with the crucified Christ and in the real presence of the risen one, we can live with unanswered final questions, without proffering hasty and premature answers, and without sinking without answer into brooding despondency.

Ideas about the end of history can be distinguished according to whether they deal with the *goal of history* (*telos*) or *history's end* (*finis*). If world history has a predetermined goal, then that is its completion, and history moves progressively–stage by stage, or dispensation by dispensation–in the direction of this goal. According to the biblical traditions, a goal of world history is the reign of the Son of Man (Dan. 7) or the Thousand-Years *Kingdom*, where Christ with those who are his will rule in peace over the nations (Rev. 20). According to the notion held in the ancient world, the goal of world history is the *Golden Age*, which follows the Iron Age in history (Virgil). According to the hope of modernity, it is the *realm of freedom* or of *eternal peace* (Immanuel Kant). For Francis Fukuyama (at that time in the U.S. Department of State in Washington, D.C.), after socialism collapsed in 1989, capitalism and liberal democracy, i.e., the Modern Western World, became this "end of history." We call ideas of this kind about the end as the goal of history *chiliastic* or *millenarian*, and if they influence the present, *messianic*.

If, on the other hand, world history reaches its end in the end of the world, then it will be broken off through catastrophes. According to biblical traditions, this is "the downfall of the world" (*Weltuntergang* in German), according to the notion held in antiquity "the universal conflagration" (*Weltenbrand* in German), according to modern fears the nuclear annihilation, or the worldwide ecological catastrophe, or the terrorist destruction. In modern parlance, we call ideas of this kind *apocalyptic*. The end of the world they envisage does not structure the course of world history; it in fact withdraws meaning from every epoch in history. In this view, world history is a meaningless history of suffering; its end is the best thing about it.

Modern faith in progress and globalization is a secularized form of the religious salvation-history millenarianism, while modern fears about the end of the world and about its annihilation are secularizations of the apocalyptic of old. As we know, history is always a struggle for power. People who have power have an interest in the progress of history and the globalization of their power. They understand future as continuation of their own present. People who are oppressed and powerless, set back and insulted, cut down and assaulted, have little interest in the progress and continuation of their history of suffering. They are only interested in a speedy end of this world condition and in an alternative future. So we must also confront the different ideas about the goal or the end of history with the critical question: *Cui bono?* Whom does it serve?

The Goal of History: Globalization

No hope has fascinated people as much as the image of a Thousand Year's Realm of Peace, and none has caused so much havoc. Christians expect Christ's kingdom of peace, Romans awaited the Golden Age, modern men and women look for "the end of history" in a world condition without history and without conflicts.

The first Christian fulfillment of this hope presented itself in the astonishing turn of events under the Roman emperor Constantine, when persecuted Christianity became first a "permitted religion" in the Roman empire and then, under the emperors Theodosius and Justinian, Rome's all-dominating imperial religion. Paul promised that those who have suffered with Christ will reign with him (Rom. 8:17; 2 Cor. 1:6–7; 2 Tim. 2:12). With this in mind, the political turn of events was interpreted millenaristically as the turn from martyrdom to millennium. The Holy (Roman) Empire was praised as Christ's millennium of peace. The Christian emperors saw their religious mandate in the conversion of the nations through their subjugation to Christ's end-time kingdom of peace. There was one Pantocrator in heaven, and his image on earth was the one Christian Caesar and his undivided world monarchy.

The political theology of this universal Christian world-monarchy springs from the application of the so-called "image of monarchies" in the book of Daniel: Four bestial and violent empires rise up out of the sea of chaos (Dan. 7). But at the end, the humane kingdom of the divine Son of Man descends from heaven, to bring everlasting peace, righteousness, and justice on earth. The fourth bestial empire was the empire of Rome, which followed the Babylonian, Persian, and Greek empires. With the Christianization of the Roman Empire, the end-time kingdom of Christ begins, according to this political reading of Daniel. The imperial kingdom of Christ will reach to the ends of the earth and to the end of time. This formed the messianism of the Christian Empire, the Christian World, and the Christian Age of humankind.

The fulfillment of the same messianic hope assumed another form in the epochal consciousness of what we call "modern times" (*Neuzeit* in German). "Modern times" are the "Third Age" of Humanity, as the philosophers of the Enlightenment called their present, applying to their own epoch the prophecy of the twelfth-century Italian visionary Joachim of Fiore, who referred to a coming "third age of the Spirit." "New Time" is always the end-time too, for after the New Time nothing can come but the end of time. This modern epochal self-consciousness led to the idea that the European domination of the world is indeed the messianic fulfillment of world history.

America was and is for the millions of immigrants "the New World," where freedom reigns for everyone. There are messianic elements built into the "American dream" and consequently into American politics. The seal of the United States, as well as every dollar bill, bears the mark of "the New World Order" (*novus ordo seclorum*). What this promises is not only a new world order, but *the* New World Order. Just as is the case with the European idea of modern times as "New Time," the American "New World Order" is universal in its intention; it is a new age for humanity and a new order for the whole world.

What is the role of America in the world today? Henry Luce called the twentieth century "the American century" and he was right: the U.S.A. decided, through its military interventions, the two World Wars, and since the downfall of the Soviet Union in 1989 the U.S. has been the only remaining superpower. But there is more at stake: While the communist experiment to form out of many nations the new "sovietman" has failed, the American experiment is still going on and is going well. America is a country of immigrants from all the nations of the world: *e pluribus unum.* Regardless of America's own internal problems in being "one out of many," immigration has made America into the central land of humankind, and this centrality continues. Thus, the American experiment is an experiment of humankind and not only of Americans. The peoples of the world are waiting for the fulfillment of the original promise of America for the world: *Novus ordo seclorum.* This New World Order cannot be an American world empire, but only the universal realization of the declaration that all human beings—and not only American human beings—are created free and equal. This is the vision of a world peace order based on human rights and the rights of nature, as the declarations of the UN proclaim.

The last prophet of the Western "end of history" for the time being had been Francis Fukuyama.[1] As supporter of the undoubtedly strange interpretation of Hegel put forward by the Russian philosopher Alexandre Kojeve in Paris, he saw the "end of history" dawning with the collapse of socialism in the Soviet Union. It is the triumph of the West, he maintained, that since 1989 there has no longer been any real alternative to Western capitalism and liberal democracy. In pluralistic capitalist democracy, humanity has finally found what it was seeking for in all its social experiments. We now live for the first time in "a world without alternative." What was once living history, full of destruction but also full of creative conflicts, can now only be visited in history museums.

Fukuyama's "end of history" was an illusion. The protest of people ground down and humiliated, as well as the protest of a violated earth, will not leave the world in the condition in which it is now. According to Hegel, the sign of the "end of history" is not lack of alternative, but freedom from contradiction. The terror of September 11, 2001, brought a terrible "end of the end of history" to all of us. Indeed, 1989 had been the end of the East-West conflict and the Cold War, and it produced the illusion of a world without alternative. As a result, it became easy to think that now *globalization* of what we want and what we are would be our future. Many spoke of the One World, the global village, the world community, the civilized world, and so forth. However, the globalization of production, markets, finance, big business, communication-systems, and modern culture did not bring peace to the world, but instead this globalization produced more and more conflicts. The neoliberal aggressive capitalism produced inequality, while democracy has always been based on equality. The Coca-Cola-ization, McDonald's-ization, and Hollywood-ization of the world destroyed local cultures. If we want peace, we need a globalization of justice and respect. Otherwise, we will never reach "the new world order," but only a world of chaos and terror. Only a just order can be a foundation for a united humanity.

The End of the World: Terrorism

The fear of a catastrophic end of the world is very often merely the reverse side of the hope for the glorious fulfillment of its history. When that hope collapses, generally all that is left is this fear.

In the biblical traditions there were not only prophetic hopes; there were always apocalyptic prophecies too. We talk about apocalypses when prophetic prophecies reach out beyond Israel's future and take on worldwide political scope or cosmic dimensions. Then a "new age" of humankind or a new creation of the cosmos is promised. According to Daniel 7, a worldwide humane kingdom of the Son of Man is promised. According to the apocryphal book of Enoch, "this earth will be smashed to pieces and everything upon it will be destroyed, and a judgment will come upon all"; afterwards, "the throne of God will be visible," "the Son of Man will come," and heaven and earth "will be created anew" (54:4).

The biblical apocalypses about a threatened downfall of the world go back to the story of Noah's flood (Gen. 6–9). In the Noah story, God decided to destroy human beings together with the Earth because of the wickedness of the powerful and the evil in human hearts. God would then make a new covenant with Noah, the one just man who was saved from the downfall. In this new covenant, there would never again be an end of the world (Gen. 9:11). But behind this remembered fear of the end of the world is the still more profound fear about God, the fear that God could "repent" (be sorry and regret) having created human beings at all, and that God could withdraw creative resolve altogether. A God who turns away completely would leave the world to sink into chaos and nothingness.

In distinction from the Bible's apocalyptic traditions, the phrase "apocalypse now" is used today to describe human-made catastrophes: the nuclear catastrophe, the ecological catastrophe, or the terrorist catastrophe. These interpretations are, however, completely wrong, because they push human responsibilities off of humans and onto God. Human beings must take responsibility for crimes against humanity and crimes against nature. The biblical apocalyptic traditions are full of hope, while the self-annihilation of the human race and the annihilation of the living space of this Earth are nothing but extermination without any hope.

It is not surprising that today the apocalyptic interpretation of crimes against humanity that threaten us all are producing a new *apocalyptic terrorism.* It is only a short step from passive expectation of the world's end to an active ending of it. That is the anarchism we know of old. In the nineteenth century, Michael Bakunin, the father of Russian anarchism, proclaimed the slogan: "The pleasure in destroying is also a creative pleasure." With this motto, he justified the murder of czars and the suicides of terrorists. "Without destruction there can be no construction" was Mao Tse-tung's command to the cultural revolution in China. It cost millions of people their lives and reduced China's finest cultural monuments to rubble. In Cambodia, the mass murderer Pol Pot took Mao's motto seriously. His Khmer Rouge murdered the older generations so as to build a "new world" with the young. They left behind two million dead in the killing-fields of a devastated country.

Apocalyptic terrorism can lead to the mass suicide of sect adherents. In 1978 in Jonestown, Guyana, it was 912 people belonging to a People's Temple sect. In 1993 in Waco, Texas, it was 78 adherents of a Branch Davidian sect, as well as 52 members of an end-of-the-world sect in Vietnam. In 1995, 53 members of a Sun Temple sect in Canada and Switzerland committed suicide. In 1997, 39 adherents of a UFO death cult killed themselves in San Diego. More recently in Uganda, hundreds killed themselves or were killed in a Catholic apocalyptic Holy Mary cult.

Apocalyptic terrorism can also lead to mass murder of other people for the sake of a supposed better future. Genghis Khan felt called to mass murder as "the retribution of God": "I am the revenger of God," he told the people of Sarmarkand before the massacres began. The poison-gas sect of Shoko Asahara apparently believed itself to be called to the final apocalyptic battle.

Since Tuesday, September 11, 2001, we are confronted with a new type of *apocalyptic terrorism*. The suicide–mass murder at the World Trade Center in New York and the Pentagon in Washington was a shock for many. As far as I can see, the new qualities are these:

1. One may become a murderer for money or out of conviction, but one becomes a suicide-murderer only out of conviction. The new terrorists are neither sick nor desperate, but they are obviously radical Islamists in a demonic way. They feel themselves to be martyrs of their faith, and believe that they will be much revered by their families and peer groups.
2. What kind of conviction motivates them? For decades, the U.S.A. has been accused by fanaticized masses in some Islamic cities as "the great Satan." This rhetoric has portrayed the Western world as the wicked world of the infidel for its secularity, materialism, pornography, destruction of families, drug dependency, women's liberation, and related practices. "The great Satan" is nothing else than the apocalyptic enemy of God. Whoever weakens and humiliates this Satan is on God's side and earns paradise.
3. The idea to fight with God in the final battle against God's satanic enemies takes away any inhibition about killing innocent people, elevates the ecstasy of power, and turns suicide into a divine service. These Islamist suicide-terrorists must feel like God when they are destroying the godless. Because they feel themselves to be divine executioners, they need no justification for their mass murder, and the meaning of their terrorism is— terror, nothing else.
4. *Islamist terrorism* is not terrorism out of oppression and starvation. They often come from good families in rich countries in the Near East, not out of the slums of Africa or Asia. The motivation must lie in a special kind of hitherto unknown Islamist apocalypticism and in the old Islamic assassin tradition from the tenth century.

No God and no religion can justify this new suicide–mass murder. This is in my opinion pure nihilism and will bring the terrorists into what was earlier called hell.

The biblical apocalypses have nothing to do with these kinds of modern/ anti-modern apocalyptic terrorism. On the contrary, the biblical visions keep hope alive for God's faithfulness to the creation in the terrors of the end-time: "The one who endures to the end will be saved" (Mt. 10:22). "When these things begin to take place, stand up and raise your heads, because your redemption is drawing near" (Lk. 21:28). Prophetic hope is *hope in action.* Apocalyptic hope is *hope in danger*, a hope that is capable of suffering, a patient, enduring, and resistant hope.

What Shall We Do?

What happened on September 11, 2001, in New York and Washington has indeed changed the situation of humankind. Everybody's life is threatened;

no one is secure anymore. The political has become the personal and the personal the political. Religion is no longer "a private matter." Retreat into privacy can lead to public misery.

Generations after World War II were brought up in a peaceful world, at least in the West, and could concentrate on their personal careers and private happiness. Politics could be neglected by many. Some called the eighties therefore "the Me Decade" and analyzed "a culture of narcissism" in the affluent classes of the Western world. In Germany, a "fun-society" (*Spaßgesellschaft*) came into being, where one could hear young people saying: "I want to have my fun and please myself, and that's the meaning of my life." All of this has found a brutal end. There is no personal life any longer without danger. Personal life has no meaning without political engagement in the necessary resistance against public terror and death, as well as the no-less-necessary work for justice worldwide.

Christian hope is the power to begin a new life. "In my end is my beginning." We know what it means to stand up after failure and start anew. What is more difficult is to stand up and start a new beginning after success. The development of the Western World (and now the whole present Modern World) is a success story of the modern, scientific-technological mind. Its globalization after 1989 into the One World was very successful—at least for us, but unfortunately not for everybody. The ghastly ditch between the First World and the Third World has deepened. Millions of homeless migrants are wandering around, knocking at the doors of rich countries. The mortality of children in Africa is growing. The losers of the globalization of our modern world are crying out for their right to live and to have freedom. We must, I believe, start *a new globalization:* a global action against poverty and hunger, a global liberation from oppression, and a global respect for cultural identity. Globalization for tomorrow means the renunciation of the arrogance of power in the Western World and a compassionate solidarity with all the wounded and suffering people on Earth.

Dialogue between world religions is necessary, but it is not the problem of the day. A "clash between civilizations" is not the challenge we are facing at this moment. The "war" that has come over us since September 11, 2001, is the terrorist reaction of a radical wing of Islamic fundamentalism. These groups are reacting against the conditions that the Modern World imposes on all of us in order for different religious communities to live a peaceful life in a common civil society. Religious communities can live in the Modern World under three conditions:

1. the separation of church and state, or religious and civil communities;
2. individual religious freedom; and
3. dignity and human rights for women.

Modern Islam (or Islam in modern societies) has agreed to these conditions and has given up the Shariah and the Jihad. Fundamentalist Islam is, on the contrary, a reaction against these three conditions of the Modern World. They want a Muslim state with exclusion of non-Muslims and the subjection of women. They revitalize for this goal the Shariah and call for a Jihad against the modern states—in the West and also in the Arabic world.

There are only a few states on Earth where those three conditions of the modern world are not accepted and practiced. All members of the United Nations have agreed to live by these principles.

The modern world is an open world, as discussions about postmodernism or the ecological revolution show, but it can offer peace between religious communities only under the three conditions mentioned. This is because these three were the conditions for overcoming the religious wars in Europe in the seventeenth century. They gave birth to the modern world then, and they are essential for the peace and modernization of the world today.

21

In the Face of Evil
Understanding Evil in the Aftermath of Terror

Luis G. Pedraja

I stood transfixed before my television on the morning of September 11, 2001, watching the tragic events of that day unfold. Along with millions of Americans, I watched helplessly, trying to grasp the magnitude of the tragedy, unable to articulate a cogent response. In the days that followed we began to respond. We prayed together, we volunteered our time and gave from our hearts, hoping to find our way through the darkness that hung over us like a cloud. We searched for hope, for answers, for a light to guide our way. We responded with faith, charity, patriotism, anger, and courage.

Yet, as we sought to find meaning and answers in the wake of the terrorist attacks, our language turned toward religion in an unprecedented way in this day and age. Politicians joined community leaders publicly in prayers, attending nationally televised prayer services and interfaith gatherings. Public discourse on religious themes, such as Muslim-Christian dialogue became the norm. Even more perplexing was the unabashed manner in which national public policy and discourse began to develop a discourse revolving around a terminology of evil in connection to the events surrounding 9/11.

From the very beginning, assumptions and characterizations of the events, the surrounding circumstances, and the perpetrators as evil began to emerge, each with implicit and often unexamined theological implications. For instance, in his address to the nation on that fateful night, President Bush characterized the acts as evil, saying, "today, our nation saw evil, the very worst of human nature."[1] This rhetoric culminated in the President's characterizing the perpetrators of these events as "evildoers" and describing his newfound mission as that of ridding "the world of evildoers."[2] Furthermore, he adds later in his remarks of September 16 that "we've been warned there are evil people in this world," and that we are dealing with a "new kind of evil."[3] These remarks are coupled with others in the same speech that make use of religious imagery with reference to God's grace, prayer, "the Lord's Day," and the more troubling remark comparing the fight against this "new evil" to a crusade.

Theologically, these remarks can be at times telling of the way we understand evil and troubling in our uncritical characterization of evil. For instance, what does it mean for the President to say we are facing a "new kind of evil," or more significantly, to say that the "evil folks still lurk out there"?[4] Our public discourse on evil is facile at times, propagandist at others. We use the terminology of evil, but we seldom take the time to fully examine and comprehend the meanings and assumptions with which we inscribe our notions of evil. While the events of September 11, 2001, are troubling and must be understood in terms of our discourse about evil, it is essential that we carefully examine our understanding of evil in light of the terrorist attacks of September 11, 2001, and the ensuing conflict that came in its wake.

Evil as Human Agency

In the wake of September 11, it is not difficult for us to understand evil in terms of human agency. The very words of President Bush on that day echo an understanding of evil in terms of human agency, "the very worst of human nature." One of the clearest manifestations of evil can be found in the nature and acts of humanity. But this calls us to make some clarifications in our understanding of evil in human nature. First, we must determine whether it is our nature that leads us to act in evil ways or our actions that engender evil in us. Second, we must understand the nature and source of human sinfulness and how human beings, created in the image of God, can become demonic in their actions, perpetrating great evils against one another.

In a certain sense, these questions are not separate questions, but inescapably conjoined. Much like the old question of which came first, the chicken or the egg, we must contend with the question of whether we are evil because we do evil acts or whether we commit evil acts because we are evil. Ultimately, the discourse following September 11 reveals this connection in our failing to distinguish between these two notions by speaking of the terrorists in terms of both the evil ones and the evildoers interchangeably. In speaking of evil ones, we understand evil as an intrinsic characteristic of those that committed the acts; evil is part of their nature. But when we speak of them as evildoers, we characterize their acts as evil, making evil the result of their agency.

In a sense, both ways of looking at the problem of evil as human agency are correct. According to Paul, we are all sinners, predisposed toward evil

(Rom. 3:23; 7:9–20). Although created in the image of God, we have chosen to perpetuate evil and in a sense changed our very being by the evil that we do. In practical terms, there is no distinction in the outcome. In the age-old controversy between Augustine and Pelagius, Augustine holds that our will is so corrupted that it cannot will to do good, Pelagius that although difficult, we could choose good over evil. Yet, side by side, whether our nature is corrupt or free to choose, the actual reality is that regardless of our will the outcome is the same: we do evil.

Whether we say that someone is evil because they do evil acts or that they do evil acts because they are evil, the consequences are the same. However, there is a difference in how we understand the person and the nature of evil as rooted in human agency. If we are evil, then evil must inevitably be the result of our actions. On the other hand, if we become evil through our actions, then we have a choice, even if it is a primordial choice as individuals or as a race. Nevertheless, if the practical consequences are the same, maybe the actual relationship between the two is more closely tied together than we imagine. This is particularly true if we think of human nature not as a static essence, but as a dynamic and relational being. In my book *Jesus is My Uncle: Christology from a Hispanic Perspective*, I introduce the notion of ontopraxis.[5] Rather than speaking about being (ontology) and action (praxis) as two separate concepts, I propose that we look at them together. Who we are affects what we do. At the same time, what we do also affects what we are.

In isolation, the question of whether being precedes action or action precedes being is nonsense. Action must be rooted in a being. But what if being is also rooted in action? In practice the question of which precedes the other is only applicable to God, in whom being and act already coincide, rendering the question moot.[6] Everything else already exists in a complex of relationships where being and action go hand in hand. Our actions as individuals affect our very being. They change who we are. As do the actions of others. For instance, if I decide to plunge from a bridge, the status of my being is likely to change. At the same time that our actions change our being, we then become more likely to act in accordance to our actions. Being and act are irrevocably interconnected, one affecting the other and vice versa.

We are sinners because we sin and we sin because we are sinners. Yet, this reality itself is rooted in our very nature as human beings and in the very concept of human agency. By virtue of being created in God's image, by being creative and free, we bear the capacity for doing both good and evil.[7] Our very freedom is what gives us the capacity to choose evil.

But why do we choose evil above good? Theologians throughout the ages have pondered this question. At times, the answer implies that we are no longer free to choose between good and evil.[8] Who we are has been corrupted by sin in such a way that our freedom only enables us to choose between evils.[9] Nevertheless, this inherent sinfulness and predisposition toward evil is not an essential part of human nature as originally created by God, but rather the result of our willful action–human agency.[10] According to Augustine, we are born in sin, yet God did not put sin in humanity.[11] Whether originally the corruption of human nature was through a primal rebellion against God or the result of our own choosing, humanity was not intended toward evil, yet evil persists, and it persists at our hands.

If evil is not intrinsic to human nature, then what lures us irresistibly toward evil? Somehow, the destructive power of evil–its darkness, our willful desire to assert our freedom by rejecting all limitations and rupturing all relationships–draws us to itself. It seduces us in a way that often defies explanation. Commenting on Paul's dilemma in Romans 7:19, Tillich writes:

"It is our human predicament that a power takes hold of us, that does not come from us but is in us, a power that we hate and at the same time gladly accept. We are fascinated by it; we play with it; we obey it. But we know that it will destroy us if we are not grasped by another power that will resist and control it. We are fascinated by what can destroy us, and in moments even feel a hidden desire to be destroyed by it."[12]

The destructive power of evil seduces us; we gravitate toward evil like a moth drawn to the flame that will devour it. Traditionally, theologians locate this propensity toward evil as a result of pride, of our desire to be like God.[13] Yet, they are careful to distinguish that this propensity is not of God's doing, but the result of our will's being bent away from God. Tillich's use of "predicament" instead of a more essentialist term, such as "human nature," indicates that our propensity toward evil is the actual condition in which humanity finds itself. But it falls far short of stating that it is the natural human condition.

Ultimately, the root of the seduction of evil lies in the nature of power and freedom accorded to humanity by virtue of our being made in the image and likeness of God.[14] We assert our freedom and our power in opposition to God, for in our imaginings we believe that only in rebellion, in asserting our will against God's, do we find our freedom and power.[15] But the root of this lies in our basic misunderstanding of the nature of God and in confusing freedom and independence. Our desire for power and freedom mistakenly confuses freedom with independence, power with dominion. Independence, by its very nature, assumes a lack of dependency, a self-sufficiency that does not necessitate any relationship with another.[16] It also asserts itself in terms of power as control or dominion, a mastery of self and others so that relationships to others are under our control. Ultimately there is a closure of our self to the other.

Freedom, on the other hand, is an ability to choose. In making our choice, we decide between different alternatives, yet our choices by their very nature always occur in relationship to another. We inevitably depend on something or someone beyond ourselves.[17] In a sense, freedom depends on choices, possibilities that lie outside us, often beyond our control. Hence, we exist in relationship to another. Power then does not lie in self-sufficiency or in asserting control over another, but in the ability to give freely to others. This form of power is what lies at the root of love, which at its very heart is the freedom to be in a relationship to another and open to the other.[18] It is this freedom of human agency that empowers us to respond to the needs of others, to rush to their aid even at our own peril, and to give bountifully to others out of care and love.

However, our freedom can easily become driven by hatred and bent on destruction, an all-consuming desire. Søren Kierkegaard, the Danish philosopher, describes this hatred as a demonic rage:

"He prefers to rage against everything and be the one whom the whole world, all existence, has wronged, the one for whom it is especially important to ensure that he has his agony on hand, so that no one will take it from him –for then he would not be able to convince others and himself that he is right."[19]

This hatred turns our freedom into the demonic, raging against all and believing that in our destructiveness, we are within our right. Evil, understood as the result of human agency, comes from us, from the choices we make. As our hatred, coupled with our freedom, drives our choices and actions, we engage in a destructive rage that consumes everything around us, and ultimately, also consumes us.

Evil as a Projection

Evil can be more than a mere question of human agency. It can also become a form of projection. In this sense, we can speak of evil as a projection in two ways. First, evil is a form of projection in the philosophical sense, as a form of moral value projection unto a morally neutral or ambivalent slate.[20] In this category would fall the thoughts of thinkers such as Rousseau and Hobbes, where social mores and conventions corrupt natural innocence or impose our value judgments upon those who are different and other from us. I would even include in this category Friedrich Nietzsche, who in his treatise *On the Genealogy of Morals* gives an account of how he "ceased to look for the origin of evil *behind* the world" and to view it as a value judgment of humanity.[21]

According to Nietzsche, the notions of good and bad come not as a result of sacrifice, but as an imposition of value. The determinant of good is the nobility who are powerful and define themselves in those terms, while bad becomes associated with the plebian and common.[22] Yet, this later notion becomes inverted by a "slave revolt in morality" that begins with *ressentiment*, a sense of resentment of those in power and of higher noble status by those of lower status.[23] Thus, we project a value judgment that limits their power, nobility, and self-assertion in an effort to level the other into the mundane, ordinary nature of ourselves. Evil becomes a creation of our resentment fueled by hatred.[24]

While I may not agree with Nietzsche's assessment of the problem of evil as a value judgment forced by the weak on the strong, he does provide an example of a projection and construction of evil that is applicable to the discourse of evil that follows the events of 9/11. In our rhetoric following 9/11, we began speaking about our enemies as evil and as the "evil ones." At the same time, enemies of the United States have painted the U.S. with the same brush. Each projects their respective value judgments upon the other, whether rightly or not. Although not motivated by Christian ideals, Nietzsche does address the possibility of loving one's enemies in terms of respect for one's adversaries and hatred as the motivation for picturing our enemy in terms of evil, leaving us with a very plausible indictment of our motivations in rendering such projections: "He has conceived 'the evil enemy,' '*the Evil One*,' and this in fact is his basic concept, from which he then evolves, as an afterthought and pendant, a 'good one'–himself."[25]

The projections of evil upon the other as a value judgment often has little to do with identifying evil in a person or in their acts; it is but a ploy to portray the other as morally inferior and in contrast assume our own moral superiority to the other. It is a way of taking a morally superior stance and to understand who we are as implicitly good in contrast to the other, who is evil. At the same time, in doing this, we easily avoid our own complicity in evil and elevate our own sense of goodness.

This leads me to move from a purely philosophical understanding of evil as projection, to a second form of projection of evil as a psychological or propaganda tool evident in our discourse following 9/11. In the wake of 9/11 our discourse on evil gravitated toward two forms of projections of evil as value judgment. One, coming from certain segments of the religious establishment, was quickly condemned by the media and political leaders. The other was taken for granted. Yet, both projections of evil had the same effect of distancing ourselves from evil and asserting our own sense of being good in contrast to the other, whom we have pictured as evil.

The first was the comments voiced by Jerry Falwell, Pat Robertson, and certainly echoed by others, that blamed the attacks not on the acts of the terrorists per se, but on the moral decline of the U.S., particularly its tolerance of abortion, gays and lesbians, feminism, and groups advocating for these causes, such as the ACLU and People for the American Way.[26] This argument is troubling in several ways. First, it raises a question of culpability. If God allows these events to happen or has lifted divine protection from the United States, it raises questions of theodicy, implicating God to some degree in these events. The notion that somehow calamities befall us as a punishment for sin is popular with many clergy and laity, and are to some extent substantiated by biblical accounts of the flood (Gen. 6:5–7) and of Sodom and Gomorrah (Gen. 19).[27]

Nevertheless, while no one is blameless before God, we cannot assume that the victims of 9/11 were somehow guiltier than the rest of us, deserving such a horrific death. Nor do biblical accounts always support this position. Job's tribulations are a test, not punishment. Those killed when the tower of Siloam collapsed were no worse sinners than the rest (Lk. 13:1–5).[28] Other

New Testament passages indicate that God is both loving and forgiving, extending grace over punishment. While sin might be directly to blame for the tragedies that befall us as a direct result of sinful actions perpetrated against us by free human agents, to claim that God would indiscriminately punish people for the sins of a nation is questionable. Of course, one might say that the tragic events of 9/11 are not a punishment from God, but rather the result of God lifting divine protection from the nation. However, implicit in this discourse is another questionable assumption, an assumption that somehow the U.S. is a Christian nation or favored by God. While there are hopefully many Christians in the U.S., the nation itself, as well as its politics, is not necessarily Christian, but merely defined by a form of civil religion. The United States might be privileged in wealth and power, but that does not necessarily imply that we have incurred God's favor. Nor should any nation assume a privileged status before God, lest they fall as the result of their sinful pride. Actually, if there is a sin that pervades our nation, it is not to be found in the groups listed by Falwell, but in our pride.

Another troubling characteristic of the remarks is the tendency to project the blame and the notion of evil on a group or community that appears as different from us. It is easy through our rhetoric and discourse to project our moral values upon those who are different from us or with whom we disagree. As Nietzsche's remarks allude, in characterizing others as evil, we portray ourselves in contrast to them as good. This is troubling because it is always easier to find or assume evil in someone else. It is infinitely harder to find the evil within. In his comments on September 16, 2001, President Bush stated, "Evil folk still lurk *out there.*"[29] The question that remains is whether there is not evil inside as well. In projecting evil to some external adversary or group of people, we intentionally distance ourselves from evil and present ourselves as aligned with the good and with God. In doing so, we forget to look at the sin that lurks within our own souls, nation, and history.

Perception, Relation, and the Rhetoric of Evil

The President spoke of the events as a "new kind of evil" and as never seeing "this kind of evil."[30] Implicit in these remarks, one would expect an assumption that there is a typology of evil and this is a new form never before seen, yet there probably is no assumption behind such remarks. In later remarks, he would speak about nuclear and biological weapons as "evil weapons." Yet, while the intent behind those who create weapons might be evil and their use may be an act of evil, it is difficult to speak of a weapon, an inanimate object, as being "evil." For that matter, the U.S. has nuclear weapons and has actually used them against civilians twice in its not-too-distant past. Yet, those weapons and their use were not characterized as evil, per se, in our history books. Their use against Hiroshima and Nagasaki might at most have been seen as a necessary evil that would end the greater evil of a war. By the same token, current discourse about the U.S.'s war against Afghanistan and against terror has not been presented as evil, at least not in the U.S.

Defining evil is a complex task, often compounded by different perceptions and understandings of evil. The discourse regarding evil that became commonplace after the terrorist attacks indicates the difficulties of trying to understand evil and what we mean when we use the word or ascribe it to something, such as the events that occurred, the people who committed the acts of terrorism, governments that threatened us, and even for people within our midst whom we perceived as sinners.

The way we talk about evil can be a matter of perception, relationship, or even rhetoric. I have grouped these three categories together because they bear many similarities and connections, such as their reliance on interpretations. For instance, perception is ultimately a matter of interpretation. Based on our experience, moral sensibilities, or even on the outcome of events, we interpret certain acts, events, and things as evil. People, events, and things that are detrimental to us, we characteristically consider as evil. People, events, and things that benefit us, we might perceive as good. But what happens when something we perceive to be in our best interest, that will be good for us, is something that is detrimental to someone else? What do we do with competing interpretations of good and evil? Is "collateral" damage in a war, the supposedly unintentional killing of innocent civilians, not an evil for those suffering the attacks? This is the complexity of evil we seldom want to face in making facile identifications of evil.

Our interpretation of events, actions, and situations rely on a multitude of frameworks of valuation. For instance, an assessment may be based on utilitarian perceptions of the benefits and detriments to us. It may also depend on how far removed an event or situation is from us. A tragedy occurring in our backyard might be perceived as worse and bathed in a rhetoric of evil, while a tragedy in another country might only be seen as tragic. Genocides in Africa and the Balkans might disturb us, but seldom elicit the visceral response from us that the events of September 11 elicited. At the same time, some might look at September 11 and, while recognizing the tragic nature of the events, speak of a greater good coming from them, such as greater national unity or a renewed interest in faith. Ultimately, as we seek to understand horrific events, we ascribe value to them and perceive them in relation to our moral intuitions, to particular outcomes, or a particular worldview. Thus, when the President speaks of weapons as "evil," he might very well be characterizing them in light of their outcome or use, that is, based on the destructive consequences of their use.

To some extent, we might also interpret evil in relation to some standard or norm, so that evil can only be understood in light of something else, such as goodness. The resurrection gives us a new perspective for understanding the evil and suffering of Jesus' crucifixion. Thus, life can triumph in spite of death and suffering. Love can overcome hatred. According to Augustine, for instance, as well as other Neo-Platonists, evil is a matter of both perception and relation. For him, evil is not really a thing. In other words, it does not have an existence apart from beings that do evil. Evil is a privation, absence, or lack of goodness, with no ontological reality.[31] Thus, evil might be found in terms of a perversion of the will and a bent toward evil, but not as a being or in the nature of a being that can be said to be solely and purely evil.[32]

In the works of Iraeneus, the early church theologian, evil was an instrument for developing moral character in humanity. Even in Islam, evil can be interpreted as a matter of perception and relation, serving to develop moral character and to bring forth greater goods, both in this world and in the rewards of the afterlife for the victims of such evils.[33] In other words, what we call evil is merely in terms of its relationship to good. When we say that a greater good might come from some great evil, we might be unknowingly echoing a notion that evil might be necessary for an appreciation of good or even to bring forth a greater good.

However, knowing that an evil might bring forth a greater good does not mitigate the pain and suffering of those afflicted by the evil. The sense of unity found after the terrorist attacks and the renewed interest in religion in some people are of little solace to those who lost loved ones in the attacks. At the same time, this does not mean that we should never talk about something good coming out of great evil. We just need to be careful to understand the implications of what we mean. The key is in how we conceive of the relationship between evil and the good that comes from it. It is one thing to say that evil is necessary for a greater good to come about, another to say that God can transform evil in such a way as to bring forth some good from it and by providing new possibilities for good in the midst of evil.[34]

When we understand evil in terms of perception or as relative to something else, we place evil in contrast or proximity to something. When we speak of evil in this way, we define evil, not as an essence in itself, but in terms of its relationship to something else, something that is valued as better or good. In perception, we understand evil in terms of its significance to us or to our world. We also interpret whether something is evil, sinful, or bad on the basis of our own worldview and moral sensibilities. In this sense, evil is primarily a matter of subjective valuation. The distinction between projection and perception is subtle, but perception is a matter of interpretation, while projection is a matter of imposing our sense of values on the other.

When we interpret evil in light of some higher good, we define evil, it would seem, in terms of something objective. But that need not be the case, especially if the definition relies on our utilitarian interpretation of goodness determined by what is good for us or in accordance to our worldview. For instance, what we understand to be the good is not necessarily what others might understand to be good, particularly if we are speaking in terms of American values versus the values of another country or culture that does not share our same views.

There is, however, a third construct of evil that can also shed light on the discourse of evil that followed September 11, evil as a rhetorical construct.

Rhetoric develops an argument that favors a position over another. In our day of media savvy, we can compare rhetoric with propaganda and "buzz" words. Ultimately, understanding evil in terms of rhetoric involves not merely a projection or a perception, but a construction. It is common practice in times of war to portray your enemies as evil, while characterizing your own causes as just and righteous. I suspect that much of the references to evil in our discourse during times of war are tinged by rhetoric, including the discourse that followed the events of September 11.

The danger of developing a rhetoric of evil regarding our enemies lies in its argumentative character and its frequent service to propaganda aims. By demonizing our enemies, we can easily forget our common humanity. The people who die in a war, on both sides of the battles, are human beings, created in God's image. Seeing them as evil allows us to justify our hatred and treatment of them. It makes it easier for us to kill under the guise of eradicating evil, justifying even our own evil and atrocities against our enemies.

Often, rhetoric combines with power and power-driven agendas, allowing us to force our projections, perceptions, and characterizations of evil upon others, especially upon those who are weaker or different from us. Power combined with rhetoric has justified many wars of conquests, crusades, and the oppression of populations we portray as inferior, sinful, or even as evil. Using rhetoric to ensure that our perceptions and projections of evil prevail against others is clearly problematic, for we may in the process see evil where there is only good or mistakenly believe that our cause is a divine cause, sanctioned by God. Jesus was accused of being in league with the devil by some of his adversaries, and others understood his death as necessary and just to preserve peace and to silence what they perceived as heresy (Lk. 11:14–15; Mk. 14:60–64). In the name of God and goodness we often bring forth great evil and destruction. Hence, we must be careful in our characterization of others as evil, lest in seeing their sin we miss our own evil (Mt. 7:3).

Structures of Evil

In examining the discourse of evil, my focus has been on characterizations of evil that can be construed in terms of individual persons or acts. But at times, we must contend with evil as a reality that transcends a given individual or group of persons. There are times when evil takes on a life of its own beyond a particular event or easy identification in terms of an individual human agent. In this sense, evil becomes imbedded in the very fabric and structure of society.[35] Evil breeds evil, as our acts of defiance, sins, and injustices become institutionalized in economic systems, social and political structures, and the laws of the land. These evils become perpetuated in inequalities that plague us continually across the ages. As Jon Sobrino writes:

> Over and above a certain natural sin (original sin) and a personal sin (individual sin), the proclamation of the Reign and the difficulty of seeing it implanted evinces the presence of a "sin of the world," which

is fundamentally historical and structural, communitarian and objective, at once the fruit and the cause of many other personal and collective sins, and its propagation and consolidation as the ongoing negation of the Reign of God. Not that structures commit sin, as liberation theologians are sometimes accused of saying; but structures manifest and actualize the power of sin, thereby causing sin, by making it exceedingly difficult for men and women to lead the life that is rightfully theirs as the daughters and sons of God.[36]

As sin becomes entrenched in the structures and systems of society, evil continues to be perpetuated, making it more and more difficult for any of us to escape its grip upon us.

Of course, these concepts are not new in themselves. The stoics believed that evil and sin were present in the world that surrounded us as part of the world of the senses, making it easier for us to fall prey to sin and evil ourselves.[37] This is perfectly understandable, as we see cycles of violence and abuse lead to further violence and abuse in families. As we are surrounded by wanton acts of violence, we slowly become desensitized to it, accepting violence as the norm and committing violence with greater ease. Economic injustices and inequalities keep some from prospering, continually struggling under inhuman conditions of poverty, while others prosper, or should I say profit, at their expense. Unjust economic practices eventually make it more difficult for some to overcome their situation in life. In desperation, as they are deprived of dignity and the bare essentials of life, some resort to drugs and alcohol to numb the pain, while others resort to crime and violence.

According to Latin American liberation theologies, poverty is the result of such unjust economic practices and sinful systems imbedded in our society.[38] Oppression and sin throughout history have created unjust social systems that rob people of their livelihood and dignity. The natives lose their land to the power of the European invader and must work the land not just for their own sustenance, but also to bring a profit to the conqueror. The cycle continues, as the conquerors get richer while the conquered get poorer. The children of the conquerors inherit the wealth; the children of the conquered inherit their enslavement. Eventually, the inequality is insurmountable, and the wealthy see their ill-gotten gains as the fruit of their labors, their rightful inheritance, not as the result of a violent past. They pass laws to protect their property and enlist the resources of the government and military to enforce those laws, securing their place. But we innocently, or maybe conveniently, forget the legacy of violence and sin that has created the present circumstances. The evil of our ancestors becomes entrenched in an unjust social structure we now take as a norm. In that sense, evil becomes structural in nature.

Injustice, sin, and evil are not always easily located in an individual. At times we create our own monster and in the process become monstrous ourselves. When it is in our own interest, we train and equip treacherous individuals to fight on our behalf, and we call them freedom fighters.

Eventually, when their interests come at odds with ours, our rhetoric shifts, and we call them terrorists. Our dealings with other nations, our international policies, are ultimately self-serving and geared toward our interests. But because we do not live in isolation, what we do unto others eventually affects us. When we ignore the needs of our neighbor to tend to our less serious needs for comfort and luxury, we breed resentment and hostility toward us. Our society today is so driven by consumerism and capital that our government tends to place the interests of corporations before the interests of the people it supposedly represents. There is an inherent evil in the economic practices that would deprive people of their livelihood, firing them, not just to safeguard profits, but to increase the profit margin that a company can present before its investors. Yet, we seldom speak of such evils in our society.

What surprises me, although it should probably not surprise me so much, is that our public discourse following the tragic events of September 11 has not addressed the problem of systemic evil. We cannot limit evil and the consequences of evil to the actions of terrorists or to our enemies. Evil also abides in the very fabric of our society, as we perpetuate violence, engage in unjust economic practices, use laws to discriminate against those who are different, and continually suppress the voices of those at the margins of society. We cannot separate the violence in Palestine, U.S. policy in the Middle East, the global economy, racial discrimination within our borders, consumerism, and systemic oppression of large segments of humanity for economic gain from the events of September 11 and our public discourse on evil. When the President speaks of a calling to eradicate evil, we need to look deeper and further than terrorists.

In the Face of Evil

In the Spanish language, there is no word for evil. The closest words we have are words such as "*mal*" (bad), "*maldad*" (badness), and "*maldito*" (bad or damned). In Spanish, there is a sense of malice, but malice is always located in the motivations and free agency of an individual. However, there is no word that carries the level of abstraction and strong emotional connotations of the word evil. Yet, is this level of abstraction necessarily a benefit in our understanding of evil? We might speak about evil in many different levels of abstractions, but ultimately evil is concrete and particular in its manifestation. Evil does not exist as a detached ethereal force, but as enfleshed in concrete individuals and actions. Even the evil entrenched in our social structures and systems originates in human agency and continues to be perpetuated by continual human acts of evil. Even if we speak of evil in term of demonic powers, there is a concrete location for evil in actual beings or in the way power affects the world.

Furthermore, the consequences of evil and evil acts are also very real and concrete. The acts of the terrorists on September 11 are not abstract. They are real and particular, impacting the lives of many individuals. To speak of evil in abstract terms does little justice to the real impact and consequence of evil upon our lives and upon the lives of countless others. In Spanish, the words denoting evil as bad always place evil not only in the concrete, but also in light of its consequences and its relationship to our determination of good. They place the discourse of evil within the context of its effects and concrete actualities.

While the discourse about evil in the aftermath of September 11 has brought the discussion to our doorstep in light of this tragedy, the manner in which we have framed our language about evil is still quite superficial. Saying that we will not rest until we eradicate evil is a noble sentiment, but it cannot be the work of an individual or a nation. Nor can we simply define the evil we are fighting as something out there, circumscribed by violence and found in our enemies. Our fight against evil must be more thorough and willing to examine the social and systemic manifestations of evil in which we all are complicit through our participation in them. When standing in the face of evil, sometimes words fail us in framing a response and understanding the horrors that we face. But, we do know that we must respond. That we must stand in the face of evil and not shrink from our calling to do justice, to love others, and to overcome hatred and sin. But we must begin by being willing to look in the mirror and by recognizing that often the face of evil is ours as well.

22

Theologies of War
Comparative Perspectives

Max L. Stackhouse

In times like these, we must look at basic concepts of religious ethics that have shaped our social history and are shaping our present situation. We must look at these religiously based concepts because we have been shocked into the renewed recognition that religion shapes the fundamental motivations of people and guides their actions more than our secular analyses admit. Thus, we turn not only to those motifs that are frequently accented in worship to deal with our quest for meaning in the face of absurdity, and to honor those who have suffered, sacrificed, and lost their lives; nor do we turn only to the classical dogmas as they seek to spell out the systematic content of our beliefs as they turn our minds to truths about good that are beyond the present evidence of evil; but we turn to those theologically informed ethical motifs that can guide our sense of responsibilities in society in times of crisis. These are not always addressed directly by piety or dogma, although life under God's care takes place in social, political, economic, familial, and professional spheres of existence, and our traditions develop understandings of these spheres of life in ways that predispose our social histories. Indeed, in a day of global influences, including the globalization of terror, we must try to survey, to understand and evaluate these issues from a comparative point of view, even as they clash.

Religion is, in ways that many analysts have ignored, the core inner logic of cultural and social traditions. Each religion shapes its host society over centuries and draws some of its religious insights from the historical experience of the societies that host it. Yet, religion always points to that which involves at least a claim about transcendence over society, even though it also is inevitably embedded in a particular social history. The relative transcendence allows it to selectively embrace, reject, or refine aspects of the culture of which it is a part, according to the deep presuppositions and inner logic of the reigning religion itself. From this vantage point, religion inevitably shapes widely held values, inclines institutions toward some and not other dominant patterns, and establishes in the mind of the people, and often in the law, various ideals of the right and the good that are not fully operational in society. The precise normative shape of the deepest presuppositions are ever in dispute, of course, for there are disagreements within each religious tradition, and most societies have more than one religious tradition. In this respect, it is not unlike schools of thought in academia, disputes of principle among political parties, competing convictions as to artistic excellence, or various alternative approaches to medicine or law. Still, the one that comes to dominance in a civilization because it is most able to form and sustain the institutions of the common life is the one that is most able to shape the deepest presumptions about truth and justice, the views of the right order of the regime, the concepts of the correct form of production and distribution in economic life, the characteristic patterns of child rearing that become typical of particular cultures, the artistic expressions of conviction, and, indeed, the attitudes toward war and peace.

When we begin to compare the religious ethics of various traditions, we find that there are a great number of areas that tend to overlap or converge, even if there are other areas that to tend to clash. Where there are disagreements, it is important to assess whether these are of high importance so that they must be settled, or whether the differences are incidental and thus do not involve basic contradictions that would induce social implosion, unbearable inner tensions, or religious collapse. If there are disagreements that genuinely threaten religious commitments and moral fabric, it is not surprising that violent conflict breaks out. As George H. Williams once said: "Religion is high voltage; it can energize or it can electrocute."[1]

Ordinarily, the great religious ethical traditions of the world and the great civilizations that they spawn share a common commitment to peace. We can see that in the way in which the key terms for peace are honored in most religious and cultural traditions – *shalom, eirene, salem, pax, mir, Friede,* and their international counterparts. With slight nuances, they all refer to a state of minimum conflict, the relative absence of coercive force, and the practice of nonviolent resolution of conflicts–all guided by a pervasive sense of justice or equity that is integral to the morals, manners, dispositions, and practices of the common life. In this past century, several icons of peace have been greatly honored–Albert Schweitzer, Mahatma Gandhi, Martin Luther King, Jr.,

Mother Teresa, the Dalai Lama, to name key examples who come from different religious backgrounds. While none are angelic in all respects, many see them as, in some regards, model figures. In contrast, people of many faiths have also adopted negative icons of those who have initiated war, destroyed cultures, and undercut the prospects of a viable society by subverting peace with demonic forms of violence–Hitler, Stalin, Pol Pot, Idi Amin, and a host of local tyrants.

At the same time, there are heroic figures who are known above all for their conquests that showed not only military prowess, but the defense of threatened peoples or the expansion of cultural horizons when cramped possibilities inhibited human development. Think of the Spartans at Thermopylae, of Alexander the Great, Charlemagne, Joan of Arc, or Winston Churchill, to cite only some memorable figures from the West. Few churches, temples, monasteries, religious orders, or mosques have not celebrated the sacrifice of those who have given their lives for the protection of their loved ones, their country, and their faith. For while all seem to know that peace is good and that destructive violence is evil, most also recognize that there is at least an episodic need to fight the forces of evil in order to establish the relative prospects for a just peace that are possible in human history. The questions become when, and how, and under what kind of religiously legitimating justification, under what conditions, and to what ends should they do so. Today, three basic theories of war are in contention, and it is important that we engage in the exploration and, in some measure, the comparative assessment of these three views. I refer, of course, to those of Judaism, Islam, and Christianity.

The "Peoples of the Book," as the Muslims say, share the fact that they are religions of revelation. That is, they hold that at the center of their faith is a divine disclosure of truth and justice. The disclosure transcends the capacity of humans to discover or invent or infer by empirical observation and rational analysis of life. Indeed, they all claim that God has taught humanity how to live in the midst of life's evils and wrongs in ways that humans could not find or construct alone. This applies also to the use of violence, and this is what we shall survey.

Jewish Roots

The deep roots of all these traditions are in the Hebrew scriptures. In Joshua, Judges, Samuel, Kings, and Deuteronomy, we find the idea of the Conquest as a duty under God. God as the "Lord of Hosts" accompanied the Hebrew warriors as they carved out a new space for themselves in a land inhabited by others. This idea has echoed in later Judaism, in Christianity, and in Islam, and is sometimes called "Holy War," although it has taken various forms, as we shall see.

The basic plot is familiar: after a long period of subjugation under Pharaoh, the Children of Israel were led by Moses on an exodus out from under their slavery. After wandering in the wilderness for many years, and being formed into a new people under a Holy Law given by God, they were commanded to take possession of the land that God promised them. In the process, it was understood that God would be with them and approve their deeds. As the lore has been taught for centuries, Joshua fought the battle of Jericho and Gideon blew the ram's horn to call the warriors to battle against those who occupied the land. Moreover, when others threatened the land that was taken, Samson took the jawbone of an ass and slew the enemies of Israel. Later, Saul, the troubled warlord, and then David, the shepherd boy who defeated Goliath, were anointed kings to establish a new political order to secure both the religious ethic, the new society, and the land. Under David and his successors, a major policy change established a standing army–although echoes of the older tradition were preserved and reappeared in the stories of the Maccabees centuries later.

The old warrior ethic had significant ethical contours to it. In fact, under the impact of Zionism and the reestablishment of Israel after World War II, extensive and detailed rereadings of those ancient texts were undertaken by modern Jewish scholars. On the basis of their research, a number of modern Israeli leaders developed the ideas of "the sanctity of arms" *(kedushat haneshek)* and "purity of arms" *(tohar haneshek)*. This is the idea that when the people or the faith are under threat, it is a "holy duty" to take up "righteous" arms to establish a safe society in the promised land.

The "holy duty" is not to be undertaken in the name of some general or king to whom loyalty is pledged. Nor are they to fight for booty or career. The purpose is not human aggrandizement, but God's purposes and sovereignty. Moreover, the idea that God is the Lord of Hosts does not only mean that God is with the hosts of warriors as they take up righteous arms to defend a people under threat, but that there are limitations on how they should behave as a company of servants of the divine will in the midst of history's conflicts. Like their ancient forebears, they are to maintain ascetic discipline in matters of piety, sexuality, diet, and sanitation. Moreover, they are not to indulge in personal hate or retribution against the enemy. "'Vengeance is mine,' saith the Lord." Combatants may be tough-mindedly calculating in the determination of "military necessity," but personal cruelty is forbidden, for if the former is understandable to both sides, the latter breeds lingering hate. These provisions were not invariably observed either in ancient Israel or in the Zionist reconquest and formation of modern Israel. In the ancient texts, for instance, we have examples of soldiers triumphantly smashing the heads of the babies of the enemy against a stone. And David exploited Uriah's dedication to the old ethic by commanding him to fight in a way that assured his death, so that David could indulge his attraction for Bathsheba–who apparently put herself in a position to attract David while Uriah was under ascetic discipline. Moreover, the people began to celebrate the empire David was constructing, and began to celebrate his victories instead of the Lord's sovereignty. "Saul has slain his thousands, but David has slain his ten thousands." All this meant that David, once the very model of a priest-king who established a measure of security and peace, could not build the temple he had planned. He had unjust blood on his hands—a fact that evoked prophetic criticism. Nathan, the first of the prophets after Samuel, courageously stood before the king and condemned him. In contemporary life, some Jews both within and beyond Israel have also been prophetically critical of Israeli policies and of the unjust blood it has shed—a fact that has, does, and must play a role in international affairs and the policy decisions of every major power in the current situation. While it is, arguably, not the task of religious ethics to set public policy, it is its task to remind all parties of the larger, deeper issues, and as necessary to speak prophetic word of protest against evil. Indeed, to speak of prophecy leads us to both Christianity and to Islam, for they are also heirs of the prophetic tradition and have developed concepts that overlap with the idea of "righteous" arms. We shall here take Islam first, for it is closer to ancient Judaism on this point.

Islam

The term that is often used in Islam for "holy war" is *jihad*. It does not, however, necessarily mean that. The root of the word is *jahada*, which means "to exert onself" or "struggle"—especially to achieve good or defeat evil. Characteristic ways in which this exertion takes place are within the heart of the believer, for the uplift of society, and in intellectual argument to defend the truth and justice of Islam ("the *jihad* of the pen") against its detractors. These uses are peppered through the *Qur'an* and the *Hadith*, although they seem to be most pronounced in those parts which derive from the early period in Mecca. In this context, Muslims were to fight only when provoked, in self-defense and in defense of the new revealed faith, although they were to practice *jihad* in these other ways. When Muhammad was driven out of Mecca, however, he had to defend his fugitive band of believers in Medina, and later felt commissioned to expand the reign of Islam over surrounding territories and peoples. The term also became used for military conquest in every *dar-al-harb*—"domain of war" in territories or among peoples where Islamic rule is not acknowledged or is overtly repudiated, rejected, blocked, or defiled. Such a domain differs from the *dar-al-Islam*, a territory where Islam and its peace prevails, or, in some interpretations, is at least given due respect and place—as, for example, British India or most Western pluralistic societies where Muslims can build mosques and practice the faith with full civil liberties.

In several interpretations of the *Hadith*, the collection of traditions about Muhammad and his life, teachings, and leadership, and in the *Shariah*, the Islamic form of civil and religious law, however, there are indications that the more military meanings of *jihad* have been given a priority, for it has been sometimes assumed that able-bodied men will take an active role in expanding the rule of Islam over the entire world. And, indeed, the history of Islam for several centuries was one of expansion by *jihad*. In this case, Qur'anic instructions to "raid in the name of God" and to "slay idolators wherever you find them" have episodically gained priority in the service of the prophetic expectation that not only pagans, but Jews and Christians should become

Muslims. That is, they will "submit," the root meaning of "Islam"; with the corollary that one who has submitted is a "Muslim." And to what are we to submit? Above all, it is to Allah, whose very thoughts are set forth in the *Qur'an* as delivered by God through Muhammad. It is this aspect of Islamic thought that inclines many to identify Islam as constitutionally "fundamentalist," although this term was clearly developed in the West to apply to a particular, heretical mode of Christian thought that involves a "divine dictation" theory of the Bible. In fact, this view of revelation is closer to the juridical traditions deriving from Mosaic traditions of revelation than to those deriving from Christian ones. Moses received the commandments of God and brought them to the people. He did not himself in any way compose them. Indeed, the *Hadith* suggests that Muhammad could neither read nor write, so he could not have done so. The content of the *Qur'an* is closer to the kind of revelation portrayed by Moses on the mountain than to that given in the accounts of the life, death, and resurrection of Jesus. There we find a radical monotheism with divine dictation understanding of revelation; in the latter we find the roots of what became a Trinitarian view of God, and a characteristic recognition of human agency in the composition of scripture. The first words of the New Testament gospels are "The Gospel according to Matthew" followed by others "according to" Mark, Luke, and John. And these books are followed by many letters "of" Paul, Peter, Timothy, and so on. These are held to point authentically to the living word, Christ, and not only to the words themselves as thoughts of God. Although Christians accept the Ten Commandments and other direct "words" as authentic disclosures of God's laws, purposes, and mercies, and seek to be guided by them, Christians also recognize the interplay of divine inspiration and human authorship in the midst of an ongoing revelation in human life and history and an internal pluralism in the very being of God.

However, Islam differs from Judaism in at least one major respect. Neither the ancient Hebrews nor modern Judaism seeks to convert the world–even if they are convinced that they are to be "a light to the nations." In this the Old Testament heritage is more like many primal religions, and like Hinduism and Confucianism insofar as they develop great spiritual and ethical teachings that can edify all but do not press toward the conversion of all to their faith. Islam does, and in this regard can be seen partially as ancient Judaism gone universalistic. In this it is more like Buddhism and Christianity, which are also universalistic in aspiration. These three religions are constitutionally missiological; they think that they have a message that can be, should be, and even must be taken to all the world for its salvation. This has created one of the critical issues for Islam. In its first several centuries, it did spread rapidly–largely by conquest in the name of *jihad*, but also by the relative superiority of its moral and spiritual vision compared to many fractious, animist, and pagan traditions it surpassed or absorbed. Indeed, after the death of Muhammad and the rise of the Caliphite tradition of Islamic empire, the Muslim traditions spread by *jihad* not only east through Persia and Afghanistan to the borders of

China and India, but north into the Balkans, and west across North Africa into Spain. It was, to be sure, stopped temporarily in France by Charles Martel in 732, but continued its expansion elsewhere. Over time, it created a complex civilization with highly developed art, literature, philosophy, and science that clearly surpassed the medieval West and rivaled the great empires of Hindu, Buddhist, and Confucian kings to the East.

But at the height of its powers, it began to falter. Not only did the divisions between Sunni and Shi'ite traditions divide it internally, bringing a great split in the fundamental theory of succession and leadership, but El Cid began the repelling of the Muslim rulers in Spain in 1080. The Roman Catholic pope about that same time also called for the knights, princes, and kings of Europe to mobilize a crusade to defend against Islamic expansion and to recover the Holy Land. Several were undertaken over the next two centuries, some of them harshly bloody and others merely disastrous, although it is clear that the the Christian West was, in part, revitalized by its common effort, its contact with Islamic culture, and the opening of trade routes that gave access also to India and China. Some hold that the Christian crusaders learned their sometimes rapacious techniques from the previous *jihad* tradition of the Muslims, but one would be hard put to assess which side was most vicious in these brutal encounters. Still, Islam continued its growth over the next several centuries, primarily by extending to the East into what is now Malaysia, Indonesia, and the Southern Philippines and the South toward Central Africa– now more by the influence of Sufi traders than by conquering warriors. Those who know Islam in this mode know it mostly as a religion of spirituality and peace.

Of greater world-historical significance is the fact that Islam's expansion was, in fact, basically stopped in the West. The West began itself to expand, in spite of Islamic efforts to engage in a reconquest of the West in resurgent efforts that led to the fall of Constantinople in 1543 and the attack on Vienna in 1683. Subsequently, the Christian West sent missionaries to most of central and southern and eastern Asia as well as Africa. They also sent colonizers and modes of medicine, science, and technology that, for the first time since the height of Islam, surpassed that of Muslim culture. When the Ottoman Empire, the last of the great Caliphite regimes was overthrown in 1924, only residues of the unified theocracy remained–the Saudi, Jordanian, and Moroccan kings, plus the scattered emirates and sheikdoms stand as pale echoes of the old grandeur in spite of the international wealth that flows to them on the undertow of the industrialized West's need for oil.

Moreover, Protestant forms of the Christian democratic West pressed, on theological grounds, for the desanctification of all political orders, the separation of "church" and "state," the nurture of Enlightenment values such as scientific methods in all things, the full education of women, the equal rights of all religions before the law, the freedom of the press, the historical-critical study of sacred texts, and the subordination of religious law to international standards of constitutional law. These "modern" developments, as they hit Islamic society, proved to be extraordinarily disruptive.

While many proximate factors surely influence the contemporary rise of militant, fundamentalist Islam, the longer and deeper drift of history has cut channels of shame, insult, and challenge to the most sacred convictions of Islamic prophecy. The creeping doubt as to whether the revelation and prophecy are really true evokes apoplectic reactions to the suggestions, by lapsed Muslims such as Salmon Rushdie, that it may not be, entirely. And when the West protects such intellectuals and scholars, supports the establishment of a Jewish state engaging in a "reconquest" in the midst of Islamic peoples, tilts toward India where resurgent Hinduism has also repudiated Islam, or encourages what is viewed as sexual freedom and cultural liberty through an "enlightened" media that is almost unavoidable anywhere in the world, and then supports Islamic political leaders who lead dissolute, secularized lives while oppressing their subjects who fall further into economic, cultural, and intellectual sloughs of despair, a rebirth of militant, virulent forms of *jihad* is quite unsurprising. The extent of sympathy for the rebirth of militant *jihad* from West Africa throughout the Arab world to East Asia, and the gleeful, barely muted, empathy from the ideological factions who joined the recent liberation movements against Western hegemony is notable.

Yet it is not at all settled as to what this rise of *jihad* movements means. Is it a Reformation of Islam–a populist turning back to scripture and disciplined morality against the waywardness and pretense of most official representatives of the tradition? Is it a theocratic parallel to those "heaven stormers" of the Radical Reformation who wanted to institute the Kingdom of God on earth by force? Might it be like certain of the "Cathari" movements in late medieval Catholicism or certain pietist movements in the later Reformation that democratized the residual feudalism of the West? Or, is it possibly comparable in any way to the Ku Klux Klan and the White Supremacists in America who claim the symbols of Christianity as their own, but who have been disowned and repudiated by major Christian bodies and the constitutional, democratic societies that they have endangered?

We may not be certain, but we do know that the terrorist actions they have perpetrated cannot be passively accepted by Christian theology or ethics, by the non-Christian traditions that, like Christianity, seek a just peace, or by societies that hope to claim a religious or moral legitimacy.

Christianity

For all the continuities of Christianity with Ancient Judaism, signaled by the early demand of the church that the scriptures must include the Old Testament, there has been, in principle, no accepted doctrine of "holy war." That is not to say that some Christians did not invoke Imperial power to protect the faith, or that some in the crusades did not seek to legitimate their actions by appeal to the "conquest texts," or to undertake behaviors that have close similarities to the most militant Islamic practice of *jihad*. Clearly they did. This can be seen also in Christian pogroms against Jews, among conquistadores against the Indians in Latin America, during the wars against native Americans in what is now the United States and Canada, and by

European believers who settled the land in southern Africa, not to mention the entire colonial experiment. But key aspects of the Christian perception of reality cut against this temptation and not only make these practices anomalies in Christian ethics, but helped prompt the protest against these very actions–which were seldom uncontested. In fact, Christians have long acknowledged that such actions demand a confession of sin, even if they were undertaken with the best intentions, for they violate the first principles and the ultimate purposes of God as understood through Christ.

It is also the case that Christianity does not have, or even claim to have, a complete social philosophy. It is not a tribe or an empire, even if some believers have acted tribalistically and imperialistically. While every area of life is touched and guided by the faith, and while much is drawn from the Hebraic traditions, much has also been drawn over the centuries from the social and historical experience of other peoples–not only the Greeks and the Latins, but the northern Europeans, the Slavic lands, and, increasingly, that of the developing peoples around the world. It is a continually growing tradition, as the history of theology makes clear. In each of these areas, Christians have sought to enter public life, to participate in political, economic, cultural, and even military life, not only with a clear conscience but with a sense of Christian duty. Christians with the capacity and opportunity to lead have a responsibility to establish, so far as it is possible in human affairs tainted by sin, a viable just peace and to resist, with force if necessary, the forms of unjust violence that erupt out of that sin. And insofar as Christians undertook this responsibility, they began to articulate the terms on which this can and should be done–terms that can be found in such theological giants as Augustine, Thomas, and Calvin, and in more elaborated form since.

While some strands of the tradition rejected such participation and adopted a stance of "pure spirituality" and pacifism (e.g., some Gnostics, many monastics, and, among Protestants, the "peace churches"–Mennonites, Brethren, Quakers, etc.), the main traditions of the Christian churches have developed the doctrine of "just war and unjust war," a doctrine similar to what the later Jewish tradition called "righteous arms" and to some aspects of the Islamic tradition when it speaks about justifiable self-defense. The most important implication of this development is that Christians are called to take responsibility for the common good, to shape the polity toward a just peace, in ways that may include the assumption of public offices. This proto-democratic impulse runs deep in the tradition and gave rise not only to the election of pastors and bishops, but eventually, to modern "secular" polities in which believers are also citizens, and which may also include direct participation in those political, police, or military spheres of life where the use of coercive, even lethal force could be required. Although there are various ways of articulating this common theme, the Roman Catholic, Eastern Orthodox, Lutheran, Calvinist, Anglican, Methodist, and some Baptist Christian traditions tend to share it.

To call this teaching a "Christian" doctrine does *not* mean that war, if conducted in the name of Christ or Christianity, is just. Nor does it parallel in status certain other Christian doctrines that attempt to spell out the best way to think about complex matters of faith. Rather, it is a set of assumptions, principles, and conditions that are intended as moral maps by which we can find our way through the thicket of ethical, empirical, and spiritual issues to guide us if and when life presents the possibility that coercive force may have to be utilized.

The primary assumption is this: God wants everyone to live in peace, and to be nonviolent toward the neighbor near or far. The just war theory, in this presumption, recognizes the insight of the monastic and the peace church believers, who know that war is always a departure from the way humanity is intended to live by God. But it demands recognition of the facts that we cannot live in pretended innocence in this life, that violence erupts in the midst of human history, and that sometimes the use of forceful means in necessary to overcome that violence and reestablish the relative peace that is possible. Christians account for this eruption of violence by a doctrine of "The Fall" (into sin) which is not shared by the Jewish and Islamic traditions. Most Christians hold that this doctrinal assumption gives Christianity a more realistic assessment of both human nature and the prospects of human history than is present in its sister traditions. It means also that most Christians have been sharply critical, even punitive, toward the Gnostic and "peace church" traditions when they hold that pure believers can attain a spirituality that is above the struggles for a just peace in history, or that the community of faith can and should embody a kind of holiness that is most virtuous when it denies a duty to engage in the responsible ordering of the common life, and thus to engage in the use of force. Such believers and churches, according to the majority tradition, are parasitic on the larger civil society where God also reigns in principle and where God's laws and purposes are also to be approximated. God is not only concerned about the pure heart or the holy church, but the course of human history and the redemption of the world.

While some variations exist in parts of the tradition, the chief principles that guide those who are seeking to discern whether or not to use coercive means *(jus ad bello)* can be stated in this way: Because of the presumption of peace, the turn to coercive means must be a *last resort*. Alternative ways to resolve the dispute must be explored with patience. Of course, in the case of an immediate attack, when life, welfare, and the faith that holds the culture together is under threat, a response of self-defense or counterattack is warranted. All this is to say that it must not only be a last resort, it must be a *just cause*. Of course, a person or a community cannot simply claim that it is a just cause; it must be a defensible claim—one that would hold up to public scrutiny. That is why, in the face of the recent attack, it is justifiable for the world community to ask the U.S. to give credible evidence that we know who is behind it before they will judge the reaction to be justifiable. Further, the response must be by *legitimate authority*. It is not for some independent militia or angry mob to take such actions upon themselves; the use of coercive force demands the existence of a viable political order. What authority is legitimate is not always easy to discern–as, for example, the African National Congress argued against the regime of South Africa. Decisive here is the fact that the question of what kind of an authority is legitimate–both in the legal *and* the moral sense–must be engaged, a question that implies the existence of an accessible, transcendent norm, a knowable higher moral law than the positive law or social convention. And, even if this is determined, practical calculations have to be made: One is whether there is a realistic *hope of success*–a just peace is not established by futile suicide. The other is that a case has to be made that *more good than harm* is likely to come of it–no just peace is aided by actions that make the problems worse.

Supposing that all the demands of these principles are met, it is still not judged moral to engage in war by any and all means. While the lust for victory in a justifiable war may lead to such a temptation, the doctrine demands that conditions be put on the action as it is engaged *(jus in bello)*. Legitimate authority must *announce the conditions* under which action is to be undertaken. Opponents are thus offered options to change their course of action. Even then, every effort must be made to *discriminate between combatant and non-combatant*, even if the enemy hides among civilians; and in engaging combatants and the machinery intended for use in the war by them, *proportionate force* must be used. One ought not, as the saying goes, "burn the house to kill a mouse."

Still further, even in the midst of battle, and most certainly when prisoners of war are captured or disarmed, combatants must *treat the enemy as human*. Torture, mutilation, mass execution, vengeful retaliation for past ills are clearly ruled out. Finally, victors must *confess their sins* if they have contributed to the causes of or unjust conduct in the war, and seek ways at battle's end to *take steps toward reconciliation and the establishment of a just peace*. This does not mean that the aggressors in the war cannot be punished; it means that the eternal replaying of old conflicts breeds new ones. Even if we cannot forget the tragedies of the past, we can reach toward, or invite, the holy gift of forgiveness.

Many of these provisions have been embodied into international law, for they capture something of universal significance in bringing a decent civility to police and military action. Clearly they played a role in many recent conflicts, were used to foment "just revolutions" in the process of decolonialization, and to protest against nuclear weapons during the Cold War–as was forcefully stated in the U.S. Roman Catholic Bishops' pastoral letter on the subject. And now, we face the issues again–this time not against a nation, but in a conflict with an extralegal network that lives under the protection of an illegitimate government and claims divine sanction. In my view, the Christian doctrine has provided a universalistic basis on which to shape the moral consensus of the world's nations. The justifications for going to war are clear. Whether we can conduct the war with the simultaneous patience and restraint needed to keep it just remains an open question.

It is not the role of any state to conduct a holy war, for no state can be holy even if it has a duty to be just. Neither can or should the church attempt to engage in holy war. It has other, nonviolent purposes. But the church can and should draw on the deepest, widest, and most Godly theological traditions it can discover and offer legitimating guidance to a nation or an international consensus when it is on the right track, warn it of the dangers that it is likely to encounter, and engage in prophetic criticism when it is off the track. Indeed, and this is most difficult for many to grasp, the church can and must seek to assess the relative adequacy of relative claims to prophetic insight that seek to legitimate a world historical movement. While we engage in the justifiable attempt to defeat or constrain terrorist violence, we must also take on the deeper, more difficult, and much more subtle task of trying to discern whether, or in what measure, the revelational claims of Islam are valid. Is it true or false prophecy? That is beyond the confines of this comparative analysis; but it must go on the theological agenda.

The implications are, quite likely, decisive for our attitudes, actions, and policies in this century.

23

The Last Word?

Marjorie H. Suchocki

It would seem that in times of overwhelming tragedy, evil has the last word for those who have been destroyed. Hatred, vengeance, and violence have overwhelmed them, without possibility of their own participation in the continued good of humankind. No matter what good may yet rise from these ashes, they do not participate in that good. For them, evil seems to hold grim triumph.

But the Christian witness calls this evidence into account. It has done so in a variety of ways. Sometimes the argument is that these dreadful evils are necessary for some ulterior purpose that is just too mysterious for us to see. Other times, the argument claims that such evils are required in order to teach the rest of us compassion–the good actions that the tragedy evokes are well worth the price. Yet again, there is the harsh perspective that tragedy is meant by God as a punishment for individual or collective evils. Each of these responses is representative of streams within the Christian tradition, but to many of us they ring hollow. They seem to force our God into the mold of a sadistic parent or teacher or even a sort of divine terrorist. Such images fly in the face of much else within the Christian tradition. And indeed, there is an alternative way of understanding and responding to these tragedies. To understand tragedy from the perspective of a Christian process theology is to refuse to give evil the last word.

And What Is Process Theology?

To explicate this, I offer a simple description of the model used by process thinkers. Everything that exists does so through a dynamic process that can be summarized in three steps. First, there is the powerful influence of the past, surging in a vast multiplicity of ways toward new formations of the present. Second, there is the powerful influence of the future, combining with the past to offer new possibilities for present becoming. Third, there is the becoming present moment itself, creatively integrating its past and its future in order to become itself. Out of this complex dynamic process, all things become what they are in a myriad of combinations, ultimately resulting in the world.

My experience as a teacher at Claremont School of Theology gives an illustration of this process. My students can easily name a variety of influences that brought them to this school. Their families, their previous educational backgrounds, influential friends, perhaps pastors or teachers—each student can tell a story of the streams of influence in the past that brought her or him to this place. But even more important than their pasts are their visions of the future. They are willing to take on three or more years of graduate school, with all its financial and physiological and spiritual demands, primarily because of something that has never before been for them. They have visions of what they might yet become—pastors, teachers, counselors, administrators! The vision of the future is powerful enough to influence them—even more powerful than their pasts. But each student finally made the decision for him- or herself. Each combined past and future influences to become a present self—a student—for the sake of what yet might be. Past influences, future possibilities, and present decision account for who they are now. This is not some "special case" in the universe, but rather it is an illustration of what is always the case: everything, including ourselves, exists in and through this dynamic dance between past and future, creating the present in the process.

Another way to express this universal rhythm is to say that to exist is to receive influences from the past, to interpret these influences according to the possibilities of the future, to integrate these influences within the becoming self, and then to offer the results of this integration to new moments of becoming. Each one, upon its completion, becomes the past for the ever-successive present. The process is receiving, integrating, giving; receiving, integrating, giving; receiving, integrating, giving, again and again and again. This process is itself the creation of time, for no sooner does the present become, than it takes its place as part of the past, joining in the call for the next moment of becoming.

The peculiar twist of this model that makes it so useful for theologians is that the model names God as the power of the future. Have you ever mused about the status of possibilities? Where do they come from? How come the influence of the past doesn't result in nothing more than a mere repetition of itself—or perhaps just random chaos? How come there is order in this whole process—why not just random energy events, bouncing off of each other—why is there creation instead of chaos? The answer, of course, lies with possibilities. While in many cases possibilities are quite limited, for complex creatures like ourselves possibilities can take us far beyond our past. I see it daily with my students—and recognize it also in my own life. It's as if there is a power for going beyond the past in this universe, a power calling us forward to visions never yet realized. Process theologians call this power "God." God is the source of possibilities, and thus we say God is the power of the future. God works with the world as it is in order to bring it toward what it can be.

But take it one step further. How would God know what possibilities are right for each and every new becoming in so vast a place as the universe? Process theologians answer that only a God could do this—a supremely relational God, who feels every single energy-event in every moment of its completion. God *feels* the world as it is, and therefore knows how to lead it toward its next best moment. God feels the world's past, and therefore can provide it with its future. But in between this power of the past and God's power of the future is the power of each becoming existent reality itself. Finite freedom and responsibility exist between these two poles of past and future

Notice, then, that there are three sources of creativity within this understanding of existence. The past has a creative effect upon the present through its power of influence. And God most certainly has a creative effect through the power of the future. And the becoming moment creatively unifies past and future to become itself. Creative power is a shared thing, not a simple thing. And therein lies the tale of the world's tragedy and the world's grandeur.

Whose Fault Is It Anyway?

If the world involves, in every moment of its existence, three creative powers, then no single power can be called the reason for evil. All things take place within a deeply influential context, and responsibility is always shared. Think of the power of the past in this illustration: I live in California, and sometimes in late winter or spring we get awesome morning fogs that totally envelop the landscape—even the freeways. Drivers can barely see each other, and must creep slowly in order to avoid accidents. Too often in such conditions an accident does happen—and then! It's never just one car involved, but the hapless drivers behind do not see the problem in time to stop, and car piles into car, creating a horrendous scene. Who is at fault? Obviously responsibility is a shared thing, with poor visibility, the need for transportation in a variety of forms, and various driving skills all combining to create the mess. Likewise, sometimes when an evil event happens all kinds of other events plow right into it, compounding the problem. The power of the past can be overwhelming. And sometimes, in the case of evil, that power is such that it leaves little freedom for the present moment to go beyond it, just as those stricken drivers can hardly avoid plowing into one another.

But what of the power of the future? Isn't God responsible for getting us out of this mess? God works with the world as it is in order to bring it to where it can be. The way the world is on those foggy freeways is such that those who drive on them can only receive a good that is conditioned by these circumstances. Alfred North Whitehead framed it like this: Sometimes even the best is bad. If you are in that line of traffic, maybe the best you can do is to pull to the side and stop—but what if there is another car bearing down on you in that other lane? What then? Your "best" is relative to your situation. And not even God changes that. Is God responsible for evil possibilities, then? And the answer is, "relatively speaking." If the world could bear a better possibility, God would give it. God always gives that which is best under these conditions, but sometimes even the best is bad.

And then we have the driver: Is the driver ultimately responsible? The problem word, of course, is "ultimately," for the driver's responsibility is relative to that which is really possible in the situation. But what each driver does in the situation participates in creating the situation as a whole, and to that degree, each driver is responsible for what he or she does with the possibilities given by God. God faithfully gives the best that the world can bear in each and every moment. But what the world can bear develops in an intricately interwoven web of shared responsibilities. To the question, Whose fault is it? the answer can only be that responsibility is shared.

So, then, shall we move away from this innocuous example and apply the question of fault to our ongoing tragedy called "September 11"? The quick and easy answer, the one that gratifies us most, is that clearly this is the fault of the terrorists themselves. They, and they only, chose to do this evil; they, and they only, chose to terrorize and murder and destroy. In a process world, the only problem word is the "only." Responsibility is a variable thing, but it is always a shared thing. The terrorists are at fault; they chose their deeds; they are responsible. But their responsibility exists within a web of contributing causes. To explore responsibility fully requires inquiry into the circumstances that made suicide (they called it martyrdom) an acceptable option for them because of the evils that their suicides would create (of course, they called these evils goods).

Other essays in this volume have explored some of these contributing causes, these shared responsibilities. To our horror, we learn that our own national policies and private goods are not untainted in the global situation that fosters terrorism. We are all a part of the past for everyone else, and the contributions of who and what we are combine in a multitude of ways to create an ethos, a climate, a consequence, a mattering in this world. We are not those terrorists, nor do we bear the same responsibility: but we have a share in the responsibility of creating this world where such horrors could happen, and even be named good by some. So to our question, Whose fault is it? we answer, "The terrorists and their supporters, to a major degree, and also, to varying degrees, many others, including ourselves."

But what of God's responsibility? If God is the power of the future, the source of possibilities, where is God's power in the midst of terrorism? What is God doing about it all? In this model, the answer has to be that God is operative the way God is always operative. God creatively offers possibilities for what good is possible in these circumstances. We must assume that God offered the terrorists alternative ways of dealing with their dreadful hatred, their too-easy blaming of America for all their ills. But a history of hatred is hard to overcome when moment by moment an individual chooses to reinforce the hatred rather than change, gaining satisfaction from the very intensity of the hatred. Like those cars piling into one another on the foggy freeway, successive moments of hatred plow into themselves, intensifying, clouding one's ability to perceive anything else. And when hatred is accompanied by visions of a future where hatred itself is glorified, then God's call to alternative futures is easily overridden. Of course, in the nature of the case, we have no way of knowing whether or not God's call was successful for some, who chose as a consequence not to become terrorists. We may have been spared from this horror for as long as we were because of God's call to would-be terrorists to do otherwise—but this is speculative. We only really know what happened with those who rejected God's call. The terrorists of September 11 successfully overrode God's call to a future of inclusive well-being. That God continued to work with the terrorists is given; that not even God is always successful is evident. What we do with the past and with the future finally falls to us.

Is That All? Shall We Feel Sorry for God?

Is that it? Has God just plain failed, end of story? Should we all feel sorry for God? In an awesome sense, we should, certainly in the context of a model where God feels the world in order to call the world to a new future. In this relational universe, God is the most relational of all, continuously feeling the world in all of its bits and pieces just as the world feels itself. What we make of ourselves is what God receives feelingly. We have enough trouble on our finite level with the pain caused by our openness to others, for to love someone is to experience their tragedies as our own. We are told in the Christian tradition that God loves the world, but we have seldom followed this to its awful consequences for God. For God to love us is for God to feel us, and for God to feel us is to know directly who and how and why we are. God, then, has to feel the terrorists and their hatred; God has to feel the terror of the persons on the planes; God has to feel the fiery agony of metal and mortar impacting upon flesh and blood. We might have known this through the suffering of God on a cross that is so central to our tradition, but we have shrunk from pushing that revelation to its universal dimension: God feels the pains of the world. Do we dare, then, to feel compassion for God?

Yet this act of God is the dynamic means of our redemption, in a most pragmatic way. Because God feels each tragedy from every dimension exactly as it is experienced by every participant, God can lead those involved in the tragedy toward what goods are yet possible. Is there heroism? God is in that heroism. Is there compassion, leading one to go more slowly toward safety—risking never reaching safety—in order to help another? God is in that compassion. Is there love yearning toward another in one final cell phone call home? God is in that yearning love. Is there courage in going up the stairs out of duty's sake in the hope of rescuing even one? God is in that courage. Or, in Pennsylvania, when passengers learn through cell phone calls that this is not simply one more inconvenient hijacking, is there bravery in daring to intervene, forcing the plane down in a field instead of into one more of our buildings? God is in that bravery. God feels the tragedies, more than us all, and in and through those feelings gives us hope, and possibilities that are the best that can be in a situation that defies all sense.

But we who call ourselves Christians should know this. The cross in so many of our sanctuaries symbolizes the awesome reality that God identifies with us in our pain, our sin, our grief, our sorrow. Incarnation has always told us that God is not a far-off God, surveying the world as if we were some alien thing under a microscope. Incarnation tells us that God is in the midst of us, experiencing with us. And the cross tells us that God does not restrict that presence to the joyful places of life, but that God is with us in our most agonizing places of pain, loneliness, terror. If we know compassion at all, why should we not dare to experience compassion for the God who feels it all—every little bit that we throw the divine way? Should we not care for the fact that God must feel our tragedies as we feel them? We at least experience them one at a time, but God experiences them all. God experiences the despair of stricken lands, the hunger of swollen bellies, the grief of wailing orphans, the hatred of fanatic terrorists, the fear of their targets. And because God experiences them, God knows and offers what forms of redemption are possible.

What Kind of Redemption?

There are two kinds of redemption. One kind is that which I have been at pains to delineate: the redemption that brings about what good is yet possible in human history. We often call this "the kingdom of God" in history, and it always is like a beacon before us, a vision of a peaceable kingdom. Through us, and our cooperative openness to God's leading, what good is possible can be done. God works through us, setting up support systems of care for the grief-stricken, financial aid for the newly jobless, blood for the injured. God leads us in the rebuilding toward a new and more inclusive good—if we will but receive these possibilities, accept them, and integrate them into who we are and have been.

Of course, it's also possible for us to be as filled with hatred and vengeance as are those who seek to terrorize us. We can give back in kind and more so, matching fear for fear, horror for horror, death for death. We can grimly enter the spiral of hatred, increasing its power in this world. But there is nothing in the witness of Jesus Christ that encourages us to think that hatred and destruction, whether from others or from ourselves, represent the call of God to a redemptive future. Rather, like our Lord we are to look for ways of inclusive well-being, seeking compassionate ways that reflect the nature of God in each context.

It is part of the transformative work of God in the world that God, who experiences the entirety of the past, gives back to the world ever-new possibilities for a better future, which the world then must decide whether or not to actualize. This is the continuous salvific work of God in this world. This form of salvation does not erase the past, as if it had never been. Rather, it offers ways to transform the past, to move beyond its evil effects, to achieve what is good in spite of the evil. There is tragedy in evil, since it would have been far better had it never occurred. But the world cannot stop the salvific grace of God, not even when the world insists on its forms of evil. God is an ever-present source of what good is yet possible. It is then up to us to respond to the good, working along with God to redeem the past.

And that response of doing what good is yet possible is the redemptive work of God in this world. Now, it is also the redemptive work of the people who go and do those things. Insofar as we respond to God's future, we become co-laborers with God, God's instruments, God's partners, in working toward what forms of transformation are possible. Of course we also have the capacity to refuse to work redemptively with God, and to the extent that we refuse, we become participants in the continuing evil effects of that which has been so tragic.

So, then, a process way of understanding the redemptive power of God in history is to say that God feels our tragedies with us. Whitehead called God "the Great Companion, a fellow sufferer who understands." God knows our histories so well, so experientially, that God is capable of leading us toward that which is transformative in the next moment. It may be baby steps, and it will never ever seem like enough. But it is transformation, and it is the work of God. God takes the circumstances as they are, and brings us through toward what can yet be.

Everlasting Redemption

The Christian witness affirms the partial redemptions that can occur in history as God leads us beyond tragedy—but what of those who experience the finality of evil? We are back to our initial question: is evil, for them, the last word? One of the reasons why process thought has been so important to me is because process gives me a way to conceptualize that ultimate answer to evil, resurrection.

Remember the essential dynamic: God, the ultimately relational One, receives the world feelingly. If God feels the world, how much of the world does God feel? The witness is that God feels the world as it feels itself. God's feelings are not partial, not shadowy copies of the real events, but a reenactment of every event that occurs, only now within the divine nature. God is the resurrection of the world.

A biblical text says that it is a fearful thing to fall into the hands of the living God, and process thought implies this as well. God's feelings of the world are integrated into the depths of the being of God: and if God feels us as we are, resurrects us as we are, then our destiny is to experience God's integration of us within the divine nature. This could be heaven, but it could also be hell. Clearly, we are in a speculative realm, but within the process model we must apply the dynamics of existence to the existing God. On a finite level, to exist is to receive the energy of the past and to integrate that energy within the self according to some vision of the future. Applied to God, God receives the world so fully that God resurrects the world, and then integrates the resurrected world into the depths of the divine being according to the divine character. On a finite level, integration is a process of evaluating, contrasting, judging that which is received according to what might yet be. Applied to God, God evaluates, contrasts, judges the world according to God's own character till the world is conformed to God.

Imagine what this would mean for the resurrected world in the life of God. The resurrected world would know itself from the divine point of view. Every resurrected reality would experience God's evaluation of itself. But of course God resurrects all things continuously, so one not only would know oneself from the divine point of view, but one would know oneself as one was experienced by all others. "We shall know as we are known," says a text in 1 Corinthians, and this indeed would be judgment. The theology suggests that God is both heaven and hell.

If we imagine what this would be like for those hijackers, it means that in God they would experience themselves as having acted against the will of God. In God, they would experience the feelings of terror they caused in every one of their victims. The agony they caused is the agony they feel, and in God, they will be conformed to the divine judgment. God's judgment on them will be their self-judgment as well. But this judgment in God is not an end in itself, but a means to the end of redeeming the world, even its hijackers. In history, we have the power of going against God; in God, we do not have that power. We *must* be conformed to the divine image, transformed into the insistent depths of a God whose "nature and whose name is love." Evil, even terrible evil, is felt by God in order to be redeemed by God—partially in history, but fully within the divine nature.

If we are resurrected into God, and integrated into the depths of God through this process of judgment, then the ancient text of 2 Peter 1:4 is true: we shall be made "partakers of the divine nature." In God, therefore, we shall experience with God God's continuous feelings of the world. We shall know the multiple continuations of history. In my own family history, I had a wonderful son-in-law who died from leukemia. Before he died, when he knew there was very little hope of recovering from the disease, he wrote letters to his boys. Six-year-old Graham shared his letter with me. Butch said to him, "When you are on a hill on a summer day, and you feel the breeze, I'm in that breeze with you. And when you are sad, and crying, I feel your tears with you." In a process frame of reference, this is not simply poetic, it is true. Those who are taken into God participate in God's own feelings, and God feels the world. In and through God, Butch is still present to his children. In and through God, who is our resurrection and life, those who have been taken into God participate in God's transforming influence toward those they still love here on history's journey. Only in God, their finite loving has been joined to God's infinite loving.

So evil does not have the last word, not even for those who have been destroyed emotionally and/or physically by evil. God is the power of resurrection. In times of terror, Christian faith, mediated and expressed through process theology, affirms that God is not mocked. God offers possibilities for transformation in history, and we are called to be co-workers with God in actions that create what good is possible, even in the midst of tragedy. History is the sphere of whatever finite redemptions are possible. And God's own self is the final and ultimate sphere of redemption, for God everlastingly overcomes evil within the divine nature through the power of resurrection. This is our faith and our hope, the final Word, through which we live.

Part 4

Just War and Just Peace

24

The Danger of Violence and the Call to Peace

Lisa Sowle Cahill

There can be no question that international terrorism commits an immense offense against the global common good and that nations suffering terrorist attacks on their own soil are the victims of unjustified aggression and have a right to self-defense. It cannot be denied that religious ideals and identities often have been distorted to justify mass violence against innocent persons— not only in the terrorist attacks on the United States in September 2001 but throughout history, and frequently by Christians. Yet the recent widespread international and interreligious repudiation of terrorist violence proves that such violence is never an authentic representation of the core values of the world's major religious traditions.

Defining the appropriate response to terrorism, whether by its victims, by a coalition of nations, or by a global representative body such as the United Nations, is not easy, however. Quick resort to the rhetoric of *war* by U.S. leaders disguised the moral ambiguity and often self-defeating character that all too often attends a violent reply to violence. Violence in the form of military action is morally ambiguous because it redresses assaults on life by further destruction of life; it virtually always transgresses the boundary between the innocent and the guilty; and those who are least powerful and least in control of state decisions are usually those who suffer most in time of war. War is self-defeating because it creates a spiral of violence that ends only when one or both parties have suffered such death, suffering, and loss that the capitulation of the less to the more powerful is unavoidable. On Veteran's Day weekend 2001, National Public Radio[1] presented an interview with a hero of World War II, Sergeant William "Wild Bill" Guarnere, a member of the U.S. Army's airborne rifle unit, "Easy Company." The company's exploits and the soldiers' mutual loyalty have been commemorated in the book *Band of Brothers*[2] and in the HBO documentary *We Stand Alone Together*. In response to the interviewer's question about the moral Guarnere would draw from his own experience, this venerable, much-honored veteran of what is arguably the U.S.'s least questionable military venture advised, "Stay away from war. War is hell. The losers lose, and the winners lose."

That point was made a long time ago by the theologian most responsible for the classic Christian formulation of just war theory, Thomas Aquinas. Aquinas revealingly entitled his presentation of so-called "just war" criteria with a question: "Is it always a sin to wage a war?"[3] Aquinas built on the dubious idea of Augustine that with the right intention, government-authorized killing can be a loving form of punishment of sinners, and Augustine's more plausible idea that war can be justified to restore peace. Aquinas himself put the emphasis on protecting the common good and enumerated three basic criteria for going to war: it must be declared by "the authority of the sovereign," not private individuals; it must be fought for a "just cause"; and it must be done with a "rightful intention," that is, to advance good and avoid evil, not out of hatred or to seek revenge. In the premodern period most of the emphasis in the moral analysis of war was placed on the conditions under which it could be initiated *(jus ad bellum),* though Aquinas does treat whether ambushes and deceit can be used as means in war (answering yes, because they are expected). With the twentieth-century advent of weapons of mass destruction, much more importance has been accorded to criteria limiting the means used in war *(jus in bello),* the foremost among which is the principle of noncombatant immunity.

Over the centuries, these criteria have been developed, refined, and restated in different ways. The U.S. bishops' 1983 pastoral letter *The Challenge of Peace: God's Promise and Our Response* and their 1993 anniversary statement *The Harvest of Justice Is Sown in Peace* provide useful summaries of just war criteria.[4] The latter document poses the question of the "justifiable use of force," then subsequently reminds readers that the just war tradition "begins with a strong presumption against the use of force" that may be overridden only to preserve peace, human dignity, and human rights. The criteria are expressed as follows:

- *Just cause*—"force may be used only to correct a gross, public evil, such as aggression or massive violation of the basic rights of whole populations."

- *Comparative justice*—"while there may be rights and wrongs on all sides of a conflict, to override the presumption against the use of force, the injustice suffered by one party must significantly outweigh that suffered by the other."
- *Legitimate authority*—"only duly constituted public authorities may use deadly force or wage war."
- *Right intention*—"force may be used only in a truly just cause and solely for that purpose."
- *Probability of success*—"arms may not be used in a futile cause or in a case where disproportionate measures are required to achieve success."
- *Proportionality*—"the overall destruction expected from the use of force must be outweighed by the good to be achieved."
- *Last resort*—"force may be used only after all peaceful alternatives have been seriously tried and exhausted."

To these criteria of going to war are added three important criteria of means in war: *proportionality* of specific means within even a just war to specific outcomes; the most uncompromising criterion of just war, the *immunity of civilians* and prisoners of war from direct attack; and *right intention* in regard to specific actions against specific targets.[5]

Virtually every one of these criteria calls the recent U.S. response to terrorism into question, as many commentators have already demonstrated.[6] John Langan, for example, highlights three areas in which moral justifications seem most vulnerable: consistent *discrimination* between military targets and civilian ones, such as residential areas and parts of the social "infrastructure" necessary to the survival of everyone, not only terrorists; an *intention* truly focused on justice and peace, not on retaliation and revenge; and *proportionality* in the sense of reliable, long-lasting results that avoid both the wholesale destruction of Afghan society and the quick resurgence of terrorist enclaves.[7]

Langan also notes that "the enemy" in this case is not so easy to define or locate. Is it Osama bin Laden, Afghanistan, or the Islamic world in general? Certainly an undifferentiated approach to Islam and Muslim cultures is part of the problem and not the solution. Morally and religiously, such a simplistic attitude would reflect only the ignorance and arrogance of those adopting it.

President George Bush and other leaders have defined as part of their military target all those states that "harbor" terrorists. The target fails to address the social, economic, and political reasons for the appeal of fanatical ideologies of martyrdom to young men in Afghanistan, as well as the no doubt complex relation between the country's religious and political institutions and terrorist cells. Osama bin Laden may seem like an obviously justifiable target, yet evidence about his direct ties to the events of September 11 have not been made public. Nor is it clear that he is accessible, especially without violating the lives of innocent civilians. More than 8000 bombs had been dropped on Afghanistan by the beginning of November 2001. Bin Laden was still at large. While U.S.-supported Northern Alliance forces had wrested control of several key cities away from the Taliban, to the apparent jubilation of much of the population, there were news reports and photographs of summary executions of prisoners of war and possibly of civilians. The future political leadership of the country was in a state of extreme uncertainty as warlords resumed roles of authority in some areas of Afghanistan, and tensions between ethnic groups within the country and between Afghanistan and Pakistan made the possibility of a multi-ethnic ruling coalition very fragile.

In the wise words of Bryan Hehir, "It is better to forfeit the rhetorical bounce that comes from invoking war and define more precisely what we can and should do. Enough to say we need an internationally coordinated, long-term effort to erode the basis for terrorism in the life of states and nations...War is an indiscriminating tool for this highly discriminating task."[8] And the broad response called for must do more than stamp out existing terrorist activities; it must place those activities and a "just war" response in a bigger social context that includes not only the religious and cultural but also the socioeconomic causes of violence, terrorism, and war. We will return to this point shortly.

First, let us note that there is one more criterion of just war that casts doubt on the present enterprise: legitimate authority. Modern applications of just war theory typically assume that it is nation-states that declare war and nation-states among whom it is conducted. Osama bin Laden is not a head of state. Indeed, one of the sources of outrage against bin Laden is his personal arrogance in setting events into motion that caused the deaths of more than 3,000 innocent people. And since neither he, his family, nor his lieutenants inhabit any parliament, capital, or royal residence, he makes a very elusive target. But the criterion of legitimate authority also pertains to the U.S. response. A key argument for the validity of a military response has been the magnitude of the danger of terrorism to the "global community." Agreement that this is so is no doubt behind the willingness of former adversaries such as Russia and China to cooperate with the United States, Britain, and other allies in ridding the world of a common danger. Yet if terrorism is a common problem and a common threat, does the authority to define and lead a response appropriately reside with one nation, especially the one with the strongest and most passionate interest in the current state of affairs? George Bush, apparently under the influence of Secretary of State Colin Powell, has moved from a unilateral approach to an increasingly multilateral consensus-building on the need for a sustained military effort in Afghanistan, and has agreed to the involvement of international troops in the engagement. At the same time, the United States continues to assume that its policy, objectives, and military capacity will control the parameters of the war effort.

A month after the terror attacks, the one hundredth Nobel Peace Prize was awarded to United Nations Secretary General Kofi Annan and the United Nations. Gunnar Berge, the Nobel committee chairman, stressed that the selection committee "wishes in its centenary year to proclaim that the only negotiable route to global peace and cooperation goes by way of the United Nations."[9] Shortly after the attack, Kofi Annan called for a cooperative approach channeled through the UN, going beyond military options to other measures, such as "the extradition and prosecution of offenders and the suppression of money laundering," according to existing UN conventions. Unless measures such as international negotiations with Afghanistan and other affected countries and investigation of the possibility of prosecuting terrorists before the International Criminal Court have been fully explored, killing as a solution to terrorism can hardly be defined as a "last resort." The question raised by Annan is whether one nation can claim authority to judge when a spectrum of options has been adequately investigated, and then to determine the nature and extent of a military "solution." According to Annan, "all nations must join forces in an effort encompassing every aspect of the open, free global system so wickedly exploited by the perpetrators of [September's] atrocities. The United Nations is uniquely positioned to advance this effort. It provides the forum necessary for building a universal coalition and can ensure global legitimacy for the long-term response to terrorism."[10]

While people and governments around the world were sympathetic to Americans in the face of the terrorist assaults, skepticism about the validity and wisdom of U.S. claims to be starting a "just war," especially without taking a long, hard, and self-critical look at the underlying causes of terrorism, were also in evidence. An interesting example in Catholic circles is a concluding document published by the Synod of Bishops that met in Rome in October 2001. Addressing terrorism in a manner politically acceptable to all signatories turned out to be a challenging task. "The sticking point was how to send a moral SOS to the United States and others in the West to alleviate the social injustice that the bishops called a root cause of terrorism, without seeming in any way to justify terrorist attacks."[11] After a debate in which U.S. bishops objected that the phrase "we absolutely condemn terrorism" did not go far enough, the document's editors, bishops from France and Brazil, came up with a redundancy that seemed to pacify the Americans: "We absolutely condemn terrorism, which nothing can justify."[12] Beyond condemning terrorism, the international episcopal body made strong statements about social inequality as it denounced the existence of "structures of sin." Specifically, the message states that "80% of the population of our planet survives on only 20% of its income," while "1.2 billion people 'live' on less than $1 a day!"[13] "Some endemic evils, when they are too long ignored, can produce despair in entire populations," the message continues. "How can we keep silent when confronted by the enduring drama of hunger and extreme poverty, in an age when humanity, more than ever, has the capacity for a just sharing of resources?" Reminding readers that Catholic ethics go beyond justifying wars to a commitment to the common good in all its forms, the bishops assert that "a drastic moral change is required. Today the social teaching of the Church has a relevance that we cannot overemphasize. As bishops, we commit ourselves to making this teaching better known in our local churches," a commitment that one hopes the U.S. episcopacy will take with increasing seriousness.

A sign that they will do so is their November 14, 2001, pastoral message "Living with Faith and Hope After September 11."[14] Tensions remain, however, even within this document. Beginning with a lengthy quotation of the Beatitudes (Mt. 5) that calls peacemakers "children of God," the bishops juxtapose gospel ideals and just war principles. "Jesus' life, teaching, death and resurrection show us the meaning of love and justice in a broken world. Sacred Scripture and traditional ethical principles define what it means to make peace." On the one hand, the document not only begins but also concludes with a call to peace: "Our community of faith has the responsibility to live out in our time the challenges of Jesus in the Beatitudes–to comfort those who mourn, to seek justice, to become peacemakers. We face these tasks with faith and hope, asking God to protect and guide us as we seek to live out the Gospel of Jesus Christ in these days of trial." On the other hand, the bishops raise questions about the applicability of just war theory on such issues as proportionality, effectiveness, and especially noncombatant immunity, but they repeatedly assert the right of the United States to use military means of defense, and they refrain from condemning any particular component of U.S. military action in Afghanistan.

Commendably, the bishops assert that "we still need to address those conditions of poverty and injustice which are exploited by terrorists," and call for "a long term focus on broader issues of justice and peace...Our nation, as a principal force for economic globalization, must do more to spread the benefits of globalization to all, especially the world's poorest. The injustice and instability in faraway lands about which we know too little can have a direct impact on our own sense of peace and security." Any clear note of repentance for American responsibility for perpetrating and benefiting from injustices is missing, however. The bishops do call for efforts to alleviate the long-standing humanitarian crisis in Afghanistan, especially the threat of starvation this winter, and for cooperation with the United Nations "to help Afghans rebuild the political, economic, and cultural life of their country after this war is over." The bishops' most pressing agenda seems to be to hold together the poles of "a just war now and a just peace later." But does the attempt to justify and support war militate against the goal of eventual peace?

What must be kept in mind, and often is not, is that just war theory as such is not very good at posing the comprehensive question of long-term causes of war and peace, since it is usually styled as a set of criteria to be applied prospectively when some authority contemplates declaring war. What is left out of the picture is the fact that "war" usually erupts in the midst of long-standing hostilities that have already involved violence on both sides. The United States supported Afghan rebels and even trained Osama bin Laden to fight against Russian rule–then pulled out and left Afghanistan to its own devices when the Soviet Union fell apart. U.S. actions or U.S.-supported actions in Iraq, Saudi Arabia, and Palestine have caused deaths and symbolize the United States' "bullying" to many in the Middle East. Here, as elsewhere in time of war, no party to violence can claim full innocence.

In any event, no war can be declared "just" until it is over, if then. The scenes and strategies of war change over time and in response to unforeseen turns of fortune. Information about "what really happened" emerges only considerably after the very events requiring moral assessment. Hence, just war criteria serve in the nature of the case more to judge, restrain, and in some minimal way to limit war by prodding the consciences of those who see war as advancing their interests, than truly to declare war "just" before the fact.

Skepticism about the probability that any specific act of war can avoid being sinful, much less promote peace, no doubt lies behind the constant efforts of John Paul II to hold up gospel ideals of forgiveness and solidarity as a reply to violent conflict, even though he has never explicitly repudiated the idea that in theory a war could be justified. Whether the whole enterprise of defining violence as just is an effective means to peace or whether it simply provides an ideology of self-justification to those with military power is a question that goes beyond just war criteria in the abstract. Hence the title of Aquinas's treatment.

A statement on a "Culture of Peace," given to the United Nations by Archbishop Renato Martino, permanent observer of the Holy See, reflects the need for a different emphasis in the Christian approach to war.[15] A substantial citation of this document can summarize and illustrate the orientation of the current papacy and Vatican representatives to the issue of just war and the importance of substituting the call for peace, backed up by practical initiatives of dialogue and social change at all levels.

According to Martino, "Peace begins within hearts. It is not simply the absence of war…but rather it helps to direct our reasoning and thus our actions toward the good of all. It becomes a philosophy of action that makes us all responsible for the common good and obliges us to dedicate all our efforts to its cause…Peace is first known, recognized, willed and loved in the heart. Then, in order to establish a culture of peace, it must be expressed and impressed on humanity, on its philosophy, its sociology, its politics and its traditions." He quotes the pope to the effect that calls for peace will be ineffective if unaccompanied by practical efforts, especially if they are followed by justifications of "exceptional" violence. Pope John Paul II, in his January 1983 "Message for the World Day of Peace," puts the initiative for action in the hands of both leaders and citizens. Those who are responsible for peace include "those who preside over the destiny of peoples, international officials, politicians, and diplomats…the citizens of each country. All are in fact called by the need to prepare true peace, to maintain it or to reestablish it, on solid and just foundations."

Martino does not minimize the difficulty of sustaining dialogue in situations of long-standing grievance: "Situations of conflict exist in today's world where a just solution may have been refused over time, by both parties involved. This has fostered feelings of frustration, hatred and temptations to vengeance to which all must remain attentive." John Paul II's advice on this point is offered:

"We all know how hard it is to settle differences between parties when ancient hatreds and serious problems which admit of no easy solution create an atmosphere of anger and exasperation. But no less dangerous for the future of peace would be the inability to confront intelligently the problems posed by a new social configuration resulting in many countries from accelerated migration and the unprecedented situation of people of different cultures and civilizations living side by side."[16]

Martino continues by excluding "acts of revenge" in retaliation for wrong done, as well as "reprisals, which strike indiscriminately at the innocent," and "continue the spiral of violence."

We must rather remove the most obvious elements that spawn the conditions for hatred and violence and which are contrary to any movement toward peace. Poverty along with other situations of marginalization that engulf the lives of so many of the world's people… are breeding grounds only waiting to be exploited by terrorists…The world must recognize that there is hope. Building a culture of peace is not preposterous, nor a utopian dream. It is, rather, an attainable reality which, even though just beyond our realization, is still a worthy and reachable goal…His Holiness reminded the young people of Kazakhstan that they should, "Know that you are called to be the builders of a better world. Be peace-makers, because a society solidly based on peace is a society with a future."[17]

In summary, just war theory developed originally and rightly as a marginal aspect of Christianity's social stance. Christians should never be champions of military solutions to social problems, even when they have been the victims of violence. Rather than being a "justification" of war, just war theory is a compromise solution to conflict in which a deplorable situation of mutual killing is subjected to minimal moral restraints. Just war theory gives Christians more reasons to question war and resist it than reasons to endorse it and to participate in it. Just war theory is based on the premise that violence in defense of self or the common good cannot be absolutely excluded as an extreme measure in extreme circumstances. It is also based on the premise that resort to war is *usually* sinful, in causes, motives, means, and outcomes. Before, above, and surrounding any moral acceptance of war should be a commitment to peacemaking and to the negotiated resolution of conflict as practical responsibilities and options.

Given the realities of politics, even thinkers within the Catholic common good tradition, committed to a basic optimism about humanity's ability to establish just and peaceful social institutions, must acknowledge the intransigence of self-interest and self-deception in human affairs. Moral rhetoric can be misused to conceal the real motives of individuals and nations, and to facilitate rather than inhibit resort to violent coercion by those who have such means within their power. Thus, especially from a Christian perspective, just war criteria should never be employed as though they fully justify any use of killing as a tool of political change. Set against the horizon of gospel ideals and the ideal of a good global society, the justice of warfare will always fall sorrowfully short. Politicians, heads of state, military commanders, and ordinary patriots are sure to provide war with all the "justification" required to meet any emergency, real or imagined. In the hands of Christian political thinkers, just war theory should be used in critique of any existing or projected program of violence, not to confer a blessing.

The only condition under which war should be advocated directly, albeit ambivalently, by Christians is when violent coercion seems the only available measure with potential to rescue innocent lives from more powerful political groups that in a given immediate context have assaulted the innocent. In such a case, military action would best be multilateral and might better be seen as a "police action," rather than as a war against a state or government. Some instances of so-called "humanitarian intervention" would meet this criterion, and it is according to this criterion that the United States' refusal to take or instigate action against the emerging genocide in Rwanda in 1994 can be condemned. Even in such instances, however, the Christian analyst must always be mindful of the selectiveness with which "just causes" are adopted, of the ease with which just war rhetoric can become an ideological tool of national self-interest, and of the likelihood that the actual violence to ensue will exceed the bounds of moral justifications. The ultimate consideration in Christian social ethics, especially when mortal violence is in question, is whether a "preferential option" is being made for justice for those least able to advance their own cause. Moreover, violence must be limited to the minimum necessary to change the situation so that other measures can gain effectiveness.

25

How to Fight a Just War

Jean Bethke Elshtain

From President George W. Bush to the average man and woman on the street, Americans are evoking the language of justice to characterize our response to the despicable deeds perpetrated against innocent men, women, and children on September 11. When they do this, they tap into a complex tradition called "just war." The origins of the just war tradition are usually traced to St. Augustine's fourth-century masterwork, *The City of God*. In that great text, Augustine grapples with the challenge to violence of Christian teaching. He comes to the conclusion that wars of aggression and aggrandizement are never acceptable. But there are occasions when resort to force may be tragically necessary, though violence is never a normative good. What, then, makes it justifiable? For Augustine, the most potent justification is to protect the innocent—those in no position to defend themselves—from certain harm. If one has compelling evidence that harm will come to persons unless action involving coercive force is taken, a requirement of neighbor love may be a resort to arms. Self-defense is trickier. According to Augustine, it is better for the Christian as an individual to suffer harm rather than to commit it. But are we permitted to make that commitment to non-self-defense for others? No, surely not.

The upshot of Augustine's reflections, refined over time, is that a primary rule for those committed to just war is noncombatant immunity or the so-called principle of discrimination, meaning that noncombatants must not be the *intended* targets of violence. A further implication is that a carefully worked out act of mass murder against noncombatants of one's own country is an injury—an act of war—that demands a response. That response involves just punishment, not in order to inflict grievous harm on the noncombatants of a country whose operatives have harmed your citizens, but in order to interdict wrongdoers to prevent further harm and to punish those responsible for the harm that has already occurred, in a world political theorists describe as one of self-help. In so doing, one reaffirms a world of moral responsibility and justice.

When a wound as grievous as that of September 11 has been inflicted on a body politic, it would be the height of irresponsibility, a dereliction of duty, a flight from the serious vocation of politics, were one to fail to respond. The Christian tradition tells us that government is instituted by God. This does not mean that every government and every public official is godly, rather, that he or she is charged with a solemn responsibility for which there is divine warrant. Surely it is an exercise in bad faith to accept this warrant but to disdain its effective use, even as one enjoys the benefits of that civic peace— the *tranquillitas ordinis*—for which government is responsible. A *political* ethic is an ethic of responsibility. The just war tradition offers a way to exercise that responsibility. This way of thinking rejects both the "anything goes" ethic of Machiavellian *realpolitik* and rejects as well an ethic that foreswears action if that action commits the country to the use of armed force in a responsible and limited way. Apropos the latter stance, it must be asked: Why are the practical alternatives to the use of armed force to preserve and protect civic peace so inadequate? Can one cry "peace, peace" when there is no peace and no possibility of such because those who have decided that an entire country is composed of "infidels" fit only for destruction are not going to cease their efforts to kill as many of those infidels as they can? What is the plausible alternative to protect the body politic? Too often one is offered pieties cast in the form of moral superiority rather than possibilities or policies.

In the immediate aftermath of the events of September 11, I said to a friend, "Now we are reminded of what governments are for." The shepherd is charged with protecting the flock. None of the goods human beings cherish, including the free exercise of religion, can flourish absent a measure of civic peace and security. If evil is permitted to grow, good goes into hiding. Evildoers that lurk and plot in the darkness and secret, that operate stealthily, and that refuse to accept responsibility for wrongdoing perpetrate harm beyond the immediate violent event. It is they who would force good into hiding as we retreat behind closed doors. What good do I have in mind? The simple but profound good that is moms and dads raising their children, men and women going to work, citizens of a great city making their way on streets and subways, ordinary people buying airplane tickets in order to visit the grandkids in California, men and women en route to transact business with colleagues in other cities, the faithful attending their churches, synagogues, and mosques without fear. Make no mistake about it: this quotidian idea, this basic civic peace is a great good. It is not the peace of the kingdom promised by scripture. That awaits the end-time.

Beating swords into plowshares and spears into pruning hooks, a world in which "Nation shall not lift up sword against nation, neither shall they learn war any more" (Isa. 2:4), is a vision connected with certain conditions, as Kenneth Anderson reminds us in a recent article. For the prophet tells us that the condition of eschatological peace is one in which the Lord's house has been established everywhere and all "go up to the mountain of the LORD...For out of Zion shall go forth instruction, and the word of the LORD from Jerusalem" (Isa. 2:3). We are not there yet, to put it mildly. As Martin Luther observed: "If the lion lies down with the lamb, the lamb must be replaced frequently."

The ordinary civic peace that horrific violence disrupts and attempts to destroy offers intimations of eschatological peace and is a good to be cherished and not to make light of. It is a good we charge our public officials with maintaining. If we live from day to day in fear of deadly attack, the other goods we cherish become difficult. Human beings are fragile, soft-shelled creatures. We cannot reveal the fullness of our being, including our deep sociality, if airplanes are flying into buildings and cities become piles of rubble composed in part of the mangled bodies of victims. We can neither take this civic peace for granted—as we have learned so shockingly—nor shake off our responsibility for helping to respect and to promote the norms and rules whose enforcement is constitutive of civic peace. Augustine taught us that we should not spurn worldly vocations, including the tragic vocation of the judge—tragic because he or she can never know with absolute certainty whether punishment is being meted out to the guilty and not the innocent. But we depend on judges and others to uphold a world of responsibility, a world in which people are not permitted to "devour one another like fishes," in Augustine's pithy phrase.

Public officials are charged with protecting a people. As those extra-ordinary firemen in New York City said, simply: "It's my job." The same holds for our military: it is their job and it is our sons and daughters who do it. This is their right authority—another vital dimension of the just war tradition and one aimed at limiting freelance, opportunistic, and individualistic violence. Responding justly to injustice is a tall order, for it means that it is better to risk the lives of one's own combatants than to intentionally kill "enemy" noncombatants. It is often difficult to separate combatants from noncom-batants, but try one must. The restraints internal to the just war tradition encode the notion of limits to the use of force. Many of these rules and stipulations have been incorporated into international agreements, including several Geneva conventions. During and after a conflict we assess the conduct of a war-fighting nation by how its warriors conducted themselves. Did they rape and pillage? Were they under careful rules of engagement or was it a free-for-all? Was every attempt made to limit civilian casualties knowing that, in time of war, civilians are invariably going to fall in harm's way? It is unworthy of the solemn nature of these matters to respond cynically or naively to such attempts to limit the damage. As theologian Oliver O'Donovan put it at the time of the Persian Gulf War: Just ask yourself whether you would rather have been a citizen of Berlin in 1944 or a citizen of Baghdad during the Persian Gulf War? The answer is obvious, as every effort was made in U.S. targeting strategy to avoid civilian targets during that conflict.

Since the Vietnam War and the restructuring of the United States military, pains have been taken to underscore the codes of ethics that derive from the just war tradition in our military academies and in the training of our soldiers, sailors, marines, and flyers. No group in this country pays more attention to ethical restraint on the use of force than does the United States military. We do not kill or even threaten to kill more than 3,000 civilians because that number of our own civilians have been murdered by perpetrators who scarcely deserve the name of either soldier or warrior. We put soldiers into combat rather than unleashing terrorists. The soldier puts himself at risk as surely as the firefighter. In contrast to the terrorist, he seeks to search out and to punish those responsible for planning, aiding and abetting, and perpetrating an evil deed. Just punishment is different from revenge. Revenge repudiates all limits; just punishment observes restraints. The course thus far charted by the administration is admirable in its complexity and its restraint. The use of military force is planned as one part of an overall strategy that involves decoding messages and following and cutting off money flows. One sign that the President and his advisers are aware of the need for restraint is their renaming a mission that was first dubbed "Operation Infinite Justice" with a more modest name that does not suggest a utopian goal. Another sign is the President's repeated insistence that our response is not aimed at a whole people or nation or way of life but is, instead, directed at those who defame their own religion, drag their own people into harm's way, and perpetrate an ideology that has as its end the deaths of babies, people in wheelchairs, moms and dads, brothers and sisters, uncles and aunts, grandmas and grandpas, friends and lovers, going about their daily routines. And why should they die? Simply because they are infidels–they are Americans. It matters not if you are white or black, young or old, male or female, able bodied or with a disability, gay or straight, Christian, Muslim, or Jew–you die. The aim of terrorism is terror. The terrorists did not issue a set of demands. They did not demand negotiation or else. They simply murdered. That is why one does not negotiate with them. There is nothing to negotiate about if the end your opponent seeks is your complete obliteration. At some point, the word breaks off and the call to responsible action begins.

This is an extraordinary moment in our nation's history. On September 11, we sustained a greater loss of life in a single day than ever before in our history, easily topping the previous norm for a day of death–the Battle of Antietam. Americans tell us they are prepared for this different kind of war. But the numbers of those who support action against terrorism begins to waver when the question is put as to whether this force would be acceptable if "innocent men, women, and children" are the victims. No war, as I have already indicated, can be fought without putting noncombatants in harm's way. The American people favor doing everything possible to limit this damage, and in this I heartily concur. One reason the country wearied of the Vietnam war was the realization that fighting a guerrilla war meant that we could not distinguish combatants from noncombatants and that, even without horrors like the My Lai massacre, our soldiers were put in the impossible position of regarding everyone as "the enemy." So: Respond we must, and respond we shall. We are obliged to stop those who use civilians against other civilians by turning a great symbol of human freedom of movement–the commercial airplane–into a deadly bomb. We will put our combatants in harm's way to punish those who put our noncombatants in harm's way and who have no compunction about mass murder. That is the burden of the just warrior. And that is his and her–and a nation's–honor.

In the dark days of Nazi terror, a brave young German theologian, Dietrich Bonhoeffer, who had been moving–remarkably so for a German Lutheran of his era–toward pacifism, committed himself to a conspiracy to assassinate Adolph Hitler, to cut off the head of the snake. He asked: Who stands fast? Bonhoeffer observed that the great evil that had appeared among the German people had "played havoc with all our ethical concepts." He was particularly severe in his criticism of those who "flee from public altercation into the sanctuary of private *virtuousness*. But anyone who does this must shut his mouth and his eyes to the injustice around him. Only at the cost of self-deception can he keep himself pure from the contamination arising from responsible action." Obedient and responsible action. One who cares about these, Bonhoeffer taught us, asks the following question: How is the coming generation to live?

We know what happens to people who live in pervasive fear. It isn't pretty. It invites lashing out and severe isolation from a desire to protect oneself. It encourages harsh measures because, and in this Thomas Hobbes was right, we simply cannot live as human begins if we live in constant fear of violent death. Recently, my daughter and I found ourselves discussing the need for a family plan should there be a biological or chemical attack. The International Criminal Court or International Human Rights Tribunal is not going to protect us from that–or anything else. The world of international relations is not the same as a domestic legal jurisdiction that has, by definition, a punitive and enforcing arm. So we are forced to ask the question: Who would pick up all the children, the grandchildren? Where would we rendezvous? Should one buy gas masks? Should one discuss any of this with two five-year-olds and a seven-year-old? Already, JoAnn, Christopher, and Bobby are drawing pictures of planes flying into buildings, and asking, "What happens if Grandma's plane is hijacked?" We reassure them, knowing that the correct answer is: There is no more Grandma. Of course, we all must die one day. But we are called to life. Christians are taught that their Savior came that believers might have life and have it more abundantly. There are times when the call to live demands action against those who deal in death. I do not believe this is contrary to our tradition. I believe it is consistent with it and with the fact that believers are claimed by a God of mercy who is also a God of justice.

26

The Just War Doctrine and Postmodern Warfare

Peter J. Haas

The just war doctrine, as we have inherited it in the Western world, was forged pretty much in its final form during the twelfth and thirteenth centuries of the Common Era in light of the tremendously brutal encounters that made up the crusades. The doctrine's classical articulation is usually taken to be the one in the *Summa Theologicae* part 2, question 40 of Thomas Aquinas (1225–1274). To be sure, the theory was refined and expanded on several times in the sixteenth through eighteenth centuries, largely in response to the religious wars between Catholics and Protestants in Europe. Although thinkers such as Francisco de Vitoria (1548–1617), Hugo Grotius (1583–1645), Samuel Pufendorf (1632–1704), and Christian Wolff (1679–1754) made important contributions to the doctrine, in basic outline it remained as Aquinas had framed it. This is important because, as I shall argue below, the theory was formulated to address the particulars of war as Aquinas would have known them. Warfare has changed so considerably since that time that the doctrine, while useful for heuristic purposes, has little practical application, and in fact may be counterproductive. The current "War on Terrorism" will serve as a case in point.

Let me explain. The basic problem, as I shall spell out below, is that the theory as we have it makes distinctions that are no longer applicable. The result is that applying just war doctrine nowadays, in the postmodern world, makes it impossible for all practical purposes to conduct any war in a just

236

manner. While this might in itself be a desirable outcome, it is hardly helpful. The just war doctrine was not designed, after all, to make all wars impossible, but rather to try to establish some moral limits on the conduct of war when these inevitable clashes between humans occur. The result of declaring all warfare, by definition, immoral is that it puts all postmodern warfare beyond the pale of moral reasoning altogether, and as such does more harm than good. It in essence says that once you have entered a war, you have crossed into territory in which everything is possible because morality does not function there. The Holocaust is a stark reminder that we do not dare go down that road again. Much more helpful would be a doctrine that will actually guide our thinking in the conduct of war, that is, one that will help us learn how to fight a postmodern war, or a "war against terrorism" in a way that is more moral than it might otherwise be. While I can not develop such a theory here, I hope to begin the discussion by trying to lay out as clearly as I can why I think the received doctrine has failed.

Let me begin with a brief discussion of the origins of the just war doctrine. Our discussion should begin by noting that the very existence of such a doctrine ought not to be taken for granted. Warfare is by its very nature a chaotic and brutal enterprise. Once a battle has been started, the need for survival and victory become paramount. Whatever other rules might be around quickly succumb to these imperatives. Thus, the very notion that there could be limits, moral or otherwise, on the fighting of war is on the surface an oxymoron. By not only conceiving of the possibility of a doctrine of just war, but by actually framing such a doctrine, Aquinas and the others performed a major conceptual feat. They made it possible to think morally about a subject that is inherently amoral, if not in fact positively immoral. At the same time, their efforts had some very practical and partisan ends. They wanted to find some way within Christian tradition to allow good Christians to go to war and engage in all its necessary brutality without giving up their salvation. Or to put it in more modern terms, they wanted to make it possible for soldiers to return from battle with their humanity and moral agency intact. But there was another intellectual breakthrough as well. The framers of the just war doctrine succeeded in extending the domain of moral thinking into the very heart of battle, and so brought even this aspect of human activity under the ethical gaze. This is an achievement of significant import.

A closer look at these motivations will be helpful. The occasion that provoked Aquinas and others to even attempt to put together such a doctrine, as I noted, was the crusades, which brought out the question of the extent to which Catholic religious, and eventually all Catholics, were allowed to participate in battle with, and especially in the massacre of, "infidels." These were, after all, people who were ideally to be converted to Christianity, not sent to eternal damnation without having been saved. More pointedly, men in religious orders were expected to take an active role in leading the soldiers and in gaining and holding the religious sites of Christianity. Yet in the struggle to spread the word of Christianity, retrieve Christian holy sites that had been re-paganized (as they saw matters), and suppress unbelievers and heretics, some warfare, with its attendant killing, deceit, and so forth was inevitable. But these attendant activities were precisely what Catholic religious were expected to overcome. Hence, a level of cognitive dissonance was reached that had to be addressed. This is why Aquinas and others attempted to sort out what limits, if any, might apply so that good Christians could still operate within the church even in the heat of ferocious battle.

In its classical articulation, the doctrine revolved around two concepts: *jus ad bellum* and *jus in bello*. The first addressed itself to the question of when it is right or just to go to war in the first place. After all, Jesus was the Prince of Peace and counseled turning the other cheek. War would seem, and has been seen by many Christian groups, to be outside the bounds of Christian activity. But it also has been in general understood that, all this notwithstanding, in some cases fighting an enemy is necessary. There are surely cases in which the entry of Christians into war is biblically sanctioned. Self-defense when wantonly attacked by another is the showcase example. Few Christians would argue, for example, that fighting off an attacker is against religious principles. Protecting Christian holy sites, such as churches, might be another example. The doctrine of just war has as one of its main goals to define these situations. This having been accomplished, the doctrine turns to the second area of concern, *jus in bello*. Assuming we are now engaged in a war for proper reasons, are there any limitations on how one may fight the war on the tactical and strategic level? The general answer is that yes, there are such limits. The Christian warriors still need to maintain their Christianity, even in the context of battle. Such limits have come down to us in the form of general principles that we still routinely invoke. They include the duty on the part of commanders to distinguish between soldiers and civilians, to ensure that the damage inflicted is commensurate with the military need, to do whatever possible within the mission to limit collateral damage, and to ensure the fair treatment of prisoners of war.

With these two pivotal concepts on the table, a third area of speculation opens up, namely, the relationship between the two. Is it possible, for example, to enter into a war unjustly, but then to conduct that war in a just manner? This aspect of the doctrine has received little sustained attention. The reason is that in the classical theory, it is taken for granted that to fight a war justly means, among other things, that you are already in the war for a just cause. How, after all, could one fight justly for an inherently unjust cause? But the question still has importance; we do not necessarily want to say that if you are in a war unjustly, then moral considerations no longer apply. We would like to think that even if the war is for whatever reason unjust, it is still possible for the soldiers engaged in it to act as moral agents. The complementary question is also important. Is it possible, or permissible, to enter into a just war and then proceed to fight it unjustly? This last question can be restated in an even more pointed fashion—is it morally permissible to enter a war against an evil justly and then, in the name of morality, limit yourself such that you suffer unnecessary casualties or even lose the war, thus allowing evil to triumph? Must a just war be fought justly "at all costs"?

These doctrines and the arguments spun off by them have, as I said, proven to be tremendously helpful to us as we think about war and how to wage it. So I am hardly in favor of jettisoning them entirely. On the other hand, I want to argue that they are not applicable to the present war because they rest on assumptions about warfare that are no longer true. I want to start with *jus in bello* (fighting war justly) and move from there up to *jus ad bello* (the justice of entering into war).

One of the most significant changes in warfare in the modern period has been the shift from the notion of war as a series of battles between two armies to the notion of war as a series of battles between nations. By nations here I mean to use the word in its nineteenth-century sense of a people as a whole. When Napoleon launched his attacks against the rest of Europe in the beginning of the nineteenth century, the Grand Armee was not simply the commander's private band of fighters, but the forward edge of the French nation. Set into motion was the process of slowly but surely erasing the distinction between civilian and military. The process was well under way by the American Civil War. In this encounter, the soldiers were themselves often little more than civilians temporarily in uniform while civilians, though not actually in uniform, often were actively engaged in supporting and staging the war. In fact, when Robert E. Lee turned over his sword to General Ulysses S. Grant at Appomattox Court House, it was not so much the loss of the army that made the confederacy collapse. The real battles that ended the war were not those surrounding Lee's army in Virginia, but the destruction of Atlanta and the attack on Savannah. In short, the confederate armies were doomed once they had been cut off from their civilian base.

This process reached a sort of logical conclusion during the middle of the twentieth century. Consider our conduct of World War II. Our strategy for bringing down the Nazi regime was designed only in part to deal directly with the German army in the field. Considerable resources were used to fight the military-industrial machine behind the field army. So we bombed factories, rail lines, civilian population centers, oil fields, and so forth. Our final blow to the military might of Japan, on the other side of the world, was not a devastating defeat of the Japanese military in the field, but the nuclear bombing of its civilian centers. These were not random acts of violence. They were responses to what warfare had become, a massive mobilization of the nation in which the field army was but the tip of the iceberg. Clearly, by mid-century the notion of a separation between military and civilian had ceased to be meaningful. In a corresponding development, we fully mobilized our own home front. There was hardly a sector of the civilian economy that was not engaged in some significant way with supporting the war effort. So even though armies were still engaging each other on the fields of battle, the real power behind these armies was back home in the civilian sector. More and more, calls for war planners to attack only the military and not civilians were becoming detached from reality. In fact, military doctrine has come to recognize that the best way to defeat the enemy in war is not to attack the army directly, but to go at it indirectly–to cut off its supplies, communications, reinforcements, and political support. A textbook example of how this works was the Israeli victory in the Sinai peninsula in the 1973 Yom Kippur war. A battalion task force, by simply blocking a supply route into the peninsula, led to the collapse and surrender of the entire Egyptian Third Army within a matter of days. The personnel and equipment largely survived.

We face today the next stage in the logic of that development, a kind of postmodern style of warfare. The kind of battle in which fixed field armies engage each other within strict parameters of time and space is a thing of the past. We saw this taking clear doctrinal shape in the kind of war in which we were engaged in Vietnam, for example. In that war, there were often no fixed front lines, no clear distinctions between civilians and military, no clear points or moments of engagement and disengagement. Every person was a potential enemy who could attack at any time and in any place. A more contemporary example is the Israeli-Palestinian struggle today, and of course the war against terrorism. All these are far removed from the type of warfare that would have been waged in the Middle Ages. They were and are much more accurately understood as struggles of one nation (or a people, a clan, or even an interest group) against another. Even concepts such as defeat and victory take on different meanings. We won virtually every military engagement in Vietnam, yet we ended up leaving the country in defeat. The same happened with our involvement in the Middle East. We were able to bring overwhelming military power to bear on our opponents in Lebanon in the late 1970s and early 1980s and yet were forced out by a confusing resistance movement of "mere" civilians who, with their bomb-laden cars and trucks, wreaked more havoc on our troops than any army had since the Korean war. The Israelis have been able to deploy massive military might against the Palestinians, defeating them in the classical military sense again and again, but for all that they have been unable to impose their will. We are finding the same blurry boundaries in our current war against terrorism. This struggle is not really about defeating any particular army in the field, even though there may be some military engagements that look like classical warfare. Rather, we are trying to defeat a shadowy network that is only loosely organized and that is ready to engage in endless guerilla-type tactics to bring pain and disorganization to the West. In short, postmodern warfare is becoming more and more a conflict between peoples in which actual soldiers in actual uniforms with actual rifles play only a minor, even marginal, role. The teenager with bombs tied to his belt, or the civilian truck driver heading for the Marine barracks is the real threat, not the easily identified soldier guarding an intersection. But the current structure of the just war doctrine does not give us adequate tools to deal with these ambiguities.

My point in all this is to demonstrate that one of the basic assumptions of classical just war theory, namely that one can distinguish between military and civilian, is simply no longer operative. With the collapse of that pillar of the just war doctrine, much of the rest of the structure falls as well. Consider, for example, the call for limiting unnecessary collateral damage. Exactly how is this to be measured? Beginning with World War II and moving forward steadily since then, even the military has blurred the distinction between what is and what is not a military target. A few examples will suffice to make my point. One of the major early air battles of World War II was the bombardment of Ploesti in Rumania. Ploesti was not a military target per se, but an oilfield. Another example: the civilian interstate highway system in this country was designed in part with military uses in mind. This blurring of distinctions can go even further. In the case of war, civilian hospitals will be "federalized" to back up the armies' limited hospital infrastructure; manufacturing plants that now turn out civilian goods will be dedicated to military material, and so on. And what about the common practice we have seen in the Middle East, and are now seeing in Afghanistan, of using civilian institutions–schools, hospitals, old-age homes, private dwellings–to house soldiers, store ordinance, and conduct military training? Exactly what damage is unambiguously collateral and unnecessary? How can military targets really be sorted out and segregated from civilian ones? The point is, in postmodern warfare they cannot.

This blurring of definitional lines has not only made the commander's job more difficult, it actually burdens her or him with additional moral responsibility. A basic premise of modern armies is that every unit commander is morally obligated to protect the troops. That is, no commander should knowingly send soldiers into a lethal situation unless and until all that can be done to protect them has been done. How does this obligation play out in the situation of postmodern warfare? In a situation in which the disposition of the enemy is unknown, in which any person or any building could pose a danger, the conscientious commander has little choice but to stop making useless distinctions on the basis of an age-old doctrine. From the vantage point of a commander about to send dozens of young soldiers into a village, whether in Vietnam or in Afghanistan, how much suppression fire is too much? In theory the need to maintain proportionality, to limit damage to the needs of the mission, is a splendid concept. But putting the concept into action in the modern battlefield involves impossible calculations of probability.

All of the aforementioned problems are exacerbated by the high lethality of today's arsenals. Warfare is no longer conducted through hand-to-hand combat with axes, spears and arrows, attacks that can be aimed with fairly good precision. The United States is fighting the Taliban in Afghanistan with long-range missiles, massive carpet bombing sorties, and heavy artillery. The Taliban are fighting back with ground-to-air missiles, artillery, tanks, and rockets. These are hardly precision weapons. It is rarely the case anymore that the death of an enemy soldier is caused by a face-to-face confrontation. More than likely, the missile, rocket, or bomb that causes the casualty was fired by an operator who never sees the results. The modern battlefield is not only lethal but largely anonymous and indirect.

The upshot of all this is that the notion that in some way war in the twentieth century can be fought morally as outlined in the classical just war theory of *jus in bello* must simply be abandoned. Warfare as it has evolved today is inherently and unalterably unjust in those terms. At the end of the day, no rules really apply any longer once we are in a state of war. To be sure, limits may be imposed for propaganda or public relations reasons. But ultimately, the "rulelessness" of war will win out. The prime example may be the attempt of the Israeli military to develop a modern theory of "clean" warfare, known in Hebrew as *Tohar HaNeshek*. The doctrine was refined, tested, evaluated, and included in soldiers' training. But once put to the test in real battle, it proved to be little more than window dressing. Modern war is not compatible with the just war doctrine, at least as it is classically conceived.

With this in mind, I want to turn attention to *jus ad bellum*. There is, of course, the question of whether or not it makes sense at all to talk about a just war if we know that in any case the war will be fought unjustly. Yet it might be worthwhile to reconsider the criteria for declaring war justly. Do these criteria at least still have some legitimacy today such that they can give us some guidance?

The answer is, by and large, yes. The conditions for declaring war justly still seem to bear some weight even today. But their application, especially in light of what fighting a war really means in today's terms, is far from clear - cut. In what follows I want to look at the seven common criteria that define *jus ad bellum*. I shall argue that they fall into three groups—those that seem reasonably applicable today, those that seem reasonable but hard to apply, and those that seem out of date.

There appear to be three criteria that are likely to continue to be applicable for postmodern warfare as we are now experiencing it: just cause, competent authority, and right intention. The first calls for engaging in war only in order to confront "a real and certain danger." This might include self-defense, for example, or as a means to preserve human life and dignity. In the present war on terrorism, this criterion has in effect already been invoked. The government has announced that this war against terrorism is a war to preserve our way of life. To be sure there can be arguments as to whether or not bombing Afghanistan or hunting down leaders of al Qaeda really leads to a preservation of our way of life, but this is a claim that can at least be argued, and insofar as it is being addressed, this first criterion seems still to function for us. The second criterion that I think fits this category demands that the declaration of war be announced by a competent authority. The original idea here was to limit individuals' rights to declare war willy-nilly on neighbors or enemies for any reason, no matter how personal. In our time, the conduct of war is by necessity the function of government and so almost by routine will fill this criterion. The last of the three in this category encompasses the other two, as well as the demand for comparative justice. This criterion demands that we go to war with the right intention. The point is that it is not enough for a war to meet certain requirements of justice formally, but that it must in fact be entered into with a proper goal in mind and with the conviction that this goal can be achieved only through warfare. That is, we need to be convinced that the stakes are sufficiently high that all objections to going to war are overcome. As to the case at hand, if the government is sincere in its belief that declaring war against the Taliban or against al Qaeda is the only way to protect our way of life and that that goal is a worthy one, then they have fulfilled this criterion.

My second category contains two criteria that seem reasonable even today, but are becoming impossible to apply because of the developments in warfare noted above. These two criteria have to do with comparative justice and proportionality. The first of these asks us to consider whether the values that are at stake for our side are worth fighting a war over. In other words, do we have sufficient cause to justify killing? This is of course intimately tied up with the second, proportionality, which asks that the costs incurred be proportionate to the good expected to be achieved. There are two problems with applying these criteria to postmodern wars. One is that warfare as it has developed today is a very blunt instrument, one that can not be wielded with much precision. In the current conflict, for example, our real battle of values might be with Osama bin Laden and the al Qaeda organization. But there is no way for us to fight these enemies without engaging their protector, the Taliban government. But the Taliban government itself is not a threat to us. We are engaging in warfare with it to get at the "real enemy." There is even a further remove. To get at the Taliban, we have to bomb Afghanistan. Although we can fully intend to hit only "military" targets, the fact remains that such a surgical distinction no longer is realistic, for the reasons mentioned above. So we may have overwhelming justice on our side going after al Qaeda, but in the actual structure of the war, in which we are perforce bombing, or at least endangering, "civilian" targets, that justice and that proportionality are being diminished. The second problem is that modern and postmodern warfare must have as the goal the elimination of the enemy's ability to fight. That is, there are no intermediate stages of victory (though we tried this in Iraq). So there is no way rationally to maintain proportionality. Either we win all the way or we do not. Thus, while we in the postmodern situation still pay some heed to these two criteria, it seems to me that their actual application in war is going to be crude at best.

Finally, there are two criteria that I think are impossible to apply to postmodern war. These are calls for resorting to war as a last resort, and only if the war has a rational likelihood for achieving its objectives. Not only are we not fighting armies but "peoples," but we are fighting not over concrete territory so much as over ideas and cultures. So it is hard to know what it means to "win" outside of a complete genocide, a chain of logic the Nazis tried to follow out to its conclusion. So we can very legitimately ask if any postmodern war, especially one aimed against a concept such as "Communism" or "terror" is really likely to succeed in some objective sense. The answer is most likely that no postmodern war will ever be fully successful. That is because we are no longer fighting just a discrete army, but mass movements. We might well be able to wipe out this or that particular organization, but we will never be able by force of arms to destroy or eliminate the underlying social, cultural, religious, and economic causes that lead to conflict. A war might buy us time and a greater degree of security, but it will never eliminate terrorism, for example. To demand that a war bring about full closure to a problem in order to be just is making an unreasonable, in fact impossible, demand.

Where does all this leave us? My argument has been that the kinds of questions posed by the classical theory of just war, and the realities it assumes for coming up with answers, are not fully applicable to warfare as it has developed over the last two centuries. Distinctions and definitions taken for granted in the theory as it took shape from the thirteenth century onward simply are no longer operative. That does not mean that the theory as it now stands is completely worthless. It still has the power to raise important and thought-provoking questions, questions that are still important and even urgent, as my first and to some extent my second category indicate. But the theory in its present form cannot in its fullness function well as a yardstick for whether this war on terrorism or any other modern or postmodern war is really moral or just.

The problem we face today is very much the same one faced by the framers of the just war theory six hundred years ago, namely that war is by its very nature unjust. Strictly speaking, there is no way on purely moral grounds that most acts absolutely necessary to warfare would ever pass muster. On the other hand, its framers well understood that sometimes war is necessary, and sometimes may even be commanded. The just war theory was created precisely to get out of that conundrum. It was designed to allow warfare to happen when necessary, to discourage resort to war in other circumstances, and to circumscribe what could be done should war in fact break out. The framers did an admirable job given warfare at the time. We today need to find a way to retool the old theory to take into account the changes that have occurred in the last two centuries. This essay is not the place to do that. But in thinking of the current situation in light of the just war theory, we should also be aware that the theory itself is in need of revision. We are called on not only to make moral judgments about this war but, maybe even more difficult, to rethink exactly what just and unjust mean for war in the world, and for the forces within it.

27

Christian Nonviolence

Stanley Hauerwas

Oftentimes when you are a pacifist, people think you have nothing to say other than, "War is bad, and this one is bad too." I hope to suggest Christian nonviolence—at least the Christian nonviolence I have learned from John Howard Yoder—has some things to say to help us understand better what is confronting us. I think one of the things that confronts us (if you ever really wanted to know what political correctness is) is that we are now living in political correctness. Those who express any concern about the American response to September 11 are assumed to bear the burden of proof. That is real political correctness.

That we live at a time of such political correctness is partly because Americans have suddenly found community. I am often supposed to be for community. Thus, I am described as a sectarian fideistic tribalist. The use of *tribalist* means that I am considered a communitarian. I always say I'm not a communitarian: I'm a Christian. I'm not a communitarian, because communitarianism in America, against the background of a liberal society, always means nationalism. The "we" that is constructed in nationalism means that people suddenly find themselves in unity across class, race, and ethnic divides, and this is extremely dangerous. Hopefully the "we" won't be any deeper a loyalty than what we give to a professional football team. However, how this rediscovery of the "we" is used could be extremely dangerous.

If you attempt to step back and ask, "Why do these people hate us?" there is very little space for that kind of question right now. If you ask, "Do you think they really attacked the World Trade Center because they hate American freedom?" it is again a question that cannot be raised. If you say, as an entertainer did, "Well, it doesn't look to me like those people were cowards. I think cowards are people that set off missiles from the middle of the ocean to attack civilians," then you are not heard on the air. These reactions are quite understandable, given the horror of the attack on the World Trade Center. But we need a space to get our breaths. I should like to think that the commitment to Christian nonviolence helps us to create that space.

I am not only a representative of Christian nonviolence but also teach in a university. So my thoughts concern both constituencies. First, the church, which seems captured by the identification of God and country. Red is a color of the Christian tradition. It's Pentecost. White is a color of the Christian tradition. It's Easter. Blue is the color for our mother who gave birth to Jesus. In the church, we never put them together. That red, white, and blue have now become Christian colors is an indication that the church has been captured by a very different narrative than the story of Jesus' birth. It seems the churches have a choice to either be pro-government or irrelevant.

How can the church be at this time a people of patience who take the time to step back in the face of terrible events? Of course, since as I noted I am supposed to be "a sectarian fideistic tribalist," I should have an easy answer, such as: "Well, it's part of the continuing accommodation of the churches to America." It is certainly true that I represent the Tonto principle of Christian ethics. When Tonto and the Lone Ranger found themselves surrounded in North Dakota by the Sioux, the Lone Ranger looked at Tonto and said, "This looks pretty tough, Tonto, what do you think we ought to do?" And Tonto said, "What do you mean 'we,' White man?"

The "we" that distinguishes Christians from Americans, moreover, has everything to do with death. Christians are a community shaped by the practice of baptism that reminds us there are far worse things that can happen to us than dying. The identification of the Christian "we" with the American "we" is an indication that the Christian "we" of baptism has been submerged in the American fear of death. The willingness of those that flew the planes into the World Trade Center to die seems incomprehensible to us. It is almost as if the desperation that drove them to these terrible acts is a parody of our unwillingness to die.

The recent debate about stem-cell research mirrors the action of the terrorist understanding of life: any means can be used to keep us from dying is the flip side of the view that any means can be used to kill people. For example, consider that Strom Thurmond (who is allegedly against abortion) thinks that with stem-cell research he's going to live to be 168, get married, and have another kid! It's no wonder that South Carolina is one of the centers of the United States military bases. Why? Strom Thurmond. Of course, that we do not know how to comprehend death for ourselves or other people has everything to do with being so wealthy.

Our wealth makes us stupid just because it allows us to live in the world without learning the pain our wealth creates in our neighbors. For example, we would not fund stem-cell research if we were a country trying to keep people from dying of hunger. We now assume the legitimacy of our government comes from funding stem-cell research to keep us from dying rather than from securing justice for the poor. Part of the space Christians can provide at this time is the space given to us as a people who have learned through baptism that the worst thing that can happen to us is not death, but dying for the wrong thing. Christians are told by our Savior that we must prepare for death exactly because we refuse to kill in the name of survival. That is what I think Christians can do at this time.

The university should be a space for exactly the kinds of questions I have been raising throughout this chapter. The university names the time and space to free us from the assumption that the way the world is is the way things have to be. For example, the university could be a place where the "just war" shapes the study of state actions. What would it be for political science departments to teach international relations from a just war perspective? What would that look like in terms of the world in which we exist? At Duke, we talk a great deal about being a global university. I don't believe it for a moment. We are a university of the United States of America and cannot imagine serving the world in any way other than through doing what is good for the United States of America.

I think the misery of the American public and the world in which we live can be seen nowhere better than in the suggestion (in many ways quite understandable) that we must take up our responsibilities as citizens and respond to terrorist attacks by shopping. A people who know nothing better to do than to shop turn out to be the most determined killers, because at last something interesting has dropped in their laps, and they don't know how to think about it. May the church and the university be judged accordingly.

28

Organizing Nonviolence

Jim Lewis

In October of 1990, I returned from Iraq. I had gone there as a member of a peace delegation sponsored by the Fellowship of Reconciliation. We returned with five American hostages who were being held at that time by Saddam Hussein. The trip to Iraq was intended to mobilize both presence and visibility to an effort for a negotiated settlement over Iraq's invasion of Kuwait rather than an all-out war. On returning to the United States, all of us on that delegation returned to the communities from which we had come. Once home we began to organize those communities to work for a nonviolent resolution to the problems in the Persian Gulf.

On January 28, 1991, just as the United States was bombing Baghdad, columnist Charles Krauthammer wrote:

> If the war in the Gulf ends the way it began, with a dazzling display of American technological superiority, individual grit, and (most unexpectedly for Saddam) national resolve, we will no longer speak of post-Vietnam America. A new post-Gulf America will emerge with self-image, sense of history, even our political discourse transformed.[1]

That was ten years ago.

After the September 11 attack on the World Trade Center and the Pentagon, we could well say that we are indeed living in post–Gulf War America, where political discourse has certainly changed.

For the past seven years I have been working on organizing poultry plant workers on the Delmarva Peninsula as they are attempting to address the injustices in the poultry industry. I have now moved back to West Virginia, the place where I served Episcopal churches for fifteen years, to live in the mountains I love, amidst the people I love. I can tell you for certain that the people I left behind in West Virginia this morning are shocked and surprised by what took place on September 11.

Gazing at a television set, watching buildings in New York City crumble right before my eyes was indeed shocking and surprising. Recovering from that initial shock, however, I must say that I am surprised that it didn't happen sooner.

I am forced to remember a trip I took into a village in El Salvador, a village that had been totally destroyed, and in which many Salvadoran peasants had lost their lives. I found in that village the remains of an undetonated bomb, a bomb that had been made in the United States, a bomb that served as a reminder of the military support given by the United States to a repressive military government that killed more than a hundred thousand people. Leaving that village, I wondered, "How much longer before these people strike back?"

Traveling in the Middle East and seeing Palestinians being killed by Israeli bullets made in the United States and subjected to tear gas from the United States, I wondered, "How much longer before these people strike back?"

Knowing, as I do, how my nation, the United States, has supported governments around the world that have killed and oppressed their own people for their own interests and ours, I have wondered, "How long before these people strike back?"

The news coverage on CNN describes this conflict as "America's New War." But I don't think it is a new war at all. We may see it as a new war, to the extent that our shores have been hit, but this so-called "terrorist war" has been going on for a long time. If you have the stomach for it and are willing to take a look at the dark side of United States military and covert activity, read Michael McClintock's *Instruments of Statecraft*.[2] The author documents the military policy carried out during the Cold War years in which the U.S. tried to defeat communism by engaging in what we called "counterinsurgency" and "counterterrorism."

This military strategy involved using all the terrorist tactics we accuse our enemies of employing in order that we might defeat them. Since the Cold War was seen as a war of good versus evil, such tactics were considered justified, yet often done covertly by our military and our CIA. It included the financing of right wing, military governments to defeat indigenous forces attempting to bring about political and economic change. Covert action by our CIA, political assassination of foreign leaders, training at U.S. military bases for foreign military personnel who were terrorizing people in their home countries, and supplying military aid were all part of ugly, often secret activities engaged in by the U.S.

McClintock has painful yet important things to say to us about our own hidden history as a nation. For example, in 1947 the passage of the Aid to Greece and Turkey bill allowed President Truman to send civilian and military advisers into that part of the world to influence the outcome of the Greek Civil War. That action was a preview of our engagement later in Korea, Vietnam, and the various conflicts in Central America, to name but a few places where the U.S. became trapped in war and terror.

In 1955, despite Geneva Convention prohibitions, the U.S. became involved in the newly independent nation of Laos. At that time I was a Marine infantry officer stationed in Okinawa who was becoming aware of the illegal involvement in Southeast Asia that eventually involved us in drug smuggling, killing, and CIA dirty tricks that finally led us into an all-out war in Vietnam. Of note: The U.S. had just come away from an encounter in Guatemala that resulted in our overthrowing the first democratically elected president in the history of that nation. That illegal activity on our part led to the deaths of more than one hundred thousand Guatemalan peasants at the hands of a repressive United States–backed regime.

In 1961, at Fort Bragg, a military base located in North Carolina, "atrocity research" was initiated. It was a study of the personality traits associated with people who kill. Out of that study came the very procedures for combat readiness units we now call "special forces." Commando teams of specialized military units were shown films of people being killed in violent ways. This training was designed to prepare soldiers to disassociate themselves emotionally from the people they would kill. Scores of soldiers were trained to kill without remorse using whatever means necessary, using the same tactics and methods we associate with terrorists.

President Carter and President Reagan poured enormous sums of money into Afghanistan to finance a tribal war against Russia. After ten years of military support and enormous killing, Russia limped home, the Cold War ended, and we proclaimed ourselves victorious in the Cold War. Interesting fact: Osama bin Laden was one of the tribal chiefs we supported during that period of war.

For me, military activity on our part in the Middle East was most painfully and tragically visible when we brought Marines ashore in Lebanon only to see their barracks destroyed in 1983. Two hundred and forty-three Marines were killed in that attack. The terrorist responsible for that suicide raid was acting in retaliation for the *USS New Jersey's* bombardment of a Lebanese village. The bomber responded with the weapon of terror in answer to the terror experienced in our bombing of that village. Terror for terror for terror, with no end in sight.

In 1986, a report was prepared for the House Armed Services Committee Special Operations Panel. Inside that report was a "skills chart" that listed assassination, abduction, hostage taking, random killing and maiming, and sabotage as the basic ingredients of our program of counterterrorism. It was the inevitable consequence of a nation prepared after World War II to protect our national interests by adopting the tactics of those we considered to be our enemies. In other words, fighting fire with fire, violence with violence.

As a Christian I am concerned about our journey as a nation down this path of violence and terror, both in our domestic life and in our dealings with other nations. I see our nation engaged in what could well be called the "myth of redemptive violence."[3] I would call into question the belief that injustice, violence, and terror are redeemed by injustice, violence, and terror. Thinking that we can conquer violence by being violent, we fool ourselves.

And I would say to you to think about how violence is woven into your life and the life of your nation, how it is even justified as redemptive and healing.

Early settlers in this nation used violence to build what has been called a "city on the hill," a nation with a "manifest destiny" to bear witness to our own preciousness.

We engaged in the most bloody and decisive war in this nation's history, a civil war in places such as Sharpsburg and Gettysburg, so that a national unity might be maintained.

We slaughtered millions in World War I with the justification that it would be the war that would end all wars.

In Vietnam, we destroyed villages in order to save them.

We use the violent instrument of capital punishment in order to show offenders, and others as well, that violence is wrong.

Some have beaten and abused women violently in order to teach them to conform to roles carved out for them in a male-dominated society.

Some have applied a strap to a child's back or buttocks with the words, "You know this hurts me more than it hurts you. I'm only doing this for your own good."

All of this done in the name of redemptive violence.

Edward Said, in his book, *The End of the Peace Process: Oslo and After,* writes about terrorism. He makes a strong point when he points to the fact that the term *terrorist* is too easily associated with Arab people, with Muslims and with Palestinians.

> Only when Muslims fall into line, speak the same language, take the same measures as Israel and the United States do, can they expect to be "normal," at which point of course they are no longer really Arab and Muslim. They have simply become "peacemakers." What a pity that so noble an idea as "peace" has become a corrupted embellishment of power masquerading as reconciliation.[4]

For those of us who regularly talk about peace and reconciliation, and see ourselves as peacemakers, Said's words carry a penetrating judgment as they point to our propensity as a nation to ostracize and radicalize any nation not on board with our agenda.

Only the other day I was at the mall in Charleston, where the military recruiters were busy recruiting young people for what will almost surely be a long war against terrorism. Troops are already being dispatched to the region surrounding Afghanistan. Putting troops in place for war almost certainly dictates fighting a war. I saw that happen in the Gulf War.

When I came back from Iraq, President Bush had already put close to half a million troops in place in the Persian Gulf. Despite a well-organized three-month effort all across the country to prevent a shooting war, those military forces eventually were ordered into combat.

Whether anything can be changed by organizing people across the country to resist continued military action in the "war on terrorism," I am not at all sure. But we must try. This is the moment when people must organize out of the conviction that redemptive violence is not a morally acceptable posture for our nation. A war undertaken as a "just war" must be unmasked for the myth that it is. A *just* war is just *war.* Those of us concerned about resolving this present crisis in a nonviolent way, rather than with bombs and guns, must organize our churches, mosques, temples, synagogues, and the communities where we live. If we fail to do this, I fear we will find ourselves, as a nation, victimized by our own blindness and destroyed by the very violence we have wielded as the weapon to end violence.

29

What Can We Hope for Now?

M. Douglas Meeks

The explosions in New York and Washington on the beautiful late summer morning of September 11, 2001, have ruptured history and catapulted us into terrible uncertainty. The twin towers of world trade and the pentagonal fortress, the symbols of our invincible economic and military power, revealed themselves as all along vulnerable. They stood, we now understand, only because these evil acts were something no human being would do and no human being would be capable of doing. Now we know that there are human beings who can and will do these acts with religious fervor and no remorse. We know that human beings can cause a sacrifice of burning flesh to the gods of hatred in what has been called "the greatest display of grotesque cunning in human history." We wonder whether we will look back at all our history through billowing smoke and falling debris. In reflective moments after September 11 we of course realized that there is a long history of terror and that other nations have been living steadily with terrorist acts. The shock of that day for Americans was the realization that what we have trusted to secure our future and what we had given an almost divine status is after all subject to history. What can we hope for now?

Even those who consider themselves atheists, when faced with these catastrophes could only mutter, "My God." In the first hours and days much of the nation seemed to pray with the author of Lamentations: "My soul is bereft of peace; I have forgotten what happiness is; so I say, 'Gone is my glory, and all that I had hoped for from the LORD.'" (Lam. 3:17–18). A Christian

253

response in a time of terror, however, cannot be a counsel of doom. So we continue with the Lamenter: "But this I call to mind, and therefore I have hope: The steadfast love of the LORD never ceases, his mercies never come to an end; they are new every morning; great is your faithfulness. 'The Lord is my portion,' says my soul, 'therefore I will hope in him'" (3:21–24).

Christians abide in a hope against hope that arises from God's resurrection power over death. It is a hope that does not depend on the conditions of world history, and yet it is a hope bound to God's passion for the redemption of *this* world. If we are to remain in hope for this world, besieged as it is by the threat of terror, our hope must be realistic. We are able to stay realistically in hope only because we are in the company of the crucified Jesus. We hope for the future of the one whose life began with the slaughter of the innocents; the one who himself experienced the terrorism of the state on the cross, the one who died for a world that seems ruled by violence and hatred, the one who descended into hell and therefore can stand with all who suffer from any kind of terrorism. We see in the resurrection of the crucified one the beginning of the defeat of evil and terror and thus the objective ground for staying in hope for this world.

A realistic hope after September 11 must confront the primary negation of hope: fate. Hope is life against fate. Hope is the mode of living in the contingencies of history for the sake of a future in which human beings and nature can flourish. The persuasion of fate, on the other hand, seeks to end the contingencies, struggles, and contradictions of history so that one set of perpetual conditions can reign. Fate is the darling of those who would end history with the triumph of a construct defined as universal necessity. Fate takes the place of providence. It replaces our expectation of the future on the basis of the crucified resurrected One.

At the beginning of the twenty-first century hope is challenged by two fates: Globalization and Terrorism. In the developed world, globalization has become the undisputed world narrative. But the meaning of September 11 is that there is an alternative to globalization, the world narrative of terror. The enormously difficult witness of Christians in this time of profound uncertainty is that neither globalization nor terror is fate. The world is open to the new creation of God's righteousness.

Globalization: The Fate of the Earth

In the 1990s many Americans came to believe that the globalization of democratic capitalism as defined by the "Washington Consensus" was the fate of the world. The globalization of communication, transportation, and finance systems by means of the "chip" and other dazzling technology shrank the world. We learned to live in cyber-capital, where there is no need for tolerance, or for that matter, memory, where markets are unregulated, and where investment and profit are limitless. We had the sense that sooner or later the rules of the market as construed in America would pervade every village and hamlet. The logic of this process stemmed from the very nature of the human being, and every section of the daily newspaper gave ample evidence that all areas of the world would sooner or later, mostly sooner, have market cultures and societies, much like that found in the United States. Didn't the arrival of cell phones, fax machines, and e-mail in the remotest part of the world mean that *Baywatch* and MTV were not far behind? No historical contingency could withstand the inexorable progress of this fate.

No book expressed this fate of globalization more effusively than Thomas Friedman's *The Lexus and the Olive Tree*.[1] The Lexus represents the promised luxury and incredible complexity of the global market in which economic changes in Thailand are registered in the neighborhood streets of Bethesda, Maryland, and the enormous power of hedge fund directors can affect the quality of life everywhere, and the International Monetary Fund can heal the "Asian Flu" and prevent the economic collapse of Mexico and Brazil. The globalizing processes are inevitable, argued Friedman, and it behooves people everywhere to learn and follow the rules of the global market or suffer the cruel consequences of the market's punishment. These rules are a "golden straightjacket." To be sure they restrict human life in significant ways, but they are the only security for life in the global village.

Friedman does acknowledge that the olive tree, which represents religious community, has some part to play in the global human project, but its function is mostly to give meaning and orientation amid the disruption of community and to provide compensation for the spirit that is flattened by conforming to market necessities. And, presumably, religious communities would support the "safety net" for the losers in every society which Friedman does believe is necessary to the progress of globalization. His advice, however, is something like Aristotle's in the *Nicomachean Ethics*: If you would be free, then live according to the necessity of your existence, which is in our case globalization.

The 1990s, however, also featured thinkers who questioned this view of globalization, such as John Gray in his book *False Dawn*. The "end of history" has not arrived with the victory of democratic capitalism over state socialism as Fukuyama had speculated.[2] The peculiar brand of laissez-faire capitalism, developed in Great Britain, the United States, Australia, and New Zealand in two short periods of modernity (1870–1930 and 1980 to the present) is not the fate of the world. Following Karl Polanyi, Gray argues that since the rise of laissez-faire capitalism, human communities have struggled against the economic rules that prevent the flourishing of human beings and of nature. It is not the case that the triumph of the West in 1989 brought an end to conflicts. They have, in fact, been deepened. The protest of the poor and of all those whose condition is worsened by globalization remains a negation of globalization as fate. According to Gray, we cannot turn to the past for solutions to human subjugation and natural degradation. We cannot suppress technological progress, but there will be different kinds of capitalist economies lodged in different cultures. The globalization that assumed that some people can be sacrificed for the progress of all according to a universally accepted utilitarian calculus and that there can be only one form of democracy is waning.

Whether in Friedman's or Gray's version, globalization is the major historical force. But terrorism would destroy globalization. We are now in a shortened history in which we are searching for the agents that will transform globalization toward a humane future. In the long run a humane globalization is a countermeasure to terror. The resolution and energy to work for a humane globalization depend on a hope that negates the fated character of globalization and terrorism.

The Narrative of Terrorism

Terror is not new. In fact, its seeds can be traced to the origin myths of most cultures and religions. History is full of the terror of tyrants and conquerors. The terror of Robespierre accompanied the blooming of the Enlightenment. Modernity also features the terrorism of the weak who are able to use the new forms of modern power to threaten the future of the strong. Prior to September 11 terror occupied our media for days and weeks at a time, but now it preoccupies our lives and may well change the way we think from moment to moment for years to come. It is one thing to encounter terror through the media; it is another to live in a space of danger. Terror has become our narrative.

The narrative of terror originates within the souls of terrorists. It produces a different kind of enemy that can't be seen. It is difficult to understand what motivates a suicide terrorist. We are rich and strong, but they are willing to die. The world created by our complicated exchanges does not attract them. This is their strength. The new terrorists can give the appearance of normalcy, as they so clearly displayed in the United States and Europe prior to September 11. They are not deranged, they are religious. They are radical Islamists in a demonic way. But Islamic suicide terrorists are not born, they are meticulously schooled and disciplined in hatred of secular learning and of Israel, isolated from the world, taught to yearn for the violence supposedly condoned by "holy war," and promised a place among the martyrs, a promise that is often intensified by sexual obsessiveness conditioned by complete separation from women.[3] Venerated by their families and primary communities, they think of themselves as martyrs to Islam. They form a non-exact parallel to the Ku Klux Klan, a demonic form of the Christian faith. They have condemned the high gloss of modernity's icons as a deep threat to Islam. Secularism means godlessness, and thus there are no limits to the destruction of God's own enemies–not even the slaughter of innocent people. Death at the hands of terrorists is a sign of God's last judgment. An angered, aggrieved conviction leads them to self-sacrifice in a vision of judgment and devastation.

The Life of Terror

The narrative of terror also takes place *within* those who are terrified. As they watched on TV the burning Twin Towers, people leaping from windows or crushed by the collapse of the buildings, many had what most educated Americans don't normally have: a sense of the apocalypse, the end of the world. The prospect of endless acts of terror perpetrated by hidden enemies against innocent civilians gives one the sense that the future is closed, inevitable, inescapable. Terrorism works for and by the creation of a widespread debilitating anxiety in the population. Terrorists intend to cripple "the Great Devil" by instilling an anxiety that runs through its veins like a virus.

The widespread anxiety and fear over our crushing loss of a sense of security cannot be denied. Fortress America has been breached. If a plane full of New York–Los Angeles commuters can be turned into a missile of war, everything is suddenly dangerous and nothing is completely secure. We are not impervious to the rage of the world. It's not that we have never known terrorist attacks, such as Pearl Harbor, the 1993 World Trade Center bombing, the downing of Pan Am flight 103, and the East Africa U.S. Embassy bombings. We have lived with the terror of organized crime, militias, Jim Crow and lynching, the anti-abortion terrorist movement, lone terrorists like Timothy McVeigh and the Unabomber, and the misfit youths who have terrorized their fellow students. The difference is not simply a matter of scale. The difference is that our defense and security systems have failed. How are our national security systems supposed to thwart bad intentions if hijackers are now suicidal? How are our lives supposed to be secure if the very wonders of our technology, our vaunted machines of transportation and communication, are turned against us in such a deadly way? How can we remain "first" in the world if the greatest inventions of our minds and products of our industrial prowess no longer set us apart but rather are the means of our vulnerability? How can people carry on daily life with the knowledge that massive systems such as nuclear energy plants, water systems, and electrical grids are exposed to terrorist attack?

We are learning that we are vulnerable in ways that we have not considered for a long time. We are vulnerable, for example, because we do not know how to live with anxiety. We have become used to a life of calculating our risks and pricing our decisions day by day. We are told that terrorists are planning new attacks in the near future but that we should live our lives as we would otherwise live them, only with heightened vigilance. Such general warnings make it impossible to assess the odds of danger in everyday life. We are urged to shop, travel, invest in the stock market, and attend NFL games as usual while keeping an eye open for trucks that might be carrying explosives or letters with no return address. We feel anxious because we can't calculate the odds. Even if more and more Americans live their lives by the "lottery," these risks are too great.

We are learning that we are vulnerable, because we Americans don't know our neighbors. We have thought that the more global we become the less local we have to be. Why does one need neighbors if one is wired into the Web? If one trades in the cyber-market, why does one need the local market? But terrorists now know that Americans don't know their neighbors and that they can therefore take up residence anywhere. Even those in gated communities are learning that it is not enough to be fenced from the poor, the ignorant, the ill, and the disturbed if the life systems they share with all other citizens are not invulnerable.

We are learning that our secularity is making us vulnerable. We don't know Islam. We don't know the faith, the daily discipline, the hopes and the fears of Muslims. The Enlightenment expectation was that religion would wither away once reason became capable of securing a universal peace. In the latter part of the twentieth century many Americans tended to think that religion would become superfluous once the market could decide all crucial questions of value. These assumptions are dangerous historical mistakes. We live in the most religious and spiritual time in the history of the globe. And we live in a time when fundamentalism has erupted in all religions in all parts of the world. Most fundamentalists are seeking to lead a religious life. But there is an extreme and violent fundamentalism of which we remain ignorant at our great peril.

We are learning that our cultural ignorance is making us vulnerable. And this is true not only in the case of our intelligence and diplomatic officers but of all our citizens. American schools and universities were for two decades awash with the preachments of multiculturalism, but on the whole our population is less prepared with linguistic and cultural abilities to understand and communicate with, for example, the languages, customs, lifestyles, and values of Islamic Arabic cultures than it has ever been.

We are learning that we are vulnerable to the life sciences' being turned into tools for mass murder. Shortly after the September 11 explosions anxiety was deepened by the prospect that anthrax spores could be spread by crop dusters and then the news that it had actually been spread through the U.S. Postal System. But is anthrax the real threat or will it be something else? What if the real danger is Ebola virus or plague or smallpox? Human beings lived with smallpox for at least 3,000 years, suffering the dread of its hideous arrival and the horror of its indiscriminate killing. It is estimated that smallpox reduced the central Mexican Aztec population from 25 million in 1519 to 3 million in 1568. In 1979 the World Health Organization declared it officially eradicated. With all the marvels of modern medicine, smallpox is the only disease human beings have been able completely to wipe out. Its return as a biological weapon would be a medical and moral catastrophe.

Fighting Terrorism Justly

The language of war mobilizes a population. Immediately after the terrorist attacks the language of the Administration was full of talk about a war on terrorism. As it moved toward military engagement it had to find some restraints on its war language. It drew back from the idiom of crusade and "infinite justice," goals that necessitate unlimited means. We hear constantly that this is a war unlike any before it. This assessment makes it all the more difficult to justify. But all wars have to be justified or they subvert humanity altogether.

The just war tradition is often said to be irrelevant in the modern practice of war and in any case is certainly not sufficient for informing the church as to how it should carry on its peculiar commission in time of war. The rules of just war apply to states that despite their self-interest intend to behave morally in war. Can the rules of just war be applied to terrorists? Terrorist networks are transnational and nongovernmental. As non-state agents they attack innocent civilians. But if the responses to terrorism are not measured by the rules of just war, these responses will inevitably mimic terrorism, which is, of course, the desired result of terrorist acts.

The life of terror in our souls is tempted with revenge. Desire for retribution is an expected first response to the deaths of innocent people caused by a willful, meticulously planned act executed with no apparent feeling of common humanity. The nation is suffering appropriate grief and anger, but it is also faced with the call for retaliation. The *lex talionis*, the law of revenge, is the oldest law we human beings know. But since Cain spilled the blood of Abel and the soil cried out in horror, we have known that revenge simply continues the vicious cycle of violence. In fact, no terrorist can ply his trade without revenge. Terrorists should be brought to retributive justice, but revenge abroad or at home will reward the terrorist's acts with a spiral of violence that continues to escalate with more terror.

The single just cause of war is "wrong received." Preemptive wars have been generally unacceptable unless the immediate intent of the aggressor could be added to the just cause. In the situation of terrorist attacks both injury and threat are substantial. Thousands of innocent, noncombatant civilians were slaughtered merely because they occupied a building of high symbolic value. The overwhelming reason the international community has agreed with the just war attribution to the military actions in Afghanistan is the firm conviction that al Qaeda and other transnational terrorist organizations are close to their objective of developing nuclear, biological, and chemical weapons, insuring their capability to murder millions rather than thousands of innocent human beings. This threat of course affects all nation-states and all peoples. Impending threat of enormous scope is thus added to profound injury as a just cause.

But a just cause does not by itself make a just war. There must be just means as well. The basic premise of just war thinking is that only evildoers are subject to attack. In order for there to be a judgment of just means there has be a distinction between the terrorist in international networks and the societies in which they are operating. Because military actions are directed at nations who harbor terrorists, it is more difficult to distinguish innocents in civil society who are neither terrorists nor supporters of terrorists. We do not know and may never know how many innocent civilians have been killed in the long-range, laser-guided "precision" bombing in Afghanistan. But there is no doubt that every innocent who is killed turns more moderate Muslims in the direction of Islamic fundamentalism.

Globalization as Just Peace

Fighting new forms of threat to personal and national security invites a rethinking of what security means in the twenty-first century. It is a moment in history in which we can realize that overcoming terrorism does not depend merely on the increased security of the United States. It depends on the increased security of the global village. If anyone in the world is insecure, we are insecure. If anyone's life is threatened, so is ours. Insecurity on which terrorism feeds stems from poverty. Insecurity feeds on newborn babies who live only a few months. Insecurity issues from the arrogance of some nations thinking themselves messianically superior to others.

Fighting terrorism requires changing the way we live and changing our relation to other nations. An effective response to terrorism requires a just military dimension, but it demands much more. Military means alone cannot defeat terrorism. It may be possible, though not likely, that the present military action will break the international network of Islamic fundamentalist terrorists. But the conditions out of which international terrorism finds resonance and support will still exist. And those conditions will give a perverted justification to future terrorists. Are we to have one preemptive war after another? Is it really possible to spread Western military technology and troops to all Islamic countries? The limit of the just war doctrine is that it does not deal adequately with the complex menace of terrorism. A just peace doctrine is a global requirement in face of the long-term impending threat of terrorism. Just diplomatic-political, economic, and social means of struggle against terrorism are as important as the military–in the long run, more important.

Three dimensions of a just peace doctrine particularly crucial to opposing terrorism as fate are: (1) the relationship of religion and democracy, (2) the practice of our own democracy, and (3) changing the way we participate in the global economy.

RELIGION AND DEMOCRACY

The United States has a long and rich history of practicing democracy. There is much that people all over the world could learn from this history. But can American democracy be exported ready-made for "nation building" in Islamic countries? Does democracy have to be secularizing? A fear of many Muslims is that democracy will wipe away Islam, as it seems to have undermined Christianity in Europe and the United States. Democracy does not necessarily mean secularization; it means systemic criticism of privilege.

The simple fact is that Islam, Christianity, and Israel are going to have to live together, or their distorted extremes will destroy the possibility of human existence at all. Western democracy prevents any religion from governing society, but it should not undermine religion. The Protestant Reformation, the Catholic Reformation, and the modern Revivals all spoke of "Christianizing" the societies in which they existed and reforming the nations. Our extreme secularization in which we think the market and democratic procedures can solve all problems has precluded this language. But in principle no democratic government should work against the Christianization of society. In the United States this would mean of course that the "Islamization" and "Israelization" of society would have to be given place–as well as the forces that work for the secularization of society in a "religious" way.

Is it possible for Islam, Israel, and Christianity to live in the same complex space? Yes, of course it is. It has happened before. It has to happen again in Israel and Palestine, or there will be no end to one of the primary causes driving Islamic fundamentalist terror. Jerusalem, again, is the focus of our hope for a space that the religions of Abraham can inhabit mutually in peace. Christians should work with Muslims and Jews to make the Islamization and Israelization of societies possible. Most theologies of world religions have not prepared us well for this kind of work or for the new crises of world religious fundamentalism. The tendency in these theologies is to discern the universal in all religions in order to preclude the danger of the particular in each religion. But this is to construct a new philosophical religion that turns out to be the *philosophia perennia* of the West. No believing Muslim or Jew wants to come to a table for conversation and common life at which the essence of Islam or Israel is already determined.

Never before have we needed so much the criticism of religion. But the most historically effective criticism of religion comes from within the religion itself. Our hope for the Middle East is that an Islam true to itself will be given freedom to pervade the societies and cultures and contend with a fundamentalist Islam that for several decades has been used and protected by despots, sometimes with the geopolitical blessings of the United States.

DEMOCRACY IN AMERICA

There was a time when most Islamic peoples looked to the United States as a hopeful sign of their future. Fundamentalist Islam profits in its agenda of hatred from undemocratic actions in Western countries. Since September 11 democracy has suffered several severe blows in the United States as the Administration has grasped "emergency powers" that flout the Constitution. In a few short weeks we have moved toward a defensive society in which foreign and domestic security experts direct how we must live. The U.S.A. Patriot Act was passed without serious debate in public or even in Congress. The Freedom of Information Act was abridged by decree. A new directive allows eavesdropping on lawyer-client conversations. And, as if the war on terror changed their accountability, the commission on Social Security reform and the energy task force are meeting *in camera*.

The Administration has decreed military tribunals that would operate under secret procedures with no requirement to reveal to the public the evidence, verdict, or punishment. Terrorists who commit suicide cannot be tried in military courts, so that leaves resident aliens and immigrants as suspects. They have a very different status than the handful of German spies who sprang to these shores from submarines and are said to be a precedent for military trials of civilians; that is, until proved guilty, they are protected by the law of the land. If the legal and civil rights of Americans, citizens or resident immigrants, are lost, then the terrorists have already won. "Homeland Security" that deconstructs constitutional rights promotes insecurity.

GLOBALIZATION AND OIL

Perhaps nothing will be more difficult for Americans in the struggle against international terrorism than changing the way we participate in the global economy. It is so difficult because it means changing the way we live. The United States' contribution to world security and a new world order should begin with its relation to oil. Oil seems to be our fate. America's passion for the automobile subjects us to a dangerous and doomed appetite for oil. Since the 1930s oil has been responsible for much of the United States' international entanglements and especially the unrest in the Middle East. Why is the United States so much hated in the Arab world? Why does it have a reputation as a bully in the Islamic world and beyond? One reason is that our demand for foreign oil has led us into one unsavory marriage of convenience after another. We have overlooked oppression in oil countries as we have bolstered leaders who would keep order and keep the oil flowing.

Saudi Arabia is a good example. The ruling family, the al-Sauds, built Saudi Arabia on defending the faith, but also on petrodollars. The terrorists of September 11 and their captains are not leaders of the oppressed and the starving. The majority of the terrorists came from Saudi Arabia, the land where the prophet Mohammed and the faith were born, the land of Mecca and Medina, which welcomes millions every year in the hajj (pilgrimage). Osama bin Laden, like many of the known terrorists, first expressed his hatred of Saudi Arabia, his own country. How can one so clearly lacking in religious credentials gain followers for jihad? Without democratic forms of dissent among Middle East Islamic countries, Islamic fundamentalism is the only form of legitimate dissent. Islamic governments have allowed or promoted anti-Americanism in order to deflect criticism of themselves.

The cycle in oil prices has been a major source of world instability in the past three decades. Recently the price of oil plunged from $30 to $17 a barrel. If the price holds at this level it would transfer $100 billion per year from oil sheiks and American oil magnates and would do more for the economy than any of the tax breaks for corporations and the wealthy that politicians are trying to justify as post-terrorist economic stimulus. The reality, however, is that this price drop threatens more instability in the oil-rich countries and thus increases conditions in which terrorism can grow. Is there no end to the dangerous consequences of this vicious cycle?

Oil continues to be a major source of America's strategic vulnerability. According to President Bush, "National security depends on energy security." But the most effective war for national security would be the war against our own oil gluttony. America consumes 25 percent of the world's oil while possessing less than 4 percent of global oil reserves. Even opening the Arctic National Wildlife Refuge to drilling would provide a mere 140 days' worth of fuel. Deregulating controls and increased drilling will not solve even our short-term energy problems, much less our long-term ones. We have to be more inventive about easing our reliance on all oil, foreign and domestic. Much more money should be put into research into fuel efficiency and developing wind and wave power, biomass research, and photovoltaic modules that can convert even diffuse light into electricity. In order to produce cars that can get 70 miles per gallon it would probably have to become unpatriotic to drive an SUV. Fighting the fate of terrorism includes the almost unthinkable changing of American consumer desire.

These three dimensions of working against the fate of terrorism for a just global peace in some sense require more fortitude than does waging war. They require a hope that resolutely negates the fate which declares that the living together of the religions, the continuation of democracy, and a just global economy are all impossible. Ground Zero in lower Manhattan is a sign like that of the prophets that the world's cities could end in a pile of rubbish to be hissed at (Jer. 19:8). Those who cry out to the Lord of Peace will find the city's security and welfare in God's justice and will therefore be found among "the builders who outdo the destroyers of the city" (Isa. 49:17).

30

New Wars, Old Wineskins

Susan Brooks Thistlethwaite

Only justice can stop a curse.
ALICE WALKER

Sometimes it takes a poet to get it exactly right. Only justice will actually, finally, stop terrorism. Violence only creates more violence. As the Christian community struggles to reflect theologically and ethically on massive terrorism in this new millennium, it must recognize that the older paradigms of just war, crusade, and even pacifism are not adequate to hold all that must be said in this time. It is also time to recognize that these three paradigms have never adequately addressed the nature of violence and what it takes to bring about peace with justice. Martin Luther King, Jr., as though speaking directly to the days and weeks following 9/11, explains,

> The ultimate weakness of violence is that it is a descending spiral, begetting the very thing that it seeks to destroy. Instead of diminishing evil, it multiplies it. Through violence you may murder the liar, but you cannot murder the lie, nor establish truth. Through violence you murder the hater but you do not murder the hate. In fact, violence merely increases hate. Returning violence for violence multiplies violence, adding deeper darkness to a night already devoid of stars.

Darkness cannot drive out darkness; only light can do that. Hate cannot drive out hate; only love can do that.[1]

Just war, pacifism and crusade are not adequate to address the point King is making. Just war seeks to reduce violence by setting limits on entry into war and on the conduct of war, but it does not ultimately take account of the fact that *violence actually increases violence*. It was not "the last Just War"[2] that finally brought peace to Europe in the twentieth century, it was the Marshall Plan that permitted the economic stability and democratic structures necessary for peace to endure. Afghanistan needed a Marshall Plan after the Soviet Union pulled out of the Afghan war, and the United States did not act. We let poverty and oppression rule, and now we are reaping the results.

Pacifism would set an absolute limit on the use of violence, but pacifism does not address the fact that peace must be *made* by the structuring of economic and political forces that can sustain the conditions of human well-being necessary to peace. Crusade, of course, has never pretended to limit violence, and no major Christian denomination today supports the validity of the crusade paradigm.[3] We have only to note the complete rejection of George W. Bush's use of the term crusade in the days following 9/11.[4]

The Christian community will advocate no fundamental change unless a clear and unambiguous alternative to the spiral of violence and revenge is offered. Current public religious, political, and military discourse merely mirrors the enemy.

The last weeks have not been devoid of statements from political, military, and religious leaders. Here is a sample: "We will win this conflict"; "The nation should know that we have a just cause"; "To every soldier, I say this, 'Your mission is defined...your goal is just'"; "May God's peace and blessings be upon him and his companions"; "May God continue to bless America."

This collection of statements was offered by the Reverend James Vijayakumar in a sermon to the United Church of Christ Council for Theological Education on October 10, 2001. He went on to say, "Obviously, it doesn't seem to be difficult to identify the speaker here, does it? After all, we have heard it several times from President George W. Bush. Well, it is not as easy as it might appear. President Bush is not the only speaker, but we go one more here. President Bush spoke only 50 percent of the words I read. The other 50 percent came from the mouth of Osama bin Laden. Not surprising, I guess. But if we may have a quick quiz, try and see which words could have been uttered by whom. Remember it is 50/50. I will read them again: (GWB): 'We will win this conflict.' (OBL): 'The nation should know that we have a just cause.' (GWB): 'To every soldier, I say this, "Your mission is defined...Your goal is just."' (OBL): 'May God's peace and blessing be upon him and his companions.' (GWB): 'May God continue to bless America.'"[5]

If you mirror your enemy in your moral arguments defending war, you will surely become your enemy. And becoming your enemy absolutely ensures that lasting peace will not result. Three days after the attacks, Howard Zinn, respected historian and author of numerous books, including *A People's History of the United States,* said, "The images on television horrified and sickened me. Then our political leaders came on television, and I was horrified and sickened again. They spoke of retaliation, of vengeance, of punishment. I thought: they have learned nothing, absolutely nothing, from the history of the twentieth century, from a hundred years of retaliation, vengeance, war, a hundred years of terrorism and counter-terrorism, of violence met with violence in an unending cycle of stupidity. Will we now bomb Afghanistan, and inevitably kill innocent people, because it is in the nature of bombing to be indiscriminate? Will we then be committing terrorism in order to 'send a message' to terrorists? Yes, it is an old way of thinking, and we need new ways. A $300 billion military budget has not given us security."[6]

The Just Peace Paradigm

Just peace is a new way of thinking. It is an emerging fourth paradigm beyond just war, pacifism, and crusade. It attempts to address precisely the areas overlooked in both just war and pacifism. Just peace proposes a positive practice for the making of peace through the establishment of economic well-being and democratic structures, while at the same time offering proven strategies for reducing conflict once violence breaks out and for bringing hostility to an end.

During the 1980s the major Christian bodies, the United Church of Christ, the Presbyterians, the Catholics, and the United Methodists, all produced documents that called for developing new approaches to peace and justice and for developing a new paradigm for a just peace. They "proclaimed similarly that while the two predominant paradigms of limited resort to force, just war theory and pacifism, are still necessary, we also need a positive theory of just peacemaking."[7]

New strategies from the conflict mediation movement, from the civil rights movement, the struggle against apartheid in South Africa, human rights efforts of nongovernmental organizations and grassroots movements, and new theological insights about power and powerlessness from liberation struggles around the world also contributed to the formulation of just peace theory.

In the 1990s further work was done on refining a just peace paradigm. A group of Christian ethicists, biblical and moral theologians, international relations scholars, peace activists, and conflict resolution practitioners started meeting and talking together about the drastic change in the nature of war and the development of new methods that had proven effectiveness in making peace more likely. Over four years, twenty-three of these scholars and activists, myself included, met and developed a more fully fleshed outline of just peace. These practices of just peace are: (1) nonviolent direct action; (2) independent initiatives to reduce threat; (3) cooperative conflict resolution; (4) acknowledgement of responsibility and seeking repentance and forgiveness; (5) advancement of democracy, human rights, and religious liberty; (6) fostering of just and sustainable economic development; (7) working with emerging cooperative forces in the international system; (8) strengthening the United Nations and international organizations; (9) reducing offensive weapons trade; (10) encouraging grassroots peacemaking groups.[8]

The just peace paradigm is not magic. One does not simply follow this recipe and presto, peace will result. Not every one of these strategies is appropriate for every situation; not every strategy will bear fruit immediately. On the other hand, we have been told as Americans by our leadership that the struggle to defeat terrorism will take a very long time. Peace also takes a long time to establish. The good news about taking time to establish just peace is that peace that is structured tends to endure and to resist the corrosions of further violence. Violence, as I have emphasized repeatedly, only begets more violence.

Just peace is not a theory, it is not a set of abstract principles, it is not a theological doctrine. We have described just peace as "practices." These are normative practices or "practice norms" because "they bring peace, they solve problems, they promote justice and cooperation in a world whose wars are immeasurably destructive. We see historical evidence that when these normative practices are carried out, they can accomplish the goals of justice and peace."[9] We don't imagine that these ten practices reduce violence and establish justice. We describe the ways that in history these practices *have already been used* to bring about greater justice and peace. That is the strength of just peace. It exists.

As not all just peace practices are immediately applicable to all situations, I will not fully describe all ten in addressing the current crisis. I would identify six that seem immediately applicable. These are: Taking independent initiatives to reduce threat; acknowledging responsibility for conflict and injustice and seeking repentance and forgiveness; advancing democracy, human rights, and religious liberty; fostering just and sustainable economic development; strengthening the United Nations and international organizations; and reducing offensive weapons and weapons trade. The first two would impact the conflict as it is being conducted today. The latter three are ways to bring an end to hostility, a reduction of support for terrorists, and a changed international climate that will not arm renegade terrorists or terrorist regimes.

Taking Independent Initiatives to Reduce Threat

In 1962, Charles Osgood, a social psychologist, proposed what he called "independent initiatives" as a strategy that had already had success in breaking the spiral of violence in situations of conflict.[10] Osgood argued that "in a relationship of distrust and heightened threat perception, nations are blocked from initiating peacemaking steps and misperceive peace initiatives from the other side as insincere manipulation."[11]

Independent initiatives must have certain characteristics to be successful: they have to be real actions, not just words; they have to be visible and verifiable; they move outside slower processes of negotiation; they should not leave the initiator weak and open to attack; they must be done more than once; if the other side does respond with verifiable steps of their own, further initiatives should be undertaken in response; the timing of each initiative should be announced and the time course met; there should be a clear explanation given of why the initiative was undertaken.

Examples abound of the ways in which independent initiatives have been used successfully to negotiate peace. In 1955 the Soviet Union set Austria free, and NATO agreed to Austrian neutrality and nonoffensive military force. Presidents Eisenhower and Kennedy acted unilaterally to halve atmospheric testing to achieve the Partial Test Ban Treaty in 1963, perhaps one of the most famous examples of independent initiatives.

How might independent initiatives work in relation to this "war on terrorism"? Unfortunately, initial opportunities to avoid war and to avoid conflict with Muslim states have been squandered by the Bush Administration both in the failure to make public verifiable evidence and in the refusal to negotiate. Rahul Mahajan, national board member of Peace Action and a specialist on South and Central Asian Affairs, has said, "The refusal to negotiate or provide evidence violates international law, especially since the administration is claiming the right to engage in actions that will result in civilian deaths."[12] It is even now not too late to publish verifiable evidence that Osama bin Laden and el Qaeda are responsible for the September 11, 2001, attacks in the U.S. and that the Taliban are directly responsible for supporting terror. The Muslim press has repeatedly accused the United States and its allies of having no such evidence. Independent verification would answer these questions directly.

Having ruled out negotiation, the United States effectively closed the door to avoiding war. War has indeed resulted. The pope had called for "peaceful negotiations and dialogue" in the current crisis. Bishop Thomas Gumbleton of Detroit has said, "Some have rushed to portray us who are opposed to the Bush administration's plans as naïve and lacking realism. But if you look at the facts, it is clear that it is we who are the realists and those who would rush to war and escalate the cycle of violence are completely out of touch with reality and with the lessons of history. Our administration is warning us that the next attack might be in the form of germ warfare. What kind of insanity is it to pursue a course of action that might escalate into biological warfare? The only way to peace is to talk, to negotiate and to build understanding. Yet, President Bush has flatly ruled out the possibility of negotiations and dialogue. What does he hope to gain by issuing ultimatum after ultimatum and refusing to negotiate?"[13]

Bioterrorism has indeed resulted. Ironically, as of the date of submission of this book chapter, November 15, 2001, it is not known who has sent the anthrax tainted mail, but it is suspected that it is being sent by a lone American.[14] Yet the anthrax scare has been used to stir up war hysteria against a shadowy Arab enemy in a much more extreme fashion than the early knee-jerk response to the bombing in Oklahoma City. Ultimately that terrorist attack as well was perpetrated by a home-grown American, trained for attack by our own American military. Again, lack of evidence hurts American credibility.

Since the bombing began, this "war on terrorism" has been pursued in an unusual way in that, while dropping bombs on one part of the Afghan countryside, Americans are dropping food on another part. This is a tentative step toward independent initiatives. The recognition of the massive starvation the Afghan people face and their almost complete helplessness in the face of what is happening in their country has resulted in the food aid. It is a recognition that the United States knows, at some levels, that we cannot make war on people so helpless.

It is critical to recognize, however, how far short of independent initiatives this step actually falls. The food drops are dangerous, they are inadequate, and they cloak the collateral damage against civilian populations that is happening.

Doctors Without Borders, the internationally respected medical aid group, has expressed concern that the food-drops are dangerous. "Besides being a drop in the bucket, airdrops are problematic for many reasons. Without aid workers on the ground we have no way of ensuring that the food gets to the needy. It's likely that women, children and other vulnerable segments of the populations are not able to get to the food. Also, airdrops could pose a danger to the intended recipients, as Afghanistan is the most heavily mined country in the world. And last, we are seriously concerned about the mix-up of the military effort with the humanitarian action. Recipients should know that the aid they are getting is free of political agendas. The Geneva Conventions define humanitarian action as neutral, independent and impartial."[15]

The simple fact is that the Afghan people face massive starvation this winter if food aid is not delivered. The airdrops are not coming anywhere close to meeting the need for food. The United Nations estimates that 7.5 million people need food immediately. They live in remote village areas where the roads are not good in the warm weather; they are impassable in the winter. A three-year drought has meant the people have already eaten their seed corn for food. They have nothing.[16]

The apparent collapse of the Taliban and the success of the Northern Alliance does not guarantee that Afghans will be fed. Already food aid to the civilian population has been taken by the Northern Alliance and given to their troops. Colin Powell has said, "One of the great tragedies of Afghanistan right now is that a lot of these people were condemned to death long before the eleventh of September by the droughts, by the situation, by the collapse of the agricultural system."[17] Aid workers need to be let back in with a UN-mediated coalition protecting them. Winter is closing in rapidly, and the window to save millions is closing.

If we do not go all out to try to save the Afghan people, the deep hatred of the power and arrogance of the United States, already prevalent in the Arab world, will have increased, virtually ensuring that terrorism will accelerate.

Acknowledging Responsibility for Conflict and Injustice and Seeking Repentance and Forgiveness

One of the enduring truths of the peace movement is that people convinced of their own innocence cannot make peace. The role of acknowledgment of responsibility in conflict and injustice and seeking repentance and forgiveness is to develop the conditions whereby people party to a conflict can look at themselves and not just at the other.

In *Just Peacemaking,* Alan Geyer writes,

Peacemaking, whether in personal, group, or international relations, requires a variety of capacities for self-transcendence:

Transcendence of one's own interests and perspectives for the sake of understanding the interests and perspectives of the other side, which calls for the virtue of *empathy.*

Transcendence of one's pride and defensiveness, which inhibit the acknowledgment of injuries done to others—a capacity for *repentance* and perhaps restitution.

Transcendence of one's own grievances and desire for vengeance over injuries inflicted by others—a capacity for *forgiveness.*[18]

There has been a long and heated debate about whether these principles of responsibility and forgiveness should apply to nation-states as well as individuals. In just peace practices, the debate is moot. Nations have acknowledged responsibility and sought forgiveness—to good effect in the international arena. Many examples could be cited. One that is particularly relevant to our current national deprivation of rights to Arab Americans is President Gerald Ford's 1976 proclamation revoking Executive Order 9066 (1942) which interned Japanese Americans in concentration camps. Ford declared that an "honest reckoning must include a recognition of our national mistakes as well as our national achievements."[19] I am certain that a future President will need to make the same statement regarding our treatment of Arab Americans and indeed Arabs.

In a *Newsweek* magazine special report, "Why They Hate Us: The Roots of Islamic Rage and What We Can Do About It," by Fareed Zakaria, there was, for a mainstream publication, an unusual attempt at self-transcendence.

The official U.S. response to the "why they hate us" question has been, "We stand for freedom and they hate it. We are rich and they envy us. We are strong and they resent this."[20] The kind of blind pride that causes us to tout our own worth is the complete obverse of the kind of self-examination Geyer describes. Zakaria points out that Muslim countries do not hate us for our freedom, our wealth, and our strength; they hate us for the role we have played in *depriving* millions of freedom, wealth, and strength. Our freedom, wealth, and strength have been achieved on the backs on others.

It was not always the case that Muslims hated the United States. In the 1950s and 1960s, despite the Six Day War, President Richard Nixon was cheered wildly on the streets of Cairo when he visited Egypt. What has happened in the interim is that American oil interests in the Middle East have drawn us into supporting thugs and tyrants. The Shah of Iran, who tried to move his country into modernity and in the process made it a client state of the United States, ruled through torture and a complete contempt for routine civil rights for citizens of his country. Our oil interests deadened our capacity for empathy for the suffering of millions at the hands of these American client dictators.

Our continued boycott of Iraq has produced untold suffering in that country. While a boycott appears nonviolent, eleven years of deprivation has produced incredible suffering in that country. "Iraq has polluted water, lack of medicine and malnutrition, all due to the sanctions. The UN sanctions committee currently has 'holds' preventing delivery of $4 billion of humanitarian supplies."[21] But American compassion has been nonexistent for the Iraqi people.

We have consistently undermined efforts in Middle Eastern countries toward more liberal societies in the name of "national security." Elaine Hagopian, professor emerita of sociology at Simmons College and authority on the Arab world, has said, "Since World War II, when the U.S. took over where the colonial powers left off, the U.S. in essence has undermined democracy…As grievances have built up in the Mideast, the fanatic figures, whether they are bin Laden or the Egyptian Islamic Jihad, are able to offer an outlet for that anger."[22]

That anger deepens when the United States offers unqualified support, at least in public, for Israel's iron-fisted rule over the occupied territories. Since election of the militaristic Ariel Sharon, assassination and an accelerated policy of devastation of Palestinian homes and businesses have been the norm. This is a dramatic change from the Israel of Yitzak Rabin, who warned, prophetically, "You don't make peace with your friends, you make peace with your enemies." Rabin was assassinated by a Jewish fundamentalist for daring to try to make peace with the Palestinians. But Israelis will never have security unless they do make peace with the Palestinians; the Palestinians will never have security unless they make peace with the Israelis.

Without memory of what we have actually done and continue to do in the Middle East, Americans are without empathy for the anger that is fueling terrorism. This is especially obvious in the complete rejection by administration leaders such as Donald Rumsfeld of any American responsibility in the bombing campaign. At his October 29 press briefing, he said, "[R]esponsibility for every single casualty in this war, be they innocent Afghans or innocent Americans, rests at the feet of the Taliban and Al Qaeda."[23]

Without self-awareness of our own role in the world, Americans have no way of letting go of blind pride, of finding compassion, and therefore of taking responsibility for their own actions. Thus, we have no way of actually addressing terrorism at its roots. Terrorism is a *response,* and unless and until we can find a way to understand the forces that have been set in motion by our own actions, we *will be* perpetually at war.

Advancing Democracy, Human Rights, and Religious Liberty

Instead of fostering democratic regimes throughout the world, the United States has consistently supported corrupt and oppressive dictators to further American political and corporate interests. This is true in Asia, Africa, and Latin America.

The just peace paradigm advocates the promotion of democracy, human rights, and religious liberty as the long-term solution to world peace. As Bruce Russett notes in his chapter on this norm, "democracies rarely fight each other." This is due to the "pervasiveness of normative restraints on conflict between democracies." This is true of nonindustrial as well as industrial democracies.[24]

Why then would the United States not promote democracy around the world? One reason is that democracy is profoundly destabilizing in the short term. It takes time for societies to build up democratic institutions, to educate citizens in democratic process and to foster a climate of tolerance. Totalitarian regimes are able to suppress the multiple ethnic hatreds that abound in many countries. The period of transition to democracy is very rocky when long-suppressed peoples are able to tell one another precisely how much they hate each other. This can make the establishment of participatory democracy, where one has to learn the art of compromise, quite difficult.

In the Middle East, the dominant religions, Islam and Judaism, have a fundamentalist thrust not only in a religious, but also in a political sense. Islam currently is the political framework for the Taliban, as is evident. These are totalizing worldviews.

Secularization, as happened in the West, has only come to the Middle East in the form of a hasty grab at the surface of modernity—consumerism. The infrastructure of a free market, political parties, accountability in government, and the rule of law is dangerous for the ruling, for the most part monarchial, regimes. Television and McDonald's are not the stuff of societal transformation. For many people in the Middle East this looks like valueless chaos.

Hence the turn to Islam. Fundamentalist Islam offers the rule of law, a structure to daily existence, and an alternative to all things Western. Arab societies are going through a massive population bulge. More than half of the people are under 25. The young men are undereducated, have no jobs, and migrate to the already overcrowded cities. What Americans fail to grasp is that Islamic fundamentalism is a politics of protest. But in an ironic twist of fate, it is a politics of protest fostered by the very corrupt regimes that have failed to provide even the most modest means of life for their ordinary citizens. This is the kind of devil's bargain the monarchies of the Persian Gulf, especially Saudi Arabia, have made. It deflects protest against its shoddy record on political process, human rights, and the economy by building and funding fundamentalist religious schools that teach that the real enemy is all things Western.

We must take the risk of democracy in our foreign policy. It took the attacks on September 11 for Americans to notice the ongoing tragedy of

Afghanistan, and particularly its treatment of women. It took this tragedy for us to notice that 70 percent of Pakistanis can't read and that their *yearly average income* is $200.

As the Taliban has collapsed and we work toward a coalition government, will we promote democracy, human rights, and religious liberty? Will the rights of women be reestablished? Will aid organizations be let back into Afghanistan to help to stem the tide of starvation? The Northern Alliance are not saints. The last time they were in power they pursued a policy of genocide against the Pashan, killing more than 50,000. Their record on human rights for women was no better than that of the Taliban. We will have to put pressure on them to create a civil society. Will we let the need for a base in Afghanistan once again overwhelm the cry of the dispossessed?

But even as we concentrate on the Middle East, we are creating conditions ripe for terrorists in other parts of the world. Millions of American dollars support the School of the Americas, the American training ground for our terrorists. Linda Panetta, regional director of School of the Americas Watch, said "I've just returned from Colombia, where I met impoverished farmers who told us about how their loved ones had been taken, tortured, even had their bodies dismembered because they spoke out against human rights abuses and environmental degradation from the U.S. sponsored fumigation campaign." The School of the Americas has recently changed its name to the Western Hemisphere Institute for Security Cooperation. Its game has apparently not changed.[25]

We will not be free of terrorism unless and until we stop funding terrorism around the world and stop training terrorists. We must never forget we trained Osama bin Laden. Instead of planting the seeds of our own destruction, we need to promote democracy, human rights, and religious liberty. They are ostensibly our core beliefs as Americans. We need to actually take the risk of democracy around the world.

Fostering Just and Sustainable Economic Development

Just and sustainable economic development follows upon democracy as a normative practice of just peace. It is defined as "processes of change in people's relationships to their environment which increase their well-being, standards of living, or quality of life."[26]

Globalization is not proving to be a route to just and sustainable economic development around the world. As Ben Lilliston, communications coordinator at the Institute for Agriculture and Trade Policy, has said, "The form of globalization represented by the WTO will do little to lessen the threat of terrorism. In fact, it is driving greater divisions between the rich and the poor— between developed and developing countries." Why? The developed countries pursue a not often even hidden global agenda of making economic dependents of developing nation-states. In agriculture, this struggle in the WTO is over trade rules that do not "address dumping of agricultural products in the international system. The lack of competition in international commodity markets ensures an asymmetric division of profits; that benefits agribusiness rather than producers or consumers."[27]

No less an authority on international economics than Edward Herman, professor emeritus of finance at the Wharton School at the University of Pennsylvania, has said, "Many have opined that a distaste for 'Western civilization and cultural values' fuels terrorism, but large numbers outside this country believe that Western civilization has hurt them badly. Corporate globalization has unleashed an impoverishment process on the Third World."[28]

The global trading system rewards the haves and does nothing to create the conditions to improve the lot of the have-nots. When one looks at the relative success in Asia of economic development, it is important to note that "in successful East Asian economies, especially Taiwan and South Korea, major land reforms occurred prior to the market opening and state protection of infant industries, and these countries have continued to have among the world's best (least uneven) patterns of income distribution."[29] What is particular to these Asian countries is that they did not regard the poor as unproductive. The land reforms gave the poor access to resources and educational opportunities. This provided a solid base for the development of an internal economy. However, there have been enormous downsides, especially in regard to environmental degradation.[30]

The governments of the Middle East, with wholesale U.S. support, have pursued a completely opposite course in economic development. The rich oil oligarchies show complete contempt for the economic condition of ordinary people; several of these states spend lavish amounts on the royal family and nothing on improving the conditions of their own people. U.S. oil interests once again keep us from demanding that these client states provide a better standard of living for their people. And by no means are all these states rich. The Gulf War, in part, was over oil envy on the part of Iraq for the Rumalia oil field to which Kuwait lays claim. Other states are poor, but they regard development as something driven by the wealthy. Oil and imported Mercedes Benzes do not make economic transformation.

The United States must come to realize that just and sustainable economic development, more along the lines of the countries in Asia cited above, make more stable partners than the iron-fisted monarchies that turn the impoverishment of their own citizens outward into hatred, ironically hatred of the U.S., which has supported them. Totalitarians do not make trustworthy world partners, as we should have learned with Stalin in the twentieth century.

Strengthening the United Nations and International Efforts for Cooperation and Human Rights

"For those engaged in constructing a just peace paradigm, the traditional model of self-contained nation-states—sovereign, secure, distinct—will no longer do…the world has changed too much for this so-called Westphalian model to guide our ethical inquiry."[31] Unfortunately, the recent foreign policy of the current administration seems to have been in the direction of the "model of self-contained nation-states." The United States has become increasingly isolationist even as it pursues global political and economic agendas.

It is instructive, therefore, than even with such an isolationist bent, the U.S. is willing to turn to the United Nations in these days as the Taliban collapses. It has become clear that only the United Nations is capable of mediating the power vacuum that has been left by the collapse of the Taliban. Despite injunctions by the U.S. not to do so, the Northern Alliance's occupation of Kabul was very telling of the power struggle a new cooperative government will face. Afghanistan's basic political structure is tribal, a structure where there is no history of cooperative power sharing. The United Nations, despite some of its failures, is the only organization with enough international support to attempt to stabilize the situation. This is one time the U.S. dare not go it alone.

It is also true that as the winter approaches and starvation becomes ever more likely for millions, calls for the UN to provide peace-keeping troops to protect the aid workers have been widespread. This is another emerging role for the United Nations—to police fragile situations of truce around the world.

I said above that at the end of the Soviet-Afghan conflict, Afghanistan needed a Marshall Plan and we did not provide one. The analogy is not exact. We cannot model post-war Afghanistani recovery on the Marshall Plan. Germany already had a political and economic infrastructure and some history of behaving like a member of the community of nations. Afghanistan has none of these. The analogy is more to post–WWII Japan, where political and economic infrastructure had to be built out of the ruins of a feudal and agrarian society.[32] It is only the UN that could possibly sustain such a process of transformation. It is a critical transformation, because, if successful, it could model transformation for other Middle Eastern states.

The reader will note the number of international aid organizations whose Web sites were consulted in the writing of this article. International aid organizations, NGO's, and INGO's, are fast becoming another power in the world for just peace beyond individuals and nation-states. Organizations such as Doctors Without Borders and Bread for the World command worldwide respect because they are international groups who do not serve any interest beyond the common interest of humanity in relieving suffering. Vaclav Havel has said, "In today's multicultural world, the truly reliable path to coexistence, to peaceful coexistence and creative cooperation, must start from what is at the root of all cultures and what lies infinitely deeper in human hearts and minds than political opinion, convictions, antipathies or sympathies: it must be rooted in self-transcendence…Transcendence is the only real alternative to extinction."[33]

Reducing Offensive Weapons and the Weapons Trade

Just peace norms require long-term thinking about new wars. It is clear that the "new" wars are not between major nation-states, but are erupting out of the Third World and its impoverishment. Creating conditions that lessen impoverishment such as just and sustainable economic development and the democratic structures that permit the flourishing of economic forces are examples of long-term thinking. We must also recognize one of the most destabilizing factors in the world today is the enormous flow of arms to the Third World and the U.S. role in this.

In August 2001 the U.S. Congress issued a report that international arms sales grew 8 percent in the previous year to nearly $36.9 billion. American arms manufacturers accounted for $18.6 billion or roughly half. Of those arms, 68 percent, a healthy majority, were sold to developing countries.

This report, "Conventional Arms Transfers to Developing Nations, 1993–2000," published by the Congressional Research Service, notes in the introduction that "Despite global changes since the cold war's end, the developing world continues to be the primary focus of foreign arms sales activity by conventional weapons suppliers."[34]

But the role of military contracting for the U.S. also has a tremendous immediate impact on thinking about this war on terrorism and why we have made the choices we have in responding. The role of military contractors in promoting war is a major motor of the quick move to bombing in the response to terrorism. Major administration figures such as Dick Cheney are themselves arms manufacturers. Michel Chossudovsky, professor of economics at the University of Ottawa and author of the book *The Globalization of Poverty*, writes, "The imminent shift from civilian into military production would pour wealth in to the hands of military contractors at the expense of civilian needs. Behind the Bush administration is the power of the 'big five' military contractors (Lockheed Martin, Boeing, Raytheon et al.), increasingly in partnership with the oil-energy giants, which are behind many of the regional wars and insurgencies along strategic oil pipelines."[35] Whatever else the war on terrorism is today, one thing that is documentable is that it is enormously profitable, as the stock of arms manufacturers attests on Wall Street.

This is not even to mention the role of the proliferation of nuclear arms and the dangers we run from that. In the fall of 2001 we were debating whether terrorists had nuclear weapons. Nuclear states such as Pakistan have been drawn into this conflict. The devastation of the World Trade Center was horrific. It pales by comparison when we think of nuclear devastation. The world must get control of its nuclear stockpile and begin to destroy it. Severe controls must be in place for those who would seek to produce nuclear materials. We must continue to pursue nuclear nonproliferation treaties.

Conclusion

"There is nothing new under the sun," says the prophet, and in many ways that is true. But this war on terrorism is new in the sense that we have not seen this scale of terror before in human history. A threshold has been crossed, and we will not be able to go back to the norms of conventional wars.

Christian moral thinking on war and peace must respond. The tenets of just war theory no long apply in terrorism. There is no recognized authority, there seem no definite combatants, and we, at least, seem blind to the distinction between combatants and noncombatants. Pacifism challenges us, as always, to refuse violence. But it does not tell us how to actually achieve the things that make for peace on a global scale.

The just peace paradigm offers ten practical strategies that have proven effective in reducing violence and creating long-term structural changes that will eliminate the conditions that produce terrorism.

The thinking of Mohandas K. Gandhi and Martin Luther King, Jr., loom large in the creation of just peace norms. When the world needed it, they showed that seemingly intractable violence could be transformed into greater justice and peace. Terrorism appears to be such intractable violence. But it is not. Peace is always possible. We can always take a step toward it. These steps are not without risk, but war is a profound risk.

Jesus cries over Jerusalem, "Would that you knew now the things that make for peace." We do know some of the things that make for peace. And shame on us if we do not employ them.

Part 5

Life and Faith after September 11

31

Dust and Spirit

Karen Baker-Fletcher

When my grandmother, Kathryn Jett, passed over ten years ago, I found great comfort in the notion of her body mingling in the dust, for reasons I could not explain. I never imagined that would be comforting, but it was an image that came to me in dreams, with all of her—body and spirit riding on the wind, through trees, earth, and water in the warmth of the sun. I later found some of my answers as to why this image was so comforting in Julie Dash's work on Gullah culture, with its earthy, cosmological emphases. And this is where I came up with the concept of sisters of spirit, sisters of the dust and Jesus as Dust and spirit. My books *Sisters of Dust, Sisters of Spirit* and *My Sister, My Brother* (with Garth Baker-Fletcher) cover my earlier reflections on this theme.[1]

I continue to work with this understanding of life and spirit, especially in light of the September 11 attack on the World Trade Center. "Dust" sent me into intellectual and faith crisis as I watched the unbelievable, as it happened, on my television screen. Within twenty-four hours, my husband and I learned that his cousin, Andre Fletcher, a firefighter on site, was missing after entering the first tower that collapsed. Andre's twin brother, Zachary Fletcher ("Cary"), also a firefighter, whose job it was to get people out of the second tower, had not been heard from. We prayed, by phone, with his parents and a dear aunt daily that they both would emerge from the mass confusion. We knew the firefighters were working non-stop. Twenty-four hours or so later, we called our New York family again. Cary had just walked in the door, sent home to rest. Andre was still missing. The next day, Cary went back, looking for his brother and others, hoping for recovery.

It seemed as if Andre were missing forever, until one day, his station had a memorial service for him and his crew, none of whom ever emerged from the dust, rubble, and ashes. They had all been assigned to shut off valves in the sub-basements of that second tower, far below the areas where digging left hope. The heat alone down there is unimaginable...

"Dust" will never be the same for me. I fear that I must confront its hellish aspects, what it means for us in the midst of destruction, face the fact that it is not always a helpful image. I have debated letting go of this image of dust forever. I have decided that is not an option. To do so, I'd have to deny the problem of existential evil that both of these men and their peers faced head-on. I decided the only way out of evil is to confront it and to admit that "dust" continues to be an image of life, but it is also an image of our perishing, which is painful. When we are able to lay our loved ones' bodies to rest, it means one thing. When bodies are desecrated by violence, the whole earth cries out for justice. Below I offer a more academic, intellectual reflection.

Dust as Metaphor

What do I mean by "Jesus as Dust and Spirit" in reflection on incarnational theology and the embodiment of the Spirit in creation, in women, in human beings? And is dust still a helpful metaphor during a time when we are daily assaulted by images of the mass gravesite that holds the remains of those whose lives were taken in the terrorist destruction of the World Trade Center? After 9/11 the metaphorical description of Jesus and humankind as dust and spirit lends itself to more complex, discomfiting, even horrifying understandings. This is not the burial any of us would have chosen for our loved ones. It is far from the beauty of the rippling sea and wind in trees or vast white sands of Nana Peazant's island in Julie Dash's acclaimed film *Daughters of the Dust.*

It is far from Nana Peazant's good soil for planting. It is easy to refer to Jesus as incarnating the Spirit of God in his very earthy, dusty, bodiliness when our images are aesthetically pleasing. To be human and divine is to acknowledge that we are made of earth, water, breath, and heat. Images of natural beauty come to mind. When we think of Jesus as embodying the Spirit of God in this way, we place emphasis on living life abundantly. It is the life of Jesus that is most important in such use of the metaphors.

Daughters of the Dust seems almost romantic in our new world context. So let's be honest and more real. All metaphors are limited. Our experiences of the tragic influence our ability to receive a given metaphor as positive or negative, healing or destructive. The image of "dust" was problematic for some before 9/11. Its underside is even more palpable after waking up to terrorism and war. It must be addressed. As Sallie McFague has observed, every metaphor contains an "is" and "is not." When we say a person is "like a fox" we do not mean that the person *is* a fox. When we "say that 'God is mother'" we "also say 'God is not mother.'"[2] We refer to that which is unseen with images from the visible world. Let's consider the metaphor of dust in light of the evils of terrorism and war. Do I think war is just, or good? There are a multitude of reasons why we may say it is existentially necessary. However, it is always metaphysically and ultimately evil, because violence begets violence, begets further destruction, begets further desecration of earth and sky and life. In truth, it is existentially evil. We delude ourselves if we imagine that our existential, physical decisions do not affect the soul. Isn't this the reason why soldiers hate war more than anyone? They know they risk not only their lives but the well-being of their souls. And they are willing to do this in the hope of defending their nation. So, I have no sense of self-righteousness about war as evil. I have too many loved ones in the military, too many friends with sons and daughters sent on missions overseas. Existentially, war simply exists and always has. I suspect that there will always be war somewhere in the world, whether I like it or not, whether it is good or not, whether it is just or not. I'm willing to admit that the persistence of evil is not in our control in spite of all of our attempts to restrain it. My prayer is always, "God help us all." I had come to this conclusion long before 9/11. But, back to the image of "dust" as it pertains to a theology of life.

Every metaphor has limitations in its effectiveness. "Dust" has multiple meanings for us in our everyday lives. We don't always want to be around it or near it. Certain kinds of dust are toxic, especially many of the synthetic dusts that pollute our air. Natural types of dust are equally unhealthy; for example, the dust from coal causes black lung disease. The dust and debris of war is caused not by creative aims but destructive aims. In order to be honest, we must respect that dust is not always healing nor does it always lead to wholeness. Therefore, dust as a metaphor has limitations. To speak of God as dust positively is to speak of God within creation in its most healing and aesthetic aspects. I would not want to say that God is not in the dust of coal. Everything in creation has a purpose, but we humans frequently abuse and distort it for our own gains.

In process theology, we talk a great deal about the primordial nature of God and God's initial aim in relation to God's consequent nature. The primordial nature of God tends toward the good, toward the well-being of all creation. The consequent nature of God refers to God's response to the existential problems we humans create by participating in evil, which is a distortion of the good and of God's initial aim. Everything that is may be turned toward good or evil. Why does evil exist? I can address the problem of theodicy more fully in another paper. However, let me state the following here. I hold that God shares power with us, and we are created in freedom to choose whether or not we will participate in God's initial aim. Thus, evil results from our decisions not to participate in God's aim toward well-being for all, to understand more wisely our interrelatedness to the entire cosmos, and to engage in creative events rather than destructive ones.

Images of the dust and smoke rising from the earth and rubble of Ground Zero remind us of bodies lost, mixed in dust and smoke, or in subterranean hot waters, a violent, improper burial. The bodies and the dusty earth of New York City have been desecrated by the will to evil in the name of goodness as many other parts of the world have also been desecrated in body, earth, and Spirit. When I look at pictures of the dust and rubble of the World Trade Center and remember a cousin who died in those towers on 9/11, I am horrified. I don't want to be a sister of dust in that way. That is not what I meant. The truth is I never fully considered the underside of the metaphor, leaving the idea of it in a state of ambivalence and a kind of faith crisis. I struggle with the metaphor, finding both hope and despair in it, no longer hope alone. There is the hope of new life and despair of unmerited suffering, the unmerited grace of the Spirit and the unmerited perpetration of evil, a struggle with who or what God is and is not. So, we approach the metaphor with greater honesty and awareness. Some of us will continue to find hope and a celebration of life in it. Some of us may find it no more healing than the glorification of the cross or images of the crucified Jesus. Glorifying the cross, some Africans have argued, is like glorifying an electric chair. As our world changes, old meanings become more complicated and shift; our images of self, Spirit, incarnation, and creation shift as we reevaluate them to recover new meaning.

Scientific Meanings of "Dust" in Feminist/Womanist Process Theology

I still hold on to understanding self and creation as made from the most elemental aspects of the cosmos, infused with Spirit, which is the source of all life and in all life and makes life possible in spite of the will not to participate in God's creative aims and the will to engage in destruction, violation, and desecration of self and world. The fact that this elemental part of us has been desecrated holds within it the truth that our bodies, our selves, our spirits, our Earth have been created good and have sacred worth and value. It is because of this truth that we can even refer to violent acts as desecrating acts. Desecration of life and the dust that emerges from devastating physical destruction does not logically lead to the conclusion that our bodies, ourselves, our planet, are any less sacred than they ever were. The dust of violence is a cause for grieving, because body and earth have been dishonored, blown to the winds, stuck in the rubble, vaporized, disrespected, with all too many stuck in an unchosen gravesite.

What does it mean to be People of Dust and Spirit when we grieve over such violation of body, earth, and Spirit? What does it mean to embody God, like Jesus, as Dust and Spirit as we consider the violation of our bodies and the earth? We've considered "dust" as metaphor. Let's also consider it as a reference to the scientific makeup of this planet, creation, and ourselves. I have chosen dust as a metaphor for very specific scientific and biblical reasons.

In Genesis 2, God creates "adamah," earth creature from the dust of the earth. Scientists find that we and other creatures are made up of basic elements from earth and sea. We are water and physically we are made up of the same quantum energy particles found in a piece of wood, a rock, the earth. We are in some respect the same song in a different, some would say more complex, key. McFague has observed that scientifically we are made from "the dust of stars" if we take "the Big Bang" theory seriously. In a similar fashion, to refer to human beings as people of dust and spirit seeks to respect the most elemental aspects of our creation. To say that we are *of* dust and spirit means that we come from it, are made up of it, are born and created from it.

Yet, at times I have written that Jesus represents God with us *as* Dust and Spirit, straying somewhat from a scientific understanding to suggest a more narrow metaphorical statement that connotes Jesus as representing God who is *like* dust and spirit. For most of the body of my text, I then speak of Jesus as God who is *in* the dust of the earth.

It would be more consistent with my meaning to say that Jesus represents God who is with us in the very earthiness of our bodies and the dustiness of creation. My point is that if we build on Genesis 2, which is supported by Whiteheadian physics and feminist/womanist understandings of the integration of the physical and the spiritual, the God whom Jesus represents is not simply like Dust and Spirit, but is also God who is Spirit in and through every infinitesimal part of creation. If Jesus embodies God in Jesus' message for healing and salvation or wholeness, as human and divine, then we are talking not simply about enfleshed God, but flesh that according to Genesis 2 is created out of the dust of the earth and breathed on by the Spirit.

Both Dust and Spirit still function as metaphors to describe the most infinitesimal, elemental, empowering aspects of reality. Dust functions as a cultural and biblical visceral image for describing spiritual/physical aspects of our makeup that cannot be seen. Spirit is a scriptural and theological term that also refers to this same infinitesimal, unseen source of all life. I employ process metaphysics to undergird a feminist/womanist theology that respects the interrelatedness of all life. I won't enter into a full discussion of actual events and occasions here. To put it most succinctly, we are all physically composed of quantum particles of energy. We are made of the same stuff as rocks and trees and other creatures on Earth. We are composed not only of water and earth and air but of energy and the source of all energy, which womanist theologians often call "the Spirit."

Conclusion

I would like to conclude with the following theological presuppositions for further thought.

(1) When God created earth, the waters, the night and the day, the animals, and the plants, the Spirit that hovered over the waters looked at all that had been created and continuing creation and said it was good.

(2) The will to evil is existentially real. Patriarchy is existentially real, and one of the problems of patriarchy globally is its ability to employ violence in the name of that which is good. We women are not immune to being seduced by this way of seeing the world, especially when we feel threatened by harm.

a. Violation of the body and earth is always evil, even when the ends we seek—e.g., the cessation of violence or the elimination of terrorism or the end of evil—are good. Violation of body and earth violates the Spirit of all parties involved. As Marjorie Suchocki observes, feminist process thought acknowledges that we are made of the same stuff as rocks and trees and other creatures of earth and sea.[3] God, who is Spirit, moves in and through all that is, "like water" coursing around, in and through all that is, connecting us in ways that we tend not to recognize or acknowledge in the business of our everyday lives. This is what makes it possible to feel deeply hurt and touched not only when our loved ones are violated but when perfect strangers are victims of violence. Our hearts sink because we remember that they are a part of us, that the evil perpetrated against one evokes a sense of violation in all of us.

b. When we choose war, in order to stop violence against us, we inevitably find ourselves hurting on all sides—soldiers, mothers, sisters, aunts, daughters, sons, fathers—as we desperately seek a way out of the absurdity of hurting one another in the name of justice and keeping the peace. We hurt on all sides. As Suchocki puts it, it is as if we are connected by thin blue threads that are not visible to the human eye. We are profoundly interrelated, which is why prayer really can effect change as our response to the world changes and when it is felt or experienced within the larger creation. It is also the reason why we hurt when we see strangers hurting.

(3) Jesus was a stranger who became "God with us," "Immanuel." Those who follow Jesus as a profound incarnation of the fulfillment of human potential and possibilities are able to feel with the stranger, to care for the stranger, the stranger within ourselves and the strangers in our everyday midst, those who don't look like us, talk like us, those who are hungry and homeless and as frightened as we are. This is what is most liberating for followers of Jesus, who is Dust and Spirit, the ability to empathize with another's pain even as we seek healing from our own. Jesus the stranger, who is dust and spirit, is more than a fulfillment of what we might become, but a remembrance of our original creation. As we realize our interrelatedness we become increasingly aware that it is true that when one is hurt, all are hurt; when only one of us is free none are free; when one works toward participating in God's initial aim of well-being for all creation, there is a ripple effect in the universe.

(4) Life has been violated. It has been desecrated. But ultimately the best of it is carried forward in the memory of God and does not perish. This memory is part of us, physically and spiritually, consciously and unconsciously, waiting for us to participate in its movement toward fuller realization of possibilities for life and well-being. It is not separate from anything that is. It is in all that

is, even in those we may choose to hate because they chose evil in the name of good. What is evil except some distortion of the good? My prayer is that we look at and learn from the human ability to distort the meaning of "God," "goodness," and "righteousness." In the midst of war, let us not say that war is good. When our nation feels it must retaliate in this way to end terrorism, let's be honest and say that war is evil and sometimes our beloved nation with all its loved ones chooses to participate. Let us say we are praying for our souls and the planet, because existentially there are many in our beloved national family and in the world who cannot envision another way. Let us persuade our nation that there is another way through understanding and compassion rather than through self-righteousness, because we are all part of the same human condition.

(5) Strangely enough, this womanist theologian likes the war novelist and journalist Tom Clancy, for one reason. He can admit that war is rarely if ever moral, and yet we humans engage in it as a means of survival and preserving certain ideals. I like his honesty, not his solutions. I like the fact that he does not try to justify war by saying it is moral. I am troubled, however, that he apparently sees no other way. I mention this popular writer because for a number of years I have noticed his popularity among middle-class Americans as I travel on airplanes. I think it is important to be aware of what people are reading in popular culture. Otherwise, how can we respond to the variety of ways of thinking in popular culture with understanding? I'm not saying all readers take Clancy's fiction and nonfiction writings seriously. But we do need to be aware that his is one way of thinking that sells more books than we do! As theologians, how might we respond to this particular way of thinking? How might we persuade those who think this way to find other ways? That is our most difficult task, isn't it?

32

What Is the War on Terrorism Doing to Us?

Tony Campolo

These are the best of times, and they are the worst of times. They are the best of times because there has been a rebirth of patriotism in the best possible sense of the word. It is not the kind of patriotism marked by arrogance, such as that displayed at the Los Angeles Olympics. That was when we waved our fingers in the faces of the world and yelled, "We're Number One!" We are no longer telling other peoples that we are better than they are; but we *are* saying we are proud of America's ideals and that we believe in the values that undergird our basic institutions. It is patriotism that takes pride in the fact that we are predominantly a nation of immigrants composed of various ethnic groups, each of which has struggled hard to become one nation under God.

It is the best of times in that there has been a rebirth of heroism. We no longer hear the rhetorical question, "Where are the heroes of our age?" We know where they are. They are the police and firefighters who rushed into burning towers while hundreds of people rushed out to safety.

But these are also the worst of times. We see some practices and policies emerging that give evidence of a primitive residue within us. Just when we thought that racial profiling was about to be vanquished, we see it suddenly reappearing. What is most disheartening is that those who had been most victimized by racial profiling prior to September 11 are now among its most adamant supporters. Many African Americans now advocate profiling Arab people. How soon one-time victims forget what they endured and themselves become the victimizers. Right now there are over a thousand Arab men being held—indefinitely—with no specific charges being leveled against them and without benefit of legal counsel. They are enduring this breach of civil rights for no other crime than being deemed "suspicious." The FBI is willing to admit that out of that thousand-plus Arabs, only ten are deemed to have any direct connections with terrorists.

What fears must they be experiencing? What must their families be going through when, in most cases, they do not even know where these men are? And what is wrong with us that we are not outraged by all of this?

I am old enough to remember when tens of thousands of Japanese people were rounded up and put in concentration camps for no other reason than that other Americans deemed them "suspicious." We later said that their imprisonment was wrong and that we would never do that kind of thing again. But we *are* doing it again! And if that is not enough, there is a ruling that, in cases of suspected terrorists, the lawyer/client privilege to private discussions can be breached. The government is claiming the right to listen in electronically on such discussions.

Friedrich Nietzsche once said, "Beware when you fight a dragon, lest you become a dragon." I have to wonder if in our war on terrorists, who, as our President claims, "hate our freedoms," we have come to abridge the freedoms and rights we all hold dear.

What has made it the very worst of times is that it is becoming more and more difficult to get away with talking about Jesus within the church. If you dare to quote Jesus in some Christian gatherings, you are likely to encounter hostility. Instead of hearing "Amens" when reciting the words of our Lord, there is a good chance you will face a stony and angry silence. If, without the required apologies, you should quote what Jesus had to say about how to treat enemies, it should be expected that one or more in the congregation will stand up and walk out. This is not a time when there are ready ears for words such as, "Love your enemies and do good to those who would hurt you." Instead, we want to hear, "An eye for an eye, and a tooth for a tooth."

This is not a good time to quote the golden rule or to repeat Jesus' saying, "Be not overcome with evil, but overcome evil with good." We find that there are many who do not want to hear Jesus telling us that "those who live by the sword will die by the sword." Instead, we want to listen to those stories out of the Hebrew Bible about the God who orders people to wipe out every man, woman, and child of those nations that would stand in the way of God's chosen people (who all too easily we think of as ourselves).

At times like these, we want leaders who will not negotiate with our enemies, and we are turned off by those Paul called to a ministry of reconciliation. Nor do we want anyone to cite the beatitude, "Blessed are the peacemakers, for they shall be called the children of God." We cheer when one of our senators tells us that God might have some mercy on our enemies, but they will get none from us, and we readily forget the Jesus who tells us that only those who *do* give mercy can expect to receive God's mercy.

After I used such sayings from Jesus during a recent Sunday morning service, an irate man scolded me by saying, "This is not the time to say those kinds of things. Statements like that are politically dangerous."

Upon reflection, I thought to myself, when did Christianity cease being politically dangerous? Because when it did, it ceased being Christianity!

Least of all, we are not about to listen to a Muslim mullah from Iran who tells us that we will only end terrorism when we get rid of the poverty and injustices that breed terrorism. We want to believe that terrorism is simply the doing of evil men and that if we can flush them out of mountain caves and kill them, we will be rid of this evil. But even if we articulate such convictions, we know down deep in our hearts that killing the followers of Bin Laden will not end terrorism at all. We know that if we are to end terrorism, we will have to address the conditions that nurture terrorism. We know we must eradicate the poverty that gives rise to the resentments upon which terrorism feeds. Unless we take action against injustices that, in many cases, are blamed on America, we know that the killing of terrorists will only make them heroes in the eyes of the oppressed.

There really is no way to end terrorism without dealing with what is being endured by the Palestinian people. We do not have to compromise the claims of Jesus for a homeland or abandon our most faithful ally in the Middle East to be committed to doing what is right for the Palestinian people. We all know that it is wrong when Israeli tanks rumble onto land belonging to Palestinians, level their houses, and then build huge Jewish settlements on that land. The Israeli government itself acknowledged that the land belonged to the Palestinians when its leaders signed the Oslo Accord. When Palestinian children throw rocks at soldiers who come with the tanks, those soldiers fire on them with live ammunition. We would never tolerate live ammunition being used on rock-throwing children in our country, but we say hardly a word about it when the Israeli soldiers do it.

The worst part of all of this is that we know that such injustices against the Palestinians could never happen without our nation's tacit support. Consider the fact that half of all the foreign aid our government gives away in any given year goes to Israel, and Israel uses a good portion of that money to buy planes and tanks and guns that we sell to them. We are the people who provide the arms that make it possible for Israel to do to Arabs what we would never let Arabs do to Jews.

It saddens me that a primary reason why those in Washington are afraid to stand up for justice on behalf of the Palestinians is because of the unwavering and unquestioning support that the state of Israel gets from the Evangelical community. We Evangelicals (and I am one of them, even if they do not want me to be one of them) have political clout, and the people in Washington know it. President George W. Bush knows that without our support he would not be in the White House. He, along with other lawmakers, knows that there are fundamentalists whose theology motivated them to lend unquestioned support to believing that the rebuilding of the temple in Jerusalem is a necessary prelude to the second coming of Christ. Politicians know the power of televangelists and radio preachers who claim that, if we do not stand with Israel in all that it does, God will not bless America. I have already stressed that we must support the survival and prosperity of Israel, but support does not mean turning a blind eye toward Israel's injustices against the Palestinians.

Please do not get the idea that I am suggesting that the Palestinians are innocent victims. Their own terrorist attacks have wiped out that designation. Nevertheless, they are victims, and if we are going to win the war against terrorism, we must stop the injustices being meted out against them. There is a solidarity among Muslim people throughout the world, and injustice against one of their nations is deemed an injustice against them all.

Second, we must stand against sacrilege against Islam. Most of us do not understand that Saudi Arabia was designated as holy ground by Mohammed and that the U.S. military base situated there is considered a desecration to Muslims everywhere. We also fail to understand how the Infatada, with its rock-throwing rebellion, is a reaction to an "in-your-face" trampling of one of the most sacred places of Islam by the present day Prime Minister of Israel.

A couple of years ago, Ariel Sharon led an army of a thousand soldiers to the Holy Mount where the Jewish temple once stood. The Holy Mount, which now sits on Palestinian land, is believed by Muslims to be the spot from which Mohammed ascended into heaven. Today it is marked by one of the primary mosques of Islam. It was a sacrilege to every Muslim in the world of Islam when Sharon went up there with a thousand soldiers at his side and attack helicopters overhead. What Sharon did should also have outraged Jews. What most of us do not know is that when the state of Israel was formed in 1948, the Jewish rabbis decided that no Jew should set foot on the Holy Mount until their messiah comes. The reason for this is that since the time when the temple was destroyed, no one knows the exact location of the Holy of Holies. You may remember that the Holy of Holies was that special place in the temple where the high priest of Israel went once a year to offer the blood of a lamb on the Mercy Seat with the hope that it would atone for the sins of Israel. No one other then the high priest was ever to set foot on this holy spot. No Jew should set foot on the Holy Mount until the messiah returns, because only he knows the exact location of the Holy of Holies. So why did Sharon go up there? You know why? To use his power to rub the noses of the Palestinians into the ground. There must be repentance for what happened there if the war on terrorism is to be won.

Finally, and perhaps most important, we must give ourselves to alleviating poverty. Consider the fact that more than 4,300 people died on September 11 because of the horrific work of terrorists, but also consider that during the twenty-four hours that made up that same day 30,000 children died either of starvation or diseases related to malnutrition. As third world people watch their children die like that, they believe that there is an affluent nation across the ocean that could help them, and doesn't. It is no wonder that they call our nation "The Great Satan." The fathers of those dead children are viable recruits for terrorism by a madman who is obsessed with bringing down our nation.

To address poverty we can begin by pressing our leaders in Washington to end the embargoes against countries such as Iraq. None of us is so deluded as to think that such embargoes are going to bring down the likes of Saddam Hussein. The people of Iraq are not turning against this totalitarian dictator as a result of the embargo. In reality, the embargo is probably strengthening Hussein's hold on power. Even more importantly, however, the ugly consequences of the embargo are that tens of thousands of children in Iraq are starving, and many die because hospitals lack the necessary medicine. Again, I quote the scripture, which says, "If your enemy hungers, feed him …and if he is sick minister unto him."

The President is right when he says that the war against terrorism will be long and hard. I will only add that it will never end until we work for the justice required by the Hebrew prophets, give respect to Islam, and live out the lifestyle of love and forgiveness prescribed by Jesus in the Sermon on the Mount. Until then, there shall weeping and gnashing of teeth.

33

A Dispatch from Security

Amy Laura Hall

I heard the news while in the woods of North Carolina, on retreat. The serene setting in which I first learned of two towers, four planes, and thousands of people has stayed with me as an absurdly apt marker for my thoughts on the matter. I now write these words while ensconced in my office. Mine is a problematic missive from a safe distance.

We were comfortable—blissfully, blessedly, obscenely so. I was leading a clergy conference, and we had decided to make it a family holiday as well. Walking the trails under tall trees, surrounded by green-tinted sunlight, my husband, my daughter, and I took deep breaths and thanked God for the gift of such a day. Our cushioned lives in Durham seemed almost chaotic in contrast. "Do I have to go back to kindergarten?" my daughter asked, "Mommy, can't we just live here?"

Later that day, while I was lecturing on God, greed, and desire in the *Confessions*, my husband and daughter were sitting in the center's library, reading *Ramona the Brave*. John saw people in the hallway gathering intently around a small radio, and he and Rachel followed. In shock, he only thought after some time that he should move her away from the words, away from the report that rendered us speechless. I recall a tangle of impressions as I both heard the news and noted my daughter's state. Rachel is not a child prone either to silence or to babble; she is conspicuously loquacious. In reaction to the unspeakable, she had begun shifting back and forth from catatonic silence to jumbled syllables, perhaps attempting to make some sense by way of nonsense.

My own reaction was a motherly inversion of my daughter's fear. I immediately attempted to shut out the words that had shattered our idyllic holiday, to recreate a setting in which such things do not terrify. I vowed then and there to summon her back to speech, to her usual, intrepidly interpreting self. "The sky is not falling, my love." "We are safe." "We are far, so very far, away from those buildings." "Let's eat some bread and peanut butter, go for a walk, remain here, not go back." Rachel's previous query returned with new salience, "Mommy, can't we just live here?"

Although the conference participants prayerfully decided to return to their parishes, my husband and I remained, seeking to sustain the lull that we now yearned for with a palpable intensity. It was surreal, playing with Rachel, eschewing the radio, wishing to listen and to speak of the matter, but daring not even to whisper of it in her presence. But around the edges of the next day, I was working, silently, on my own interpretation. From the safety of the wooded hills, I summoned forth again and again an image. "Come, let us build for ourselves a city, and a tower with its top in the heavens, and let us make a name for ourselves…Come, let us go down, and confuse their language there, so that they will not understand one another's speech."

This mantra became soothing, almost as pacifying as the verdant setting itself. They have built a tower, a tower that intrudes upon the heavens, a tower to make a name for themselves, and God has crumbled the tower and their name. When I offered this interpretation in hushed tones to my husband, after Rachel was sleeping soundly, he stared, horrified, and implored me to keep it to myself. But I constructed this heuristic, piece by piece, brick by brick, in the quiet hours that followed the dreadful day. Do not worry, my love, come back to speech, resume your courageous discernment, we are a long, long way from New York City.

I was able to prop up my edifice, seeming to scrape the heavens with my trenchant observations, until we returned. Leaving that place of retreat, increasingly bombarded with verbal descriptions of the mind-numbing, visual images I had tenaciously avoided, I could no longer methodically add brick upon brick. Sitting in my car, weeping uncontrollably while listening over the radio to another mother's tears, I glimpsed that there was no plausible, no righteous, no truthful way to climb over the suffering. I knew then that I had misunderstood my task as a mother and as a theologian. Faced with the unutterable, faced with my own daughter's incapacity for coherent speech, I had sought to craft space for a meaning that spared us both. I believe now that there is no such meaning.

If there is a way faithfully to receive speech in the midst of this, I suspect it is inextricably bound up with much I tried to avoid. Other Christians have in various eloquent ways suggested that this event brought the suffering of the world to our very doorstep. We have received a fleeting glimpse of the eviscerating images that haunt the drawings of a Palestinian child. We have briefly overheard the screams with which a Rwandan survivor wakes herself nightly. But the vision and the hearing have been blessedly ephemeral. A stark contrast to which we were all privy remains: one woman in Manhattan wails against God with profound, gut-wrenching indignation while an Afghani woman, asked whether she fears American reprisal, tells us that she can imagine nothing beyond the numbing pain that is her life.

Are we therefore to wish for more bloodshed here in our land so that real meaning might abound, so that we might identify in solidarity with the wretched of the Earth? Before I seek masochistic solace in this answer, I must recognize that there is something right, even truthful, in the first woman's rage. We were not created to be silent when splattered by the blood of our young. Lamentation, even indignation, is a response for which we seem to be hardwired, unless we have become deadened by distance or perpetual pain. That many children of Palestine and Israel are, out of fear, wetting their beds at midnight in spite of the soothing lullabies sung to them at dusk is a genuinely terrible thing, a thing we should not wish on anyone—even ourselves. We are not meant to eke out an existence at the edge of hell. Contrary to the heroic words that reverberate still around the rubble, most of us do not heartily thrive as chaos ensues. Most of us jump, or push.

No, wishing for suffering for the sake of sustained solidarity makes little sense. The Marxist in me, the part of me that dearly loves Amos and Micah, longs for America to reap fully what we have sown. But then I sing "Over in Killarney" as Rachel falls asleep. I watch her eyelids flutter and then, slowly, fall, and I wonder at my hubris.

Seeking the space within which our children may learn the alphabet and gain the security to sleep through the night is not in itself contrary to the will of God. To suggest such a simple thing has been the error of many a left-leaning talking head. What is suspect, and what we in America must learn vulnerably to detect, is the comfort we have gained at the expense of others. Our security and pleasure are, in a profound way, wrongly obtained. As we tuck our children in at night, in Little Mermaid sheets made by malnourished women in Sri Lanka, amidst the soft glow of a Snoopy nightlight manufactured by children in Matamoros, we are sheltering them with the worn limbs of our neighbors. Only alongside this utterly disturbing realization may we begin to rebuild.

And inasmuch as we protect ourselves daily from the cries of those on whose labor we feast and rest, we tempt the wrath of God. I sit and type these words while wearing a pair of pants made in Bangladesh, and the tag inside is a fine example. Next to the words "Made in Bangladesh," the designer has sprightly added, "BELIEVE THAT LIFE IS FUN." So much of American culture exists at the intersection of these two claims. With money gained from global capitalism, we may purchase well-priced goods in the global market. And we may enjoy them, truly enjoy them, as we watch productions meticulously orchestrated to wipe away any inkling that our comfort is causing another to suffer. Watch protests on the evening news, and we will intersperse images of happy families at McDonald's. Or listen to wailing on *All Things Considered* followed shortly by *A Prairie Home Companion.* Believe that life is fun, and it may be so.

I suggest that another searing image from the past few months must continue to burn into our moral imaginations and complicate our speech. In the photograph, a group of Muslim men hold up a sign, "Americans, think, why do so many people hate you?" We may mark as the triumph of NFL culture that so many Americans respond defiantly, "Because they're jealous of us, that's why!" Others sentimentalize the heroism of the event in order to apply a safely innocuous veneer: the real message of 9/11 is not about hate but the triumph of human love. Either way, we seek the same false solace I sought in the hills of North Carolina. Reerecting our national manhood or reestablishing domestic tranquility—each response requires an ignorant distance from the wounds we inflict.

No, we cannot just live in retreat. Americans cannot continue to live here, in a world that is falsely, resolutely secure. Rowan Williams, in a forthcoming piece called *Writing in the Dust,* has put this point to us very well:

> We want the goods that unrestricted markets can bring (unrestricted in the sense that no one other than the prosperous restricts them). But we have yet to come to terms with what the greater part of humankind believes to be the corollary of this: that the prosperous will be seen as the makers of poverty. In the global village, the one who becomes rich is seen as the thief of his neighbour's goods.[1]

The language with which we must speak in the midst of potential chaos cannot be wrought of the stuff of the past. And yet, as I write this, America is in a building frenzy everywhere, seeking to restore our comfort, seeking to remind ourselves and our children of the false words that have brought us to a point of such profound greed and avoidance.

I believe that the way into meaning, if there is such, will be different than the means by which I have so often forged it. Hoping for clarity, I must know myself confused. Wishing for security, I must find myself exposed. In all this, I believe that I must know myself newly, frightfully, vulnerable. While I may will this for myself, I have no earthly idea how to will it for my small child. May I reasonably hope that God will provide such, perhaps that God has provided such in the Word who is the condition for the possibility of speech itself? If the meaning in all this cannot be gained in the midst of retreat and comfort, then how may I speak? If meaning cannot be *gained* at all, my speech must somehow be a testimony to the radically contingent, fragile, *reception* of words themselves. And if I cannot receive such testimony apart from the tears of mothers in New York and in Afghanistan, if my testimony is tied up with, God help me, the tears of my own child, my life must, somehow, be transformed.

In the meantime, I suspect that mine is merely a false dispatch, a confused missive from ill-gotten security.

34

In a Time Such as This[1]

Ada María Isasi-Díaz

The Twin Towers once stood about forty miles from Drew University, where I teach ethics. A few days after the September 11 tragedy, when the Manhattan bridges opened and I was able to get to the university, I took time in my classes to analyze what had happened. Virtually every person I have talked to or heard in the news has used four words to describe what they feel, to describe their reaction to the tragedy: anguish, pain, fright, and loss. The students also expressed these overwhelming feelings and emotions.[2] Again and again I keep asking myself and others, "How did we get from anguish, pain, fright, and loss to the bombing of Afghanistan? Answer me this," I insist. "How come it is considered patriotic to exact vengeance instead of extending forgiveness? How come it is considered patriotic to curse those responsible for the tragedy of September 11 instead of feeling compassion for them?"

Answers like "We must not show weakness" or "We need to make sure that something like this never happens again" simply do not ring true. Such responses avoid looking at all that happened before September 11. They refuse to take into consideration what led to that day of disaster. These answers avoid analyzing U.S. policies that so devastate a significant number of people that they are willing to follow orders at the expense of their own lives. When the nightly news, for example, has shown non-Afghan men crossing into Afghanistan to join the Taliban forces, the same thought came to me: Why are they willing to risk their lives? I can understand that a few men, and even more than a few, are fanatics bent on destroying others to forward their cause. But when there are significant numbers of people who are willing to follow those extremists, something is happening that the rest of us cannot dismiss or ignore.

Virtually every opinion I have read or heard that has dared to question the response of the U.S. government (a point at which I find myself in this article right now) has made it clear that what happened on September 11 is not being condoned in any way whatsoever. I join them. I denounce all violence; I denounce all taking of human life and, therefore, unequivocally, I denounce and protest, I abhor and condemn what happened on September 11. But precisely for the same reasons that I cannot in any way whatsoever excuse what happened then, for those same reasons I denounce and protest, I abhor and condemn the bombing of Afghanistan and any and all actions that are death-dealing instead of life-giving. If we designate as fanatics and extremists those who planned, approved, and executed the dreadful acts of September 11, what do we call those who bomb a country where the majority of its citizens are women and children, a country with no means of defense against such bombing?

The people of New York City, soon after September 11, turned Union Square into one big altar full of candles, signs, and symbols of their anguish, pain, fright, and loss. At the edge of the zone in lower Manhattan closed for many days after the tragedy, Union Square became a sort of open-air church where we went to be with others, to console one another, to see if we could help one another understand what had happened, to attempt to help find ways of moving on with our lives. I happened to go on the evening that city officials had decided it was time for us to move on, to go back to being consumers, a role they have reminded us of repeatedly since the early days after the tragedy. The night a colleague and I went there, the city had cleaned the place, filling dozens of garbage bags with the mementos and symbols the people had created to ritualize their fright and pain, their loss and anguish. But New Yorkers are a fierce brand of people. There they were, setting up the altar again, posting signs, lighting candles, discussing and preaching, crying and finding comfort in the arms of strangers. Nothing impressed me more that day than a flyer pasted in different areas of the park that said, "Not in my son's name." A mother refused to allow her son's death to be used by the authorities as the reason for bombing Afghanistan, as the reason for the U.S. to engage in acts strikingly similar to those of the terrorists on September 11.

Another day begins. The sun is about to rise above my horizon, a horizon crowded with the buildings of upper Manhattan. But for those of us who live in this city, for the time being there is no longer "just another day." Instead, the precariousness of life that became so palpable on September 11 has made us fill our days with such intentionality that every day now has its own features, characteristics, and goals. Each day has to be faced specifically so we can live through the anguish, pain, fright, and loss that subsume our lives. And each day, which we now live so carefully, gives us the opportunity to understand ourselves, individually and as a people, in a very different way from the lighthearted reflections of those lazy days of last summer. As I drive across the George Washington Bridge, I turn to look at the scarred skyline of Manhattan and pray for those who died and their families. The fully armed men who patrol the sidewalks of the bridge remind me of the other military personnel carrying out the orders to bomb Afghanistan and those who are ready to invade it and carry out ground combat. Those who patrol this Manhattan bridge with machine guns remind me how the illusion of safety has disappeared from my life, how from now on I stand with the millions of women, children, and men who day after day, all around this world of ours, live in danger of dying an untimely death.

Knowing in a Different Way

I have purposefully laid out the themes of this article in a long introduction that is different from the one traditionally used in academic discourse. I have done this in an attempt to gather first feelings and emotions, and only secondarily, understandings and reasons. I follow this structure to highlight the role of emotions and feelings in learning and in the work of ethics. The anguish, pain, fright, and loss so prevalent in our lives nowadays make it more obvious than ever that emotions and feelings play a role in what we know, how we know it, how we process what we know, and how we allow it to impact our lives. I am here trying to go beyond the mere assertion that our worldview or ideology, the position from which we know, and the implications of our knowing affect or determine what we know. In a way my assertion is simple, not at all extraordinary or new, but inescapable all the same: Our emotions and feelings, and not just our ability to reason and to understand, are central elements of our knowing. Our emotions and our feelings, as a matter of fact, put us in touch with reality in a way our intellect does not. The wrenching emotions and feelings that the September 11 catastrophe aroused in us do not cloud our thinking and understanding, but rather illumine it. Without them our knowledge is incomplete, our understanding is severely hampered, our reasoning is faulty. It is precisely our emotions and feelings that make it possible for us to be involved in such a way that we can claim to know, to have learned something from the situation we have experienced and about which we have some information.[3]

To know reality, I believe, one has to be, first of all, enmeshed in a situation; one has to be impacted and affected by it.[4] Many things we come to know are not part of our immediate experience. In this case solidarity becomes key, for solidarity is what allows us to become enmeshed in situations that are removed from us experientially, but that impinge on our lives. The farther something is from our experience, the more difficult it is for us to be touched by the reality of things instead of merely being in touch with ideas about reality. To be touched by reality, one has to be in touch with its materiality, and since our personal experience is limited, since our touching others and situations in which we are not involved is limited by the finitude of our humanity, the only way we can come to "touch" this reality is through a deep sense of solidarity. Emotion, then, makes it possible to become enmeshed in the materiality of situations and other people's lives in ways that intellect does not.

I did not know personally, as far as I have been able to ascertain, anyone who died in the Twin Towers, the Pentagon, or the airplane crash in Pennsylvania. Yet the physical immediacy of what happened, its enormous scope, the images seared into my mind by television replays, the surreal image of smoke rising from lower Manhattan, the absence of the Towers in the Manhattan skyline, the increased security at airports and train stations—all this enmeshes me in what happened and makes it possible for me to know this devastating reality in a much better way than if I only read about it.[5]

The second necessary element of knowing involves taking responsibility for what has happened in the sense of shouldering what it requires, what it demands, what it exacts from us. This is the ethical component of knowing that one cannot effectively evade. And here is where we need to look carefully at what public officials, the government, and the media have done with us, with you and me personally. For what has happened is that our anguish, pain, fright, and loss have been abducted and turned into violence. What has happened is that we have been told that the best—and only?—reaction possible is a violent one, one that demands retribution. Let us be very clear: retribution is but a thinly disguised version of vengeance, and vengeance is never an ethical action. It is wrong to seek vengeance in and of itself. Furthermore, it has been proven time and again that vengeance generates only more violence. Violence does not satisfy those seeking to exact some sort of payment for what they have suffered.

The day after the disaster, I went out in my neighborhood in upper Manhattan to buy fruit and vegetables. I went into the little neighborhood stores where I have been going for the last twelve years. The sense of anguish, pain, fright, and loss was so obvious. People looked at each other and simply sighed. We sensed that we each knew what the other was thinking, what the other was feeling, what concerned us all. The usual assertiveness and impatience of New Yorkers were gone. Incredulity seemed to have replaced our brashness, and all we could do as we looked at each other was shudder. Then I returned home to the lone functioning television station[6] to face the barrage of violent language that had become standard by then, to watch how our emotions were being hijacked by the government in an attempt, I believe, to keep us from thinking about how part of the responsibility for what happened lies squarely on the shoulders of this nation. Government officials could have chosen to react in some other way, but instead, all we heard from them was an immediate declaration of war, language that debased others, that offered no solution but vengeance, and that equated patriotism—love of country—with military action. Indeed, they continue to assure us this is the only possible solution. Would we not know better and understand more clearly what happened on September 11 if our anguish, pain, fright, and loss had been channeled a different way? Would we not know better if our emotions had been used to help us understand those who were attacking us instead of turning them into enemies that we, as a nation, vow to destroy, that we, as a nation, vow to obliterate from the face of the Earth?

The anguish, pain, fright, and loss we feel can very well be placed at the service of making us go beyond our regular pattern of analyzing and dealing with situations in which we are involved, in which we place ourselves always at the center, making ourselves the main point of reference. The profound emotions that gripped us on that frightful September 11 have made us vulnerable, and when we are vulnerable we are able to allow into ourselves what in our regular state of mind we persistently keep out: people, events, and ideas that challenge our priorities and make us lay aside our rational/ cost-analysis/how-does-this-benefit-me way of confronting reality. Here is an opportunity for us to go beyond ourselves and in so doing to grow in the best ways possible. Here is a moment where the intensity of emotions and feelings has made it socially acceptable for us to lead with our hearts. It could have been possible or easier for us to break through our usual way of thinking and to shoulder part of the responsibility for what happened. We might have understood it in a different way. However, this new and untried way of thinking was immediately made impossible by the leaders of our communities, who have had one unswerving message for us: the best way, the only way, to cope with the situation, to act in a responsible way, is to endorse a military response. Because our anguish, pain, fright, and loss were transformed into feelings of revenge, our knowledge of what took place on September 11 has been distorted. It has been perverted. War is the one and only ethical response that has been envisioned and endorsed by our governmental representatives and, yes, even by most of our church leaders. This leads us to ignorance of what really makes our political actions questionable.[7] The total unwillingness of those who speak for us and to us to look for alternatives to a violent response to the events of September 11 has left us bereft of moral decisions that enhance life and expand goodness and kindness, trust and love, solidarity and compassion in our world.

Acting in a Different Way

The third element of knowing reality has to do with the action-oriented pole of knowing, for we have long left behind the idea that we can know in the abstract or that we can claim to know and understand and not do anything about it. Here I affirm that *not acting* on what we claim to know is not neutral. It is a positive something in the sense that it results in our endorsing the way proposed. This action-oriented moment of knowing follows on the heels of the ethical component of knowledge that requires us to take responsibility for reality in order to really know it. Perhaps here is where we can begin to unmask and deconstruct the "knowledge" of September 11 that has been elaborated by the government and the media. As we reject the military solution, as we attempt to influence the way the U.S.A. as a nation is acting, we begin to create a different narrative—a different discourse—of what happened September 11. We begin to honor the anguish, pain, fright, and loss that we experience day in and day out; we begin to allow ourselves to lead with our hearts and to come to know reality in a different way. But we cannot do this unless we act in a different way. The "official" interpretation of what happened is so potent and pervasive that we cannot just sit in front of our television sets and attempt to think differently from what we are being told. We have to allow ourselves to act into knowing, to feel into knowing, in a different way. This is the ethical and epistemological challenge facing us. Our responsibility is to act differently so we can know differently. How do we "act-know/know-act" in a way that makes us agents of life, of fullness of life, instead of dealers of death? Knowing that how we act toward others and what we know is constitutive of who we are, how do we love ourselves in the present situation so that we can love others?

Thich Nhat Hanh, a Vietnamese Buddhist monk, prophet of peace, spoke at Riverside Church shortly after the September 11 tragedy. In his address he took our anguish, pain, fright, and loss and led those present to a different place from where we have been directed by the government and the media. Instead of using violent language and war images, the Buddhist monk helped his audience to lead with their hearts, to be in touch with and to understand the desperation behind the acts of September 11. To be in touch with and to try to understand the situation that gave rise to the attacks in no way means condoning what happened or attempting to excuse from responsibility those who planned the attacks and helped carry them out. However, it does mean that we take responsibility for asking the hard questions instead of leaving them for others to ask and then condemning them for doing so. It means that we honor our anguish, pain, fright, and loss, but that we do so knowing that we now simply join the vast numbers of people all over the world, as well as marginalized groups in this country, who feel and have felt this way for generations. Thich Nhat Hanh took our anguish, pain, fright, and loss and made us realize that the way we respond to what has happened definitely colors our understanding of those events, understanding that we then turn into a rationalization for what we do. The Vietnamese Buddhist monk proposed that we respond differently from the present course. He suggested that instead of bombing Afghanistan we should flood with aid that country and other countries in that part of the world that are poor beyond our comprehension. This aid, coming from people made vulnerable by fear and pain, would not be self-serving, aid with strings attached, to help us to control others in a more efficient way, but rather, respectful aid that would enable those nations to stand on their own.

In a time such as this, Thich Nhat Hanh's presentation suggests, how different our world would be if instead of becoming cheerleaders for war the United States would lead the world in efforts to respect one another and our different ways of life! To be able to act in such a way, we have to know "those people" as intrinsically connected to us, as indeed they are, and ourselves intrinsically linked to them, as indeed we are. To submerge ourselves in the process of "knowing differently-doing differently" we have to recognize, appreciate, and cherish the common interests that we have as human beings. To "know differently-do differently" we have to realize that the globalization process, which we find of so much benefit to us in this country, also creates an interdependence that carries with it the same responsibilities characteristic of all mutual relationships.

If our knowing does truly depend on our ability to be in touch with the reality we claim to know, and if it depends on our taking responsibility for it, it is no less true that our knowing depends also on our taking action on the reality in which we are enmeshed and for which we are responsible. All reality that touches our lives in some way changes us and is changed by us. Therefore, what we do following on what we comprehend throws light back on what we have understood. The way in which we are actively present in any given reality affects how we know that reality and, consequently, what that reality is for us, what it means for us, how it affects us. Concretely, if we had spent the millions of dollars the bombs dropped over Afghanistan have cost us for humanitarian aid for the people of Afghanistan, we would come to know what happened on September 11 in a different way, a difference that would then ground our future actions in this moment in history. Yes, if we had been convinced to act humanely, even if we were not very sure it was going to be effective, even if we were not convinced that it was going to stop future acts of terrorism in our world, if we had acted differently, we would know ourselves and the tragedy that we suffer differently. We would know those who inflicted such wounds on us and the tragedy that they suffer in a very different way.

The anguish, pain, fright, and loss that have been turned into a patriotism that exacts nothing but vengeance and leads only to violence should instead lead us to compassion. Yes, compassion for those who have hurt us, compassion for those whose way of thinking and believing led them to overcome the human instinct for self-preservation, is a befitting way, a moral way to be present in the reality that we know as September 11. Compassion is an ethical attitude and praxis that in a time such as this is indeed redemptive, not only for those to whom we show compassion but also for ourselves who have the opportunity to be compassionate.

In Times Such as This: Compassion

Compassion in a time such as this is indeed a brave and courageous act. Compassion in a time such as this is not an extraordinary act. Neither is it an inappropriate response for public–political–acts. Compassion is a necessary disposition and way of acting in the present circumstances, for it helps us to understand the needs and relationships that are part of this situation. Furthermore, it is my contention that without compassion we cannot see the real consequences of the response the U.S. government to the September 11 attack.[8]

Compassion demands of us beneficent actions that must arise from a concrete concern for the good of others. Compassion is what in ethics we refer to as a virtue, that is, a habitual disposition concerned with choosing both how to act and how to feel.[9] Compassion, as well as any other virtue, does not exist in the abstract. One who is compassionate is so only because she or he does compassionate acts, and such acts are born from a way of feeling, from a disposition that has to be rooted in the heart as well as in the mind. How do we acquire such a disposition? How do we become compassionate people? How do we act in a beneficent way toward those who have harmed us? How does being compassionate help us to know the dreadful reality of September 11?

The virtue of compassion does not arise solely from an act of the will. Neither does it come solely from a kind heart. The virtue of compassion—feeling and action combined—needs to be practiced time and again so it can become second nature. The practice of compassion starts with our ability to feel with and for others and, in order to do that, we have to value the other, we have to believe that those "others" have something to contribute to us and to the world, something intrinsic to our well-being. We act in a compassionate way, and we have concern for the good of "others," for their sake as well as for our own sake.[10] To have compassion toward others, therefore, we need to allow ourselves to be vulnerable, or rather, we need to recognize that we *are* vulnerable instead of pretending that we are impenetrable and self-sufficient. Vulnerability is openness to being affected, moved, and convinced by someone else. Openness here refers to an attitude and a belief that our truth is not necessarily the only truth and even that our truth might be wrong, which means that the truth of other persons might be right.

Again, I am not suggesting, by asking us to be compassionate toward those who attacked us, that we condone what they did. I am asking us, however, to leave behind the imperialist position that rules every aspect of the U.S.A. as a nation and of our lives as a people. The U.S.A. is a great nation, but to others it may be only the most powerful, not necessarily the greatest. Most probably, they believe that their own nation is the greatest! For us, this may be the best system in the world, but for others—with other cultural and historical backgrounds—this system may not necessarily be the best system. We have every right to defend our way of life, but not at the expense of other people, of placing them all at the service of our way of life, of imposing upon them our way of life.[11] We need to see ourselves in relation to these "others," and we need to respect their ways of life and their beliefs.[12] The anguish, pain, fright, and loss that the events of September 11 have caused give us a window of opportunity for being vulnerable to others and therefore, for feeling the need to be compassionate. Anguish, pain, fright, and loss can indeed provide for us the opportunity for "emotional thinking," for turning to others in a different way, for de-centering ourselves and considering the situation as others see it and in view of others. September 11 provides us with a rich opportunity to practice courageously the virtue of compassion, a virtue that is needed if we are to attain the fullness of humanity for which we were created. We may not be in the habit of being compassionate, but here is an opportunity to move in that direction, an opportunity we cannot waste, an opportunity for which we will be held accountable.

We must be compassionate and concerned for those who attacked us and hurt us in such a grievous way if for no other reason than because of the interconnection that exists among us. In this day and age the interconnection among all peoples is more obvious than ever. Globalization is a reality at many levels of our lives. Consider communications: there is almost instantaneous accessibility to worldwide information, and one can reach almost every corner of our planet in less than forty-eight hours. Think of the economy: before Wall Street opens in Manhattan, we are told how it will be affected by markets in other parts of the world. Of course, the economy of the U.S.A. buoys up or drags down the economies of many other countries. What about ecology? Acid rain does not stay inside any given country's borders; global warming does not occur in only one area of the planet; and the deterioration of the ozone layer responds to practices in many different countries. Consider health: the AIDS epidemic certainly has no boundaries. These realities affect all humanity regardless of the country in which we live. Therefore, compassion for those who attacked us, being concerned about them and acting toward them in a beneficent way have specific and immediate repercussions for everyone. We should indeed be feeding the people of Afghanistan, not as part of a propaganda blitz aimed at turning them against the Taliban, but out of a deep sense of compassion. The Afghanis have suffered and continue to suffer in unspeakable ways, partially because of our own dealings with them—using them as chess pawns—for several decades. Our lives are very much intertwined with theirs; we have furthered our cause, our economic well-being, and our political influence by using the Afghanis.[13] It is now obvious that we have explicitly tied their destiny to ours. In a time such as this, when thousands are in refugee camps, when so many Afghani men have died that a disproportionate number of women and children make up the population, when they are facing such a harsh winter and widespread famine, in a time such as this, we are called to be compassionate. We do have an option other than the one we have embraced. As a nation we must reverse ourselves and become compassionate toward Afghanistan.

Finally, compassion is a much more life-giving way of channeling the anguish, pain, fright, and loss that we all feel. Compassion respects and honors those feelings, while revenge and vengeance betray them. Violence and revenge lead only to more violence and play into the hands of those who have done violence to us. Religious leaders expressed this concern immediately after the September 11 tragedy. We must "face deep and profound questions of what this attack on America will do to us as a nation…We assert the vision of community, tolerance, compassion, justice, and the sacredness of human life, which lies at the heart of all our religious traditions…Let us make the right choices in this crisis—to pray, act, and unite against the bitter fruits of division, hatred, and violence. Let us rededicate ourselves to global peace, human dignity, and the eradication of injustice that breeds rage and vengeance."[14]

In a time such as this, we must honor our anguish, pain, fright, and loss and work to increase goodness in the world instead of violence. In a time such as this, we must concentrate on being as generous as possible, on being as compassionate as possible for the sake of all of humankind. We are always called to be the best we can be. We are always called to be life-giving and not death-dealing people. In a time such as this, let us grow in stature in the eyes of our children and of the rest of the world. Let us welcome and embrace the call and the grace to be compassionate.

35

Christian Intellectuals and Escapism after 9/11

Charles T. Mathewes

In the wake of September 11, the intellectual and religious left was presented with two basic strategies for responding to the horrendous events. One option was to put as much daylight as possible between the causes that leftists support–reducing poverty, reining in corporate rapaciousness (particularly in the Third World), environmentalism, anti-globalization, "social justice," among others–and the unspeakably nefarious, utterly despicable acts of the terrorists: to insist that the left's basically liberationist and egalitarian aims fundamentally have nothing whatsoever to do with bin Laden's fanatical, fascistic fantasies. The other option was to attempt simultaneously to avoid directly affirming the attacks, while still indirectly associating them with the left's agenda–to suggest that the attacks are in some sort of way driven by the same basic problems that drive the left, that Osama bin Laden and Mother Jones are in some fundamental way working for the same causes, if only because they oppose the same thing–namely, U.S. hegemony.

What in the world made almost all leftist intellectuals, seemingly independently, choose the second strategy?

To think that there's any affinity between the left and al Qaeda is wantonly to ignore the facts of the case. While many leftists associate bin Laden with their own criticism of U.S. policy toward Israel and Iraq, in 1990 bin Laden offered to defend Saudi Arabia with his own troops *against* Iraq (which is, after all, nobody's model of an Islamic state); and the word on the Arab street is that bin Laden isn't really serious about the Palestinians, that he's a Johnny-come-lately to the cause. What really drives bin Laden crazy is the U.S. military's defiling presence in Saudi Arabia, the Holy Land of Mecca and Medina. If he can throw in some solid anti-Israel grievances as well just to amplify his voice (larded with a heavy dose of sheer anti-Semitism, hard to distinguish in almost all Arab and Muslim—and much European—discourse about Israel), well, then, so much the better. And needless to say, bin Laden is hardly a Gramscian "organic intellectual" resisting U.S. hegemony; indeed, al Qaeda is inconceivable without globalization. So there's not really much at all in the way of a common agenda between bin Laden and the intellectual left. Before September 11, I doubt any leftist would have thought to say anything about bin Laden except to condemn him in the strongest terms for his antihumanism, his sexist absolutism, and his vicious intolerance. And they would have been right. With friends like these, who needs enemies?

That's the meat of the problem I want to address here. Today the left does not worry about who its friends are, because it's too busy hating its enemies. If you kill and oppress your own people, you're probably a bad guy. But if you manage to kill U.S. civilians in large numbers—well, hey, that's understandable.

The root problem this reveals is a *religious* one, and it must be addressed as such, on explicitly religious grounds. The problem revealed is the difficulty of resisting our perennial temptation to construe the world in fundamentally dualistic terms, whether "agonically" as in the "clash of civilizations" talk one hears so frequently from the right wing, or more "victimologically" as one hears regularly from the left. The problem is that the left still believes in the devil but no longer has faith in any God: They still are organized around a base hatred of capitalism, even after the God of socialism has so dramatically and publicly failed.

It is no small irony that, of the three groups in whose words and deeds I am most interested—the terrorists, the Bush administration, and the intellectual left—only the Bush administration managed, in the wake of September 11, blessedly not to conform to expectations. That should be the cause of some serious, concentrated reflection on the part of intellectuals on the left. That it has not yet sparked such reflection should itself be a further topic of rumination. And also shame, and a rich, and livid, sense of betrayal by many who, like me, think of themselves as on "the left." But here I want to focus on the rumination.

The Effective Gnosticism of Modern Intellectual Life

To begin with, note how the idea of "America" operates, in much leftist discourse, in a fundamentally metaphysical way, without any further analysis, as an analytically functional concept. The left's interpretation of the events promotes the worst possible picture of the United States, straining credulity wherever possible, accepting what incredible rumors fit their dogmatic metaphysics of American evil (Mossad pilots in the planes; faked or decades-old footage of Palestinians dancing in the streets; the idea that the attacks were "preemptive strikes" [!?!] unleashed out of fear that the U.S. was about to attack bin Laden–though at the magnificent incoherence of this last even some of the true believers blink). The point is not the individual credibility of the stories themselves; rather, their attraction lies in the way they fit the preset ideological frame within which the left's intellectual program is trapped. Many people, myself included, have worried about an incipient dualism in public discourse in the United States between "America" and "terrorism" expanding to fill all imaginative space in the current situation; in this view, "you're either with us or against us." This attitude asphyxiates genuinely critical thought before it can even begin. But the dualistic rhetoric of "American capitalism" or "American consumer culture" or "American culture"–a rhetoric for which the left bears some considerable responsibility, and to which it remains stubbornly loyal–functions in no way fundamentally different from this purportedly "patriotic" dualism. All such rhetorics are rhetorics of demonization, rhetorics which various extremist groups, not all of them Islamic by any means, employ to guide and justify their actions.

Nor, unfortunately, do I think that the parallels rest entirely on the conceptual level; they infiltrate the psyches of those who employ them as well. Several days after the attack I heard a good friend in my discipline expostulate, with something not unlike enthusiasm, about the damage inflicted on "America" by the terrorists. What struck me was not that he was expressing any terrible sincerity at the thought of thousands of people dead in flames, concrete, and rubble, for I know my friend better than that. What struck me was that his enthusiasm was in a certain sense entirely *ideological,* entirely caught within the circuit of a worldview awesomely immune to any incursions of reality, such as exploding jetliners, torn body parts, or people falling, flaming, from the sky. It was not dead people he was clucking over but an attack on an idea, an attack which, it was clear, did not entirely displease him. The bodies seemed to be merely incidental, a distraction from the fundamental essence of the act.

The crucial thing that this reveals is the left's lack of a genuine vision or alternative, a positive picture of what they want. But this is not simply a failure of imagination; it reveals the left's basic attitude toward "the way the world is" to be one of *revulsion,* a hostile, disgusted recoil from reality. Connected with this is an incipient demonization, a Manichean sensibility operating just as much in leftists' reactionary rhetoric as in the knee-jerk patriotism (larded with heavy doses of consumer-oriented sensationalism) piped through our televisions from the mainstream media corporations. To understand how we might avoid succumbing to these temptations, it will help us to gain some clarity on what has gotten the left to this point: the point where they take a terrorist event such as this to be, if not good news, at least well deserved, and to build their public pronouncements around condemnations of condemnations of it–around "anti-anti-terrorism," if you will. That is, we need to understand the deep causes of this fundamental and reflexive revulsion.[1]

It is easy to tell oneself that the roots of the left's current escapism lie in historical events, particularly in the contingencies of the student unrest of the late 1960s. This is certainly the view of various right-wing critics who trace a straight line between (what they see as) the sillinesses and naive self-righteousness of those years and the stance of the "tenured radicals" thirty years on. And one can admit that this view has some analytic power without signing on to any larger "conservative" (actually libertarian) agenda. The contemporary left has been marked by its history in debilitating ways. One need look only as far as the Cold War, in the left's opposition to Western powers in favor of the "actually existing socialisms" of the Soviet bloc: This opposition burdened the left with a history of dualism, premised on a quasi-apocalyptic faith in the always just-over-the-horizon revolution of the proletariat, construed messianically. And it is important to note the rise of the New Left and its failure to be fully defeated by the disillusionments of 1968 and what came after. The idealists of that era, unwilling to rethink their self-righteousness, constructed an ever-more ornate, rococo palace of desperate cynicism. This cynicism allowed them to keep their beliefs but only at the cost of immobilizing them, along with all other beliefs; they could not admit the possibility of legitimate political success at all, for such success would give the lie to their cherished belief that theirs was the only possible, "ultimately" right way.

The cynicism gained its most theoretically sophisticated and respectable formulation in the works of Michel Foucault throughout the 1970s; but the *Weltanschauung* was captured beautifully by The Who's song, "Won't Get Fooled Again," when Roger Daltry sings, "Say hello to the new boss, same as the old boss." This cynicism deflates political energies, by changing the focus of one's political attention toward paranoia (which is now flourishing on the left at least as respectably as it does on the right), a paranoia about any and all uses of power. But this cynical, paranoid account is also, ironically, *consoling*, because it gives metaphysical legitimacy to a sense of futility or failure on the part of intellectuals. Such leftists identify strategy with purity, and made the best (or what they thought was the best) the enemy of the good. If their apocalyptic fantasies of complete liberation could not succeed, they would not admit that projects of less grand scale could really accomplish anything "substantial" either.[2] All of this is importantly true and, as Napoleon is reputed to have said, to understand someone's politics, one need only recall what the world looked like when the person was twenty. Much of the left's odd political reactions have to do with the fact that "the left" is largely guided by people who turned twenty in the sixties and early seventies.

But the events of the 1960s are not the root cause of the left's hostility to real political life; those years merely aggravated a deeper constellation of forces pressing intellectuals (on left and right alike) to accept a picture of themselves as fundamentally *distanced* from the "material realities" of power. Most prominent among these forces were what I would call the effective *Gnosticism* of modern intellectual life.[3] As society differentiated in the modern age, and the division of labor entailed the specialization of tasks and skills, the "surplus" intellectual capital—that "intellectual labor" which was not directed toward some office (in several senses) in the modern economy—grew ever more otiose, and felt ever more deeply its own obsolescence. Apart from the badges of office, apart from the degrees, the cafés, the gnarled prose, it is essential that the intellectual appear as an *idler*. This modern clerisy (to which I, and probably you, dear reader, belong) has thrashed about, looking for some justification for itself at the same time that it has grown to resent the way in which it sees itself rendered *pointless* by modern social systems.

Intellectuals' responses to the inescapable recognition of their own extraneousness have been manifold. Think of Habermas's ideal of the intellectual as a sort of discursive border cop; or think of Foucault's intellectual archaeologist; or (closer to home) think of theologians such as John Milbank, who take the theological task to be the imagination of new forms of conceptual theological "strangeness" which may well spark a new "cultural imaginary" on the part of the churches. While these responses vary on their faces, they share very telling deep structural similarities. Most importantly, they all recognize that intellectual workers are "distanciated"; in a way, indeed, their status as "intellectuals" *just is* this distance. To be an intellectual in the modern world is always to be tempted toward an absolute estrangement.

And this is where Gnosticism comes in. Many thinkers have argued that the modern world, with its mind-body dualisms and its belief in technological salvation, is in some ways inherently Gnostic.[4] My claim is less ambitious though more concrete: Contemporary intellectuals are tempted toward patterns of behavior that lead to attitudes and beliefs that are *functionally* analogous to those of the Gnostics of late antiquity. As I use it, Gnosticism is not most basically a doctrinal marker of, say, a literal metaphysical dualism; that is merely its superficial designate. Rather for me Gnosticism signifies a certain existential recoil from the world, a sense that the world is not properly one's home. Note that here the priority is given to negation, to the *denial* of a home, rather than the affirmation of some other home (presumably "elsewhere," in some heaven—maybe Paris?); that affirmation comes, if it comes (and sometimes it does not), as a secondary step, a deduction or postulation from the more primordial recoil. This is not to deny the many and profound differences between ancient Gnostics and modern intellectuals, perhaps especially the difference that the ancient Gnostics at least *chose* their marginality; it is simply to point to one important analogy between them.

A Christian Response to Gnosticism

It is understandable that so many Christian intellectuals have succumbed to the siren song of this modern demi-Gnosticism. After all, Gnosticism has been as close to a perennial temptation for Christians throughout history as one is likely to find. Given the fact that both positions spend so much of their energy and symbolic resources exploring the "felt wrongness" of the world as we find it, the mutual attraction of the positions is predictable. Nevertheless, they diverge radically in their basic accounts of this felt wrongness, regarding both its origins and how we should respond to it. While the Gnostic temptation is to recoil from association with the world conceived as a "cesspit of corruption," Christianity insists that any such recoil is itself a further expression of the problem we face. It is part of the genius of Christianity fundamentally to resist all such recoils from the world and the metaphysical dualisms they entail. So Christian thinkers might understand themselves to have a role to play here, in disarming such tendencies toward escapism and demonization. Let me explain what I mean by exploring in more detail what I think is the most attractive (and at least roughly orthodox) Christian account of evil and sin.[5]

The central differences between Christianity and Gnosticism emerge from reflection on the basic Christian claim that creation as a whole is fundamentally absolutely good. From our phenomenological experience of the world's felt wrongness, the Gnostics attempted to deduce a metaphysical cleavage running through creation—or rather, they sought to endorse our temptation to recoil indiscriminately from creation by rationalizing that recoil through the confabulation of such a base metaphysical dualism. Against this, Christianity diagnoses that recoil as part of the problem and insists that we ought to resist it; its metaphysics of being and goodness, its "monarchic axiology," is best understood as an attempt to elaborate in a metaphysical vernacular its resistance to the tendency to recoil. Hence the traditional Christian accounts insist either that "evil" is what God ultimately uses for our improvement, or (more radically) that evil is itself ultimately *nihil*, nothing, sheer flight and ultimate futility. Perhaps the greatest image of this in Christian thought is the presentation of Lucifer in Dante's *Inferno*: There the arch-fiend and origin of evil is nothing more than the first inmate of Hell, ensnared in an imprisonment of his own devicing—for he is trapped, half-buried in a lake of ice which freezes ever more solidly the more he beats his wings to escape it. The profundity of such images of evil, and the metaphysical accounts that elucidate them, originate in and gain their determinate meaning not from sheer speculative intelligence but from the centuries-long attempt to think through the intellectual consequences of Christianity's basic resistance to the recoil that Gnosticism endorses—a resistance better described as a more primordial affirmation of the world as under the holy providence of a single Sovereign God.[6]

One worry about this is that it may be fundamentally just as escapist as the Gnostic temptation it implicitly opposes, because it can seem simply a metaphysical consolation prize for those too weak to face the fundamental indifference (or worse) of the world. (This is the worry of critics such as Marx, Nietzsche, and Freud.) By so totally emphasizing the goodness of creation it may, such critics worry, distract us from confronting the hard problems we should address, and it can even seduce us into thinking of ourselves as essentially *victims* of the Divine sovereign's inscrutable will.[7] (It is worth noting and reflecting on the resilience of our desire to see ourselves as victims.) Alongside the *privatio* account of evil, then, the tradition has consistently insisted on the fundamentally *accidental* character of evil's entry into creation.

This accidental character of evil has been one of the deep truths communicated (or meant to be communicated) by the Christian doctrine of sin. But the language of sin operates not only to exonerate God from culpability; it also operates to diagnose our root problem. The fault is not only accidental, it is *inexcusable*, and we are at fault. Our sins cannot be simply overlooked, we must be *redeemed* from them. And that is the deepest point: Sin is a one-way street, and those who have fallen into sin cannot fix themselves.

The point of emphasizing evil's presence in the world as due to the accident of sin is not finally to make us wallow in our guilt, or drive us to despair. It means to make us recognize our own complicity in the world's failings, to be sure; but that recognition is not meant to be immobilizing or dispiriting. It means to provide a clear-eyed assessment of our predicament, an assessment that will help us identify and resist our manifold and ever-multiplying strategies of avoiding recognizing our sinfulness. The range of our avoidance strategies is awesome: In different ways it encompasses both the desperate "works-righteousness" earnestness of the Social Gospeler, who believes that we must build the Kingdom of God on Earth; and the wounded cynicism of the academic postmodern, convinced that any effort will be inevitably co-opted by The Powers That Be. (Typically each individual manifests both of these attitudes and a myriad of others as well.)

Once we have seen these temptations to be temptations, we may be frustrated and wonder what we are to do. We are called upon to wait. Our lives are to be lived in the pained anticipation of eschatological longing, a longing that our existence in the church is meant to discipline us into accepting. This "advental being" is not fundamentally a form of paralysis, however; it entails certain obligations toward the life of our societies. But these obligations are oriented rather rigorously around resisting evil, and only secondarily around promoting good. (This is because the societies are not the privileged loci of God's action, as are the churches.) So this "social ethic" is itself secondary, for the primary task is the liturgical one of the church's "becoming the church"– in Stanley Hauerwas's terms, training itself in practices in order to embody ever more fully the Incarnate Word spoken by the one to whom it refers, and to whom it also defers.

We have moved far from the surface question of intellectuals and their failings. But we have not moved *away* from this issue; we have moved ever more deeply beneath it. The key is the disposition with which one approaches involvement in society. Is one looking to realize a perfect society? Or is one aiming definitively to identify some social force as *the* origin of evil? On the view I have sketched here, such attitudes bespeak a deep misunderstanding of our position in the world, an ignorance of our own complex complicity in evil and sin. And naturally such misunderstandings will eventuate in (or, equally likely, such misunderstandings will emerge from pre-reflective behavioral patterns of) a fundamental despairing recoil from the world. It is this recoil that Christianity means to resist. Because evil is understood in this account to be fundamentally a dissent from God's will, the ultimate shape of our response to evil–a response induced in us by grace–is not paralysis but empowerment, not a metadissent from dissent but rather a real recommitment to participation in God's providential design.

How might such a dispositional program result in a different way of seeing the events of September 11?

Complexity versus Conspiracy

For starters, it would work against seeing everything in light of large-scale conspiracies by demonic forces. It would see a world marked by irony more than malice. And it would eventuate, I should hope, in a tough-minded and clear-sighted appreciation of the fact that the fixation on "America" is at least as much an obstruction to useful thinking about our current predicaments as it is a useful heuristic device.

Let me be clear. I wholly agree with the many who are terribly anxious about the effects of consumer culture on a globalizing world, about the defoliating devastation it can wreak on local cultures and economies; about the impoverishment of millions for the pleasures of other millions; and about the withering effect of consumerist attitudes on what I would call our souls. (I note, however, that these concerns are also the subject of interest of "neoclassical" economists who, we must recognize, no matter our distaste at their political beliefs, have interesting and attractive arguments about the power of capitalism for the general wealth of the world–arguments which, while the left has been growing increasingly shrill, have allowed a strange alliance of libertarians and cultural conservatives to seize the high ground.) Nor am I saying that American citizens, American corporations, and the United States government are not crucially, fundamentally caught up in unjust patterns of overconsumption and exploitation of the resources, "natural" and human, of others; indeed they are, and dramatically so.

But I fear that by too totally focusing on "America" as the cause and *locus* of all such ills, the left does not allow itself to see the real dangers, choosing instead to find and lash out against an easy target instead of facing up to the full range of problems that confront us. Politics is the art of compromise, and compromise invariably involves comparison. I do not want to dilute my message by detailing an alternative, but let me threaten to be tiresome by reminding us of some facts that ought to be accounted for by the left, but presently are simply ignored:

- the role of advanced technology and transnational capital (in the form of computer technology, international money markets, the ready availability of credit to anonymous borrowers), and the advance of globalization in general, in empowering and giving form to terror attacks;
- the vast complicity of other governments and corporations, particularly European, in the cultivation of terrorists for immediate monetary gain;
- the relative egalitarianism of the United States, in terms of race and gender equity, the traditional openness to immigrants, and the

incredible socioeconomic volatility of the populace, which generally tends to make people wealthy rather than to impoverish them (particularly in comparison to European states, in which racism and ethnocentrism are much too apparent and typically lead to violence);

- the complex reasons behind the U.S. support of Israel, which (whatever one thinks of it) is due not simply to American malfeasance and anti-Arab racism, but crucially to the powerful presence of a pro-Israel lobby in the U.S. working with determination to shape U.S. policy and to ensure a safe homeland for Jews, after learning in the twentieth century that Europe was not that safe homeland; and the rather simpler reasons for the lack of such political pressure in European countries, which come down to the fact that the European nations have no large Jewish lobbies, because the anti-Semitism in those countries led to the mass extermination of the Jews in the Holocaust (remember that, fellas?), which also convinced most Jews who survived that Europe was not, after all, a good place for them to be;

- the deep history of these conflicts, which did not spring full-grown into creation *ex nihilo* in 1989 by the rapacious unleashing of U.S. consumer capitalism on a quaint and innocently preconsumerist world. After all, it was not the U.S. that invaded Afghanistan in 1979, and the bioweapons that are likely to make their first, unimaginably horrific appearance as a terror weapon in the near future (irrespective of the anthrax threat, which may well be incidental to the terrorist attacks), are not drawn from U.S. military labs, where experiment and development was halted by President Nixon (Nixon!) in 1969, but from the secret, illegal, and fundamentally evil ventures of the "actually existing socialisms" of the Cold War era.

To attend to these issues need not dilute the criticism of the residents of the United States for their excessive consumption of the world's resources. I do think this criticism needs to be made, and made strongly. But I fear that that criticism has been allowed to exhaust the space of critical thinking in ways that short-circuit thinking by collapsing into demonology. And so the left comes to resemble, not a "cosmopolitan" worldview, but a parochially anti-American one (and even worse, a *European* anti-Americanism). And such a left is neither critically perspicacious, nor rhetorically effective, nor—what is for me the worst thing—appropriate for Christians.

Conclusion

The left does not have much in the way of intellectual respectability remaining. The damage it suffered in the Cold War, which (as Susan Sontag once said) proved *Reader's Digest* right and *The Nation* wrong, has been disastrous for our public life as a whole; for there is no vital left-wing intellectual alternative to the various right-wing ethnocentrists and "true believer" economic libertarians. And it seems to me that the left's attempts in the last few years to find and specify a useful opponent in "America" have been unfortunately successful in deflecting their criticism in a wrong direction. For they have created–or participated in the creation of–a symbolic monster that too simply collects all the attributes of absolute evil and none of the complexity that actually attends human affairs.

To do better, we need a less Gnostic left. But that will involve resisting the structural seductions of Gnosticism, which will be hard to do outside of explicitly religious frameworks such as Christianity. I cannot speak for all intellectuals, but I think this means that, in practical terms, then, to be better "intellectuals," left-wing Christian intellectuals must be better Christians.

36

Wounds of Hurt, Words of Faith

Mary Elizabeth Mullino Moore

The world is acutely aware of brokenness in this moment of time. If no other blessing comes from the terrorist acts of September 11, 2001, the United States has been awakened to tragedy, evoking a collective sense of the horrible realities that many people in this world face every day of their lives. Two dangers lurk in this awakening. First is the danger that people in the United States will be preoccupied with our own loss and will not see connections between our tragedy and other tragedies around the world. Second is the danger that we will seek healing and unity by collective retaliation, rather than by allowing our vulnerability to awaken us to the pain of others and to our own participation in wounding others through economic and political policies.

Today is a day of wounds and words. Collectively we face *wounds of hurt*, and, in our diverse religious communities, we seek *words of faith* that have meaning and power for this time. The myriad of worship services, panel discussions and presentations that have taken place since September 11 reveal the depth of human wounds and the hope people place in the very act of sharing words, whether in communities of faith, interreligious gatherings, or academic and political events. The relationship between wounds and words is complicated. People can use words of faith to heal or exacerbate their own wounds, and also to heal or exacerbate the wounds of others. People may allow their wounds to stir harsh words toward others or use their words to ignore, denigrate, or deepen the wounds of others. On the other hand, wounds and words can work together to deepen human understanding and religious commitment for a better world. Words, for example, can evoke empathy and understanding for others' wounds, and the experience of being wounded can enhance the respect and care in people's words.

Consider one example of the complexities of this relationship. The word "justice" can be used to declare some countries and religious communities just and others unjust. It can also be used to scrutinize the adequacy of justice in *all* countries and religious communities, and to encourage more just and humane actions by all. People have used the word justice in both ways, and in many other ways as well. Other words are similarly complex; thus, I enter this discussion with conscious awareness that both possibilities and dangers lie within human wounds and words. Both can perpetrate stubborn resistance to change or miraculous transformation; both can destroy or heal. The hope underlying this essay is for *wounds that transform* and *words that heal.* To this end, we will explore wounds of hurt, words of faith, and possibilities for ecumenical and interfaith witness to a more justice- and love-filled world.

Wounds of Hurt

Hurt is undeniable, but living with wounds is challenging. As vulnerable people, we are tempted to dwell on our hurts; indeed, people do need to mourn. We are tempted to strike out against the perpetrators of terror, and indeed, human communities do need to bring perpetrators to international justice. We are also tempted to move on and not dwell on tragedy; indeed, the human race does need to enter a new era of reflection and action. But none of these responses is adequate alone, and each can be distorted. The basic question now is how we will respond to the horrors of September 11, not just for the first weeks, but also in the months and years to come. What kind of mourning, justice-seeking, and recasting of thought and action are necessary?

We have already entered a new era, simply by being acutely aware of wounds of hurt. As Ted Brelsford said in a sermon two short weeks after the terrifying destruction of four hijacked airplanes:

> What is true about the world now was true also before September 11. But our perceptions of the world have shifted in some radical ways. Most of us did not really know the meaning of an earthquake that kills thousands in India, or the horror of terrorist attacks in the Middle East, or the dis-ease of violent hatred within one's own society...The world is the same. Now we know a little bit more about it.[1]

In these words, Brelsford points to the world situation and also to the role of knowledge. The very movement toward knowing "a little bit more" about the world awakens a sense of mourning, both for ourselves and for others. It also awakens the yearning to respond with more than tears. It raises the question with urgency: What can we do? It is no wonder that the United

States felt such appreciation for the firefighters and police officers who gave their lives to save others on September 11, and later to find those who had been killed in the crashing World Trade Towers. These people revealed an image of significant action in a moment of disaster.

The significance of this question is intensified when we consider the genuine possibility that we frail human beings might contribute to *tikkun olam* (the Hebrew expression for "repair of the world"). To consider this possibility, we turn to another sermon preached during the same week of September. On the eve of Yom Kippur, Rabbi Leila Gal Berner preached to her congregation in Washington, D.C., telling the story of a 21-year-old Pakistani Muslim man who worked in the World Trade Center and had many friends there. This young man described his experience of evacuating Building 7 and running to escape the Towers. About five blocks from his office, he turned to look as the World Trade Center fell. As people continued to run, he fell with people running all around him. He was wearing a pendant around his neck with an Arabic prayer for safety. While he lay on the ground, he described how a Hassidic Jewish man came to him and read the pendant in Arabic out loud. Then, he spoke in a deep Brooklyn accent: "Brother, if you don't mind, there is a cloud of glass coming at us, grab my hand, and let's get the hell out of here."

As the young Pakistani man told his story, he added that the Hassidic man "was the last person I would ever have thought who would help me." Yet, this was the person who led him away from the sea of glass and debris.[2] The young man concluded his story with encouraging people, when they are angry and want to retaliate, to remember these words: "Brother, if you don't mind, there is a cloud of glass coming at us, grab my hand, and let's get the hell out of here."

We see here a moment of *tikkun olam*, occasioned by the unifying experience of terror. Neither the Pakistani man nor Rabbi Berner are denying the reality of evil as they share this story; they are painfully aware of wounds that people inflict upon other people, wounds that run centuries deep. They have chosen, however, to focus on a ray of kindness and its potential to illumine other possibilities for repairing the world. Rabbi Berner concludes by drawing the connection with *tikkun olam:*

> In one instant of profound humanity, in one flash of profound goodness,...the shards of glass, deadly splinters caused by indescribable evil were redeemed and they became shards of light, sparks of the Divine, manifest in one human being...Don't let anybody ever tell you that what you do will not bring *tikkun olam*, the healing and redemption of our shattered world.[3]

Rabbi Berner's words expose the challenge of exploring wounds of hurt. She exposes the possibility that words of faith–such as *tikkun olam*–can interpret the torn-apart world and its potential for repair. Words of faith can also guide human actions toward hope.

Words of Faith

The discussion of wounds has led naturally to *words of faith.* What words do we need, and how might we express and interpret these words during troublesome days such as these? One temptation is to find sound bites that give hope. Certainly many of these have appeared across the United States in the weeks since September 11; billboards and bumper stickers carry such words as "God bless America" or "United we stand." Some sound bites are particularly prominent in Christian communities, such as "Trust in the Lord," "Turn your life to Jesus," or "God is our strength." Some churches have argued over whether and how to display the United States flag, or to what extent to focus sound bites on the U.S. and to what extent, on explicitly religious language. One church marquis near our home has two lines, "God bless America" and "Jesus saves." Such mixing of civil and Christian religion is commonplace as people seek which words of faith are most powerful and most unifying in these days of trauma.

The effort to find appropriate words of faith is a source of conflict for many Christian congregations. Some congregations are already conflicted in their relationships with God and divided in their relationships with one another; these congregations are particularly quick to focus their unifying hopes on the nation, placing the U.S. flag at the front of the Sunday morning processional, before the candles and cross, for example. The very effort to find the most appropriate words of faith in this time stirs conflict and confusion. What words do we need in such a time?

Words: According to Matthew (22:36–39), a lawyer asked Jesus which was the greatest commandment. Jesus replied: "'You shall love the Lord your God with all your heart, and with all your soul, and with all your mind. This is the greatest and first commandment. And a second is like it: 'You shall love your neighbor as yourself.'" These are words of Jesus. More accurately, they are words of Matthew, Mark, and Luke recalling words of Jesus; they are also words of the Hebrew scriptures.

More words: According to 1 Corinthians, Paul said to the embattled Christian community of Corinth, "And now faith, hope, and love abide, these three; and the greatest of these is love" (13:13). These are words of Paul. More accurately, they are words that have been passed down as Paul's letter, words that reiterate both the words of Jesus and the words of Hebrew scriptures.

Words are very important to Christianity; Jesus is even identified as the Word of God (John 1:1). Words are thought to mediate the power, grace, and will of God. They have the power to heal–to point to God's Reign or New Creation. But words also have the power to wound, and the world has been both healed and wounded by Christian words, both now and in the past. Here I will attend particularly to three words of Christian faith. The first–love–has already been introduced by the two scripture texts. The other two–justice and peace–are also powerful words that point to God's New Creation, but they are also ambiguous words, and they can be used to wound.

Love has sometimes been used to discipline children to the point of abuse. Justice has been used to justify unnecessary war and unnecessary destruction of life. Peace has been used to force superficial harmony onto peoples—harmonies without deep and abiding justice, therefore without deep and abiding peace. On the other hand, these same words—love, justice, and peace—have been the source of great redemptive works over the centuries of human history. Consider the U.S. civil rights movement in the 1960s. The words love and justice, in particular, were watchwords that inspired and guided a movement that wrought great change in the social fabric of the United States. Consider the Truth and Reconciliation Commission of South Africa, where the words love, justice, and peace guided a truth-telling process designed to open the way for genuine reconciliation in a post-Apartheid world.

These words have no easy definitions, but some description is useful if we are to discover the potential within them. Love might be understood as a deep desire for the flourishing of life—the flourishing of God's life, another person's life, a society's life, one's own life, creation's life. To love, then, is to live in such a way that the subjects of our love are embraced by our yearning for them to enjoy fullness of life. Justice might be understood as a way of life that establishes social processes and social structures to enhance the flourishing of *all* life. To do justice is to live so that all might enjoy fullness of life without destroying the flourishing of others. Perfect justice is not possible, but any flourishing of one people at the expense of others is an affront to justice. Peace is the active pursuit of love for each being and justice for all beings, such that people and lands are brought into harmony with one another. Peace is more than the absence of war; it is the active pursuit of love and justice.

With these reflections on words of faith within Christian tradition, we turn now to the interplay of words and wounds in Christian history. This historical sweep will be overly brief, and thereby oversimplified, but it is not untrue. In the name of Christianity, European Christians sponsored crusades during the Middle Ages, motivated by a passion to convert "infidels" to Christianity. These people were not infidels at all, but mostly Jews and Muslims, mostly faithful Jews and Muslims; yet, Christian words, such as "saving the infidels," were used to destroy communities of people and undercut their sacred traditions. Unfortunately, Christian motivations were further contaminated with economic and political goals. Later, in the name of Christianity, Nazi Christians sponsored the murder of six million Jews, using Christian language to justify their actions. Both before and since that time, many wars have been waged as "just wars," justified by a righteous or urgent cause. Some of these have been judged by later interpreters as necessary wars; others have been uncovered as unnecessary acts of aggression or complicity with aggression. Even in more "necessary" wars (usually contested), the results have left a path of destruction in terms of hatred multiplied and distrust passed to later generations. The purpose of this essay is not to refute or defend the possibility of a just war, but simply to identify ways in which religious language has been used to defend acts of defense or aggression, and to do so with very mixed results.

The United States faces this very dilemma during the post–September 11 weeks. The collective wounds of hurt create an ethos that welcomes what the President has identified as "freedom-fighting" and "fighting for peace," challenging other nations to be "with us or against us."[4] What we can easily forget with such rhetoric is that freedom has more than two sides. Throughout the history of the United States and the world, every war or conflict that has been labeled with two sides has left devastation in its wake. European settlers labeled Native Americans as "other" and thereby justified killing them and diminishing their cultures and lands. White Americans labeled Africans as "other," and thereby enslaved them. The United States labeled the Soviet Union as "other" and thereby contributed to a Cold War legacy of violence, so much so that we can now recognize "our moment" only when we see a righteous cause before us. We must define freedom-fighting by more than righteous violence, for violence only breeds more violence and ensures that future generations will live in fear, mistrust, and suffering. Struggle for freedom we must, but we must struggle in international courts and tribunals. We must walk alongside others, drawing upon the wisdom of others. We must hope that the freedom for which we struggle is freedom for all persons and all lands, and not just for ourselves. In short, we who are Christians must ask what are the demands of love, justice, and peace.

We see in this discussion of words that ambiguity prevails. Christian words have been used to justify destruction and, also, to create just peace throughout history. With awareness of powerful words and ambiguous interpretations within Christian tradition, we turn now to search for hope, first within ecumenical Christianity and then within interfaith efforts.

Ecumenical Witness

The most persuasive actions for addressing wounds of hurt with words of faith will be those that bring people together with a common voice. The actions of the World Council of Churches of Christ (WCC) and the National Council of Churches (NCC) are cases in point. Even before September 11, and before bombing began in Afghanistan on October 8, these two ecumenical councils, and others around the world, were addressing their attention to the devastations of violence. In February of this year, the World Council of Churches officially announced the Decade to Overcome Violence: Churches Seeking Reconciliation and Peace 2001–2010.[5] The WCC represents the fellowship of 342 diverse churches from 100 countries and all continents of the globe.

I have discussed the Decade to Overcome Violence elsewhere, but what is important to the present essay is the powerful way in which that announcement prepared the way for ecumenical and denominational bodies to respond quickly to the tragedies of September and October 2001. Visiting teams have come to the United States, as well as to Mozambique and other places of conflict in the present world.

When the Central Committee announced the Decade, His Beatitude Archbishop Anastasios, of the Orthodox Autocephalous Church of Albania, identified Christ's power of peace as the central source of hope for Christians. He said that Christ's peace supported the Albanian churches as they responded to war victims in Kosovo. The churches offered the victims aid regardless of religious identity, knowing that most were Muslim.[6] During these same days of World Council sharing, people also identified ways in which Christianity continues to participate in violence. The Reverend Hector Mendez, of the Presbyterian Reformed Church in Cuba, identified ideological violence as a source of great trauma, explicitly naming the ideological violence of the United States against Cuba. He argued, however, that the efforts of Cuban churches in sowing seeds of reconciliation have constructed a "bridge" between Cuban society and North America.[7]

The picture we see is a picture of Christianity that sometimes stirs peace, is often contaminated, but persists in building bridges in spite of contamination. In other words, the picture is messy; it is filled with words and also with wounds. On the Sunday morning when the WCC General Secretary Konrad Raiser announced the Decade to Overcome Violence, he was sufficiently brave to recognize the failure of Christianity alongside the World Council's vision. He said:

> All of us carry the seeds of this evil within us. For us, the Decade journey must start with repentance for the violence that Christians and churches have tolerated or even justified. We are not yet the credible messengers of non-violence that the gospel calls us to be.[8]

At the time of this declaration and confession, the WCC also turned attention to possibilities of negotiated peace in the Middle East; to bombings in Sudan; to the United States' plan to provide military equipment for Colombia; to the WCC work for "justice, peace, reconciliation and reunification of Cyprus"; and to a call for peace-making in Indonesia.[9] In short, the witness to a world beyond violence was not seen as one that would come with a simple declaration.

The ambiguity was underscored when His Holiness Aram I, Catholicos Cilicia of the Armenian Orthodox Church, said these words: "Violence is evil. Yet for some, living under conditions of injustice and oppression, where all means of non-violent actions are used up, violence remains an unavoidable alternative, a last resort."[10] He proceeded to explain that this does not legitimize violence, but it does identify situations in which we cannot condemn violence "when it is used as a 'last resort' for the cause of justice and dignity."[11]

In this same opening address to the Central Committee, Aram I also advocated non-violence, recognizing the power of nonviolent resisters such as Mahatma Gandhi and Martin Luther King, Jr., and celebrating the tumbling of the Berlin Wall in a peaceful way. He explained, "Violence generates violence, while non-violence uncovers the powerlessness of the powerful."[12] At the same time, Aram I explained that some situations require "'limited and controlled' violence aimed at changing social conditions and establishing justice for all."[13] He pled for the end of violence, alongside a cry for justice for all peoples, concluding, "Peace is not just the absence of violence; it is the presence of justice."[14] In this address, one can see a dialogue going on within Aram I himself, which is the same dialogue that goes on inside Christianity. This is not a simple just war theory, but a plea for recognizing the ethical struggle of Christian people.

Likewise, Jose Ramos-Horta, Nobel Peace Prize winner for his peace efforts in the conflict between Indonesia and East Timor, raised the question of armed intervention as a last resort. Ramos-Horta urged that churches advocate for peaceful resolution of conflict, but recognize that certain circumstances, such as genocide, require intervention.[15] At the same time, he advocated the restriction of arms sales by richer nations to developing countries, blaming such sales for the deaths of four million people and the refugee status of 30–40 million others. He proposed a simple and very challenging solution: "If the richer countries—governments of the industrialised world—dedicate resources to eliminating poverty, it would go a long way toward eliminating violence."[16] He urged that wealthier countries forgive the debts of the least developed countries, and that governments of underdeveloped countries be held to lawful and ethical actions.

The claims in these ecumenical efforts are for the possibility of life beyond violence. The launching of the Decade is an act of hope, although the world offers little possibility of optimism. It is an act taken with sober consciousness of the wounds of the world, even before the terrorist acts of September 11, 2001, and before bombings began in Afghanistan on October 8. Optimism seems even more impossible now, although the urgency of hope—an act of faith—is greater than ever. The launching of the Decade to Overcome Violence is an act led by words, but hopefully not limited by them. The very announcement is a sacramental act, mediating the grace of God through the dreams and decisions of ordinary human communities for the sanctification of human life and the well-being of all creation.[17]

These reflections on the WCC Decade are incomplete, as is the Decade itself. I choose this exemplar of hope because it *is* at the beginning and because it *does* express hope that the present church can make a difference in the present world. We face a terrible irony that the Decade was launched just seven months before the September 11 attacks in the United States. The irony is amplified by the words and acts of violence that have followed. The Decade issues a global challenge, and it is inaugurated with a seemingly overwhelming challenge to find ways toward peace in a frightened world where thousands of lives have already been lost.

Interfaith Witness

From where does hope come in an international, interfaith, interethnic world? This is the critical question facing the world during a year of fear and threat. Neither fear nor threat is new, but many people in the United States are facing them for the first time on a global scale. Much can be learned by turning to peoples of diverse communities around the world.

Consider signs of determined hope in Israel and Palestine. Gershon Baskin told the story of his friend Isaac Saada, a teacher involved in peace education in Israel and Palestine.[18] Saada had confided in his friend how difficult it was to teach his children to love and hope for peace because they had seen so many terrible things. They asked their dad how he could possibly work with the Israelis. He responded to them "that we had to believe in peace and that peace would eventually come." He elaborated that "the worst thing that could happen to them and to the Palestinian people would be if they filled their hearts with hatred." Soon after saying these words, Isaac Saada died in a shelling meant for terrorists.

This story has an unhappy ending, but it does reveal a powerful hope–a hope for which Isaac Saada gave his life. If Saada's life is not to be in vain, other people–Palestinians, Israelis, Muslims, Christians, and Jews–will need to live with the same determined hope that characterized his life, even when faced with imminent danger. This is not a naïve posture, but a decision to be a force for justice and peace. Human work will not always be effective in transforming the world; many tragedies will happen along the way. Yet, hope in the face of threat may be the only pathway for transforming the harsh realities of the world. Such hope requires courage, as seen in the life of Isaac Saada. One of the principles of the Carter Center reflects the same courageous hope. In its work for peace and health around the world, the Carter Center commits itself to face "the possibility of failure as an acceptable risk." Transforming human practices is full of risk; however, building new habitats from the debris of violence may be the only way to reshape human life and witness to life-giving possibilities for the creation. If Isaac Saada could do this in the midst of shelling, the human family can do it now in the aftermath of September 11.

One interfaith community that has worked together for some years is an association of Christian and Muslim Religious Educators in the University of Birmingham, England. On October 23 of this year, they issued a press release decrying the terrorist acts of September 11 and the actions of the U.S.A. and Britain on October 5. These acts were identified as "inconsistent with the principles of the religions we represent and teach."[19] They further stated that the actions of September 11, although they were done in the name of Islam, were counter to Islam's teaching "that God is merciful and compassionate."[20] Further, they condemned the violence that Western governments had since committed against the Afghan people. Their central argument, ascribed to by both Christians and Muslims, was that human beings are created in the image of God and are representatives of God. Further, they make a practical observation about paths that are promising for lasting peace and those that are not:

We believe that violence produces more violence, and that terrorism cannot be eliminated by violence, but only by the pursuit of justice within the structure of international law.[21]

The witness of these Muslim and Christian educators is possible because they have been building relationships for some time. It is powerful because it acknowledges wounds of hurt and calls upon words of faith to analyze and address the present moment. Herein lies the challenge for the whole human family.

Conclusion

This discussion leads back to words of hope—love, justice, and peace. The path toward hope is not simple. Fellow travelers have diverse, even contrary, perspectives. On some days, the ambiguities of love, justice, and peace are overwhelming; yet we are called to travel that seemingly impassable path. We are called to continue working for peace with the simple hope that our humble efforts will magnify justice and love for all.

37

How Should Christians Respond?

Ronald J. Sider

The most important–and perhaps the hardest–task is to be Christians first before we are Americans or Europeans or Palestinians. History shows that especially in times of national crisis and heightened patriotism, Christians often equate God and country; often quickly identify perceived national self-interest with the will of God; often inappropriately apply biblical texts about the people of God to their nation.

Especially at this moment, it is enormously important that the church in the United States refuse to blur the distinction between the body of Christ and America. The first responsibility of the church–whether one stands within the just war or the pacifist tradition–is to be the church.

God has not suspended the biblical commands to "work for the good of all" (Gal. 6:10) and "love your enemies" (Mt. 5:44). They still apply after September 11. Let's ask God to show us how Christians everywhere and especially in America could take some dramatic steps to demonstrate our love for Middle Eastern Muslims, even–or perhaps especially–the people of Afghanistan.

It is also crucial that the church offer a biblical answer to the question on so many minds: Why did this happen?

Jerry Falwell, appearing on Pat Robertson's "700 Club" television show, disgraced all Christians, especially evangelicals, with his terrible comments on September 13, saying that "the pagans and the abortionists and the feminists and the gays and the lesbians [and] the ACLU" all "helped this happen."[1]

Our all-wise, all-powerful God chose to create free human beings capable of rejecting God's will and harming their neighbors. Since we are communal beings, our sinful acts regularly create terrible consequences for our neighbors. God could always prevent evil people from harming their neighbors, but that would destroy both our freedom and our very existence as communal beings. So God allows terrorist attacks and Holocausts, not because God wants that, but because God desires free persons.

God's goodness to us, however, does not stop with the gift of freedom. The cross tells us that God cares so much about the way that we abuse our freedom to defy God and devastate our neighbors that the Creator of the universe actually dies for our sins. God stands weeping, with open arms, pleading with us to repent, accept his astonishing forgiveness, and turn from hurting our neighbors. Today, perhaps, we have a special opportunity to share this wonderful gospel with gentle love and confidence. But we also need to remember that as long as history lasts, God will continue to grant persons freedom, even when they choose to do terrible things. That's why the dastardly evil of September 11 happened.

Another part of what the Bible tells us is also important, albeit easily distorted. The Creator who gave us freedom also embedded a moral order in the very structure of the universe. Whether or not we acknowledge it, some things are right and others are wrong. As Romans 1 says, violating that moral order has consequences, not just eternally, but within history. Sin–whether sexual misconduct or economic injustice, disrespect for human life or racial prejudice–has consequences that work their way through our homes and nations. Societies that defy the moral order God placed in the universe will suffer consequences.

But does that mean that we should connect specific tragedies with specific sins? People in Jesus' day thought specific illnesses resulted from specific sins. Jesus clearly rejected that view (Jn. 9:1–3). On occasion, God directly revealed to the prophets of the Old Testament that specific tragedies resulted from specific disobedience in Israel and Judah. But no Christian today dare claim that kind of special revelation. Never, therefore, should Christians today connect an evil like the terrorist attack with specific sinful acts.

To be sure, there is a truth here that is crucial. This nation, like all others, is a tragic mix of good and evil–which is *not* to say that all societies are equally good and bad; the relative difference between relatively free, relatively just America and the Taliban's unjust, repressive Afghanistan is a good to be treasured. Our nation, however, has done evil things in the world that help explain why significant numbers of people hate us. Christians in America need to be humble enough to face that honestly.

But to engage in honest self-evaluation and also to be able to condemn the attack on September 11 as evil (rather than merely personally distasteful), we need precisely the universal moral norm given by the Creator. American intellectuals who have embraced postmodernism's radical relativism cannot condemn the attacks on September 11 as wrong and immoral; they can only say some groups feel good about the attacks and others do not. It is surely illuminating that on September 22, *The New York Times* ran Edward Rothstein's editorial pointing out that the "attacks on U.S. challenge the perspective of postmodern true believers." The author clearly rejected postmodernism as "ethically perverse."[2]

Finally, we should remember a warning from Reinhold Niebuhr–often considered America's most distinguished theologian and ethicist. Every nation, he argued, regularly exaggerates its own righteousness and identifies its significant but partial goodness with the absolute righteousness of God, mistaking its standards for God's standards. Because people are both finite and selfish, every nation, even the best, overstates its own goodness and underestimates the validity of its opponents' claims. The moral pride that results produces an inability to see one's own faults and a consequent messianic triumphalism that overreaches and produces deadly backlash.

Niebuhr did not conclude that all human systems and societies are equally unjust. "The dishonest pretension of universality which accompanies every partial perspective in history…does not mean that significant choices between rival political movements cannot be made."[3] It is not only possible but imperative to distinguish between a relatively just and good system in spite of its failures and a substantially less just and more evil system that nonetheless has some valid claims.

Niebuhr's argument is urgently relevant. To speak of seeking to "eradicate evil from the world" or to label the effort to combat terrorism "Operation Infinite Justice" (a label that fortunately was soon abandoned) is to overreach. I thank God for the wonderful freedom and widespread justice of our nation. In contrast to many undemocratic, repressive governments in our world, America is a treasure to be cherished and protected.

But it is only a relative good. It has flaws. We have done evil things in the world–including in the Middle East. To acknowledge those faults and to understand that they have contributed to fairly widespread hatred of America in Muslim lands is not for a moment to justify or excuse in any way the terrible evil of the terrorist attacks.

If we are to respond wisely, we must dare to pray not only for the strength to justly combat terrorism but also for the humility to recognize our own imperfection. Moral pride will not only outrage others; it will also blind us to our faults, which if uncorrected, will prove fatal.

Gently and prayerfully, Christians today should use this teachable moment to answer the question, "Why?" To explain the moral order of the universe. To invite everyone to trust in the God who loves his free, disobedient creatures so much that God dies to overcome evil. To love even those who spitefully use us and thereby demonstrate that our highest loyalty is not to our nation, but to the Middle Eastern carpenter who is Lord and Savior of the world. And, whenever we can, to add a voice of sanity to the public debate.

38

We Must Find a Better Way

Walter Wink

Michael Kelly thinks he has killed pacifism. In an editorial in the *Washington Post* of September 26, 2001, he cites George Orwell's 1944 description of pacifism as "objectively pro-Fascist." "If you hamper the war effort on one side you automatically help out that of the other," Orwell reasoned. Applied to "America's New War," Kelly finds the logic irrefutable. "Organized terrorist groups have attacked America. These groups wish the Americans to not fight. The American pacifists wish the Americans to not fight. If the Americans do not fight, the terrorists will attack America again. And now we know such attacks can kill many thousands of Americans. The American pacifists, therefore, are on the side of future mass murders of Americans. They are objectively pro-terrorist." Hence the pacifist position is "evil."

Would that life were so simple! For what Mr. Kelly overlooks is a third way, neither passive nor aggressive. For millions of years his error has been endlessly repeated. It is the fight/flight response. But that third way has occasionally been tried, and, wonder of wonders, it has frequently succeeded. Religions pioneered the third way as a nonviolent protest against those two invidious alternatives. Starting with the Hebrew midwives, nonviolence was elaborated by Jainism and Buddhism, given political bite by Jews like the prophets and Jesus, articulated by Christians like Saint Francis and Martin Luther King, Jr., and made programmatic and practical by the Hindu Gandhi and the Muslim Badshah Khan.

Nevertheless, I agree with Mr. Kelly that pacifism must go. It is endlessly confused with passivity. In the nations in which Christianity has predominated, Jesus' teaching on nonviolence has been perverted into injunctions to passive nonresistance, which, as we shall see, is the very opposite of active nonviolence. Jesus had said, "You have heard that it was said, 'An eye for an eye and a tooth for a tooth.' But I say to you, Do not resist an evildoer. But if anyone strikes you on the right cheek, turn the other also; and if anyone wants to sue you and take your outer garment, give your undergarment as well; and if one of the occupation troops forces you to carry his pack one mile, go two" (Mt. 5:38–41).[1] As it stands, this saying seems to counsel supine surrender. If you are a woman and you are struck by your spouse on one cheek, turn the other; let him pulverize you. If you are sued for a piece of clothing, give all your clothes voluntarily, as an act of pious renunciation. And if a Roman soldier forces you to carry his pack one mile, be a chump: carry it two. And the crowning blow: don't resist evil at all.

For centuries, readers of this advice have instinctively known something was wrong with this picture. Jesus always resisted evil. Why would he tell us to behave in ways he himself refused? And that's where the trouble starts. The Greek word translated as "resist" *(antistenai)*, is literally "to stand *(stenai)* against *(anti)*." The term is taken from warfare. When two armies collided, they were said to "stand against" each other. The correct translation is given in the *Scholars Version*: "Don't react violently against the one who is evil" (Mt. 5:39).[2] The meaning is clear: don't react in kind, don't mirror your enemy, don't turn into the very thing you hate. Jesus is not telling us not to resist evil, but only not to resist it violently.

Jesus gives three examples to explain his point. The first is: "If anyone strikes you on the right cheek, turn the other also." Most people picture a blow with the right fist. But that would land on the left cheek, and Jesus specifies the right cheek. A left hook wouldn't fit the bill either, since the left hand was used only for unclean tasks, and even to gesture with it brought shame on the one gesturing. The only option, then, is a back-handed strike with the right hand against the right cheek. This was not a blow to injure. It was symbolic. The back-handed blow was intended to humiliate, to put an inferior in his or her place. It was given by a master to a slave, a husband to a wife, a parent to a child, or a Roman to a Jew. The message of the powerful to their subjects was clear: You are a nobody, get back down where you belong.

It is to those accustomed to being struck thus that Jesus speaks ("if anyone strikes *you*"). By turning the other cheek, the person struck puts the striker in an untenable spot. He cannot repeat the backhand, because the other's nose is now in the way. The left cheek makes a fine target, but only persons who are equals fight with fists, and the last thing the master wants is for the slave to assert equality (see the *Mishnah, Baba Kamma* 8:6). This is, of course, no way to avoid trouble; the master might have the slave flogged to within an inch of her life. But the point has been irrevocably made: the "inferior" is saying, in no uncertain terms, "I won't take such treatment anymore. I am your equal. I am a child of God." By turning the other cheek, the oppressed person is saying that she refuses to submit to further humiliation. This is not submission, as the churches have insisted. It is defiance. That may sound a bit idealistic, but people all over the globe of late have been taking their courage in their hands this way and resisting, nonviolently, those who have treated them thus.

Jesus' second example deals with indebtedness, the most onerous social problem in first-century Palestine. The wealthy of the Empire sought ways to avoid taxes. The best way was to buy land on the fringes of the Empire. But the poor didn't want to sell. So the rich jacked up interest rates—25 to 250 percent. When the poor couldn't repay, first their moveable property was seized, then their lands, and finally the very clothes on their backs. Scripture allowed the destitute to sleep in their long robes, but they had to surrender them by day (Deut. 24:10–13).

It is to that situation that Jesus speaks. Look, he says, you can't win when they take you to court. But here is something you can do: when they demand your outer garment, give your undergarment as well. That was all they wore. The poor man, then, is stark naked! And in Israel, nakedness brought shame, not on the naked party, but on the one viewing his nakedness. (See the story of Noah, Genesis 9.) Jesus is not asking those already defrauded of their possessions to submit to further indignity. He is enjoining them to guerrilla theater.

Imagine the debtor walking out of the court in his altogethers. When onlookers ask what happened, he tells them that the creditor got all his clothes. People come pouring out of the streets and alleys and join the little procession to his home. It will be awhile before creditors in that village take a poor man to court!

But, of course, the powers that be are shrewd, and within weeks new laws will be in place making nakedness in court punishable by fines or incarceration. So the poor need to keep inventing new forms of resistance. Jesus is advocating a kind of Aikido, where the momentum of the oppressor is used to throw the oppressor and make him the laughing stock of the community. Jesus is not averse to using shame to kindle a moral sense in the creditor.

Jesus' third example refers to the *angeria*, the law that permitted a Roman soldier to force a civilian to carry his 65–85 pound pack. But the law stipulated one mile only. At the second marker the soldier was required to retrieve his pack. By carrying the pack more than a mile, the peasant makes the soldier culpable for violation of military law. Again, Jesus is not just "extending himself" by going the second mile, as the popular platitude puts it. He is putting the soldier in jeopardy of punishment.

So you can see why I agree with Mr. Kelly. The examples Jesus gives are something more than nonresistance. They are gutsy, courageous, even defiant. So I don't regard myself as a pacifist. I see myself rather as a violent person trying to become nonviolent. Mr. Kelly and I concur that the "flight" option is cowardly, irresponsible, and ineffective. But where he is still mired in the "fight" option, I am prepared to risk active, even militant, nonviolence—a third way.

Far from proving impractical, nonviolence has been about the only thing that has been working of late. With the possible exception of the Gulf War, I cannot think of another instance where violence prevailed. And our actions during and after that war are at the root of the hatred felt by so many in the Middle East toward the U.S. (It is too early to make a judgment of history regarding the current war.) By contrast, in 1989–90 alone, fourteen nations involving 1.7 billion people underwent nonviolent revolutions, all but one (China) successfully. During the twentieth century, 3.4 billion people were thus involved. Yet most churches since the time of Saint Augustine have embraced the Roman "just war theory," convinced that nonviolence won't work, that only violence can save us.

The current crisis challenges both Mr. Kelly and me. Mr. Kelly, because he is impaled on the paradox that nothing fails like success. It goes like this: If we destroy the Taliban and Osama bin Laden, thousands will take their places. All-out war with Arab Muslims could lead straight to World War III, complete with biological and nuclear weapons. Our very lust for retaliation is proving the truth of the adage that violence only leads to more violence. At the very least, we can expect a world unsafe for Americans, even in our homeland. As President Lyndon Johnson commented, "The more bombs you drop, the more people you make mad," an insight he failed, for political reasons, to honor in regard to Vietnam.

In response to the attack on America, Attorney General John Ashcroft has proposed creating secret military tribunals in which suspects may be detained without their identities being made public, and may be held without charges being brought against them. The U.S.A. Patriot Act, so quickly signed into law after the attack, allows law enforcement authorities to enter a home, office, or other private place without a warrant and conduct a search, take photographs, and download computer files without notifying the person whose property is being searched until sometime *after* the search is conducted. Most troubling, this authority is not limited to anti-terrorism investigations but also extends to supposed criminal ones. Wiretapping has virtually been removed from the discretion of judges, and Internet communications can be intercepted. Student records (including participation in demonstrations) will be made accessible to a variety of governmental agencies, thus stifling dissent. Furthermore, the agencies receiving this and other private information have virtually unlimited use of it, thus resurrecting the specter of the government spying on its own citizens and using that power to limit free speech. This is not an empty threat. Those who demonstrated against the war in Vietnam or the nuclear madness paid a high price for their courage, and the rightness of their protests is now generally conceded by nearly everyone. This erosion of civil liberties may land us in the very "objectively pro-Fascist" situation of which Mr. Kelly warns and which the Bill of Rights was intended to prevent.

There are causes for this war, and most of them should have been taken care of years ago. Most of what Osama bin Laden claims to be fighting for should have been the basis of America's Middle Eastern policy. We should have lifted the sanctions in Iraq, which have killed upwards of a million innocent people, over half of them children under five—a war crime for which *we* are guilty. We could have easily withdrawn our troops from Saudi Arabia, since it is offensive to pious Muslims to have non-Muslim troops in their holy land. We should have used our enormous influence to stop Israelis from settling in the West Bank, and helped Palestinians secure a state. We should quit propping up anti-democratic dictatorships in the region, many of which would collapse without our support. And we should reduce our oil dependency by developing alternative sources of energy and promoting conservation.

Not that these unjust situations adequately account for Osama bin Laden's vendetta against America. The rationale of terrorists is terror, and reasons given today may shift tomorrow. The terrorist who regretted being caught before he could kill 250,000 Americans betrayed the game by admitting that it was simply to kill Americans. What we have here is a massive projection of fundamentalist Muslim shadow on the United States. We no doubt deserve censure, but not the murder of our innocents. No pretext can ever excuse the slaughter of innocents, whether Americans in the Twin Towers or Afghan civilians in the Middle East.

But the current crisis also challenges me. I distinguish between force and violence, arguing that force, rightly exercised, is the legitimate use of restraint to prevent some from doing harm to others. Violence, by contrast, is injurious or lethal harm deliberately intended, and can never be justified. I am struggling with that distinction today. Is there a continuum from force to violence, or from police action to war? How, then, do we know how much force we can use before it becomes violence? Could a UN police force, tightly networking with the combined intelligence services of the 180 nations in the UN, have been capable of apprehending the terrorists? Could we have sent in special forces to seize bin Laden and bring him to trial at the World Court? Didn't the "restrained" use of force already escalate to violence the moment President Bush called it "war"? Unless we have committed ourselves to nonviolence from the outset, these distinctions become rationalizations as the use of force inevitably degenerates into violence.

It's easy to see why Bush wants it called "war." The killing of civilians, inevitable in a war where innocents are mingled among combatants, can be written off as "collateral damage," as if real people weren't involved. I have only recently heard of several thorough accountings of civilian casualties, even though we know that high aerial bombardment inevitably has its victims.[3] And by calling it war, the full resources of the world's most daunting military could be devoted to destroying an entire sector of the Afghanistan population. Mr. Rumsfeld made it clear over and over: his goal was to kill as many Taliban as possible. Capture, trial and, if convicted, incarceration, were too cumbersome. Kangaroo courts and summary executions are more convenient. Hence the administration's reiterated warrant: Osama bin Laden, dead or alive, preferably dead.

One of the most lucid reflections on terrorism was made three years before the crisis of September 11, 2001, by Lt. Col. Robert M. Bowman, Ret., who flew 101 combat missions in Vietnam and directed all the "Star Wars" programs under Presidents Ford and Carter.

We are the target of terrorists, he said, not because we stand for democracy, freedom, and human rights [as President Bush has alleged], but because, in much of the world, our government stands for dictatorship, bondage, and human exploitation. "We are the target of terrorists because we are hated. And we are hated because our government has done hateful things." We are hated because our government denies democracy, freedom, and human rights to people in Third World countries whose resources are coveted by our multinational corporations. (I mention only in passing the lucrative pipeline Russia wishes to build through Afghanistan that could only be tapped if the Taliban were out of the way. Might that explain why, not just bin Laden, but the Taliban as well, had to be destroyed?) We are hated because we have been involved in the overthrow of democratic regimes in Iran, Chile, Vietnam, the Congo, and much of Central America, in the case of the last, repeatedly. And we have bombed twenty-two nations since 1946, not one of which became a democratic government respectful of human rights.

Lt. Col. Bowman concludes, "Only one thing has ever ended a terrorist campaign—denying the terrorist organization the support of the larger community it represents. And the only way to do that is to listen to and alleviate the legitimate grievances of the people."[4] As Uri Avnery, founder of the Israeli peace group Gush Shalom put it, "One can kill a million mosquitoes, and millions more will take their place. In order to get rid of them, one has to dry the swamp that breeds them."[5] Doing justice in the Middle East will not mollify true terrorists. But it could remove the source of much outrage, and thus dry up the reservoir of recruits for holy war.

It is natural to react defensively when attacked as we were. But retaliation will not work, else Israel would be the safest nation in the world. An Israeli cab driver unwittingly exposed the impotence of revenge when he said, "We have to beat and beat and beat the Palestinians until they learn to love us." Nicholas Lemann shows how our massive military reaction played right into bin Laden's hands.[6] Using the Spanish Basque's "action-reprisal-action cycle," the al Qaeda terrorists carried out a spectacular act of aggression that made the insurgency appear to be powerful and exciting. This action was then calculated to create a savage overreaction by the enemy that would gain international sympathy for the terrorists' cause and lead to massive enlistments among daring and angry young men. We could scarcely have cooperated better.

The Bush administration has hewn rigorously to its objectives in this war, but they are mostly short-term goals. As a person committed to nonviolence, I nevertheless find myself rooting for the overthrow of bin Laden, al Qaeda, the Taliban, and terrorism everywhere. But then I pause to reflect, and realize that the long-term prospect of our counterviolence is not so promising. The means we are using will not achieve the desired result. Unless we use our power to institute real justice, we will find ourselves with the "endless enemies" of which Jonathan Kwitny so eloquently wrote.[7]

President Bush wants us to believe in a final violence that will eradicate evil once and for all and make future violence unnecessary. But the violence we use creates new evil, however just the cause. It inculcates the longing for revenge, and for what the losers call "justice." And they will have learned from our example how to use violence more efficiently. *Violence can never stop violence because its very success leads others to imitate it.* Paradoxically, violence is most dangerous when it *succeeds*.

The problem is not merely to gain justice but to end the Domination System. In the struggle against oppression, every new increment of violence simply extends the life of that system and deepens faith in violence as a redemptive means. You cannot free people from the Domination System by using its own methods. You cannot construct the City of Life with the weapons of death. You cannot make peace—*real* peace—with war. As Gandhi observed, "The only people on earth who do not see Christ and His teachings as nonviolent are Christians."

These are trying times for those of us who affirm nonviolence. We have few practical alternatives to offer, and the perceived success of violence persuades many that we are wrong. It's too late to prevent a military response to this crisis or the wholesale killing of civilians. But it is critical that we resist the black-and-white, all-or-nothing thinking that is so emblematic of wartime, and instead try to think outside of the box. For those of us committed to nonviolence, perhaps the Third Way in this crisis is the refusal to become our enemy. Given the fact of this "war," we can still resist the chipping away at our civil liberties. We can bring our enemies to justice in a court of law, rather than a secret military tribunal. We can fight for the inclusion of women in any new Afghan regime. And we can insist on the candid reporting of civilian casualties.

The church is called to nonviolence not in order to preserve its purity, but to express its fidelity. It is not a law but a gift. It is simply offered to those who seek what God has in store for the world. The gospel is not in the least concerned with our anxiety to *be* right; it wants to *see right done.* Those who today renounce the kingdom of death do so not because they are trying to please a deity who demands obedience, but because they have committed themselves to the realm of life. They refrain from killing, not because they are ordered to, but because they recognize something of God in everyone, and realize that what we do to the least of these—our enemies—we do to God.

In the final analysis, nonviolence is not a matter of legalism but of discipleship. It is the way God has chosen to overthrow evil in the world. Therefore, Jesus does not advocate a perfectionist ethic in which our salvation depends on being nonviolent. God can forgive our failures to be nonviolent. It is not a "work" that one must achieve in order to be counted righteous. We cannot even say that nonviolent actions are in every circumstance the will of

God. How can I know, in any given situation, whether my nonviolence is not a heinous crime, or a total miscalculation of what God desires? I cannot presume on the judgment of God. I can only say that nonviolence is at the very heart of the gospel, and that the church's task is to attempt to spread this leaven into the life of the world. And I can only believe that history will finally vindicate the power of truth and love over the power of death.[8]

Notes

PART 1: OBSERVATIONS OF TERROR AND WAR

Chapter 2: Subversion, Body-Politic, Scripture:
A Question on the Limits of Power

[1] Antonio Negri, *The Politics of Subversion: A Manifesto for the Twenty-First Century* (Cambridge, Mass.: Basil Blackwell, 1989).

[2] Peter Ochs, *Peirce, Pragmatism, and the Logic of Scripture* (New York: Cambridge University Press, 1998).

[3] Stephen E. Fowl and L. Gregory Jones, *Reading in Communion: Scripture and Ethics in Christian Life* (Grand Rapids: Eerdmans, 1991).

[4] Negri, *The Politics of Subversion*, 192.

[5] Ibid., 193.

[6] Douglas Kellner, *Media Culture: Cultural Studies, Identity and Politics between the Modern and the Postmodern* (London: Routledge, 1995).

[7] Kenneth Surin, "Is It True What They Say about 'Theological Realism'?" in *The Turnings of Darkness and Light: Essays in Philosophical and Systematic Theology* (New York: Cambridge University Press, 1989), 51.

[8] Gilles Deleuze and Felix Guattari submit that, "In principle, all States are isomorphic; in other words, they are domains of realization of capital as a function of a sole external world market." See *A Thousand Plateaus: Capitalism and Schizophrenia* (Minneapolis: University of Minnesota Press, 1987), 464.

[9] Fredric Jameson argues that surface supplants depth. This is what he calls the "waning of affect," the effect of which disarms the possibility of the individual human body to locate itself and to explain its existence through history. See *Postmodernism: Or, the Cultural Logic of Late Capitalism* (Durham, N.C.: Duke University Press, 1991), 12–15, 44.

[10] John Howard Yoder, *The Politics of Jesus*, 2d ed. (Grand Rapids: Eerdmans, 1994), 199. Of course, Yoder is arguing against this liberal reading of scripture.

[11] Kenneth Surin, "Marxism(s) and 'The Withering Away of the State'," *Social Text* no. 27 (1990): 46.

[12] See Daniel Lazare, *The Velvet Coup: The Constitution, The Supreme Court, and the Decline of American Democracy* (New York: Verso Books, 2001).

[13] John Milbank and Catherine Pickstock, "Truth and Vision," in *Truth in Aquinas* (London: Routledge, 2001).

[14] The allusion is to Rowan Williams's essay "Postmodern Theology and the Judgment of the World" in *Theology After Liberalism*, ed. John Webster and George P. Schner (Malden, Mass.: Blackwell Publisher, 2000), 321–34.

[15] I am indebted to Rocco Gangle, Ken Surin, Brian Sholl, and John Milbank for their helpful suggestions while revising this paper originally delivered at the University of Virginia forum "Imperialism and Terror," October 1, 2001.

Chapter 4: Business as Un-usual: Reconstructing Divine Economy

[1] Julie A Nelson, "Economic Man," in *The Elgar Companion to Feminist Economics,* ed. Janice Peterson and Meg Lewis (Aldershot: Edward Elgar Publishing, 2000), 284.

[2] Feminist economists such as Julie Nelson, Marianne Ferber, and others have unveiled the gender-bias of economic man. Marianne Ferber and Julie A Nelson, eds., *Beyond Economic Man: Feminist Theory and Economics* (Chicago: University of Chicago Press, 1993).

[3] Al Krulick, "Gimme a Commercial Break," *Orlando Weekly*, 15 October 2001, www.alternet.org/story.html?StoryID=11709.

[4] Patrick McGeehan, "For Many Traders, the Fun Has Gone Out of Their Jobs," *The New York Times*, 13 October 2001, www.nytimes.com/2001/10/13/business/13mood.html.

[5] W. D. Davies and Dale C. Allison, *A Critical and Exegetical Commentary on The Gospel According to Matthew,* International Critical Commentary on the Holy Scriptures of the Old and New Testaments (Edinburgh: T&T Clark, 1988–97), 39.

[6] Similarly, Karmen MacKendrick notes that ascetic desire lacks respect for limits. Karmen MacKendrick, *Counterpleasures* (Albany: SUNY, 1999), 149ff.

[7]Judith Plaskow has argued that women as persons were not the addressees of the commandments. The Exodus text mentions that no women were present at the promulgation at the Sinai. Several of the Ten Commandments also appear to consider women property of men. Cf. Judith Plaskow, *Standing Again At Sinai: Judaism from a Feminist Perspective* (San Fransisco: HarperCollins, 1990), 25.

[8]Davies and Allison, *Matthew,* 47.

[9]Donna Haraway's vision of such a figure suggests that it "cannot be man or woman" but exhibits a certain queerness of gender and of economy. Donna J. Haraway, "Ecce Homo, Ain't (Ar'n't) I a Woman, and Inappropriate/d Others: The Human in a Post-Humanist Landscape," in *Feminists Theorize the Political,* ed. Judith Butler and Joan Scott (New York/London: Routledge, 1992), 85.

[10]Henry George Liddell and Robert Scott, *A Greek-English Lexicon* (Oxford: Clarendon Press, 1948). Many discussions of hysteria or the wandering womb do not list the connotation of lack and deficiency. See Ilza Veith, *Hysteria: The History of a Disease* (Chicago: The University of Chicago Press, 1965), ix; Mary R. Lefkovitz, *Heroines and Hysterics* (New York: St. Martin's Press, 1981), 13; and Aline Rousselle, *Porneia: On Desire and the Body in Antiquity* (Cambridge, Mass.: Blackwell, 1983), 69.

[11]Rousselle, *Porneia,* 67–69.

[12]Veith, *Hysteria,* 22.

[13]Daniel Boyarin, "Freud's Baby, Fliess's Maybe: Homophobia, Anti-Semitism, and the Invention of Oedipus," *GLQ 2* (1995): 117.

[14]Boyarin, "Freud's Baby," 117.

[15]I am grateful to Virginia Burrus for making we aware of this text. Roy Porter, "Baudrillard: History, Hysteria, and Consumption," in *Forget Baudrillard?* ed. Chris Rojek and Bryan Turner (New York: Routledge, 1993), 4.

[16]Porter, "Baudrillard," 2.

[17]Porter, "Baudrillard," 3.

[18]Porter, "Baudrillard," 10.

[19]Porter, "Baudrillard," 2.

[20]Catherine Keller, *Apocalypse Now and Then: A Feminist Guide to the End of the World* (Boston: Beacon, 1996), 19–20.

[21]Derek Krueger, *Symeon the Holy Fool: Leontius' Life and the Late Antique City* (Berkeley: University of California Press, 1996), 2.

[22]Krueger, *Holy Fool,* 47.

[23]Krueger, *Holy Fool,* 128.

[24]Krueger, *Holy Fool,* 2.

[25]Michael Moore, *Downsize This! Random Threats From an Unarmed American* (New York: HarperPerennial, 1997), 10, 18–19.

[26]Moore, *Downsize This,* 2.

[27]Moore, *Downsize This,* 50, 118.

[28]Transcribed from http://adbusters.org/37/nodesigns/3.jpg.

[29]Kalle Lasn, *Culture Jam: The Uncooling of America*™ (New York: William Morrow and Company, 1999), ix.

[30]Lasn, *Culture Jam,* 111.

[31]Lasn, *Culture Jam,* 7.

[32]John Briggs and F. David Peat, *Seven Life Lessons of Chaos: Timeless Wisdom from the Science of Change* (New York: HarperCollins, 1999), 8–9.

Chapter 5: Civil War, Civil Rights, World Trade Center

[1]Alice Walker, *In Search of Our Mother's Gardens: Womanist Prose* (New York: Harcourt Brace Jovanovich, 1983), xi.

[2]S. P. Reyna and R. E. Downs, *Deadly Developments: Capitalism, States, and War* (Australia: Gordon and Breach Publishers, 1999), 5.

[3]Sharon Begley, "The Roots of Evil," *Newsweek* (May 21, 2001): 32.

[4]Ibid., 34.

[5]Ibid., 35.

[6]Reyna and Downs, 4.

[7]Antonín Basch, *The New Economic Warfare* (New York: Columbia University Press, 1941), vii–viii, 5, 7, 9, 16, 21, 29.

[8]J. Maurice Clark, Walton H. Hamilton, and Harold G. Moulton, eds., *Readings in The Economics of War* (Chicago: University of Chicago Press, 1918), xi–xiv.

[9]Alex P. Schmid, "Terrorism and the Use of Weapons of Mass Destruction: From Where the Risk?" in Max Taylor and John Horgan, eds., *The Future of Terrorism* (London: Frank Cass, 2000); 128–29, n. 18.

[10]Terrell E. Arnold, *The Violence Formula: Why People Lend Support and Sympathy to Terrorism* (Lexington, Mass.: D. C. Heath, 1999), 179–80.

[11]Ibid.

[12]See René Girard, *Violence and the Sacred* (Baltimore: The Johns Hopkins University Press, 1977).

[13]Gil Bailie, "Cinema and Crisis: The Elusive Quest for Catharsis," *Image* 20 (1998): 17–20.

[14]Conversations with Diana Culbertson, Professor of Literature, Kent State University, Summer, 1995.

[15]Stephen J. Whitefield, http://www.us-israel.org/jsource/biography/arendt.html.

[16]Hannah Arendt, *On Revolution* (New York: Penguin Books, 1963), 11–19, 115.

[17]Ibid. 57–58.

[18]Lewis Baldwin, "The Highroad to Destiny," in *Martin Luther King, Jr.: A Profile,* ed. C. Eric Lincoln (New York: Hill and Wang, 1984), 99–100; Robert M. Franklin, Jr., "Martin Luther King as Pastor," *The Iliff Review* 42 (Spring 1985): 4; Martin Luther King, Jr., "Letter from Birmingham Jail," in *Why We Can't Wait* (New York: Harper, 1963), 90–91; Richard Lischer, *The Preacher King: Martin Luther King, Jr. and the Word That Moved America* (New York: Oxford University Press, 1995), 3–4, 8, 10–11.

[19]Louis Lomax, "When Nonviolence Meets Black Power," in *Martin Luther King, Jr.: A Profile,* ed. C. Eric Lincoln (New York: Hill and Wang, 1984), 165–73.

[20]Lischer, 171. See also William Donnel Watley, "Against Principalities: An Examination of Martin Luther King, Jr.'s Ethic" (Ph.D. diss., Columbia University, 1980), 352, 356, 358, 361, 364, 368, 369.

[21]Preston Williams, "Contextualizing the Faith: The African-American Tradition and Martin Luther King, Jr.," in One *Faith, Many Cultures: Inculturation, Indiginization, and Contextualization,* ed. Ruy O. Costa (New York: Orbis Books and Boston Theological Institute, 1988), 130–33; Paul R. Garber, "Black Theology: The Latter Day Legacy of Martin Luther King, Jr.," *Journal of the Interdenominational Theological Center* 2 (Spring 1975): 100, 103, 107, 113.

[22]Lewis Baldwin, "Martin Luther King, Jr., the Black Church, and the Black Messianic Vision," *Journal of the Interdenominational Theological Center* 12 (1984–85): 93–108. See also King, *Stride Toward Freedom* (New York: Harper, 1958), 223; King, *Strength to Love* (New York: Harper & Row, 1963), 62–63.

[23]James Melvin Washington, ed., *A Testament of Hope* (San Francisco: Harper & Row, 1986), 500.

[24]Ted Rall, "It's About Oil," *San Francisco Chronicle,* 21 November 2001, A25. See also Ahmed Rashid, *Taliban: Militant Islam, Oil & Fundamentalism in Central Asia* (New Haven, Conn.: Yale Nota Bene, 2001).

[25]Rall, "It's About Oil."

[26]Vladimir Todres, "Chevron pipeline to boost Kazakhstan's exports," *San Francisco Chronicle,* 28 November 2001, B3.

[27]Emmanuel Levinas, *Totality and Infinity,* trans. Alphonso Lingis (Pittsburgh: Duquesne University Press, 1969), 39.

[28]Ibid., 199–200.

[29]Ibid., 27.

[30]Ibid.

[31]Jacques Derrida, "Faith and Knowledge: The Two Sources of 'Religion' at the Limits of Reason Alone," in Jacques Derrida and Gianni Vattimo, eds., *Religion* (Stanford, Calif.: Stanford University Press, 1996), 42.

[32]Ibid., 5, 11, 15, 25, 27, 44–49.

[33]Mark Juergensmeyer, *Terror in the Mind of God* (Berkeley, Calif.: University of California Press, 2000), 3.

[34]The shaping of my essay includes reflections and sources from my students in the Ph.D. seminar "History of Theology, 1914–1965" at the Graduate Theological Union, Berkeley; including Matthew Haar Farris, research assistant, Nate Hinerman, Richard Atkins, Sylvia Sweeney, Joseph de Léon, Jennifer Hughes, Virgilio Domingos, and Luke Higgins. My partner-husband-editor-designated driver of 20-plus years, the Honorable Michael A. Kirk-Duggan guided me to the relation between international oil consortia and the current Afghan "War on Terrorism."

Chapter 6: "For This the Earth Shall Mourn" (Jer. 4:28)

[1]Reinhold Niebuhr, *Faith and History: A Comparison of Christian and Modern Views of History* (New York: C. Scribner's Sons, 1949), 3.

[2]Douglas John Hall, *Lighten Our Darkness: Toward an Indigenous Theology of the Cross* (Philadelphia: Westminster Press, 1976).

[3]Quoted by James M. Wall in *Christian Century,* 26 September 2001, 45.

[4]See the works of Douglas John Hall, including *Thinking the Faith: Christian Theology in a North American Context* (Minneapolis: Augsburg Press, 1989); *Professing the Faith: Christian Theology in a North American Context* (Minneapolis: Fortress Press, 1993); and *Confessing the Faith: Christian Theology in a North American Context* (Minneapolis: Fortress Press, 1996).

[5]Quoted in Edward W. Said, *Reflections on Exile and Other Essays* (Cambridge, Mass.: Harvard University Press, 2000), 184.

[6]Walter Brueggemann, *The Land: Place as Gift, Promise, and Challenge in Biblical Faith,* Overtures to Biblical Theology 1 (Philadelphia: Fortress Press, 1977).

[7]Barbara Kingsolver in *San Francisco Chronicle,* 25 September 2001.

[8]Quoted by Karl J. Weintraub, *Visions of Culture* (Chicago: University of Chicago Press, 1966), 269.

Chapter 7: Roots of the Taliban

[1]Judith A. Mayotte, *Disposable People? The Plight of Refugees* (Maryknoll, N.Y.: Orbis Books, 1992).

[2]Personal interview. For further information, see my *Disposable People?*

[3]Louis Dupree: *Afghanistan* (Princeton, N.J.: Princeton University Press, 1980), 316.

[4]Arthur Bonner, *Among the Afghans* (Durham, N.C.: University Press, 1987), 45.

[5]Ahmed Rashid, *Taliban: Militant Islam, Oil & Fundamentalism in Central Asia* (New Haven, Conn.: Yale University Press, 2000), 88–93.

[6]Peter Marsden, *The Taliban: War, Religion and the New Order in Afghanistan* (New York: Zed Books, Ltd., 1998), 45–46, Ahmed Rashid, 26–27.

Chapter 8: Sovereignty, Empire, Capital, and Terror

[1]For the development of this notion, see for instance Carl Schmitt, *The Leviathan in the State Theory of Thomas Hobbes: Meaning and Failure of a Political Symbol* (Westport, Conn.: Greenwood Press, 1996), as well as his other works.

[2]Michael Hardt and Antonio Negri, *Empire* (Cambridge, Mass.: Harvard University Press, 2000).

[3]See, for example, Rider Haggard's *King Solomon's Mines.*

Chapter 9: September 11 and the Ethics of Violence

[1]Francisco de Vitoria, *De indis II, sive de iure bello,* § 14; see Vitoria, *Political Writings,* ed. Anthony Pagden and Jeremy Lawrance (Cambridge: Cambridge University Press, 1991), 304.

[2]Versions of parts of this paper were read at the University of Virginia and at Mary Baldwin College in October and November, 2001. I thank participants in those discussions for their comments and questions. I am thankful also to Talbot Brewer, Roque Carrion Wam, Cora Diamond, and, as always, Ms. Isa Wiener, for their help.

Chapter 10: "Dealing in Straight Power Concepts": Justice and the Use of Force

[1]George Kennan, quoted in William L. Robinson, *Promoting Polyarchy: Globalization, US Intervention, and Hegemony* (Cambridge: Cambridge University Press, 1996), 1. Shorter versions of this paper were presented at the "Imperialism and Terror" teach-in at the University of Virginia on October 1, 2001, and at the "Why War?" symposium in the Literature Program at Duke University on October 26, 2001. I am grateful to John Milbank for inviting me to participate in the University of Virginia teach-in, and to Creston Davis for being its flawless organizer; and also to Julie Kim and Simon Krysl for organizing the Duke teach-in.

[2]I am indebted throughout to Alain Badiou, "Philosophy and Politics," *Radical Philosophy,* no. 96 (1999): 29–32, for this characterization of the essential structure that connects truth and justice.

[3]The relation between truth and falsity becomes important at this point. Falsity emerges when a fundamental undecidability is introduced between the real and the unreal. I shall say more about truth shortly, but it is important to note here that falsity is not error or confusion, but the capacity to make a potential event of truth succumb to the forces of nondecidability. On this, see Gilles Deleuze, "Doubts about the Imaginary," in his collection *Negotiations*, trans. Martin Joughin (New York: Columbia University Press, 1995), 65–66.

[4]As Thomas Jefferson once noted, Americans tend to regard their Constitution as the equivalent of "the ark of the covenant, too sacred to be touched." See *The Works of Thomas Jefferson*, vol. 12, ed. Paul Leicester Ford (New York: Putnam, 1905), 11. Quoted in Daniel Lazare, *The Velvet Coup: The Constitution, the Supreme Court, and the Decline of American Democracy* (London: Verso, 2001), 8.

[5]See Badiou, "Philosophy and Politics," 29. Badiou clearly believes that a philosophy is necessary if the possible truth of this political standpoint is to emerge. He shares Plato's view that there has to be a necessary concatenation between philosophy and politics if justice is to find its place of actualization. Interestingly enough, a similar position is taken by the emphatically non-Platonist Deleuze, who insists that such things as rights are not created by "codes and pronouncements" but "by the philosophy of law." See his "On Philosophy," in *Negotiations*, 153. The principle straddling the otherwise quite different positions of Badiou and Deleuze derives from the insight that politics cannot on its own transcend the disarray of partiality and interest (Badiou), and that political activity in the mainstream is typically constrained by having to be undertaken through the auspices of the apparatuses of the State (Deleuze). For the latter point, see Deleuze (with Claire Parnet), "Many Politics," in his *Dialogues,* trans. Hugh Tomlinson and Barbara Habberjam (New York: Columbia University Press, 1987), 124–47.

[6]For this, see Badiou, "Philosophy and Politics," 29. See also Deleuze, "On Philosophy" in *Negotiations,* 153, where it is asserted that "jurisprudence...is the philosophy of law, and deals with singularities; it advances by working out from singularities."

[7]The claim here that truth and justice are inextricably bound up with politics is of course also to be found in Badiou's work. However, I depart from Badiou's insistence that a true politics is occasional and even extraordinary, the last real example for Badiou being 1968. For this, see Badiou, *Abrégé de métapolitique* (Paris: Seuil, 1998), 17 and 167. Badiou may have succumbed to what Simon Critchley has aptly called "the seduction of a great politics," that is, the politics of an epochal transformation. For Critchley, see "Demanding Approval: On the Ethics of Alain Badiou," *Radical Philosophy* 100 (2000): 27. By contrast, "politics" in the sense used here is thoroughly quotidian, and pertains to the day-to-day functioning of social, political, and legal institutions. These institutions typically function by harnessing themselves to regimes of nondecidability, that is, they are constitutively not in the truth, and it is the task of a politics of justice to decouple institutions from these regimes of nondecidability, thereby allowing them to be in the truth and in justice. Truth and justice are in every sense achievements, not "natural" properties of political and social institutions qua institutions.

[8]For an exemplary critique of Huntington's thesis, see Edward Said, "The Clash of Ignorance," in *The Nation* (available on the Web at http://www.thenation.com on October 22, 2001). Said concludes: "'The Clash of Civilizations' thesis is a gimmick like 'The War of the Worlds,' better for reinforcing defensive self-pride than for critical understanding of the bewildering interdependence of our time" (paragraph 15).

[9]On this, see Badiou, "Philosophy and Politics," 29.

[10]The notion of "innocence" and its cognates is often used to characterize the individual who by virtue of not having done wrong should not be subjected to any form of retribution. Some may object that no one is truly "innocent," that, for example, the American who votes quite happily for politicians in favor of grossly one-sided policies regarding Israel, further bombing of Iraq, and so on, is not entirely free of culpability. For this reason it may be more appropriate to refer to the victims of the September 11 attacks as "noncombatants," in the same way that the hapless civilians now being bombed in Afghanistan are noncombatants. For a useful discussion of the question of noncombatant immunity, see Richard Norman, *Ethics, Killing and War* (Cambridge: Cambridge University Press, 1995), 159ff.

[11]The indiscriminate attacking of civilians is forbidden by the *jus in bello* provisions of international law, and the International Law Commission's Draft Articles on State Responsibility forbid the submission of the general population of a state to indiscriminate mass punishment. For discussion of this see Yoram Dinstein's classic work *War, Aggression and Self-Defence,* 3d ed. (Cambridge: Cambridge University Press, 2001), 104. Two further observations are in order

here. First, Article 94(2) of the United Nations Charter decrees that no individual state is permitted to wage war unilaterally and that only the Security Council of the United Nations is competent to authorize the use of inter-state force. Article 51 of the UN Charter permits a state to use armed force in self-defense, but does not sanction the use of force in retaliatory action on the part of a victim state against an initial use of armed force. It should be noted that the United States did not seek authorization from the UN Security Council before attacking Afghanistan, and also that it is a requirement of international law that any self-defensive action taken against an initial armed attack be constrained by the principle of proportionality. For discussion of the condition of proportionality, see Dinstein, 183ff. The danger here is that the U.S. and its allies are on their way to becoming state terrorists in their very attempts to combat the terrorist attacks of September 11. Second, in the event of war, and given the presumed applicability of the terms of the Geneva Convention to the prosecution of such a war (already declared by President Bush and other members of his administration), a captured Osama bin Laden would presumably have to be treated as a prisoner of war according to the provisions of this Convention.

[12]Here the principle adumbrated by Grotius in the seventeenth century is perhaps worth noting: It is the bidding of mercy, if not justice, that, except for reasons that are weighty and will affect the safety of many, no action should be attempted whereby innocent persons may be threatened with destruction. See Hugo Grotius, *The Law of War and Peace (De Jure Belli ac Pacis Libri Tres)*, trans. Francis W. Kelsey (Indianapolis: Bobbs-Merrill, [1925] 1962). Grotius is a "consequentialist," that is, he upholds the principle that an act (the killing of innocent human beings in this case) can be justified if it has as one of its consequences the prevention of a greater wrong, a wrong that would have occurred had the act in question not been performed. Grotius is, of course, a natural law theorist, and the position adopted in this paper does not embrace a natural law perspective, nor does it underwrite any form of consequentialism.

[13]In thinking about this question I am indebted to Thomas M. Franck's magisterial *Fairness in International Law and Institutions* (Oxford: Oxford University Press, 1995), 248ff.

[14]For the view that the killing of innocents is never justified, even in anticipatory self-defense, see, among others, Elizabeth Anscombe, "Mr. Truman's Degree," in *The Collected Papers of G.E.M. Anscombe*, vol. 3 (Minneapolis: University of Minnesota Press, 1981), 62–71. See also Anscombe, "War and Murder," in Joram Grab Haber, ed., *Absolutism and Its Consequentialist Critics* (Lanham, Md.: Rowman and Littlefield, 1994), 29–40. Anscombe's "absolutist" postion is thus opposed to the "consequentialism" of someone like Grotius (note 12 above).

[15]This would be the "absolutist" position of someone such as Anscombe and Thomas Nagel. As Nagel puts it: "Once the door is open to calculations of utility and national interest, the usual speculations about the future of freedom, peace, and economic prosperity can be brought to bear to ease the consciences of those responsible for a certain number of charred babies." See Thomas Nagel, "War and Massacre," in Haber, ed., *Absolutism and Its Consequentialist Critics,* 222. Nagel's 1972 paper delineates a modified absolutist position, since Nagel accepts that the consequences of an action ought to be taken into account when these consequences are virtually guaranteed to occur and are potentially dire. But there are cases, says Nagel, when the absolutist would experience a profound moral dilemma, since he or she would be responsible for sanctioning an evil consequence precisely because he/she has refused to break the prohibition against killing innocents in order to prevent that greater evil from occurring. The position taken in this paper is fundamentally compatible with Nagel's.

[16]Chalmers Johnson, *Blowback: The Costs and Consequences of American Empire* (New York: Metropolitan Books, 2000), 33.

[17]Ibid., 223.

[18]Here I modify the observation made by Thomas Nagel when he says in "War and Massacre" that "Hostile treatment, unlike surgery, is always addressed *to* a person, and does not take its interpersonal meaning from a wider context. But hostile acts can serve as the expression or implementation of only a limited range of attitudes to the person who is attacked. Those attitudes in turn have as objects certain real or presumed characteristics or activities of the person that are thought to justify them. When this background is absent, hostile or aggressive behavior can no longer be intended for the reception of the victim as a subject. Instead it takes on the character of a purely bureaucratic operation. This occurs when one attacks someone who is not the true object of one's hostility–the true object may be someone else, who can be attacked through the victim; or one may not be manifesting a hostile attitude toward anyone, but merely using the easiest available path to some desired goal. One finds oneself not facing or addressing the victim at all, but operating on him–without the larger context of personal interaction that surrounds a surgical operation" (228–29).

Nagel's point is that attacking noncombatants effectively makes them into objects who are used instrumentally to achieve other ends. The position taken in this paper, while it does not controvert Nagel's claim, nonetheless views every situation between attacker and noncombatant as one that involves an essentially social relation (though in fairness to Nagel this relation, in the broad sense being used here, may not necessarily have the richness that marks a "personal interaction" of the kind adverted to in the above-quoted passage). Thus, it is clear that the September 11 hijackers used, more or less effectively, various elements of the American social system to achieve their objectives, and this social system is, of course, the one to which their victims belonged. In fact, it was precisely the capacity of the hijackers to insert themselves seamlessly into the American *mores,* the *mores* of their victims, that enabled their attacks to be so successful. Hostility between parties is willy-nilly social.

[19]The Bush administration's recent announcement that it is now in favor of the principle of a Palestinian state has to be greeted with skepticism. Meaningful support for such a state has at the very least to be accompanied by a reversal of the U.S.'s "do nothing" policy on the implementation of the United Nation's resolutions 242 and 338, which call on Israel to withdraw from all the territories it has occupied illegally since the Six Day War of 1967. The U.S. will also have to help ensure that Palestinians have the right of return to lands sequestered by Israel, and that the new Palestinian state be allowed to claim east Jerusalem as its capital. Until the Bush administration shows itself to be willing to move on these and other fronts, its announcement must be regarded as a ploy in the U.S.'s and Britain's current attempts to win over moderate Arab opinion. For a lapidary discussion of this and other issues, see Perry Anderson, "Scurrying towards Bethlehem," *New Left Review,* second series no. 10 (2001): 5–30. See also As'ad Ghanem, "State and Minority in Israel: The Case of the Ethnic State and the Predicament of its Minority," *Ethnic and Racial Studies* 21(1998): 428–48.

[20]See Peter Gowan, "Neoliberal Cosmopolitanism," *New Left Review,* second series no. 11 (2001): 79–93, quotation taken from 83.

[21]Ngaire Woods, in her conspectus of this international order, concludes that "there is little indication that powerful member states have any intention of altering the hierarchical basis on which order has traditionally been maintained, even though that hierarchy will not serve to meet the more complex challenges of order in a globalized world." See Woods, "Order, Globalization, and Inequality in World Politics," in Woods and Andrew Hurrell, eds., *Inequality, Globalization, and World Politics* (Oxford: Oxford University Press, 1999), 35.

[22]Despite the accusations of guilt leveled by the American and British governments, no convincing evidence of bin Laden's culpability for the attacks of September 11 has been produced for the public, leaving the Taliban to be the visible focus of the American military campaign. There are reported videotapes in which bin Laden is said to admit culpability for the September 11 attacks. It should be noted, however, that the U.S. and its allies were blaming bin Laden and his associates for the attacks even before these videotapes were known to exist–it is this putative evidence that needs to be scrutinized and assessed by an international prosecutorial authority.

[23]For instance, Article 11 of the United Nations International Covenant on Economic, Social and Cultural Rights (1966) stipulates that "recognizing the fundamental right of everyone to be free of hunger" requires that states "ensure an equitable distribution of world food supplies in relation to need." The elimination of hunger being indispensable to human well-being, a quest for global justice will *a fortiori* involve implementation of Article 11. Here it is worth noting that it has been estimated that even if inequality within each nation were eliminated, 75 percent of global inequality would still exist. On this see Debra Satz, "Equality of What Among Whom? Thoughts on Cosmopolitanism, Statism, and Nationalism," in Ian Shapiro and Lea Brilmayer, eds., *Global Justice* (New York: New York University Press, 1999), 68. Only measures that are global in scope can remedy global misery. Interestingly enough, it was Leibniz in the seventeenth century who perceived the importance of welfare in securing the well-being of citizens:

> The greatest and most efficacious means...of augmenting the general welfare of men, while enlightening them, while turning them toward the good and while freeing them from annoying inconveniences [poverty, unemployment, maleducation] insofar as this is feasible, would be to persuade great princes and their principal ministers to make extraordinary efforts to procure such great goods and to our times to enjoy advantages which, without this [extraordinary effort] would be reserved for a distant posterity.

See Leibniz, *Memoir for Enlightened Persons of Good Intention,* 2d ed., ed. and trans. Patrick Riley (Cambridge: Cambridge University Press, 1988), 107, quoted in Riley, *Leibniz' Universal Jurisprudence: Justice as the Charity of the Wise* (Cambridge, Mass.: Harvard University Press, 1996), 223, surely the most accomplished anglophone examination of Leibniz's political theory.

[24]On this, see Bob Deacon, "Social Policy in a Global Context," in Woods and Hurrell, eds., *Inequality, Globalization, and World Politics,* 211–47.

Chapter 11: Errant Concepts in an Age of Terror

[1]John Milbank, "Intoduction," in *Radical Orthodoxy: A New Theology,* ed. John Milbank, Catherine Pickstock, and Graham Ward (London: Routledge, 1999), 3.

[2]Gilles Deleuze and Félix Guattari, *What is Philosophy?* trans. Hugh Tomlinson and Graham Burchell (New York: Columbia University Press, 1994), 36.

[3]Pierre Bourdieu, *The Logic of Presence,* trans. Richard Nice (Stanford, Calif.: Stanford University Press, 1990), 52.

[4]Pascal Boyer, *The Naturalness of Religious Ideas* (Berkeley: University of California Press, 1994), xi.

[5]Dan Sperber, *Explaining Culture: A Naturalistic Approach* (Oxford: Blackwell Publishers, 1996), 1.

[6]Ibid., 59.

[7]For a discussion of the difficulties in relying on theories of reference in the interpretation of historical change, see Edith Wyschogrod, *An Ethics of Remembering: History, Heterology and the Nameless Others* (Chicago: University of Chicago Press, 1998), 18–32.

[8]Richard Dawkins, *The Extended Phenotype: The Gene as the Unit of Selection* (Oxford: W. H. Freeman, 1982), 2. The view cited is that of D'Arcy Thompson.

[9]William James, *Essays in Radical Empiricism* (Cambridge, Mass.: Harvard University Press, 1976), 86.

[10]Richard Dawkins, *The Selfish Gene* (Oxford: Oxford University Press, 1976), 33.

[11]Ibid., 292.

[12]Dawkins, *Extended Phenotype,* 114.

[13]Dawkins, *Selfish Gene,* 22.

[14]Dawkins, *Extended Phenotype,* 1.

[15]Ibid., 83.

[16]Jean Baudrillard, *The Illusion of the End* (Stanford, Calif.: Stanford University Press, 1994), 15.

[17]Christopher G. Langton, "Artificial Life," in Margaret A. Boden, ed., *The Philosophy of Artificial Life* (Oxford: Oxford University Press, 1996), 47.

[18]Ibid., 50.

[19]Ibid., 41–47.

[20]Ibid., 88.

[21]Thomas S. Ray, "An Approach to the Synthesis of Life," in Margaret A. Boden, ed., *The Philosophy of Artificial Life* (Oxford: Oxford University Press, 1996), 136.

[22]Langton, "Artificial Life," 58.

[23]Gilles Deleuze, "Foreword," in Eric Alliez, *Capital Times: Tales from the Conquest of Time,* trans. Georges Van Den Abbeele (Minneapolis: University of Minnesota Press, 1996), xii–xiii.

[24]Dominique Janicaud, *Powers of the Rational: Science, Technology and the Future of Thought,* trans. by Peg Birmingham and Elizabeth Birmingham (Bloomington, Ind.: Indiana University Press, 1994).

[25]Ibid., 260.

[26]Nicholas Rescher, *Complexity: A Philosophical Overview* (New Brunswick, N.J.: Transaction Press, 1998), 1.

[27]Ibid., 191.

[28]Ibid., 208.

[29]Paul Cilliers, *Complexity and Postmodernism: Understanding Complex Systems* (London: Routledge, 1998), 4.

[30]Ibid., 10.

[31]Ibid., 116–17.

PART 2: VISIONS

Chapter 12: Fragments of a Vision in a September 11 World

[1]This is part of a reflection entitled "Rich Woman, Poor Woman," written by a working-class Chilean woman in 1973 shortly after Chile's elected socialist president, Salvador Allende, was overthrown in a bloody military coup. A U.S. missionary translated the work and brought it with her when she was forced to leave Chile. Source: Coordinating Center for Women, New York, N.Y.

²E-mail message from the International Center of Bethlehem, October 2001.

³David Tracy, "Saving from Evil: Salvation and Evil Today," in *The Fascination of Evil,* ed. Hermann Häring and David Tracy (Maryknoll, N.Y.: Orbis Books, 1998), 107–16, here 114.

⁴Choan-Seng Song, *Third-Eye Theology: Theology in Formation in Asian Settings,* rev. ed. (Maryknoll, N.Y.: Orbis Books, 1991), 119.

⁵Karl Rahner, *Encounters with Silence,* 5th ed. (Westminster, Md.: The Newman Press, 1965), 23, meditates on the "eloquent sounds" of God's silence. See also Barbara Brown Taylor, *When God Is Silent* (Cambridge, Mass.: Cowley Publications, 1998), 43–82.

⁶Dietrich Bonhoeffer, *Letters and Papers from Prison,* ed. Eberhard Bethge, enlarged ed. (New York: Macmillan Publishing, 1972), 219.

⁷Quoted in *Holy Name Province: 100th Anniversary* (Paterson, N.J.: St. Anthony's Guild, 2001).

⁸I learned about the custom of Lithuanian women to sew a birth-shirt, and about Jewish women's ritual practices of guarding the birthing mother against the "child eater" from *Women, Ritual and Liturgy,* ed. Susan K. Roll et al., Yearbook of the European Society of Women in Theological Research 9 (Leuven: Peeters, 2001).

⁹Cf. Kathleen D. Billman's use of this story from Exodus as an image of pastoral ministry: "Pastoral Care as an Art of Community," in *The Arts of Ministry: Feminist-Womanist Approaches,* ed. Christie Cozad Neuger (Louisville, Ky.: Westminster John Knox Press, 1996), 10–38, esp. 21–25.

¹⁰See Denise Ackermann, "Engaging Freedom: A Contextual Feminist Theology of Praxis," *Journal of Theology for Southern Africa* 94 (1996): 33–49, esp. 46–47.

Chapter 13: The Armageddon of 9/11: A Counter-Apocalyptic Meditation

¹In the interest of a counterapocalypse–neither a literal apocalypse nor an anti-apocalypse– I have mapped the effects of John's revelation in *Apocalypse Now and Then: A Feminist Guide to the End of the World* (Boston: Beacon, 1996).

²I propose counterapocalypse as an alternative to both unself-critical apocalypticism, which tends to literalize the prophetic voice, and antiapocalypse, which represses it, in my book *Apocalypse Now and Then.*

³Edward W. Said, "The Clash of Ignorance," *The Nation* (October 22, 2001).

⁴I am not in a position to invent new terminology for the twentieth-century literalist/absolutist branch of Islam, and indeed seek to solicit its non-otherness by use of the term *fundamentalist.* But I use it with the following, pre-9/11 proviso in mind: "So long as the Western world...anxiously follows the spread of the Islamic movements incorrectly termed 'fundamentalist' (Islam, with all its different faces, cannot be blanketed under the single term 'fundamentalist'), there exists in Europe a widespread tendency to view Islam as a potential adversary." Franco Cardini, *Europe and Islam,* trans. C. Beamish (Oxford: Blackwell, 1999, 2000), 1.

⁵Norman O. Brown, "The Apocalypse of Islam,"in *Apocalypse and/or Metamorphosis* (Berkeley: University of California Press, 1991), 86.

⁶Sura 70:8–10, 15–35, "The Stairways," in *The Koran Interpreted,* trans. A. J. Arberry (New York: MacMillan, 1955), 300. All subsequent translations of the Koran in this chapter are from Arberry's translation.

⁷Sura 16:77.

⁸Sura 91:14.

⁹Sura 92:12–14.

¹⁰*The City,* to which Mohammed and his followers made the founding *hejirah*, or migration, in 622.

¹¹The five pillars comprise the fundamental practices of Islam. First is the *Shahada,* or witness ("There is no god but God" *[la ilaha illa'llah]* and "Muhammad is God's messenger.") The second is the *salat,* or ritual prayer, the fourth is fasting on Ramadan, the fifth is the Hajj to Mecca. "Behind all the stress on practice is the recognition that the Koran must become flesh and blood. It is not enough for people to read the Koran or learn what it says. They have to embody the Book." Sachiko Murata and William C. Chittick, *The Vision of Islam* (St. Paul: Paragon House, 1994), 9.

¹²"Where Christians discerned God's hand in apparent failure and defeat, when Jesus died on the cross, Muslims experienced political success as sacramental and as a revelation of the divine presence in their lives. It is important, however, to be clear that when the Arabs burst out of Arabia they were not impelled by the ferocious power of Islam." Karen Armstrong, *Islam: A Short History* (New York: Random House/Modern Library, 2000), 29f. I recommend this readable text for an introduction.

[13]"After the campaigns waged by the caliphs who immediately succeeded the Prophet, that is from the 630's onwards, the expansion of Islam never resembled an inexorable military conquest…It was in fact a continuous, not always consistent process of conversion…of groups belonging to exhausted or crisis-ridden societies–for example the Monophysite Christians of Syria and Egypt, harshly treated by the basileus of Byzantium…Many nevertheless preferred to remain loyal to their own faith…and to be considered as *dhimmi*–'protected' as well as 'subject.' They thereby demonstrated, incidentally, their opinion of government by the infidel as being preferable to government by their co-religionists." Cardini, *Europe and Islam,* 4.

[14]For a study of the highly gendered and spatialized apocalypticism of Christopher Columbus as constitutive of "modernity," see C. Keller, "The Breast, the Apocalypse and the Colonial Journey," in *The Year 2000: Essays on the End,* ed. Charles B. Strozier and M. Flynn (New York: New York University Press, 1997), 42–58; or Keller, *Apocalypse,* 140–80.

[15]"He is known to have discussed Voltaire's Mahomet with Goethe, and to have defended Islam and the Prophet. His interest in the East was accompanied by a strong sympathy with the crusades," Cardini, *Europe and Islam,* 197.

[16]In the process Mehmet Ali maintained the support of the Ottoman Empire by defeating the Wahabite sect of Arabia, whose brand of Islam is still a key stream of contemporary Muslim missions in the West and extremism in the Middle East.

[17]Quote from Al-Jabarti, early nineteenth-century sheikh, cited in Karen Armstrong, *The Battle for God* (New York: Ballantine, 2000), 113.

[18]Led by Hasan al-Banna (1906–1949) until his assassination, the Brothers and Sisters sought dignity and freedom from European cultural dominance and economic destitution. Suppressed through mass imprisonment, torture, and extermination of Brothers by Jaml Abd al-Nasser, the Brotherhood became a militant underground movement.

[19]Ayatollah Kashani prophesied this at the time of the coup, marking the emergence of the U.S. as a colonial aggressor. "When Iranians looked back on Operation Ajax, they would forget the defection of their own people from Musaddiq, and believe implicitly that the United States had single-handedly imposed the shah's dictatorship upon them…There seemed to be a double standard. America proudly proclaimed its belief in freedom and democracy, but warmly supported a shah who permitted no opposition to his rule, and denied Iranians fundamental human rights," Armstrong, *Battle for God,* 229. This double standard was already becoming standard international policy.

[20]"Nobody had ever claimed before that jihad was equivalent to the five Pillars of Islam, but Mawdudi felt that the innovation was justified by the present emergency. The stress and fear of cultural and religious annihilation had led to the development of a more extreme and potentially violent distortion of the faith," Armstrong, *Battle for God,* 168.

[21]"Qutb told Muslims to model themselves on Muhammad: to separate themselves from mainstream society (as Muhammad had made the hijrah from Mecca to Medina), and then engage in a violent jihad. But Muhammad had in fact finally achieved victory by an ingenious policy of nonviolence; the Quran adamantly opposed force and coercion in religious matters, and its vision–far from preaching exclusion and separation–was tolerant and inclusive. Qutb insisted that the Quranic injunction to tolerance could occur only after the political victory of Islam and the establishment of a true Muslim state," Armstrong, *Battle for God,* 169f.

[22]See especially Leila Ahmed, *Women and Gender in Islam: Historical Roots of a Modern Debate* (New Haven, Conn.: Yale University Press, 1992).

[23]Armstrong, *Islam,* 165.

[24]Gustav Niebuhr, "After the Attacks: Finding Fault; U.S., Secular Groups Set Tone for Terror Attacks, Falwell Says," *The New York Times,* 14 September 2001.

[25]Bert Decker, http://www.boldassurance.com.

[26]Ibid.

[27]For a succinct guide to the theological and postmodern problematic of "modernity" I recommend Paul Lakeland, *Postmodernity: Christian Identity in a Fragmented Age* (Minneapolis: Fortress Press, 1997).

[28]See Walter Wink, *Engaging the Powers: Discernment and Resistance in a World of Domination* (Minneapolis: Fortress, 1992).

[29]Eve Hoffman had given sarcastic voice to my discomfort: "Still, the instant deflection of rage from the perpetrator to the target, the undercurrent of Schadenfreude evident in many statements ('What do you expect, given American foreign policy? They had it coming to them. We have to have a more complex view of where terrorist rage comes from. Americans will just have to learn why the world hates them so much') has been astonishing and dismaying…the first

impulse of many progressive commentators in the wake of the terrible events was to reach for their holsters and come up brandishing standard-issue anti-Americanism as if it were a brave new piece of subversive analysis."

[30]Richard Falk, "Ends and Means: Defining a Just War," *The Nation* (October 29, 2001): 11–15.

[31]Ibid.

[32]Ibid.

[33]Ibid., 13.

[34]To summarize: Force must be used with discrimination, with minimal damage to civilians, and remain "proportional," that is, not greater than that needed to achieve an acceptable military outcome, indeed, not greater than the provoking cause.

[35]Falk, "Ends and Means," 12.

[36]Ibid.

[37]Wink well distinguishes nonviolence from pacifism, saying it is aggressive. But when he insists on "nonviolence without reservation" as a "clear-cut, unambiguous position" for the churches, "understandable to the smallest child," leaving moral ambiguity and just war theory to governments and ethicists, I hear the apocalypse again (see Wink, *Engaging the Powers,* 229). Indeed, his uncritical celebration of Revelation as antidote to the "domination system," that is, "the Beast," in the face of his recognition of Hebrew Scripture's occasional implication in violence, outlines the blind spot.

[38]"Responsible action" accommodates the view that within nature and history there is no pure nonviolence. As Alfred North Whitehead put it, "life feeds on life." There are only kinds and degrees of violence/nonviolence. So the aim to *reduce* violence however and whenever possible may work more credibly than the aim at a purity that characterizes neither the Bible nor creaturely existence.

[39]Edward Said notes that there is "as yet no decent history or demystification" of this contest of the three, whose "bloody modern convergence on Palestine furnishes a rich secular instance of what has been so tragically irreconcilable about them. Not surprisingly, then, Muslims and Christians speak readily of crusades and jihads, both of them eliding the Judaic presence with often sublime insouciance." Said, "Clash of Ignorance," 13.

[40]Also I am grateful for insightful comments from present and former master of divinity students Bruce Nowacek and Shawn Anglim.

PART 3: RESPONSES OF THEOLOGY

Chapter 14: "Make Them as Tumbleweed"

[1]All scripture in this chapter is the author's rendering.

[2]For another meditation on these themes and this psalm, see my "Liturgies of Anger," *Cross Currents* (forthcoming).

Chapter 15: Truth-telling Comfort

[1]Karl Barth, *The Word of God and the Word of Man* (Boston: The Pilgrim Press, 1928), 186.

Chapter 16: The Theologian in the Twilight of American Culture

[1]Manning Marable, *Black America: Multicultural Democracy in the Age of Clarence Thomas and David Duke,* Open Magazine Pamphlet Series (Westfield, N.J.: Open Media, 1992), 16.

[2]Pierre Bourdieu, *Acts of Resistance: Against the Tyranny of the Market,* trans. Richard Nice (New York: The New Press, 1998); Susan Haack, *Manifesto of a Passionate Moderate: Unfashionable Essays* (Chicago: University of Chicago, 1998); bell hooks, *Teaching to Transgress: Education as the Practice of Freedom* (New York: Routledge 1994); idem, *Yearning: Race, Gender, and Cultural Politics* (Boston: South End Press, 1990); idem, *Outlaw Culture: Resisting Representations* (New York and London: Routledge, 1994); Charles Mills, *The Racial Contract* (Ithaca, N.Y., and London: Cornell University Press, 1997); Cornel West, *Prophesy Deliverance!: An Afro-American Revolutionary Christianity* (Philadelphia: Westminster Press, 1982); Morris Berman, *The Twilight of American Culture* (New York: W.W. Norton, 2000); and Michael Hardt and Antonio Negri, *Empire* (Cambridge, Mass.: Harvard University Press, 2001).

[3]Berman, *The Twilight of American Culture,* 19.

[4]Ibid., 182.

[5]Ibid., cited in John Gray, *Isaiah Berlin* (Princeton, N.J.: Princeton University Press, 1996), 88–89.

[6]W. E. B. Du Bois, *The Souls of Black Folk* (1903; New York: Vintage Books, 1990), 16, 35.

[7]James Boggs, *Racism and the Class Struggle* (New York: Monthly Review Press, 1970), 147–48.

[8]Michael Omi and Howard Winant, *Racial Formation in the United States, From the 1960s to the 1990s* (New York: Routledge, 1994), 55–56.

[9]Ibid.

[10]Ibid., 58.

[11]Bernard Lonergan, *Insight: A Study of Human Understanding* (New York: Philosophical Library, 1957), especially chapters 6, 7, and 18–20.

[12]Yen Le Espiritu, *Asian American Panethnicity: Bridging Institutions and Identities* (Philadelphia: Temple University Press, 1992).

[13]Roy Arundhati, "The Algebra of Infinite Justice," London, *The Guardian,* 29 September 2001.

[14]Audre Lorde, "The Master's Tools Will Never Dismantle the Master's House," in *Sister Outsider: Essays and Speeches* (Trumansburg, N.Y.: Crossing Press, 1984).

[15]We "others" learn to use the "master's tools." What are those tools? Among the many are coercion and intimidation; a preference for individual over collaborative and interdependent action; an eagerness for conformity and homogeneity over pluralism and difference; yielding to segregation in order to divide and rule, rather than separation in order to develop and flourish; and surrendering to co-optation rather than risking experimentation and creativity.

[16]Bernard Lonergan, "Finality, Love, Marriage," in *Collection, Collected Works of Bernard Lonergan,* vol. 4 (Toronto: University of Toronto Press, 1988), 27.

[17]*Instruction on the Ecclesial Vocation of the Theologian* (Vatican City 1990), no. 7.

[18]Ibid., no. 1.

[19]Vatican II, *Ad Gentes Divinitus,* 7 December 1965. Citations are taken from Austin Flannery, ed., *Vatican Council II: The Conciliar and Post-Conciliar Documents,* rev. ed. (New York and Grand Rapids: Costello and Eerdmans, 1992), no. 10.

[20]Ibid.

[21]*Instruction on the Ecclesial Vocation of the Theologian,* no. 7.

[22]Ibid., no. 9.

[23]*Time* (February 4, 1991).

[24]Houston A. Baker, "Scene...Not Heard," in *Reading Rodney King: Reading Urban Uprising,* ed., Robert Gooding-Williams (New York: Routledge, 1993), 42.

[25]Cited in James H. Cone, *Martin and Malcolm in America: A Dream or a Nightmare* (Maryknoll, N.Y.: Orbis Books, 1991), 89.

[26]In *The Racial Contract,* Charles Mills situates unstated assumptions about race in the context of social contract theory and examines the "racial contract" at the center of economic exploitation and uncovers how this contract "races and norms" space and human bodies and requires violence and ideological conditioning for its enforcement.

[27]Frank Lentricchia, *Criticism and Social Change* (Chicago: University of Chicago Press, 1985), 25.

[28]James H. Cone, "Looking Back, Going Forward: Black Theology as Public Theology," *Criterion* 35, 1 (Winter 1998): 27.

[29]Etienne Balibar and Immanuel Wallerstein, *Race, Nation, Class: Ambiguous Identities,* trans. Chris Turner (New York: Verso, 1991), 22, 49.

[30]"U. S. Bishops' Pastoral Letter on Racism in Our Day: Brothers and Sisters to Us" (1979), 1.3.

[31]John E. De Gruchy and Charles Villa-Vicencio, eds., *Apartheid Is Heresy* (Grand Rapids: Eerdmans, 1983), 177–78.

[32]Berman, *The Twilight of American Culture,* 71–90.

[33]Ibid., 178.

[34]Michael Hardt and Antonio Negri, *Empire* (Cambridge, Mass.: Harvard University Press, 2001), 413.

[35]Paul Tillich, *The Shaking of the Foundations* (New York: Charles Scribner's Sons, 1948), 161–62.

Chapter 17: Faith, Ethics, and Evil

[1]http://www.crimesofwar.org/expert/attack-anderson.html.

Chapter 20: Hope in a Time of Arrogance and Terror

[1]Francis Fukuyama, *The End of History and the Last Man* (New York: Free Press, 1992).

Chapter 21: In the Face of Evil:
Understanding Evil in the Aftermath of Terror

[1]President George W. Bush, in his address to the nation, September 11, 2001, White House news release.

[2]Ibid., remarks of the President upon arrival in the South Lawn, September 16, 2001, White House press release.

[3]Ibid.

[4]Ibid.

[5]Luis G. Pedraja, *Jesus is My Uncle: Christology from a Hispanic Perspective* (Nashville: Abingdon, 1999), 106.

[6]In process theology, for instance, God is in a state of becoming. Hence, the being of God changes in a dynamic of creative action on behalf of God and all creation. In Barth's thought, and in Eberhard Jüngels work, God's being is not only in becoming, God is defined in being for others. This in itself is an active choice for others. Even in understanding God as creator, we already understand that activity is part of God and constitutive of God's being as one who creates and loves.

[7]Paul Tillich writes, "He alone who is free is able to surrender to the demonic forces that turn his freedom into bondage." In "Heal the Sick; Cast out the Demons," *The Eternal Now* (New York: Charles Scribner and Sons, 1963), 61.

[8]John Calvin gives us a clear example of this position, arguing the "the will is enchained as the slave of sin, it cannot make a movement towards goodness, far less steadily pursue it." *The Institutes of the Christian Religion*, trans. Henry Beveridge, Book 2, 3.5 (Grand Rapids: Eerdmans, 1989), II, 253.

[9]John Calvin writes "all parts of the soul were possessed by sin after Adam…so corrupted that it needs to be healed and to put on a new nature as well." *Institutes of the Christian Religion*, trans. Ford Lewis Battles, as cited in *The Many Faces of Evil: Historical Perspectives*, ed. Amélie Oksenberg Rorty (New York: Routledge, 2001), 121.

[10]Ibid., 121–22. Augustine also attributes our sinfulness to our willful turning away from God, 53.

[11]Augustine, *The Confessions of St. Augustine*, trans. Rex Warner (New York: Mentor Books, 1963), Book 1, 7.23.

[12]Paul Tillich, "The Good That I Will, I Do Not," in *The Eternal Now*, 48.

[13]Augustine writes in *The City of God*, "The head and fount of all these evils is pride, which reigns supremely in the devil, although he has no flesh," trans. J.C.W. Wand (London: Oxford University Press, 1963), Book XIV, 3.225.

[14]According to Karl Barth, who addresses the nature of human freedom in his treatise "The Gift of Freedom," trans. Thomas Weiser in *The Humanity of God* (Atlanta: John Knox Press, 1960), 59–96.

[15]In Christian existentialism, this would be what Søren Kierkegaard calls despair which is conscious of being despair as a form of defiance in which the self asserts itself, being fully in control, and self determination without any form of dependence upon another. See, for instance, *The Sickness unto Death*, trans. Alastair Hannay (New York: Penguin Books, 1989), 98–105.

[16]Barth writes that "human freedom cannot be understood as realized in the solitary detachment of an individual in isolation," nor should it be understood as asserting itself. However, we often fail to understand freedom correctly and assume that it means such a self-assertion and sense of isolation. *The Humanity of God*, 77–78.

[17]Both Schleiermacher and Barth understood freedom as an ability to choose between differing alternatives. For instance, Barth writes "to call a man free is to recognize that God has *given* him freedom." Later on, he writes, "Man becomes free and is free by choosing, deciding, and determining himself in accordance with the freedom of God." Hence, human freedom is dependent upon God, and the choosing we do is between that given to us and before us. Ibid., 74, 76–77.

[18]In speaking about freedom, Barth writes: "God's freedom is the freedom of the Father and the Son in the unity of the Spirit. Again, man's freedom is a far cry from the self-assertion of one or many solitary individuals. It has nothing to do with division and disorder. God's own freedom

is Trinitarian, embracing grace, thankfulness, and peace. It is the freedom of the living God. Only in this relational freedom is God sovereign, almighty, the Lord of all." Thus, freedom is not in isolation but in relationship, in being free to be for the other. It is not "freedom *from*, but a freedom *to* and *for*." *The Humanity of God*, 71–72. Also, see 79–80.

[19]Kierkegaard, *The Sickness Unto Death*, 103.

[20]Amélie Oksenberg Rorty outlines this as one of the "faces" of the metaphysical and theoretical problem of evil in her introduction to the book *The Many Faces of Evil*, xv.

[21]Friedrich Nietzsche, *On the Genealogy of Morals: A Polemic*, trans. Walter Kaufman (New York: Vintage Books, 1967), 17.

[22]Ibid., 27–28.

[23]Ibid., 36–40.

[24]Ibid., 40.

[25]Ibid., 39.

[26]These comments were made on September 13 during a broadcast of the 700 Club, hosted by Robertson and cited in the *Washington Post*, September 14, by John F. Harris, staff writer.

[27]Some comments made in defense of Falwell and Robertson's remarks concerning 9/11 actually quote these passages. For instance, a comment registered on September 26, 2001, in the *St. Mary and Franklin Banner-Tribune* [Franklin, Louisiana] discussion site, defends Falwell and Robertson, citing Sodom and Gomorrah and the destruction of the world because of sin.

[28]For a detailed treatment of the matter, see my article "In Harms Way: Theological Reflection on Disaster," in *Quarterly Review* (Spring 1997): 5–24.

[29]George W. Bush, remarks upon arrival in the South Lawn, White House press release, September 16, 2001.

[30]Ibid.

[31]See Rorty's introduction to *The Many Faces of Evil*, p. xiv, for a summary of evil in terms of relation to some greater good in the works of Augustine and Neo-Platonists.

[32]As Augustine writes in *The City of God*, "Things solely good, therefore, can in some circumstances exist; things solely evil, never, for even those natures which are vitiated by an evil will, so far indeed as they are vitiated, are evil, but in so far as they are natures they are good." *The Many Faces of Evil*, 49.

[33]Abu Hamid Al-Gjazali, in *There is No evil in Allah's Perfect World*, views evil as part of the context of a greater universal order, thus writing "Were it not for illness, the healthy would not enjoy health. Were it not for hell, the blessed in paradise would not know the extent of their blessedness," in *The Many Faces of Evil*, 54.

[34]For a further development of this concept see my article, "In Harms Way: Theological Reflection on Disaster," in *Quarterly Review* (Spring 1997): 15–24.

[35]According to Marjorie Hewitt Suchocki, sin and evil take on a life of their own in social structures that facilitate the transmission of sin from one generation to another, perpetuating evil in our world. See particularly her chapter on this topic in *The Fall to Violence: Original Sin in Relational Theology* (New York: Continuum Press, 1995), 113–27.

[36]Jon Sobrino, "Central Position of the Reign of God in Liberation Theology," in *Mysterium Liberationis: Fundamental Concepts of Liberation Theology*, ed. Ignacio Ellacuría and Jon Sobrino (Maryknoll: Orbis Books, 1993), 355.

[37]Stoicism was an empirical philosophy with a great degree of determinism, but they also emphasized freedom and the importance of the senses upon us. As sin and evil became present in the world, they influenced us. Frederick Coplestone, *A History of Philosophy*, vol. 1 (New York: Doubleday, 1993), 388–400.

[38]Ignacio Ellacuría, "The Historicity of Christian Salvation," In *Mysterium Liberationis*, 278.

Chapter 22: Theologies of War: Comparative Perspectives

[1]This frequent comment of Williams can be found on the tape by George H. Williams, "Religion Under Hitler," *The Adams Tapes*, vol. 2 (Cambridge, Mass.: The James Luther Adams Foundation, 1990).

PART 4: JUST WAR AND JUST PEACE

Chapter 24: The Danger of Violence and the Call to Peace

[1]Interview by Liane Hansen, *Weekend Edition*, National Public Radio, 11 November 2001.

[2]Stephen E. Ambrose, *Band of Brothers: E Company, 506th Regiment, 101st Airborne from Normandy to Hitler's Eagle's Nest* (New York: Simon and Schuster, 2001).

³Thomas Aquinas, *Summa Theologica*, II–II.40. Italics added.
⁴These documents are available from the United States Catholic Conference, Office of Publishing Services, 1312 Massachusetts Avenue, N.W., Washington 20005.
⁵ *The Harvest of Justice Is Sown in Peace* (Washington, D.C: United States Catholic Conference, 1994), 5–7.
⁶The Catholic weekly magazines *Commonweal* and *America*, for example, quickly published sets of commentaries on the situation. See *Commonweal*, September 28, 2001, for essays by Peter Steinfels, Robert E. White, Bruce Martin Russett, and Jean Porter; see *America*, October 8, 2001, for a report on early episcopal responses and essays by J. Bryan Hehir, John Kelsay, John Langan, George A. Lopez, James Martin, and Robert P. Waznak. For Protestant responses by Martin L. Cook, Glen Stassen, Jean Bethke Elshtain, and James Turner Johnson, see *The Christian Century*, November 14, 2001.
⁷John Langan, S.J., "From Ends to Means: Devising a Response to Terrorism," *America* 185, no. 10 (October 8, 2001): 13.
⁸J. Bryan Hehir, "What Can Be Done? What Should Be Done?" *America* 185, no. 10 (October 8, 2001): 11.
⁹Serge Shmemann, "Nobel Peace Prize is Awarded to Annan and U.N.," *The New York Times*, 13 October 2001, A1.
¹⁰Kofi A. Annan, "Fighting Terrorism on a Global Front," *The New York Times*, 21 September 2001.
¹¹Melinda Henneberger, "Bishops' Message Condemns Terrorism and Social Inequality," *International Herald Tribune*, 29 October 2001, p. 2.
¹² *Weekend Edition*, National Public Radio, 11 November 2001.
¹³A summary of the report and the direct quotations here represented may be obtained from http://www.vatican.va/news_services/press/sinodo/documents/bollettino_20_x-ordinaria-2001/02_inglese/b29_02.html, as can the full text of the bishops' statement.
¹⁴Available at www.nccbuscc,org/sdwp/sept11.htm.
¹⁵Renato Martino, "The Culture of Peace: What a Serious Campaign Against Terrorism Entails," presented at the United Nations, New York, October 23, 2001, available at www.zenit.org.
¹⁶Pope John Paul II, "Message for the Celebration of the World Day of Peace," January 1, 2001.
¹⁷Pope John Paul II, Address at Eurasia University, Astana, Kazakhstan, September 23, 2001.

Chapter 28: Organizing Nonviolence

¹Charles Krauthammer, "How the War Can Change America," *Time* (January 28, 1991).
²Michael McClintock, *Instruments of Statecraft: U.S. Guerilla Warfare, Counterinsurgency, and Counterterrorism, 1940–1990* (New York: Pantheon Books, 1992).
³Cf. Walter Wink's use of the phrase in his book, *The Powers That Be: Theology for a New Millennium* (New York: Doubleday, 1998), and elsewhere in his writings.
⁴Edward Said, *The End of the Peace Process: Oslo and After* (New York: Vintage Books, 2001), 47.

Chapter 29: What Can We Hope for Now?

¹Thomas Friedman, *The Lexus and the Olive Tree* (New York: Farrar Straus Giroux, 1999).
²John Gray, *False Dawn: The Delusions of Globalization* (New York: The New Press, 1998), 120ff.
³ *New York Times Magazine*, 25 July 2000.

Chapter 30: New Wars, Old Wineskins

¹Martin Luther King, Jr., *Where Do We Go From Here: Chaos or Community?* (New York: Harper and Row, 1967), 594.
²Studs Turkel, *"The Good War": An Oral History of World War Two* (New York: Pantheon Books, 1984).
³Glen Stassen, *Just Peacemaking: Ten Practices for Abolishing War* (Cleveland, Ohio: The Pilgrim Press, 1998), 4.
⁴For the full text of Bush's September 16 speech and press conference in which he referred to "this crusade, this war on terrorism," see http://www.cbsnews.com/now/story/0,1597,311488-412,00.shtml.
⁵James Vijayakumar, "Identity Crisis," sermon presented to the Council for Theological Education, The United Church of Christ, Cleveland, Ohio, October 25, 2001.

[6]www.tompaine.com/opinion/2001/09/13/1.html.

[7]Stassen, *Just Peacemaking*, 4. See also Susan Thistlethwaite, *A Just Peace Church* (New York: United Church Press, 1986, reprinted by The Pilgrim Press, 2001).

[8]Stassen, *Just Peacemaking*, iii–iv.

[9]Ibid., 5.

[10]Charles E. Osgood, *An Alternative to War or Surrender* (Urbana: University of Illinois Press, 1962), cited in Stassen, ed., *Just Peacemaking*, 46.

[11]Ibid., 47.

[12]rahul@tao.ca, www.nowarcollective.com, October 1, 2001.

[13]tigdet@juno.com, in www.accuracy.org/press_releases/PR100101.htm, October 1, 2001.

[14]*The Chicago Tribune*, 9 November 2001, p. 1.

[15]Nicholas de Torrente, www.doctorswithoutborders.org, October 16, 2001.

[16]Dominic Nutt, dnutt@christian-aid.org, www.christian-aid.org, October 29, 2001.

[17]"U.S. Looking to Next Mission: Helping Stricken Afghans," *The Chicago Tribune*, November 16, 2001.

[18]Stassen, *Just Peacemaking*, 77.

[19]Ibid., 86.

[20]*Newsweek* (October 15, 2001): 22.

[21]Hans Von Sponek, former UN Assistant Secretary General, quoted in www.pbs.org/newshour/bb/middle east/jan-juneoo/iraq 5-3.html, October 30, 2001.

[22]echagop@aol.com, www.arabic.hour.org, October 12, 2001.

[23]William Hartung, www.worldpolicy.org/projects/arms, November 5, 2001.

[24]Stassen, *Just Peacemaking*, 97.

[25]Linda Panetta, www.soawne.org, October 3, 2001.

[26]Stassen, *Just Peacemaking*, 109. On the conditions that structure society for peace and justice, see Jesse L. Jackson, Jr., and Frank Watkins, *A More Perfect Union: Advancing New American Rights* (New York: Welcome Rain Publishers, 2001), chapters 10–18.

[27]www. Wtowatch.org, November 7, 2001.

[28]www.zmag.org/hermancalam.htm, September 18, 2001.

[29]Stassen, *Just Peacemaking*, 115.

[30]Ibid, 117.

[31]Stassen, *Just Peacemaking*, 146; see also Jackson and Watkins, *A More Perfect Union*, 407.

[32]Rev. David Pattee, personal communication.

[33]Stassen, *Just Peacemaking*, 187.

[34]Thom Shanker, "Global Arms Sales Rise Again, and the U.S. Leads the Pack," *The New York Times*, 20 August 2001.

[35]www.globalresearch.ca.

PART 5: LIFE AND FAITH AFTER SEPTEMBER 11

Chapter 31: Dust and Spirit

[1]Karen Baker-Fletcher, *Sisters of Dust, Sisters of Spirit: Womanist Wordings on God and Creation* (Minneapolis: Fortress Press, 1998); and Karen Baker-Fletcher and Garth Kasimu Baker-Fletcher, *My Sister, My Brother: Womanist and Xodus God-talk* (Maryknoll, N.Y.: Orbis Books, 1997).

[2]Sallie Mc Fague, *Models of God* (Philadelphia: Fortress Press, 1987), 22–23, 25–26).

[3]For her work, see Marjorie Hewitt Suchocki, *God, Christ, Church: A Practical Guide to Process Theology* (New York: Crossroad, 1982), and *The Fall to Violence: Original Sin in Relational Theology* (New York: Continuum, 1994), as well as her other writings.

Chapter 33: A Dispatch from Security

[1]Rowan Williams, *Writing in the Dust* (forthcoming).

Chapter 34: In a Time Such as This

[1]I dedicate this article to the youngest in my family: Julia, Mikey, Katie, Alec, and Caroline. Others may not agree with what I say in this article, but these children are the ones who have the right to hold me accountable for what I think and do in a time such as this. To them I owe a world where the greatest possible number of people can live to their fullest potential instead of a world where less than one third of us live at the expense of all the rest. In a time such as this, Julia, Mikey, Katie, Alec, and Caroline, you keep me honest. I thank you for this.

²Of course, another word often heard was "anger." I do not use *anger* as a point of reference in this article for several reasons. First of all, I did not feel angry, my students did not mention anger, and when I checked with close friends, they were not feeling angry. Second, all those I heard on television and radio who mentioned being angry also mentioned feeling anguish, pain, fright, and loss but not all those who felt these emotions mentioned anger too.

³I want to make it perfectly clear that I am talking here about epistemology and not only about hermeneutics, though the latter impinges on the former.

⁴I am using here Ignacio Ellacuría's explanation of the process of knowing reality. See Ignacio Ellacuría, "Hacia una fundamentación del método teológico latinoamericano," *Estudios centroamericanos* 30, no. 322–23 (Agosto-septiembre 1975): 419–21.

⁵Of course, we can and do become saturated or "sick and tired" of what we see repeatedly and then we ignore it; we do not allow it to touch us; we become callous. Here is where we rely on habits–virtues–of caring and compassion that are kept alive and operative only if we practice them. Often, the beginning of our caring and being compassionate starts with making ourselves be attentive to what we see, and so much of what we see is what we watch on television in the comfort of our homes that we have to make an effort not to watch as a mere spectator. We need to watch to know, and we need to remember that to know, we have to become emotionally engaged, which in turn leads us to take responsibility for what we know and to become involved in what we learn.

⁶I do not have cable television and in Manhattan the television antennas of the main networks were on top of one of the Twin Towers. All that I was able to see for several weeks was a local station that obviously had an antenna somewhere else and transmitted nonstop about what was happening in New York City.

⁷The use of justice as a code word for retribution, for punishing the guilty, for retaliation, is unpardonable on the lips of anyone, but particularly of religious people. The moral indignation of common, ordinary people over the misuse of the word *justice* around the events of September 11 came to the fore in a stunning way over the suggestion of some in the government to use the code name "Operation Infinite Justice" for the war against Afghanistan, an idea that they had to abandon for its blatant hubris!

⁸Jodi Dean, *Solidarity of Strangers: Feminism After Identity Politics* (Berkeley: University of California Press, 1996), 92–101.

⁹Diana Fritz Cates, *Choosing to Feel: Virtue, Friendship, and Compassion for Friends* (Notre Dame, Ind.: University of Notre Dame Press, 1997), 2. I thank the Drew University students in my course "Contemporary Ethical Issues: Love and Reconciliation" for their insights during our class discussions this fall semester, 2001.

¹⁰Ibid., 133–36.

¹¹Consider this, regarding our way of life, something that many might think quite insignificant but that has enormous repercussions all over the world. Consider how our way of life is marked by our use of paper. The fact is that all the trees of the world would disappear in two years if the whole world were to use the amount of paper that is used in the U.S.A., where only 6 percent of the world population lives. Why then should we not learn from the way of life of those who use paper in a much more limited way, instead of imposing our way on them? See Pedro Casaldáliga, "El Pregón del Jubileo," *Presencia Ecuménica* 46 (Enero-Marzo 1998, Caracas): 23.

¹²Respect for the way of life and beliefs of others does not in any way mean that we accept situations of oppression and violence in other cultures. As a woman I am very aware of the fact that in the name of cultural differences, women have been the victims of oppressive and violent practices such as genital mutilation, not being allowed to receive an education, and dress codes that are abusively confining. These I unequivocally denounce as unjust, as simply wrong.

¹³This is not the place to review in full the facts that many of us are now learning but that the U.S.A. government chooses to ignore. I only offer the following to substantiate what I say about the U.S.A.'s use of Afghanis and their situation: Osama bin Laden is a Saudi Arabian millionaire who "became a militant Islamic leader in the war to drive the Russians out of Afghanistan. He was one of the many religious fundamentalist extremists recruited, armed, and financed by the CIA and their allies in Pakistani intelligence to cause maximal harm to the Russians…though whether he personally happened to have direct contact with the CIA is unclear and not particularly important…Bin Laden…[and his followers, many of whom are not Afghanis] turned against the U.S. in 1990 when…[this country] established permanent bases in Saudi Arabia–from his point of view, this was a parallel action to the Russian occupation of Afghanistan, but far more significant because of Saudi Arabia's special status as the guardian of the holiest Moslem shrines." Noam Chomsky, "Interview with Noam Chomsky by Radio B92 in Belgrade," September 18, 2001.

This interview is available from many sites on the internet, such as http://www.medialens.org/articles/nc_belgrade_interview.html.

[14]"Deny Them Their Victory: A Religious Response to Terrorism," September 20, 2001. This statement has been signed by nearly 4,000 persons to date. The full text may be found at http://www.ncccusa.org/news/interfaithstatement.html.

Chapter 35: Christian Intellectuals and Escapism after 9/11

[1]I pass over another source of the problem, namely, the difficulty that moderns have in thinking clearly about the potential inescapability of violence in an imperfect world without falling into an amoral nihilism. See Michael Howard, *War and the Liberal Conscience* (New Brunswick, N.J.: Rutgers University Press, 1978).

[2]See Jeffrey Isaac, *Democracy in Dark Times* (Ithaca, N.Y.: Cornell University Press, 1998), and Mark Edmundson, *Nightmare on Main Street: Angels, Sadomasochism, and the Culture of Gothic* (Cambridge, Mass.: Harvard University Press, 1997).

[3]Stefan Rossbach, *Gnostic Wars: The Cold War in the Context of a History of Western Spirituality* (Edinburgh: Edinburgh University Press, 1999).

[4]Most obviously Harold Bloom (as a pro-Gnostic) and Eric Voegelin (as an anti-Gnostic).

[5]This account derives (sketchily) from my book *Evil and the Augustinian Tradition* (Cambridge: Cambridge University Press, 2001).

[6]This leaves a deep question open, namely, whether this God's power and goodness toward us completely coincide. This is a question of divine sovereignty that it seems to me the Reformed Tradition has answered in one way and the Catholic traditions have answered in another way.

[7]I worry that Marilyn McCord Adams's *Horrendous Evils and the Goodness of God* (Ithaca, N.Y.: Cornell University Press, 1999), as brilliant as it is, may tempt us toward this end.

Chapter 36: Wounds of Hurt, Words of Faith

[1]Ted Brelsford, Chapel sermon, Candler School of Theology, Emory University, Atlanta, Ga., September 27, 2001.

[2]Quoted by Rabbi Leila Gal Berner, Kol Nidre, Congregation Bet Mishpachah, Washington, D.C., September 26, 2001 (5762).

[3]Ibid. Berner concluded the thought with these words to her congregation: "For in each and every moment of our lives, we can bring healing. In each and every moment of our lives we can save a world entire. *This* is our hope, this is our challenge, *this* is how we can enter the New Year choosing life over death, affirming good even in the face of the darkest of all evils."

[4]The words are quoted from President George W. Bush, Jr.'s, earliest speeches on September 11, 2001, and soon thereafter. These were widely broadcast and published.

[5]Philip E. Jenks, "Decade to Overcome Violence Is Launched in Snow and Lights," press release, United States Office World Council of Churches, New York, February 5, 2001. See an extended discussion of this announcement and the events leading to it in Mary Elizabeth Moore, "Beyond Poverty and Violence: An Eschatological Vision," *APT Occasional Papers*, no. 5 (Fall 2001): 1–12.

[6]World Council of Churches, "Central Committee Prepares to Launch Decade to Overcome Violence," press release, Geneva, February 5, 2001.

[7]Ibid.

[8]Ibid.

[9]World Council of Churches, "WCC Central Committee Asks Member Churches to Discuss, Reflect on Concerns Related to Protection for Endangered Populations," press release, Geneva, February 6, 2001.

[10]World Council of Churches, "Moderator's Report to WCC Central Committee: Aram—Violence is Evil but May Be Necessary to Restore Justice," press release, Geneva, January 30, 2001.

[11]Ibid.

[12]Ibid.

[13]Ibid.

[14]Ibid.

[15] World Council of Churches, "Nobel Peace Prize Winner Supports Armed Intervention, but only as Last Resort," press release, Central Committee, Potsdam No. 17, Geneva, February 5, 2001. Ramos-Horta is a Roman Catholic layperson, whose own church is not formally part of the WCC, but is an active collaborator. He was the 1996 co-winner of the Nobel Peace Prize, and he presently serves as cabinet member for foreign affairs in the United Nations Transitional Administration in East Timor.

[16]Ibid.

[17]The origin and detailed analysis of this definition is developed in Mary Elizabeth Moore, *Sacred Teaching: Education as a Sacramental Act* (Cleveland: Pilgrim Press, projected for 2002).

[18]Gershon Baskin, Co-Director of Israel/Palestine Center for Research and Information, letter of July 18, 2001.

[19]D. M. Wilson, press release, "Declaration by Christian and Muslim Religious Educators in the University of Birmingham," Birmingham, United Kingdom, October 23, 2001.

[20]Ibid.

[21]Ibid.

Chapter 37: How Should Christians Respond?

[1]John F. Harris, "God Gave U.S. 'What We Deserve,' Falwell Says," *Washington Post,* 14 September 2001, C03; http://www.washingtonpost.com/ac2/wp-dyn?pagename=article &node=&contentId=A28620-2001Sep14.

[2]Edward Rothstein, "Attacks on U.S. Challenge Postmodern True Believers," *New York Times* 22 September 2001.

[3]Harry R. Davis and Robert C. Good, eds., *Reinhold Niebuhr on Politics* (New York: Charles Scribner's Sons, 1960), 130.

Chapter 38: We Must Find a Better Way

[1]Author's translation.

[2]The Scholars Version can be found in several sources, including Robert J. Miller, ed., *The Complete Gospels: Annotated Scholars Version* (Sonoma, Calif.: Polebridge Press, 1992).

[3]See the careful accounting of civilian casualties in "3,500 Civilians Killed in Afghanistan by U.S. Bombs," by Professor Marc Herold, University of New Hampshire, *Common Dreams* News Center, www.commondreams.org/news.2001/1210–01; and Meinhart Vandewal (KOBUTSU@engaged–zen.org).

[4]Public Internet communication from Lt. Col. Robert M. Bowman, Ret., isss@ rmbowman.com.

[5]Uri Avnery, "Twin Towers," *Peacework*, October 2001, 10.

[6]Nicholas Lemann, "What Terrorists Want," *The New Yorker*, October 29, 2001, 36–41.

[7]Jonathan Kwitny, *Endless Enemies: The Making of an Unfriendly World* (New York: St. Martin's Press, 1984).

[8]Portions of Walter Wink, *Engaging the Powers* (Minneapolis: Fortress Press, 1992), 216–19, were used with permission.